THE GREAT
"RED MENACE"

Recent Titles in
Contributions in American History
Series Editor: Jon L. Wakelyn

Class, Conflict, and Consensus: Antebellum Southern Community Studies
Orville Vernon Burton and Robert C. McMath, Jr., editors

Toward A New South? Studies in Post-Civil War Southern Communities
Orville Vernon Burton and Robert C. McMath, Jr., editors

To Free A People: American Jewish Leaders and The Jewish Problem
in Eastern Europe, 1890–1914
Gary Dean Best

Voting in Revolutionary America: A Study of Elections
in the Original Thirteen States, 1776–1789
Robert J. Dinkin

Good and Faithful Labor: From Slavery to Sharecropping
in the Natchez District, 1860–1890
Ronald L. F. Davis

Reform and Reformers in the Progressive Era
David R. Colburn and George E. Pozzetta, editors

History of Black Americans: From the Emergence of the Cotton Kingdom
to the Eve of the Compromise of 1850
Philip S. Foner

History of Black Americans: From the Compromise of 1850 to the End of
the Civil War
Philip S. Foner

The Southern Enigma: Essays on Race, Class, and Folk Culture
Walter J. Fraser, Jr., and Winfred B. Moore, Jr., editors

Crusaders and Compromisers: Essays on the Relationship of
the Antislavery Struggle to the Antebellum Party System
Alan M. Kraut, editor

Boston 1700–1980: The Evolution of Urban Politics
Ronald P. Formisano and Constance K. Burns, editors

THE GREAT "RED MENACE"

United States Prosecution of American Communists, 1947–1952

PETER L. STEINBERG

Contributions in American History, Number 107

GREENWOOD PRESS

WESTPORT, CONNECTICUT
LONDON, ENGLAND

Library of Congress Cataloging in Publication Data

Steinberg, Peter L.
  The great "Red menace."

  (Contributions in American history, ISSN 0084-9219 ;
no. 107)
  Bibliography: p.
  Includes index.
  1. Anti-communist movements—United States—History—
20th century. 2. Subversive activities—United States—
History—20th century. 3. Communism—United States—
1917–   . 4. United States—Politics and government
—1945–1953., I. Title. II. Series.
E743.5.S76 1984   973.918   84-3832
ISBN 0-313-23020-X (lib. bdg.)

Library of Congress Catalog Card Number: 84-3832
ISBN: 0084-9219
ISSN: 0-313-23020-X

First published in 1984

Greenwood Press
A division of Congressional Information Service, Inc.
88 Post Road West
Westport, Connecticut 06881

Printed in the United States of America

10 9 8 7 6 5 4 3 2 1

Contents

Preface

While teaching high school American history in the 1960's and 1970's, I saw that for many young people historical perspective had skipped a generation. Social and political protest was widespread and a kind of innate radicalism grew among those who were viewing the inequities of American life for the first time. Groups such as Students for a Democratic Society (SDS) attracted many more people than those who actually joined. My students, many of whom came from Harlem, were particularly fascinated by the rise of the Black Panther Party. These organizations filled a political void which had existed since the era of "McCarthyism."

The new radical groups seemed to lack historical understanding and a coherent political theory or vision. As a result, they were vehicles of protest which had little chance of resisting the heavy pressure of government persecution. The SDS largely disintegrated with its remnants seeking an "underground" existence. The Panthers were destroyed as many leaders were killed, imprisoned, or fled into exile. The students in my classes were shocked by the violent confrontations which occurred and by the apparent inability of democratic society to accommodate radical criticism. There was little recognition that government actions were a continuation of policies begun during the Cold War against another radical organization—the Communist Party of the United States (CPUSA). There were few efforts among both radical youth and nonradical observers to link the previous generation with contemporary events.

This study is an effort partially to bridge the historical gap created by the onset of "McCarthyism." It examines government efforts to suppress the CPUSA during the early Cold War years. It considers the internal dynamics and external policies of both the government and the Communist Party (CP) in order to see the circumstances which drove the communists "underground." Aspects of the origins of "McCarthyism" necessarily are examined.

I owe a special debt to Professor Vincent P. Carosso of New York University's Graduate History Department. His willingness to share a portion of his remarkable expertise and energy made it possible to sharpen skills of expression which had rusted from disuse. The staff of the Harry S. Truman Library provided expert assistance in an atmosphere of unmatched cordiality. Particular thanks are due to Dennis Bilger, Elizabeth Costin, and Harry Clark, all of whom made it possible to maximize my work in the Library's manuscript collections within a minimum time period. The Tamiment Library at New York University made its valuable resources readily available. Norman Leonard allowed me access to the transcript of the California Smith Act case in the friendly atmosphere of his San Francisco law offices. Alex and Eva Bittelman opened their home and private papers to me. This remarkable couple, who shared a lifetime of struggle, sought only to leave a portion of their wisdom to future generations. Their full story is yet to be told. Those who granted interviews—particularly Tom Clark, John Gates, and George Watt—provided valuable material available from no other sources. Their help is greatly appreciated. The same cannot be said for the Department of Justice. Its reluctance to accept the spirit of the Freedom of Information Act has been commented upon by others. It is sufficient to note here that despite six years of effort, the Department continued to deny me effective access to much of its enormous collection of material dealing with the Communist Party.

There can be no simple acknowledgment of the contribution of my parents. They lived this history and were able to retain a rare sense of rationality concerning the events which occurred. It was my father who suggested this specific project to me. He provided a necessary framework of understanding without ever seeking to impose his own conclusions. Renee, my wife and coworker since college days, made it possible for me to take the time to complete this work. Her encouragement, as well as effort and skill in continually examining the resulting manuscript, has been invaluable. My children, Mark and Lynn, accepted my absence from normal paternal duties, usually with good cheer. This work could not have been completed without their sacrifice and it is dedicated to the hope that they will help to create and be able to enjoy a better, freer world.

Introduction

Tucked away in a dusty bin of the federal courthouse in Foley Square, New York, lies a rarely opened, thirty-year-old volume of the Criminal Docket on which are inscribed the skeletal details of the indictment of twenty-one "second-string" American Communist Party leaders for violation of section 3 of the Smith Act. The specific charge listed on the docket sheet is "Conspiracy to teach and advocate the overthrowing of the Govt. of the U.S. by force and violence." Clearly handwritten in blue ink under the charge is the phrase "dirty commies."[1] The words today lie beneath a light covering of dust, but they are unmistakable and symbolize an era of political prejudice whose consequences have perhaps been more widespread than any in the history of the United States.

It is fitting that the bias of the era should be so clearly stated on the pages of a protected legal document held within a federal "hall of justice." Just as the phrase "dirty commies" invaded these judicial pages, the thirteenth juror—prejudice—was unavoidably present in the judicial proceedings of the period. A political system dependent on an independent judiciary to curb its excesses found the courts to be an inextricable part of the system itself and, as such, subject to the same stresses and pressures.

The judicial system came to be used as one element in a campaign which spread a sense of political fear throughout the United States and threatened to destroy the delicate balance which has always existed between individual freedom and the perception of national security. The period of that campaign has come to be known as the era of "McCarthyism," but its origins predated Joseph McCarthy's entrance into Washington, D.C., in 1946, and its major impulse grew quite independently of McCarthy. McCarthy took advantage, as did others, of an atmosphere of fear and insecurity which already existed in order to further his personal political fortunes, but his part was minor, although flamboyant, and, as others have suggested, merely symbolic of the age.[2]

In the same year as McCarthy's election to the Senate from Wisconsin, former Representative Martin Dies, the first chairman of the Special House Committee on Un-American Activities, wrote to President Harry S Truman suggesting that a public atmosphere existed for vigorous action against communists. Dies, who had temporarily retired from Congress two years earlier, urged the President to put into effect seven specific recommendations previously made by his committee: deport alien communists, require registration of members of "Communist organizations," refuse to recognize unions having communist officers, bar alien communists from entering the United States, fire communists holding public jobs, "cancel the citizenship papers of every naturalized Communist," and "compel the C.I.O. to get rid of its Communist leaders."[3] Dies' far-ranging program might well have been set aside as the ravings of an aging professional anticommunist, now without political power and seeking a last measure of influence. That his letter was not treated in this manner is an indication that his assessment of the political atmosphere apparently had considerable merit.

Despite the fact that World War II and United States-Soviet military cooperation had ended less than a year before, it was abundantly clear already that a new "Red Menace"—replacing the menace of the fascists—had arisen in the consciousness of the leaders of the United States, and was quickly filtering down to the people. A close observer has suggested that by 1946 the President's chief foreign policy advisers were seeking to implant a new image of the Soviet Union in the minds of the American people, one widely different from the one that prevailed during World War II. This view portrayed the Soviet Union as "an aggressive, totalitarian Nazi-like state, run by inhuman fanatics anxious to subordinate all mankind to their false creed."[4] Communists were now viewed as "almost superhuman" and "as able to capture human minds and souls for the pursuit of evil."[5]

Both during and after World War II, FBI Director J. Edgar Hoover attempted to join the external challenge of communism with what he considered to be an acute internal threat. With religious fervor, in speeches across the United States, Hoover repeatedly called for a holy war against this rising "Red Menace." Hoover termed American communism a "godless, truthless, philosophy of life" and warned that communists were infiltrating every aspect of life in the United States.[6]

He went on to describe internal communists as "panderers of diabolic distrust"[7] and ended in a stirring call for a war against the antichrist:

The danger of Communism in America lies not in the fact that it is a political philosophy but in the awesome fact that it is a materialistic religion, inflaming in its adherent a destructive fanaticism. Communism is secularism on the march. It is a mortal foe of Christianity. Either it will survive or Christianity will triumph because in this land of ours the two cannot live side by side.[8]

The rhetoric used by Hoover and others provided the atmosphere that Dies believed would lead to the acceptance of an internal anticommunist program.

Instead of ignoring the Dies letter or authorizing a polite acknowledgment, the President directed Attorney General Tom Clark to prepare a return letter over the signature of presidential secretary Matthew J. Connelly. Although giving no encouragement to the specific program set out by Dies, Clark's reply stated: "You may be sure we are watching these groups and every effort will be made to prosecute successfully whenever a federal violation occurs." The Attorney General specifically noted that federal statutes existed to deal with "persons who advocate the overthrow of the government by force and violence and all these agencies have been activated to see that their provisions are carried out." In what must have seemed a chilling postscript to Dies, a man long in the public limelight, the letter added that the President "hopes you are enjoying your return to private life."[9]

Within five years of the Dies letter and presidential response every one of his seven recommendations—and more—either had been carried out or initiated. During that span of years the United States moved from a predominant public hope that the wartime Soviet-American alliance would be maintained through the United Nations to build an era of peace and prosperity, to a cold war throughout much of the world, a hot war in Korea, and an internal war against democratic principles and freedoms.

There have been other times in which the balance between individual liberty and the right of the state to protect itself has been upset by predominant emphasis on the latter. The struggle over the Alien and Sedition Acts during the administration of John Adams—and perhaps earlier struggles over the Constitution itself—set a pattern which has troubled the United States ever since. The "Red Scare" of the post-World War I period represented a modernization of this traditional clash of values whose essential elements have remained with us ever since. The problem of balance must always exist within a "democratic" society, but it becomes acute and perhaps irreconcilable during periods of crisis. The perceived growth of domestic and foreign "Red Menaces," as well as continuing worldwide conflict, provided such a crisis in the post-World War II years.

It is abundantly clear from both public comment and internal documents that the national administration was fully aware of the historical context of the crisis and of its dangers for the maintenance of basic freedoms. The administration's concern was insufficient to stop the destruction of the balance and to maintain a sense of real political equilibrium. The resulting development of "McCarthyism," as Robert Griffith has pointed out, was not an "aberration" of American politics, but was the essence of those politics and should be considered "a natural expression of America's political culture and a logical though extreme product of its political machinery."[10]

Truman faced increasing anticommunist pressures both from within and without his administration. His historical vision of a free society clashed with a pragmatic desire to create a bipartisan response to the rise of Soviet power and expansion, and to limit the effectiveness of a right-wing assault on domestic Democratic Party programs. The President employed inflated rhetoric to achieve widespread support for his foreign policy initiatives to "contain" the growth of Soviet influence. Truman accepted a form of domestic appeasement to reduce the popular effect of right-wing charges that the administration was "soft on communism."

Neither the chief executive nor his principal advisers considered domestic communists as a political or internal security threat, yet they sacrificed the freedoms of this group in order to maintain power and to save the policies they believed necessary. Truman considered the Communist Party an inconsequential sect whose destruction could do little harm to the essential fabric of American democracy. The CP, he believed, safely could be sacrificed to the appetite of the right wing, thus protecting liberal America from a conservative flash point. There was limited recognition that the elimination of the extreme left might open the gates to a broader spectrum of political attack. The administration may well have believed, in any case, that there were few viable political alternatives.

The origins of "McCarthyism" have become a matter of widespread historical comment and debate. The continuing tempo of this discussion is vivid testimony to the importance that is attached to this period and to our inability to analyze satisfactorily the failure of democratic controls since World War II, ultimately leading to the crises surrounding Watergate. The historiography of these years has been extensive, and it continues to grow.

Most of the analyses of "McCarthyism's" origins suggest a society in which the right wing, the liberals, and the Truman administration were operating largely in a political vacuum, untouched by a viable left wing. That is not necessarily an accurate assumption. The left, through the late 1940's and into the early 1950's, was extremely active, although increasingly beset by difficulties. The development of a national hysteria with its integral fear of communism cannot be understood without considering the interaction of the left—particularly the American communists—with the rising forces of reaction.

A necessary precondition for the general restriction of individual liberty had to be an attack upon the American Communist Party. The external communist threat would be fully accepted and feared if a clear internal threat was shown. The CPUSA served as the logical link to prove the connection between external and internal dangers faced by American "democracy." If the American people would believe that the CP was simply the local agent of an international communist conspiracy, they might willingly join in a demand for repressive policies.

The reaction of the American communists in building their alliances, creating their positions, and responding to the attacks upon them played an essential part in the developing hysteria. Although small in number, the American communists aroused a public perception—and, to an extent, a government perception as well—which was a determinant in the speed with which "McCarthyism" developed and the degree to which it spread. The communists, by themselves, could not control this, but they could and did have an important influence.

The primary prosecutive weapon used against the CP in this period was the Alien Registration Act of 1940, known as the Smith Act. Under this law, the leaders of the Communist Party were indicted for "conspiracy to teach and advocate the duty and necessity of overthrowing" the United States government.

A group of nonelected government officials joined together to encourage an anticommunist program of vast proportions. There is substantial evidence to suggest that the bureaucracy of the Federal Bureau of Investigation, in conjunction with important elements in the Department of Justice and other governmental agencies, worked secretly and effectively to establish conditions whereby their views would prevail over those of many elected officials. Their influence was felt to an astonishing degree and may have been decisive in creating the conditions which allowed "McCarthyism" eventually to flourish. Much of their work was done without the knowledge of the highest officials of government, but some of it was carried on with the tacit approval of those officials, or, at least, their "benign neglect."

The anticommunist allies skillfully used the legislative branch of government, the media, the courts, and a sometimes reluctant executive branch to achieve their aims. To a degree, it would appear that elected officials rather than providing an effective brake became the captors of a highly disciplined bureaucratic structure.

This is not to suggest the presence of a group of "devils" with evil designs seeking to establish their personal power for its own sake. Far more dangerously, a network apparently grew of dedicated, highly "patriotic" bureaucrats who truly believed that the only way to save American democracy was to restrict its libertarian practices. They truly believed the United States was beset by traitors on the inside and an implacable foe on the outside. They truly believed that elected officials were too subject to the popular will and too easily manipulated to provide the strength needed in a time of clear crisis. They linked themselves to and sought to serve the interests of the essential sources of right-wing power—big business, the Church, and national patriotic organizations.

Much of our historical treatment of the CPUSA was filtered through the prism of the anticommunist bureaucracy. The communist and associated left-wing press were the only other conduits of information. They were swiftly discredited and almost eliminated in terms of their impact. It is only in the last few years, since Watergate, that material has started to become available which provides an accurate portrait of the "Red Menace" and those who created it.

NOTES

1. Criminal Docket, vol. 136 [*United States v. Flynn, et al.*], United States Court House (Foley Square, New York).

2. Robert Griffith, *The Politics of Fear: Joseph R. McCarthy and the Senate* (Rochelle Park, N.J., 1978), preface; Athan Theoharis, *Seeds of Repression: Harry S. Truman and the Origins of McCarthyism* (Chicago, 1971), 13–16.

3. Martin Dies to Harry S Truman, July 16, 1946, Official File (OF) 263 (1945–47), Papers of Harry S. Truman, Harry S. Truman Library, Independence, Mo. Hereafter cited as HSTL.

4. Leslie Adler, "The Red Image: American Attitudes Toward Communism in the Cold War Era" (Ph.D. Diss., University of California, Berkeley, 1970), 236.

5. Ibid., 331–32.

6. J. Edgar Hoover, *On Communism* (New York, 1969), 63–64.

7. Ibid., 103.

8. Ibid., 91.

9. Matthew J. Connelly to Martin Dies, August 12, 1946, OF 263 (1945–47), Papers of Harry S. Truman, HSTL.

10. Griffith, *The Politics of Fear*, 30.

THE GREAT
"RED MENACE"

I

An Internal Cold War

During the same month of Harry S Truman's sudden elevation to the Presidency on April 12, 1945, a French monthly little known in the United States published an article by French communist leader Jacques Duclos which was to shake the structure and policies of the American Communist Party. The coincidence of these two events, little understood at the time and seemingly so disparate in their importance, was to provide an essential framework for the public development of an internal cold war in the United States.

The article in *Cahiers du Communisme* attacked the leadership of Earl Browder, head of the American communist movement, for "liquidating" the CPUSA in 1944 by forming, in its stead, the Communist Political Association. Duclos sharply suggested that this action had been based on an incorrect assessment of the international situation and implied that a period of international conflict could now be anticipated rather than one of long-term peace, the perspective set forth by Browder. The Duclos article was instrumental in effecting changes within the communist movement. It was almost immediately picked up by the State Department and incorporated in an important background paper for President Truman's use at the Potsdam Conference.

The State Department analysis used the Duclos article as vital evidence in proving that American communists could now be expected to revert to a period of bitter criticism of American foreign policy, including the accusation that Truman had deserted the policies of Franklin Roosevelt.[1] The analysis went on to label communist movements as "fifth columns" and to warn against the dangers of "fellow-travelers" and "dupes." The foreign policy of capitalist-communist collaboration was over, and the State Department strongly set forward the concept that the international communist movement would swiftly seek to gain world power.[2]

The importance of the State Department analysis cannot be overestimated. It was given to an impressionable President faced with overwhelming responsibilities and crises around the world. It provided the basis of an approach which was to be reinforced consistently as the Cold War developed. The emphasis on the foreign policy danger was used to delineate an associated internal danger. Opposition to one without fighting the other was impossible. The concept of a "fifth column" not only set the image of a clandestine, clever, and traitorous enemy, but it also evoked the memory of Nazism's destruction of democratic institutions and entire nations.

Far from an isolated study, the State Department analysis received almost daily support. Shortly after Truman's assumption of the Presidency, J. Edgar Hoover commenced on a long-term project to educate the President on the internal dangers faced by the United States. In communications sent almost daily, the chief executive was literally inundated with reports from the FBI—all transmitted directly from Hoover to the President through a trusted aide. In the first year of his administration, the Hoover letters went directly to Harry Vaughan, Truman's military aide and a close personal friend since World War I. The Attorney General, Hoover's direct superior, at first had no knowledge of this connection.[3] On occasion Hoover provided Attorney General Tom Clark with the same material he had given the President. The Attorney General would send some of it on to Truman in the belief that he was presenting him new material.

Many of Hoover's letters to the President dealt directly with the American Communist Party and consisted, in the main, of material gained from FBI informants within the Party. Some of the material apparently was gathered by FBI wiretapping or other forms of "bugging," and some of it did not concern communists at all.

One of his earliest communications—marked "personal and confidential by special messenger"—concerned a meeting held in the home of Frederick Vanderbilt Field whom Hoover identified as "a financial angel to the Communist movement in this country," although not suggesting that he was a communist.[4] Much of the report consisted of quotes from concert and stage performer Paul Robeson, a guest at the gathering. There would appear to have been no purpose in sending this report to the President except as an effort to influence him in an anticommunist direction. There is no suggestion that the meeting was illegal, conspiratorial, or anything but an exercise of basic political freedom.

The fact that the FBI monitored the gathering with such apparent care and reported it to the highest political authority in the state was clearly an excessive use of its power and a forerunner of the political repression to come. Although there is no evidence that President Truman requested such reports, he neither rejected them nor ordered the FBI to stop or curb its actions. Reports such as these sometimes even included the names of important members of his administration.

A mass meeting at Madison Square Garden on November 14, 1945, sponsored by the National Council of American Soviet Friendship, was the subject of an extensive report to the President only two days later. Although the Council had support from many prominent Americans, and this rally was addressed by Undersecretary of State Dean Acheson among others, it is clear from the Hoover letter that the FBI considered the meeting to be communist-inspired and controlled. Short biographies of all speakers with the exception of Acheson were provided the President, with heavy emphasis placed on their left-wing contacts.[5]

Acheson became a particular Hoover target and was cited in mid–1946 as a possible Soviet espionage agent. Hoover wrote to the President warning that a reliable source had provided information of "an enormous Soviet espionage ring" in Washington whose major purpose was the collection of atomic energy information. Although offering no evidence of illegal acts by Acheson or any of the other suspects, Hoover noted:

It has also been made known to the Bureau through various sources in the past that the political views of Under Secretary of State Dean Acheson, Assistant Secretary of War Howard C. Peterson, and Secretary of Commerce Henry Wallace have been pro-Russian in nature, and therefore, it is not beyond the realm of conjecture that they would fit into a scheme as set out above.[6]

"Not beyond the realm of conjecture" appears to have been substituted for evidence.

The FBI political dragnet reached significantly into the ranks of liberal and left-wing congressmen. Senator Claude Pepper, Democrat of Florida, an opponent of Truman foreign policy in the early years of the Cold War, was a frequent target of FBI concern, and his more critical remarks concerning the President were quickly transmitted to the White House. Similarly, West Virginia Democratic Senator Harley Kilgore and left-wing representatives Vito Marcantonio of New York's American Labor Party and Hugh DeLacey, a Washington Democrat, were the subjects of Hoover letters to the chief executive. All Hoover's targets were accused of being "pro-Russian" or at least, anti-Truman, and of being involved in publishing ventures or speaking engagements which were opposed to administration policy.[7]

Although Hoover always maintained he did not involve himself in local jurisdictions or problems, he made an exception in order to report to Truman that the Democratic nominee for governor of Alabama, James Folsom, was heavily supported by "alleged Communists" and that statements made by him in the course of his campaign which were critical of the foreign policy of the administration "follow closely the alleged propaganda pattern of the present Communist Party line in the United States."[8] Within a year Folsom signed an Alabama law outlawing the Communist Party in his state.

A favorite Hoover interest was Henry Wallace, whose domestic activities and foreign tours disturbed the FBI Director. Hoover provided the President with at least three reports on Wallace's September 1946 tour of Latin America—not only quoting his speeches, but also noting those who sat near him, fellow speakers, and sponsors of his meetings.[9] Hoover undoubtedly was seeking to provide valuable political information to the President, particularly after Wallace left the cabinet and sought to project himself as the left political alternative to Truman.

Just as Hoover attempted to prove to the chief executive that the CPUSA represented a real threat to the government's various branches, he placed even greater emphasis on alleged communist infiltration of the labor movement. Faced with a series of major strikes following the conclusion of the war, the administration was more than willing to accept the thesis of communist involvement. Hoover fed and reinforced that thesis. His main target was Lee Pressman, the general counsel of the Congress of Industrial Organizations and a major influence in that union organization since its founding in the 1930's. Pressman, openly a left-winger for many years, was the subject of an extensive biography given the President in 1945. Terming Pressman "subject to influence if not actual control by the Communist Party of the United States," Hoover related a long list of "alleged Communists" with whom he was said to have had contact over the years as a private attorney, a lawyer in various New Deal agencies, and then in the labor movement.[10]

Within a period of several months, Hoover had reported to the President on communist involvement in strikes in meat packing plants, the coal mines, and the maritime industry.[11] The pattern in all the reports was similar. Communist Party leaders were described in clandestine meetings with various officials of organized labor and were said to be seeking to control the formulation of union policy and strike strategy. Hoover was particularly concerned with communist attempts to achieve a large measure of unity among the various maritime unions through the establishment of a Committee on Maritime Unity. He maintained that communists would then control sea transport and implied that this control would be dangerous.[12]

Hoover attempted to link communist efforts to penetrate organized labor with infiltration of the government. In a June 1946 letter, he advised that the Communist Party was seeking to place supporters in key positions in the Labor Department. Pressman, according to Hoover acting for the CP, had proposed the appointments of David Morse to the position of assistant secretary of labor for international affairs and Isadore Lubin to the post of undersecretary of labor. Although Hoover did not go so far as to suggest that either was a communist or even a "fellow-traveler," he specifically said that the Pressman group "will gain considerably in power if a new Assistant Secretary for Internal Affairs is one of their own group." The inference was clear. Hoover further charged that Pressman had succeeded already in placing several of his friends in positions of importance in Secretary of Labor Lewis Schwellenbach's department. Schwellenbach, a close personal friend of the President, was thus put in the position of being considered a "dupe" of communist elements. Hoover's charges, although admittedly "not . . . substantiated," were striking close to the President himself.[13]

The effects of Hoover's letters were clearly felt. The reports were transported quickly to the President and apparently read with some interest. When attorney Morris Ernst, a leader among anticommunist liberals, wrote to the President in November 1945 suggesting that he obtain FBI files concerning "the relationship of some top people in the labor movement to the Executive Committee of the Communist Party"— a subject which he allegedly discussed with President Roosevelt in 1943— Truman pencilled in the comment, "We have all this."[14] The Ernst letter not only suggests the effectiveness of the Hoover campaign and the receptivity of the President, but also emerges as the beginning of a remarkable concurrence of views between the FBI and anticommunist liberals.

The most extensive reports provided the President by Hoover concerned the internal activities of the Communist Party. Hoover was apparently intent on proving both the efficacy of FBI information and the dangers of the Party. As early as the beginning of 1946, he was already referring to the "conspiratorial aspect of the Communist movement in this country," although CP members had neither been convicted nor indicted on any such charge.[15] Hoover reported to Truman, again on the basis of unverified evidence, that communists had been given "secret instructions . . . to support . . . the international aims of the Soviet Union."[16] The "secret" was hardly well kept since this was a publicly proclaimed policy of the CPUSA and was to remain as a central, although perhaps destructive, element of Party policy.

The Hoover accounts stretched from detailed summaries of all the reports given at Party "plenums"—enlarged meetings of the National Committee of the Communist Party[17]—to speeches given by CP leaders in Cuba,[18] to the statements allegedly made by minor, local Party officials.[19] A central, unifying characteristic of these reports was that the FBI Director carefully chronicled critical remarks made about the President and threats of political retribution.[20]

Considered alone, the FBI reports, "confidential and secret" as they were and with the imprimatur of a highly respected national investigatory agency, would have been enormously effective in establishing an internal atmosphere of fear and suspicion. These FBI accounts were supplemented by others from various influential officials and agencies. The hand of the Bureau was often felt in many of these evaluations as well. These persons received much of their data through the FBI and, in turn, supplied intelligence to the Bureau. Hoover specifically noted, on occasion, that certain information he was providing the President was also being given to other government agencies, including the Department of State and Military Intelligence.[21] The fact of a common pool of "intelligence" and outlook heightened the impact of these reports within the executive branch.

Formal evaluations of the connection between Soviet policy and American communists were most influential. These began in mid–1945 and became extremely regular within a year. In May 1946 Clark Clifford, special counsel to the President, received a report warning against the establishment of a communist "fifth column."[22]

As the Cold War heated up, the reports escalated in their frequency and intensity. In July 1946 Admiral William D. Leahy, the President's chief of staff, in a statement on military policy to be followed toward the Soviet Union, interpolated the domestic corollary that the government "should prevent Communist infiltration into our governmental agencies, our armed forces, and the labor elements upon which our warmaking capacity depends. To this end only personnel free from Communistic tendencies and of unquestioned loyalty to the United States should be selected for key positions."[23] The inference of the possibility of existing disloyalty was clear. In the same month as the Leahy recommendations, the President requested a similar evaluation from Secretary of War Robert Patterson. His rapid response struck the same note as had Leahy. He strongly suggested "increased support" for the FBI in order to combat the threat of communist infiltration.[24]

Just as Truman solicited the views of his top military advisers, he also asked Clark Clifford for a summary of United States relations with the Soviet Union. Clifford turned to his assistant, George Elsey—influential himself in the formulation of administration policy—to do most of the basic work. Elsey went considerably beyond the seemingly limited nature of the request and proceeded to consult with the major departments and leading policy makers in the administration. Particularly sought were the views of George Kennan whose recent "long telegram" on Soviet policy and the correct United States response—setting forth the basic principles of "containment"—had been so influential.[25] Leahy and Patterson were among those whose ideas were requested, and Hoover undoubtedly had important input as well.

Clifford's lengthy report on "American Relations with the Soviet Union," delivered in late September 1946, strongly recommended a tough global military and economic response to Soviet expansionist pressures and a domestic propaganda counterpart to prepare the American people for the needed massive effort.[26] The Soviets were accused of fostering both espionage and "subversive movements" in the United States, and the Communist Party was specifically named, with little benefit of evidence, as the conduit for both. Clifford warned: "Every American Communist is potentially an espionage agent of the Soviet government, requiring only the direct instruction of a Soviet superior to make the potentiality a reality."[27] CP members were accused of specifically attempting to subvert the armed forces and of seeking to "capture" the labor movement in order to gain a strategic position from which to cripple the United States' industrial plant in time of danger.[28]

The wave of condemnatory reports on Soviet policy and the continuing emphasis on a "fifth column" had a telling personal effect on Truman and ultimately on governmental policy. Even before the series of reports in the summer of 1946, Truman had been sufficiently influenced, primarily by Hoover, to react somewhat irrationally to what was perceived as a real internal threat. Faced with a critical railroad strike in May 1946, the President sat down one evening to write, in longhand, the draft of a speech to be delivered to the American people. There is little question that the draft represented no more than an outlet for a frustrated President faced with continuing crises. It never was meant either for publication or delivery. At the same time, it indicates Truman's frame of mind as he linked communism with both the labor movement and the Congress within the setting of an international communist movement. The cooler heads of administrative aides Clifford, Charles Ross, and Samuel Rosenman prevailed as they joined to write a nonhysterical address to the American people, throwing out the presidential draft.[29] The President's reaction indicates that the cumulation of FBI memoranda and other reports, supplemented by the rising international crisis, had been most effective. No one had been more responsible for this effect than J. Edgar Hoover.

The FBI Director's aversion for, and fear of, communism was not new. It grew out of neither the World War alliance nor the expansion of communism in the postwar period. Far more important in shaping his views was the "Red Scare" of the post-World War I period, the first "Red Scare" in which he played an important role.

Hoover joined the Department of Justice on July 26, 1917, as an aide to John Lord O'Brian, special assistant to the attorney general for war work. Initially placed in charge of a unit in the alien registration section, Hoover was soon given control of a new General Intelligence Division within the administrative staff.[30] Twenty-four years old and with the title of special assistant to the Attorney General, he was assigned to write a "legal brief" on the newly created Communist Party and Communist Labor Party. Hoover later claimed that for this assignment he examined a wealth of contemporary material as well as the traditional works of Marx and Engels. The conclusions which he reached were to be unchanging through the rest of his life.

These doctrines threaten the happiness of the community, the safety of every individual, and the continuance of every home and fireside. They would destroy the peace of the country and thrust it into a condition of anarchy and lawlessness and immorality that passes imagination.[31]

Hoover's personal opportunities increased immeasurably on May 10, 1924, when Attorney General Harlan Fiske Stone appointed him, on the recommendation of Herbert Hoover, as head of the Bureau of Investigation, the direct predecessor of the FBI.[32] Aware of the excesses of A. Mitchell Palmer, to which Hoover had made a contribution, Stone attempted to insure against the establishment of a political police. He set strict rules for the conduct of Bureau activity. The Stone standard was interpreted to mean that the Bureau would be limited to fact gathering in violations of specific federal statutes and that these would be undertaken only under the direction of the Attorney General.

The major thrust of an FBI anticommunist campaign began during the administration of Franklin Roosevelt. With the United States locked into the Great Depression, with a growing radical movement, and faced with both a developing communist competitor in the Soviet Union and rising international tensions, Hoover took advantage of the situation to increase his power, budget, and anticommunist program. In 1936 he received the first substantial change in Bureau responsibilities and prerogatives. At two late August meetings with the President, Hoover claimed he was instructed verbally to conduct a survey concerning the relationship between domestic communists and fascists and "attempts by foreign agents to influence domestic affairs."[33] Hoover ordered his special agents to begin collecting information on "subversive activities" in the United States and to expand greatly FBI domestic responsibilities into an area of pure intelligence gathering which "was entirely unrelated to the enforcement of federal criminal laws."[34]

By June 1939 instructions had been issued for FBI offices to investigate the Communist Party, presumably under provisions of the 1938 Foreign Agents Registration Act.[35] Thousands of informants in defense plants and communities throughout the nation were recruited as the FBI established a rather massive system of domestic spying.[36] The outbreak of World War II accelerated these programs.

On September 6, 1939, a few days after the opening of the war, Roosevelt issued a public statement emphasizing the authority of the FBI in the areas of espionage, sabotage, and violations of neutrality laws. The President requested all law enforcement officials, regardless of jurisdiction, immediately to turn over to the Bureau any information they might have regarding these areas and "subversive activities." The statement resulted from a Hoover memorandum to Attorney General Frank Murphy requesting a strong presidential declaration on the matter of investigatory power.[37] An entirely new FBI unit, the Security Division, later known as the Domestic Intelligence Division, was created to handle those matters relating to the President's directive.[38]

The apparent readiness of the FBI for its new assignment was astonishing. Before the end of 1939 Hoover had ordered the preparation of a "Custodial Detention List" including the names of both aliens and citizens "on whom there is information available to indicate that their presence at liberty in this country in time of war or national emergency would be dangerous to the public peace and the safety of the United States Government." Lacking statutory authority for the creation of such a list, Hoover directed that all investigations relative to it be conducted strictly confidentially, and that they not be known to anyone outside of the Bureau. Broad discretion was given to Bureau offices as they were directed to gather material concerning participation in "dangerous subversive movements," although these terms were not defined.[39]

Informed a year later of the existence of the Custodial Detention List, Attorney General Robert Jackson attempted to establish some meaningful supervision, but Hoover resisted. He was finally ordered to submit FBI dossiers to a Special War Policies Unit within the Department of Justice, with guarantees given concerning the protection of "confidential informants."[40] In 1943, in the midst of the war, Attorney General Francis Biddle emphatically ordered an end to the Detention List. Noting that no legal authority existed for it, he said that the "classification system is inherently unreliable." The Bureau and the Justice Department were once again to be restricted to "investigating the activities of persons who may have violated the law."[41]

It was too late to stop the Bureau's activities or the actions of some members of the Justice Department. The instruments of democratic control effectively had broken down, and a bureaucracy built strong by the war and apparently convinced of its own infallibility began to operate independently of elected officials. Hoover directly contravened the Attorney General's intention and instructions. Within a month he had ordered the designation "Custodial Detention List" simply replaced by "Security Index." Investigations and reports continued, apparently without notification to either the Attorney General or the Justice Department.[42] By early 1946 the FBI had accumulated 10,763 names on its Index, including "communists and members of the Nationalist Party of Puerto Rico," with the former greatly predominant.[43]

Throughout World War II the FBI waged its own internal war against the Communist Party. Every member of the Party and the Communist Political Association was to be investigated fully.[44] Agents were sent to towns and cities throughout the United States to gather information on individual Party members.[45] Ordinary citizens were asked to join the CP to act as FBI informants and were told that "this job is essential to the internal security of the United States."[46] The 1943 Biddle order to deal only with specific violations of the law had no apparent effect on Bureau actions.

Toward the end of the war the FBI nominally ordered some cutbacks in its investigations of the CPA. Field offices were instructed to limit their investigations to "key figures" or "potential key figures" in the national or regional communist organizations, but there was apparently little real change in policy. Many offices continued to investigate all communists.[47] This temporary, minimal decrease in the intensity of the FBI anticommunist drive did not last long.

By the beginning of 1946 the Bureau was again ready for an all-out drive against communists. In a memorandum to Hoover, Assistant Director D. Milton Ladd recommended "re-establishing the original policy of investigating all known members of the Communist Party" and of maintaining security index cards on each. Ladd put forward the argument that the CP was simply an appendage of Soviet policy, and each member—particularly those in unions and basic industries—was to be considered a possible saboteur and espionage agent. He decried the lack of legislative authority to act against communists in case of emergency and strongly suggested that existing laws were not adequate. Most interesting in view of the long FBI investigation of the Party and its actions in the next few years was his view of the Smith Act's inadequacy as an anticommunist weapon. Ladd noted: "It might be extremely difficult to prove that members of the Party knew the purpose of the Party to overthrow the Government by force and violence." He implied that the Attorney General should be asked for new legislative authority.

The Ladd memorandum, while suggesting consultation with the Attorney General in certain necessary areas—or perhaps use of the Attorney General might be more accurate—went much further in moving the FBI, on its own authority again, into the political life of the United States. Ladd proposed a massive, clandestine propaganda campaign by the Bureau to prepare the American people for the possible mass arrest of communists. Anticipating a flood of liberal protest at the time of such seizures, he suggested a preemptive propaganda program with particular emphasis on the labor movement and religious organizations. Materials were to be distributed "indicating the basically Russian nature of the Communist Party in this country." Ladd asked that a special FBI training conference be established, including key operatives throughout the United States, to prepare them for this campaign. The program was aproved by the FBI Executive Conference.[48]

The Ladd plan was the forerunner of what in the 1960's would come to be known as COINTELPRO—counterintelligence program. This program was exposed in the 1970's as a deliberate effort to destroy selected left-wing targets through massive propaganda and internal disruption. William C. Sullivan, later head of the Intelligence Division, testified in 1975 that COINTELPRO tactics were in operation as early as 1941.[49]

The Ladd memorandum was instrumental in Hoover's determination that the Attorney General should be informed of the existence of the Security Index. Little more than a week after receiving Ladd's memorandum, Hoover sent a confidential memorandum to Attorney General Clark in which he carefully wrote that the FBI was in the process of "taking steps to list all members of the Communist Party and any others who would be dangerous in the event of a break in diplomatic relations with the Soviet Union, or other serious crisis involving the United States and the U.S.S.R."[50] This was the first hint, albeit a rather ingenuous one, received by the Attorney General of the existence of the Security Index. Years later Clark disclaimed any prior knowledge of the Index and said that while he was aware of FBI "infiltration" into allegedly subversive groups, he had no knowledge of their disruptive tactics. He admitted that Hoover was, for all intents and purposes, independent in this area. "We did not know what they were doing," he said.[51] To J. Edgar Hoover, the Attorney General's knowledge of the Security Index was a necessary prelude to the suggestion that mass detentions might be needed in the event of conflict or threatened conflict with the Soviet Union, and that new legislation specifically granting such powers should be sought.[52]

Prodded by the FBI, the Justice Department considered its options in case of national emergency. It determined that either a declaration of martial law or a suspension of the writ of *habeas corpus* could be used to meet the danger.[53] The Bureau was not satisfied with the Justice Department position. Hoover again wrote to Clark asking him to seek Congress' "statutory backing for detention."[54] The Attorney General ignored this specific request and, instead, asked for a more detailed explanation of the FBI's Security Index. The Bureau responded with examples of "Communists and Communist sympathizers whose names appear in the Bureau's Security Index," but withheld the names of "Espionage Suspects and Government Employees in the Communist Underground" for "security reasons." The Department of Justice neither challenged the withholding of information nor the FBI criteria for the Security Index.[55]

Hoover had prepared carefully for the internal cold war. World War II cooperation with the Soviet Union temporarily had limited his efforts, but never stopped them. FBI policies following the war helped set the stage for public acceptance of the increasingly bitter worldwide communist-capitalist confrontation. Tense foreign relations, in turn, allowed the Bureau's accession of greatly increased power and influence. This continuing cycle inevitably led to government programs reflecting the growing concerns of the American people.

NOTES

1. Richard M. Freeland, *The Truman Doctrine and the Origins of McCarthyism: Foreign Policy, Domestic Politics, and Internal Security 1946–1948* (New York, 1972), 138.

2. Leslie Adler, "The Red Image: American Attitudes Toward Communism in the Cold War Era" (Ph.D. Diss., University of California, Berkeley, 1970), 278.

3. Tom Clark to author, March 28, 1975.

4. J. Edgar Hoover to Harry Vaughan, November 15, 1945, Box 167, Folder C. Hereafter box numbers and folder designations will be cited as 167/C. President's Secretary's Files (PSF), Papers of Harry S. Truman, Harry S. Truman Library, Independence, Missouri. Hereafter cited as HSTL.

5. J. Edgar Hoover to Harry Vaughan, November 16, 1945, 167/American-Soviet Friendship, PSF, Papers of Harry S. Truman, HSTL.

6. J. Edgar Hoover to George E. Allen, May 29, 1946, 169/P, PSF, Papers of Harry S. Truman, HSTL.

7. J. Edgar Hoover to Harry Vaughan, May 9 and 22, 1946, 169/R and 167/Communist data, PSF, Papers of Harry S. Truman, HSTL; J. Edgar Hoover to George E. Allen, May 29 and July 29, 1946, 169/P and 168/K, PSF, Papers of Harry S. Truman, HSTL.

8. J. Edgar Hoover to George E. Allen, September 11, 1946, 168/F, PSF, Papers of Harry S. Truman, HSTL.

9. J. Edgar Hoover to George E. Allen, September 12, 20, 24, 1946, 169/W, PSF, Papers of Harry S. Truman, HSTL.

10. J. Edgar Hoover to Harry Vaughan, December 5, 1945, 169/P, PSF, Papers of Harry S. Truman, HSTL.

11. J. Edgar Hoover to Harry Vaughan, January 29 and 31, May 15 and 29, 1946, 168/M and Maritime, PSF, Papers of Harry S. Truman, HSTL; J. Edgar Hoover to George E. Allen, May 22, June 5 and 10, September 13, 1946, 169/Personal and 168/M and Maritime, PSF, Papers of Harry S. Truman, HSTL.

12. Hoover to Vaughan, May 15, 1946, HSTL.

13. J. Edgar Hoover to George E. Allen, June 4, 1946, 168/M, PSF, Papers of Harry S. Truman, HSTL.

14. Morris L. Ernst to Harry S. Truman, November 8, 1945, Official File (OF) 263 (1945–47), Papers of Harry S. Truman, HSTL.

15. J. Edgar Hoover to Harry Vaughan, February 11, 1946, 167/Communist data, PSF, Papers of Harry S. Truman, HSTL.

16. Ibid.

17. J. Edgar Hoover to Harry Vaughan, February 28, 1946, 168/F, PSF, Papers of Harry S. Truman, HSTL.

18. J. Edgar Hoover to Harry Vaughan, March 8, 1946, 167/Brazil, PSF, Papers of Harry S. Truman, HSTL.

19. J. Edgar Hoover to Tom Clark, June 20, 1946, J. Edgar Hoover to Harry Vaughan, June 6, 1946, 167/Communist data, PSF, Papers of Harry S. Truman, HSTL.

20. Hoover to Vaughan, March 8, 1946, HSTL.

21. J. Edgar Hoover to Harry Vaughan, November 15, 1945, 167/C, PSF, Papers of Harry S. Truman, HSTL.

22. "Union of Soviet Socialist Republics—Policy & Information," May 15, 1946, Russia Folder, Papers of Clark M. Clifford, HSTL.

23. William D. Leahy, "Recommended Military Policy to be Followed by the United States with Respect to the Soviet Union," July 1946, Russia Folder, Papers of Clark M. Clifford, HSTL.

24. Robert P. Patterson to President Truman, July 27, 1946, Russia Folder, Papers of Clark M. Clifford, HSTL.

25. Robert J. Donovan, *Conflict and Crisis, The Presidency of Harry S Truman, 1945–1948* (New York, 1977), 221.

26. Clark M. Clifford, "American Relations With the Soviet Union," Septem-

ber 24, 1946, 79, Foreign Affairs Russia 1946, Folder 2, Papers of Clark M. Clifford, HSTL.

27. Ibid., 67.

28. Ibid., 68.

29. Donovan, *Conflict and Crisis*, 212–13.

30. Don Whitehead, *The FBI Story, A Report to the People* (New York, 1956), 37, 41.

31. J. Edgar Hoover, *Masters of Deceit, The Story of Communism in America and How to Fight It* (New York, 1958), v–vi.

32. Whitehead, *The FBI Story*, 67.

33. Ibid., 157–58; Athan Theoharis, *Spying on Americans, Political Surveillance from Hoover to the Huston Plan* (Philadelphia, 1978), 67, 69, 261 n.14.

34. U.S. Senate, 94th Cong., 2d sess., *Final Report of the Select Commmittee to Study Governmental Operations with Respect to Intelligence Activities* (6 vols., Washington, 1976), II, 30–31. Hereafter cited as *Final Report*; Frank Donner, *The Age of Surveillance, The Aims and Methods of America's Political Intelligence System* (New York, 1980), 53–60.

35. Whitehead, *The FBI Story*, 165.

36. *Final Report*, III, 255.

37. Ibid., II, 34n, 59; Theoharis, *Spying on Americans*, 73–75.

38. Luther A. Huston, *The Department of Justice* (New York, 1967), 231–32.

39. J. Edgar Hoover to all SACs, December 6, 1939, in U.S. Senate, 94th Cong., 1st sess., *Hearings Before the Select Committee to Study Governmental Operations With Respect to Intelligence Activities* (7 vols., Washington, 1976), VI, 409. Hereafter cited as *Select Committee Hearings*.

40. *Final Report*, II, 35.

41. Francis Biddle, "Memorandum for Hugh B. Cox, Assistant Attorney General and J. Edgar Hoover, Director Federal Bureau of Investigation," July 16, 1943, in *Select Committee Hearings*, 412–13.

42. J. Edgar Hoover to all SACs, August 14, 1943, in *Select Committee Hearings*, 414–15; Donner, *The Age of Surveillance*, 162–63; *Final Report*, III, 421.

43. *Final Report*, III, 422n, 175.

44. Ibid., 421.

45. Sanford J. Ungar, *FBI* (Boston, 1976), 280.

46. Angela Calomiris, *Red Masquerade, Undercover for the F.B.I.* (Philadelphia, 1950), 15.

47. *Final Report*, III, 421.

48. D. M. Ladd, "Memorandum to J. Edgar Hoover," February 27, 1946, in *Final Report*, III, 429–30; Theoharis, *Spying on Americans*, 163–65.

49. *Final Report*, II, 66; William C. Sullivan and Bill Brown, *My Thirty Years in Hoover's FBI* (New York, 1979), 128.

50. J. Edgar Hoover, "Memorandum to the Attorney General," March 8, 1946, in *Final Report*, III, 430.

51. Tom Clark to author, March 28, 1975.

52. Hoover, "Memorandum to the Attorney General," March 8, 1946, in *Final Report*, III, 430; Theoharis, *Spying on Americans*, 44–45.

53. *Final Report*, III, 436.

54. Ibid.

55. FBI Director, "Memorandum to the Attorney General," September 5, 1946, in *Final Report*, III, 436–38.

II

The Politics of Disloyalty

The degree to which the rising anticommunist rhetoric and atmosphere of the early Cold War period can be attributed to the FBI is impossible to determine. It is perhaps significant that those groups to which the Bureau was directing most of its attention, liberals, labor unions, and religious organizations, became early centers for the anticommunist attack. The programs of these groups were to be critical in raising the level of public anxiety, leading to a necessary governmental response. The FBI demanded a substantial role in the developing federal policies to combat domestic "subversion," particularly in the area of government employment.

In May 1946, James Loeb, the national director of the Union for Democratic Action, predecessor of the soon-to-be-formed Americans for Democratic Action, developed an effective anticommunist liberal position in an influential letter to *The New Republic*. Based essentially on a pragmatic approach, Loeb emphasized his belief that no united front organization could gain power "through democratic means." Believing that communists would inevitably seek to take over any group with which they were associated, Loeb urged his fellow liberals to reject communism and cooperation with communists and, implicitly, to seek their goals through expressly anticommunist organizations.[1] The Loeb letter represented an existing division in liberal ranks. Coming in the midst of the gathering debate over foreign policy and in the shadow of the Cold War, it was a stroke of lightning against the quickly weathering face of the popular front—that loose coalition of groups on the political left.

The CIO, the practical fighting arm of the popular front, also felt the lash of anticommunism and reacted in much the same spirit as Loeb's pragmatism. Philip Murray, president of both the CIO and his own United Steelworkers, had the latter unanimously adopt a resolution in May that the union would not "tolerate efforts by outsiders—individuals, organizations or groups—whether they be Communist, Socialist or any other group—to infiltrate, dictate or meddle in our affairs."[2] Later in the year Murray brought the same message to the CIO when he asked the Executive Board to approve a condemnation of communism on the grounds that to fail to do so would make the CIO an effective target for its enemies.[3] The same message was then spread to the Conference of Progressives—an effort to unite politically the advocates of a popular front policy—at the end of September.[4] Soon after, Murray dropped any commitment he might have had to the Conference, indicating a personal break with left coalition policies. With his decision went a major portion of the Conference's possible influence.[5]

The Catholic Church spearheaded the religious reaction against communism. The leadership of the Church had followed a consistent anti-radical, anticommunist position long before the Cold War. In the development of American-Soviet conflict, it was more than ready to play a leading role. In some areas of the United States, it was the first organization to raise the banner against communism.[6] It would appear that the FBI was encouraging the Church's actions as early as 1945.[7]

Francis Cardinal Spellman, the leader of Catholic anticommunism in the Untied States, has been described as being "obsessed" with the dangers of communist subversion.[8] J. Edgar Hoover was apparently pleased to lend his presence to a furtherance of the Cardinal's crusade.[9] Early in 1946, Bishop Fulton J. Sheen, for many years a leader in the anticommunist movement, bitterly condemned "Red Fascism"—a phrase which Hoover often used and helped to popularize.[10] The Association of Catholic Trade Unionists, with the active support of the Church, also was effective and sometimes critical in destroying left-wing influence in the labor movement.[11] In this case the combination of a religious base for anticommunism, with a forceful, active labor campaign was most effective. FBI influence in all these areas was strong, although its pre-COINTELPRO operations did not exist in an anticommunist vacuum.

Rising public clamor, together with international events, made communism a campaign issue in the 1946 midterm elections. The Republican Party nationally—as it had in 1944—raised the specter of a Democratic administration in alliance with the forces of communism. The strident rhetoric of the right added to America's unrest over communism,[12] and the magnitude of the Republican victory caused many to seek a more basic cause than the traditional issues. Some perceived the electoral swing as resulting from the communist issue. Republican success in winning the House of Representatives 246 to 188 and the Senate 51 to 45, and particularly the apparent value of the communist issue in such campaigns as those of Richard Nixon in California and Joseph McCarthy in Wisconsin, were intensely analyzed.[13] The conclusion of the right apparently was that the new "Red Scare" could be an immensely effective political weapon as the presidential election of 1948 approached.

Anticommunist liberals felt an urgent need to dissociate themselves from radicalism. They had seen many liberals defeated in the election, they believed, for failure to join the anticommunist tide. They were determined not to be "redbaited" by the right wing, but to go, in fact, to the right of the right on this issue.[14]

The election results may not have proven conclusively the potency of anticommunism, but they did show that the Republican Party was ready to commit itself to the issue in preparation for the 1948 elections. It appeared certain that with control of Congress, the Republican majority would launch a series of investigations in the area of "subversion" in an attempt to embarrass the administration and to link it with communism.[15] Within a month of organization of the Eightieth Congress "there were thirty-five projected investigations, and none of these offered more bountiful political dividends than did those investigations into the field of loyalty and security."[16] The President, apparently placed in a position of critical political necessity, responded on November 25, 1946, with Executive Order 9806, the establishment of a Temporary Commission on Employee Loyalty.[17]

Most analyses of the Temporary Commission's appointment have seen it as a clear-cut response to political pressures. Some have suggested that the presidential action represented a "panicked reaction" to the 1946 election,[18] while others have seen it as at least a keen awareness of the dangers posed by the new Republican majority.[19] The pressures to establish the Commission were not so new as these analysts would suggest. They had been building for some time, although political reality may have hastened their fruition. The developing political atmosphere since the concluding stages of the war probably had more to do with the appointment of the Commission than the specific 1946 electoral defeat.

A series of events, beginning in 1945, had dramatized for the American people the dangers of government infiltration and had provided political capital for Republicans and some Democrats. In February 1945 more than a thousand classified government documents were discovered in offices of the magazine *Amerasia*. The magazine, run by a friend of Earl Browder, became the center for charges of a vast espionage ring. The fact that the documents were used rather openly in the preparation of articles on Far Eastern affairs, and that none of them ever was transferred to a foreign government did not lessen the fears that grew. These were heightened within a short time by the June 1946 report of the Canadian Royal Commission which had investigated alleged Soviet espionage within the Canadian government. The report, based importantly on the revelations of Soviet defector Igor Gouzenko, detailed the apparent involvement of Canadian citizens in passing national secrets to Soviet agents.[20] The threatened parallel to the United States could not be avoided.

Danger similar to that of the Canadian espionage case was made all the more relevant and believable by the fact that information concerning a United States government spy ring already had been provided. Elizabeth Bentley had gone to the FBI in 1945 to weave a story of espionage in high places. The FBI had sent these reports to the White House for the President's attention, although apparently deliberately omitting the name of its informant at first. Truman later suggested that these Bentley reports were "the key" to the establishment of his loyalty program.[21] The President's administrative assistant and subsequent special counsel, Charles Murphy, recalled: "These Bentley reports did indicate that communist efforts to infiltrate the government were serious, serious enough to require setting up a regular orderly procedure in government for dealing with the problem."[22]

Despite the acknowledged receipt of the Bentley reports in 1945, Truman did not act until a year later. The delay can only be understood in terms of his perception of the threat or, in this case, lack of a threat. Murphy said: "At that time not everyone had made such a fetish of anti-communism. It was the idea of just a few people that because they had some wrong leaf working for the government of the Untied States they were about to destroy us all. It was a little on the preposterous side." Discussing this in 1954, Truman fully agreed with Murphy's assessment. Murphy added that he still doubted there had been sufficient evidence to prove the existence of a government espionage ring.[23]

During the year from the initial Bentley reports to the establishment of the Temporary Commission, internal governmental pressure to act grew greatly. Tom Clark's later assertion that "the real impetus for the order came from the Department of Justice [including the FBI] rather than from any overt Congressional pressure" may well be accurate.[24] Hoover gave the President "successive reports on the supposed spy ring."[25] Clark received what he later estimated to be hundreds of memoranda from the FBI Director during the same period and said that these were decisive in bringing about the creation of the loyalty program.[26] The Attorney General, in turn, used his influence at the White House to the extent that the President later spoke of "the trouble I had with Tom Clark in the setting up of a security program . . . ."[27]

The establishment of federal loyalty precedures was not new. It had begun with section 9A of the 1939 Hatch Act[28] which denied federal employment to any person who was a member of a political party or organization "which advocates the overthrow of our constitutional form of government."[29] The penalty for violation of the law was dismissal from government service. A year later, in providing for enforcement of the provision, the Civil Service Commission defined the Communist Party as coming within the purview of the statute.[30]

In 1940 Congress began the practice of adding a rider to every appropriation act to bar the use of federal funds for the employment of advocates of forceful overthrow of the government. In passing these laws it would seem that Congress was expressing its dislike of communists rather than any real fears of radical infiltration.[31]

In the midst of war, and faced with a series of charges from Martin Dies' Special House Committee on Un-American Activities, the administration attempted to make formal its loyalty procedures. The Attorney General appointed an interdepartmental committee on February 14, 1942, to deal with charges made against federal employees by the Dies committee. With limited authority and facilities, the interdepartmental group requested the Attorney General to draw up a list of organizations coming within the scope of the Hatch Act's section 9A.[32] The Attorney General already had begun such a procedure and had sought the assistance of the FBI a year earlier.[33] The resultant list, considered confidential, was based on FBI files and was circulated throughout the various agencies of the federal government.

The initial loyalty commission was superseded within a year by a more formal interdepartmental committee established by Executive Order 9300. Consisting of five appointees, this group existed within the Department of Justice. It was given the authority to advise on and coordinate all matters dealing with "subversive activity" within the federal government, with the specific exceptions of the Navy and War departments. The FBI was to be the intermediary agency for the receipt of all complaints and evidence. The Bureau was to provide "completed investigative reports" to the interdepartmental committee which could then issue advisory opinions.[34] Although the committee was formally in existence until the establishment of a new loyalty commission, it largely disintegrated after 1945.[35]

The vacuum thus created was quickly filled by the House of Representatives. At the start of the 1945 legislative session, the House Civil Service Committee was authorized to study loyalty among federal employees and loyalty procedures. The resulting subcommittee report was transmitted directly to the President on July 25, 1946. The subcommittee, headed by West Virginia Democrat Jennings Randolph, recommended the establishment of an executive commission to "make a thorough study of existing laws and the adequacy of existing legislation."[36]

On precisely the same day as the subcommittee report went to the President, J. Edgar Hoover wrote to Attorney General Clark recommending that A. Devitt Vanech, a special assistant to the Attorney General, be designated as the Justice Department's representative on the new loyalty commission "if it is set up."[37] This unsolicited nomination by the Director was accepted by Clark some five months before the commission was established.[38] Vanech, a member of the Department for some thirteen years, was known to be very close to Hoover. Clark's quick agreement to appoint him is an indication of the decisive role played by the FBI in the formulation of administration loyalty policy. As events would later show, Vanech's presence on the Commission provided it with a strong FBI advocate and gave it a direct conduit for information. Clark later acknowledged his assistant's close relationship with Hoover, but maintained that Vanech alone would have been unable to control the Commission.[39]

The President, in an apparent attempt to limit the significance of the communist issue in the election, waited until late November to appoint the Temporary Commission. It consisted of an interagency group with one representative from each of the following departments: Justice, State, Treasury, War, and Navy, and also an appointee from the Civil Service Commission. Significantly, the Justice Department representative was designated as chairman, the only administrative procedure predetermined in the President's Order. On the same day as the Commission was formally established, Vanech became its head. The Commission was provided with a far-ranging mandate. It was to recommend a comprehensive federal loyalty program, including standards for new applicants, procedures to be established for existing federal employees, and possible new legislation. The temporary body was given little more than two months to accomplish this task. Its report was to be delivered on or before February 1, 1947.

The Commission's operation was far more limited than its comprehensive final report made apparent. Several witnesses were called to testify, but few provided very much information. FBI Assistant Director D. Milton Ladd appeared, informed the Commission that there was a "substantial number of disloyal persons in government service," but refused to provide supporting data or to be more specific in terms of the severity of the alleged problem. The Commission, dissatisfied with the information and cooperation it had received, requested an appearance by J. Edgar Hoover. Believing that full factual information was necessary before a program could be drawn, its members prepared a full set of questions for Hoover.[40] He did not appear, despite the cooperation required by the Executive Order. Instead, Attorney General Clark made an "informal appearance" before the Commission, and both Clark and Hoover later submitted statements to it.

The Hoover statement provided no evidence of the type which the Commission was seeking. The FBI Director simply alleged that "subversive or disloyal persons constitute a threat" and listed various means by which the disloyal employee might do harm to the United States. These means ranged from possible espionage, to influencing policy, to bringing other "subversives" into government, to the recruitment of other employees.[41] Later letters from War and Naval Intelligence followed almost the exact pattern of the FBI response. Despite its failure to gain concrete evidence, the Commission went ahead to complete its assigned tasks and had a draft report ready before the end of January. Vanech sent a copy of the draft to Hoover so that the FBI might propose concrete changes through the Attorney General.

The FBI Director responded forcefully to several of the loyalty proposals. The Commission had recommended that each agency and department establish its own loyalty procedures. Hoover proposed the creation of a full-time loyalty review board to oversee the entire program with centralized control and appellate jurisdiction. The Commission asked that minimal safeguards be established to protect accused employees. All investigative material used as the basis of charges was to be made available, upon request, to agency and department heads so that a fair evaluation of the importance of evidence and its sources might be made. Hoover bitterly attacked what he perceived to be a threat to the FBI's independence and its informant program. He noted that "the Bureau has steadfastly refused to reveal the identities of its confidential informants," or its means of "technical surveillances"—referring to its wiretapping and bugging procedures. He demanded that the FBI, in providing evidence to other agencies, maintain the right to select and interpret those materials to be extracted from its voluminous files as well as to evaluate the reliability of its sources without revealing them.

Hoover also wanted clarity in provisions granting Civil Service Commission investigative authority. It must remain clear, he said, that the FBI would maintain responsibility in cases involving "subversive activities" of federal employees. Examining the procedural guarantees to be provided to accused employees, Hoover emphasized that the balance must come down in favor of security rather than individual rights and that refusal of or removal from federal employment should take place if "a reasonable ground exists for believing the person involved is disloyal to the Government."[42]

The Hoover recommendations were sent to the Attorney General who, two days later, pencilled in his agreement to each of Hoover's major points and sent the document on to Vanech with an injunction to "keep me advised." Vanech's responsibility was to see that Hoover's proposals, of which he had already received a copy, would be included in the Commission's final report. Given the importance of the Hoover changes and the degree to which they differed from the draft report, the Commission was in reality required to choose between its own concepts and those of the FBI Director. It selected the latter. To provide increased pressure, Clark wrote to the Commission less than a week before the President was to receive its final report. Again, he failed to give any specific factual material for the Commission, but emphasized the seriousness of its undertaking when he wrote that "even one disloyal person constitutes" a serious danger to the United States. His letter explicitly, and now in his own name, supported each of the FBI's major proposals.[43]

The report presented to Truman on February 20, 1947, included the Hoover recommendations, with the exception that the new Loyalty Review Board would be given advisory rather than final appellate jurisdiction. The President, kept informed by Clark of the main outlines of the Commission's work, already was committed to acceptance of its recommendations.

The Issuance of Executive Order 9835 to establish the government's new loyalty program was delayed until March 21. It has been suggested that the President timed his public announcement of the loyalty program to coincide with his Cold War foreign policy initiatives, particularly the Truman Doctrine speech to Congress a week earlier. The international "Red Menace," against which the Truman administration had asked Congress and the people to do battle, was now brought home as a danger to every American.[44] Clifford Durr, at the time a Federal Communications Commission member, later wrote that President Truman had told him that "he had signed the Order to take the ball away from Parnell Thomas."[45] It is perhaps significant that Thomas' House Un-American Activities Committee was about to begin a series of major hearings into "un-American propaganda activities" in the United States. The fear that these and other hearings might be turned into a platform for antiadministration propaganda may well have been real.

Whatever the specific cause of the timing—and it may have served a combination of purposes—the Executive Order played a vital role in the developing internal cold war. It started from the premise that federal employees must be of "complete and unswerving loyalty to the United States." It accepted totally the Clark thesis that any disloyal federal employee represents "a threat to our democratic processes." The Order described a loyalty system whose objective, as Athan Theoharis suggested, was "absolute security."[46] Each department and agency was to establish its own loyalty board and rules. Every prospective employee was to undergo investigation by the Civil Service Commission, and a positive determination of loyalty would be necessary for employment. Each current employee was to be checked by the FBI for any indication of possible disloyalty. Where such indication existed a full field investigation was to take place. Investigators were to use all possible "pertinent" sources, including the voluminous files of HUAC. No definition of "loyalty" was provided, but perhaps that resulted from the President's belief—undoubtedly shared by others—that "you're either loyal to the United States, or you're not!"[47]

Perhaps the most far-reaching aspect of the Order was its requirement that the Attorney General draw up a list of "totalitarian, fascist, communist, or subversive" organizations for dissemination by the Loyalty Review Board and use in determining possible "disloyalty."[48] The purpose of the Attorney General's list was to provide the FBI with "a substantive legal basis for the . . . investigation of allegedly 'subversive' organizations which might fall within these categories."[49]

Far from resolving the dispute over the loyalty program, the Executive Order spawned an immediate, bitter struggle over investigative authority between the Civil Service Commission and the FBI. Despite the fact that the Order expressly gave major authority to the Commission and a clearly secondary role to the Bureau, Hoover, aided by Attorney General Clark and his assistant Vanech, engaged in a bitter struggle to reverse the practical effect of the Order. The major battlegrounds were in the administration's Bureau of the Budget and in Congress. The Executive Order could not become effective until a congressional appropriation was made, and the initial step would be budget estimates which would be sent to the President and then on to Congress.

Intense Department of Justice pressure resulted in a budget proposal to give the FBI full responsibility for all loyalty inquiries. The Civil Service Commission was to be limited to initial examinations of new employees, but if any loyalty question was developed, the FBI would conduct the full field investigation.[50] The Commission fought back in an April 25, 1947, letter to the President in which, while conceding to the FBI the power to deal with current workers, it maintained that allowing the Bureau to investigate prospective employees would immediately place political suspicion upon them.[51]

Truman "sided positively" with the Commission and opposed Hoover's position, despite pressure from his chief political lieutenants. Both Clark Clifford and his assistant, George Elsey, believed that Congress would support the FBI no matter what position the administration took. After a visit from the President, Elsey noted that Truman "wants to be sure & hold F.B.I. down, afraid of 'Gestapo!' "[52] Clifford was ordered to seek a more equitable agreement and succeeded in achieving a new budget proposal giving Civil Service discretionary power to turn over loyalty investigations involving new personnel to the FBI. The emphasis was that the Commission "*may,* if it wishes, call on the F.B.I."[53] The resulting budget allocation request gave the Commission double the FBI allocation to carry out the Executive Order. The President signed and sent the new budget proposal to Congress.

Hoover responded with an impressive demonstration of influence in Congress. While Clifford believed the administration would be able to push its program through, Truman disagreed. In a handwritten note to his assistant, he predicted that "J. Edgar will in all probability get this backward looking Congress to give him what he wants. It's dangerous."[54] The President was right. Congress more than reversed the requested budget allocations, providing $7.4 million to the FBI and $3 million to the Civil Service.[55] Through the exercise of its powers, and at the rather clear instigation of the Justice Department and the FBI, Congress thus settled the dispute. The FBI would now have full authority, on its own terms, for loyalty investigations.[56]

Latter day commentators have suggested that the FBI's role was not really a crucial question and have accepted Elsey's argument that the uses of investigatory material were more important than who did the investigations. The administration of the program, in this view, was of primary importance.[57] These views ignore the fact that the very base of the program was provided by the confidential information distributed by the FBI without any independent check on its procedures or sources.

There is widespread agreement that the creation of the loyalty program was a prime factor in the development of anticommunist hysteria. Historians and political scientists have differed on the degree and/or reality of an internal threat which may have been present and on the necessity for a comprehensive federal loyalty program. Few have rejected the thesis that the speed with which the program was created and the rhetoric to which it was attached were instrumental in needlessly creating the image of an internal "Red Menace."[58] The President of the United States had joined those who saw an internal communist danger. The threat seemingly was sufficiently severe to force the creation of a hasty program, and one whose objective was absolute security. Communists were to be considered so dangerous that even one in the government could endanger national security. Could it be less so in a factory, a union, or a school? Rather than quieting the demand for anticommunist programs, the President's Executive Order greatly enhanced and legitimized the existing fear.

The continual unfolding of the loyalty program, over a period of more than a year, served to maintain the generalized atmosphere of fear. Every two or three weeks, after the congressional approval of the appropriation for the program, new developments were taking place. Agencies were instructed to complete forms on employees, the forms were sent in, they went to the FBI; the Loyalty Review Board was created and held its first meeting—the measures needed by the federal government seemed interminable and overwhelming.

Perhaps most significant in the process, and particularly so since no revelations of a communist conspiracy in the government were forthcoming, was the development of the Attorney General's list of "subversive" organizations to be used as a guide for action in loyalty proceedings. The Department of Justice began with the list of forty-seven organizations which had been developed and secretly used during World War II. With that as a base, it sought to determine which organizations should be added. The procedure employed was entirely at the discretion of the Department of Justice. There was no effort to involve other branches of the government, nor were the organizations being considered for inclusion consulted. Once again the FBI played a vital role. It provided the Attorney General with summaries on groups which it deemed worthy of possible inclusion on the list. Often these summaries contained little or no identifying data as to sources. There was never a definition of the various categories into which these organizations might fall. The concept of "subversive" for one might be quite different for another.

Attorney General Clark designated James McInerney, head of the Internal Security Section of the Criminal Division, to coordinate the list procedure. The raw FBI reports were disseminated to thirty to thirty-five attorneys within the Justice Department. They used these reports to suggest what organizations ought to be included on the list. The recommendations went to the Attorney General and his principal assist-ants.[59] According to Clark, if any assistant objected to the inclusion of an organization, it was deleted.[60] The initial list of some ninety orga-nizations was made public on December 4, 1947. In releasing it, the At-torney General warned: "Guilt by association has never been one of the principles of American jurisprudence. We must be satisfied that rea-sonable grounds exist for concluding that an individual is disloyal. That must be the guide."[61]

In the context of the period, Clark's warning, if it was really meant to be such, was lost. Compiled in secret and made public with consid-erable fanfare, the list presented the American people with a bewilder-ing assortment of organizations with unfamiliar names and seemingly dangerous purposes. "Proof" was now available for everyone to see that there really did exist a "subversive" network of people and organiza-tions within the United States.

The President was well aware of the gathering hysteria. A few days before the issuance of the first list he had warned the cabinet that the loyalty program had to be based on fact rather than simply on suspi-cion. It must not be allowed to follow the road of HUAC, he said.[62] The public furor following the list's publication forced Truman to try to temper the growing fear. "Membership in an organization," he said in a public statement, "is simply one piece of evidence which may or may not be helpful in arriving at a conclusion as to the action which is to be taken in a particular case."[63] That concept was then sent to the Loyalty Review Board which incorporated it into its rules of procedure.[64]

On the same day the President apparently tried to limit the signifi-cance of the Attorney General's list, two important statements were made—one public, one private—which undermined his attempt. Tru-man declared, in the same statement, that the FBI would now conduct all loyalty investigations,[65] thus ratifying Hoover's complete victory in his struggle within the administration and destroying Truman's limited effort to curtail the power of what was swiftly assuming the propor-tions of a political police. Within the cabinet, the Attorney General was making clear that his list would be greatly expanded. He suggested that left-wing labor unions might be added, and that the Lawyer's Guild—a widely reputed left-wing organization of attorneys—was being con-sidered for inclusion. There was apparently no objection from the Pres-ident or other cabinet officials.[66] Within three years close to two hundred organizations were included.

Most of the American people apparently accepted the government's characterization of these organizations. Within a few years a former member of the Justice Department would write: "The doctrine of guilt by association which was repudiated by the Attorney General when he issued his list has become the effective policy in its general use."[67] Clark later recalled that "without our advice or approval" states, municipalities, private companies, organizations, schools, and other disparate groups began to use the list.[68]

Conservative and reactionary politicians believed the list provided the proof of the "Red Menace's" reality they had been seeking for years. Curiously, some liberal anticommunists found a common ground with them. Although indicating some distaste for the concept of such a listing, particularly without benefit of a hearing, they saw in it a convenient means for isolating those who still supported the popular front concept.[69]

The inception of the Cold War had frightened the American people and made them susceptible to anxiety over a possible internal security threat. The development of the federal loyalty program, rather than reassuring the people, intensified their fears. In acceding to the demand for demonstrable anticommunist action, the Truman administration emboldened the political right wing and added to its popular constituency. The President had dropped a ball at the top of a long, steep hill. As the ball rolled down the incline, it gained momentum. Attempts to stop it in the middle of its descent would not please the ever increasing crowd—both the public and government officials.

NOTES

1. James Loeb, Jr., "Progressives and Communists," *The New Republic*, CXIV (May 13, 1946), 699.

2. Joseph R. Starobin, *American Communism in Crisis, 1943–1957* (Cambridge, 1972), 147.

3. Mary S. McAuliffe, *Crisis on the Left: Cold War Politics and American Liberals, 1947–1954* (Amherst, 1978), 15.

4. Curtis D. MacDougall, *Gideon's Army* (3 vols., New York, 1965), I, 106.

5. Alonzo Hamby, *Beyond the New Deal: Harry S. Truman and American Liberalism* (New York, 1973), 156.

6. Ronald W. Johnson, "The Communist Issue in Missouri: 1946–1956" (Ph.D. Diss., University of Missouri, 1973), 2.

7. Donald F. Crosby, "The Politics of Religion," in Robert Griffith and Athan Theoharis, eds., *Original Essays on the Cold War and the Origins of McCarthyism* (New York, 1974), 28.

8. Ibid., 29.

9. David Caute, *The Great Fear: The Anti-Communist Purge Under Truman and Eisenhower* (New York, 1978), 108.

10. Crosby, "The Politics of Religion," 30.

11. Ibid., 35.

12. McAuliffe, *Crisis on the Left*, 4.

13. Robert J. Donovan, *Conflict and Crisis, the Presidency of Harry S Truman, 1945–1948* (New York, 1977), 237.

14. Leslie Adler, "The Red Image: American Attitudes Toward Communism in the Cold War Era" (Ph.D. Diss., University of California, Berkeley, 1970), 340; Hamby, *Beyond the New Deal*, 157.

15. Donovan, *Conflict and Crisis*, 242–43.

16. Robert Griffith, *The Politics of Fear: Joseph R. McCarthy and the Senate* (Rochelle Park, N.J., 1978), 40.

17. Eleanor Bontecou, *The Federal Loyalty-Security Program* (Ithaca, 1953), 274–75.

18. Fred J. Cook, *The Nightmare Decade, The Life and Times of Senator Joe McCarthy* (New York, 1971), 62.

19. Adler, "The Red Image," 321; Donovan, *Conflict and Crisis*, 242–43, 193; Susan M. Hartmann, *Truman and the 80th Congress* (Columbia, 1971), 17–18.

20. Bontecou, *The Federal Loyalty-Security Program*, 21.

21. Harry S Truman, Post-Presidential Conversations Memoirs 1, November 19, 1954, Post-Presidential File (PPF), Harry S. Truman Library, Independence, Missouri. Hereafter cited as HSTL.

22. Charles Murphy, Post-Presidential Conversations Memoirs 1, November 19, 1954, PPF, HSTL.

23. Harry S Truman and Charles Murphy, Post-Presidential Conversations Memoirs 1, November 19, 1954, PPF, HSTL.

24. Francis H. Thompson, "Truman and Congress: The Issue of Loyalty, 1946–1952" (Ph.D. Diss., Texas Tech University, 1970), 18.

25. Murphy, Post-Presidential Conversations Memoirs 1, November 19, 1954, HSTL.

26. Tom Clark to author, March 28, 1975.

27. Truman, Post-Presidential Conversations Memoirs 1, November 19, 1954, HSTL.

28. Athan Theoharis, *Spying on Americans: Political Surveillance from Hoover to the Huston Plan* (Philadelphia, 1978), 197–209.

29. Bontecou, *The Federal Loyalty-Security Program*, 284.

30. Ibid., 285–86.

31. Ibid., 12.

32. Herbert Gaston, Interview, April 5, 1949, Box 8, Internal Security File-Interdepartmental Committee on Employee Investigation Folder. Hereafter box numbers and folder designations will be cited as 8/Internal Security . . . . Papers of Eleanor Bontecou, HSTL.

33. Bontecou, *The Federal Loyalty-Security Program*, 166.

34. Ibid., 272–73.

35. Ibid., 20.

36. Alan D. Harper, *The Politics of Loyalty: The White House and the Communist Issue, 1946–1952* (Westport, 1969), 24.

37. J. Edgar Hoover, "Memorandum to the Attorney General," July 25, 1946, 1/ADV Loyalty Commission, Papers of A. Devitt Vanech, HSTL.

38. Attorney General Clark to J. Edgar Hoover, July 31, 1946, 1/ADV Loyalty Commission, Papers of A. Devitt Vanech, HSTL.

39. Tom Clark to author, March 28, 1975.

40. Stephen J. Spingarn, Oral History Interview, 44, HSTL.

41. Bontecou, *The Federal Loyalty-Security Program*, 300–302.

42. Director, FBI, "Memorandum to the Attorney General," January 29, 1947, 1/F.B.I. Loyalty, Papers of A. Devitt Vanech, HSTL.

43. Bontecou, *The Federal Loyalty-Security Program*, 307.

44. Richard M. Freeland, *The Truman Doctrine and the Origins of McCarthyism, Foreign Policy, Domestic Politics, and Internal Security 1946–1948* (New York, 1972), 115.

45. Cook, *The Nightmare Decade*, 64.

46. Athan Theoharis, *Seeds of Repression: Harry S. Truman and the Origins of McCarthyism* (Chicago, 1971), 102.

47. Harper, *The Politics of Loyalty*, 233.

48. Bontecou, *The Federal Loyalty-Security Program*, 275–81.

49. U.S. Senate, 94th Cong., 2d sess., *Final Report of the Select Committee to Study Governmental Operations with Respect to Intelligence Activities* (6 vols., Washington, 1976), III, 433.

50. George Elsey, "Handwritten Notes," May 2, 1947, 69/Internal Security-Federal Employee Loyalty Program, E.O. 9835, Papers of George Elsey, HSTL.

51. George Elsey, "Handwritten Notes," May 5, 1947, 69/Internal Security-Federal Employee Loyalty Program, E.O. 9835, Papers of George Elsey, HSTL.

52. Elsey, "Handwritten Notes," May 2, 1947, HSTL.

53. Clark M. Clifford, "Memorandum for the President," May 9, 1947, 69/Internal Security-Federal Employee Loyalty Program, E.O. 9835, Papers of George Elsey, HSTL.

54. Clark M. Clifford, "Memorandum for the President," May 23, 1947, 11/Loyalty investigation, Papers of Clark Clifford, HSTL.

55. Bontecou, *The Federal Loyalty-Security Program*, 34.

56. Ibid., 75.

57. Clifford, "Memorandum for the President," May 7, 1947, HSTL; Hamby, *Beyond the New Deal*, 171.

58. Adler, "The Red Image," 334–35; Bontecou, *The Federal Loyalty-Security Program*, 155; Caute, *The Great Fear*, 269; Hamby, *Beyond the New Deal*, 379; Harper, *The Politics of Loyalty*, 45; Theoharis, *The Seeds of Repression*, 12; Sanford J. Ungar, *FBI* (Boston, 1976), 86.

59. Philip B. Perlman, Post-Presidential Conversations Memoirs 2, December 15, 1954, PPF, HSTL; Bontecou, *The Federal Loyalty-Security Program*, 168–69; U.S. House of Representatives, 80th Cong., 2d sess., Appropriations Committee, *Department of Justice Appropriations Bill for 1949. Hearings . . .* (Washington, 1948), 12.

60. Tom Clark to author, March 28, 1975.

61. *The New York Times*, December 5, 1947.

62. Notes on Cabinet Meetings, October 31, 1947, PPF, Papers of Matthew J. Connelly, HSTL.

63. Harry S. Truman, *Public Papers of the Presidents of the United States 1947* (Washington, 1963), 491.

64. "Summary of the Orders of the Loyalty Board," 11/Internal Security File-Attorney General's List of Subversive Organizations, Papers of Eleanor Bontecou, HSTL.

65. Truman, *Public Papers . . . 1947*, 490.

66. Notes on Cabinet Meetings, November 14, 1947, PPF, Papers of Matthew J. Connelly, HSTL.

67. Bontecou, *The Federal Loyalty-Security Program*, 179.

68. Tom Clark, Oral History Interview, 103–4, HSTL.

69. Arthur M. Schlesinger, Jr., *The Vital Center, The Politics of Freedom* (Boston, 1949), 121.

III

The Politics of Anticommunism

If the federal loyalty issue had arisen in a political vacuum, it might have burned bright for a short while and then died from lack of oxygen. Far from a vacuum existed. Anticommunism fed the flames of the loyalty issue and was, in turn, fed by its increased incandescence. The FBI continued to stoke the fires. As each specific anticommunist issue arose, the Bureau, most often privately and indirectly, made its contribution.

In the midst of the Joint Congressional Committee on Atomic Energy confirmation hearings on the appointment of David Lilienthal as chairman of the Atomic Energy Commission, Tennessee Democratic Senator Kenneth McKellar and others accused Lilienthal of procommunist leanings.[1] Republicans began using the Lilienthal hearings to reopen the entire communist issue[2] and the President became politically vulnerable prior to his loyalty program Executive Order.

Hoover chose this opportunity to begin a series of reports to the President pinning a communist or procommunist label on leading members of the scientific community. While never directly attacking Lilienthal, to whom the President had given unqualified support, Hoover created the image of a procommunist plot within the scientific community to achieve his confirmation. The main "conspirator" upon whom Hoover fastened was Dr. Harlow Shapley, director of the Harvard Observatory. Shapley, a vice chairman of the Progressive Citizens of America and recently under attack by the House Un-American Activities Committee (HUAC), was apparently placed under intense surveillance by FBI agents who reported on his meetings and conversations. Hoover claimed that Shapley was in indirect contact with Lilienthal and that the latter had agreed that Shapley should seek to gain support for him while publicly remaining out of the controversy.[3]

Perhaps most bizarre in Hoover's reports was his allegation that Shapley, in attempting to gain backing for the creation of a federally supported national science foundation, had used a "tactical scheme very similar to the general operational procedures of the Communist Party."[4] The doctrine of guilt by association was now seemingly supplemented by the concept of guilt by operational similarity.

The fact that no crimes were even alleged by the FBI in these accounts, and that they were reporting on acceptable legal actions, apparently did not concern the White House at all. Instead of calling a halt to the memoranda, there seemed to be encouragement of them. Hoover needed no inducement in the area of science. During the Lilienthal controversy he attacked the loyalty of other leading scientists in long letters to the President. Most prominent among these subjects were J. Robert Oppenheimer, his brother Frank,[5] and Dr. Edward Condon, director of the National Bureau of Standards.[6]

An attempt was made by Hoover to link an alleged scientific conspiracy with other issues in which the FBI had an interest. Shapley, for example, was quoted as sharply criticizing the Bureau by sarcastically welcoming its agents—apparently correctly—to a Madison Square Garden meeting in late March 1947.[7] Earlier he had reportedly laid plans for an attack upon Secretary of Labor Lewis Schwellenbach as a result of the latter's suggestion to outlaw the Communist Party.[8]

Testifying before the House Education and Labor Committee on March 11, 1947, Schwellenbach had launched an anticommunist campaign which was to have important consequences. Commenting on the suggestion that Wagner Act rights should be withdrawn from unions which elect "Commmunists or subversive officials," the Labor Secretary not only agreed but said "that you do not go far enough. Why should we recognize the Communist Party in the United States?" The apparent call for outlawing the CPUSA was expanded as Schwellenbach added: "Why should they be able to elect people to public office and theoretically at least elect Members of Congress and why should we have an organization recognized which has as its purpose the overthrow of the Government of the United States by force and violence."[9]

The Schwellenbach statement was a double bombshell. It served as active encouragement for HUAC, just about to open extensive hearings on the Communist Party, and it encouraged the House Education and Labor Committee to include an anticommunist provision in the comprehensive labor legislation then being drawn. From the administration's point of view, the timing was crucial and very possibly deliberate. The next day the President was to deliver his Truman Doctrine speech. Just two days before Schwellenbach spoke, Clark Clifford had informed his assistant that Truman's speech was to be "the opening gun in a campaign to bring people up to [the] realization that the war isn't over by any means."[10] Schwellenbach's proposal apparently was the domestic equivalent of that speech.

Encouraged by friends who applauded him for taking "a poke at the Commies,"[11] and receiving the tacit approval of the administration which made no move to silence him, Schwellenbach followed up in the next week with a call for a constitutional amendment to outlaw the Communist Party.[12]

While informal discussions went on in the White House, there was never any specific consideration of the Schwellenbach proposals.[13] Questioned at a press conference at the end of March, Truman refused to comment on his cabinet officer's statements and said that Schwellenbach had been speaking for himself.[14] Truman had in the past been quoted as saying that Schwellenbach was a man who "saw right down the same alley on public policy" with him.[15] The connection of the Labor Secretary's views to those of Truman was natural and inevitable without a specific denial. None was forthcoming. Later in the year Schwellenbach was still declaring his support for a proposal to outlaw the Communist Party.[16]

Encouraged by the Schwellenbach statement, the Executive Order on loyalty, and the support of the Department of Justice, HUAC opened its next round of hearings on March 24, 1947. The Attorney General had cooperated publicly with the Committee a month earlier when he had suddenly issued a "presidential warrant" by telephone to New York for the detention of Gerhard Eisler, a refugee from Nazi Germany and an alleged international communist representative. Eisler had been under surveillance by the FBI for three years,[17] and his presence had been well known to the Committee's members. They determined to make him a star attraction at their February hearings. Claiming that he was about to flee the country—a strange charge in light of the fact that the government had been seeking his deportation earlier—J. Parnell Thomas, New Jersey Republican and Committee chairman, had asked Clark to ensure Eisler's presence at the hearing. The assistance of the Attorney General insured a violent confrontation when Eisler was denied an opportunity to make a statement, leading to fifteen minutes of shouting and his forcible removal from the HUAC hearing room.[18] Following the Eisler hearing, Thomas wrote to Clark urging government action against the supposedly uncovered "Moscow-directed fifth column." Clark replied that the Department "will as it has in the past, cooperate fully" with the Committee.[19]

The Attorney General's promise was carried out quickly, although

Clark might well have come to regret his action. On March 14 Thomas sent a telegram to FBI Director Hoover requesting him to appear before the Committee on March 28 to submit recommendations dealing with communism and specifically with proposed legislation. A few days later Hoover sent an assistant to Thomas to indicate that he would prefer not to appear since extensive testimony might require dealing with confidential sources and methods of collection. Thomas informed the assistant the "discussion of legislation was the excuse for the meeting which will be held next week but that in reality it will be a full-dress denunciation of Communism."

Hoover immediately wrote to the Attorney General outlining the situation and suggesting that the disclosure of Bureau techniques would greatly inhibit the investigation of communists. He proposed that Clark use his influence to induce the Committee not to call him.[20] Clark sent the Hoover letter to A. Devitt Vanech, once again acting as the FBI man in the Department. It was arranged that Hoover would appear before the Committee to read a prepared denunciation of communism, but would not be subjected to specific forms of questioning. The Committee was thus provided with its star expert on communism through the good offices of the administration, and its hearings proceeded on schedule.

Mississippi Democratic Congressman John Rankin opened the hearings. He had introduced (H.R. 1884) one of the two bills which were to provide the legislative excuse for taking testimony. Rankin noted: "The President's Executive Order goes a long way toward meeting the situation, or the provisions, I will say, at least, of the bill which I introduced . . . but at the same time realizing we are now in a death grapple between oriental Communism and western civilization, I think we should proceed with the hearings . . . . "[21] The Rankin bill was "to prohibit certain un-American activities," and would have barred Communist Party candidates from the ballot, forbidden favorable teaching of communism, and stopped the use of the mails for spreading "Communist ideology."

The other bill (H.R. 2122) was more direct. It was to outlaw the CPUSA.[22] Hoover did not disappoint the Committee in its real purposes. His statement was later issued as a separate document.[23] The heart of it was an exaggerated description of the "Red Menace:"

The Communist Party of the United States is a fifth column if there ever was one. It is far better organized than were the Nazis in occupied countries prior to their capitulation.

They are seeking to weaken America just as they did in their era of obstruction when they alined [sic] with the Nazis. Their goal is the overthrow of our Government.[24]

Although Hoover indicated he had "grave doubts as to the wisdom" of a law outlawing the Communist Party, on the ground that it would tend to drive the CP underground, thereby making more difficult the task of surveillance and control, he did favor "unrelenting prosecution wherever they are found to be violating our country's law."[25] While indicating no support for specific new legislation, he emphasized his belief that "such laws as we have now should be vigorously enforced, and maybe some of them strengthened."[26] This concentration on strict enforcement of existing laws and particularly their use against communists was to be a continuing FBI theme throughout the Cold War and was to be carried out largely on the basis of the Bureau's influence.

The remainder of the HUAC hearings lacked the drama of Hoover's presentation, with the exception of the appearance, at his request, of Communist Party General Secretary Eugene Dennis. The confrontation, scheduled on the same day as the Hoover statement, resulted in no testimony. Dennis was forcibly ejected from the hearing room, amidst a scene of chaos and confusion, as he refused to reply to the initial Committee questions concerning his "real name."[27]

At the end of March there was confirmation of what has been termed "the active alliance of the Administration, through the Justice Department, and H.U.A.C."[28] The Department secured the indictment of seventeen leaders of the Joint Anti-Fascist Refugee Committee on the grounds of contempt of Congress for refusal to produce their records before HUAC. A month later indictments were gained against CP leader Dennis and communist attorney Leon Josephson for contempt in their refusal to testify before the Committee.

The administration alliance with HUAC was becoming decidedly one sided. Shortly after the conclusion of hearings, Thomas wrote to Clark demanding that the Communist Party be prosecuted under either the Foreign Agents Registration Act or the Voorhis Act. The latter required organizations subject to foreign control and engaged in political activity to register with the attorney general.[29] The failure, indeed the inability of the administration to act under these laws, due to insufficient evidence, having helped to raise the level of fear in the United States, caused an inevitable reaction.

On the same day the House voted to cite Dennis and Josephson for contempt, two congressmen called for the impeachment of the Attorney General in order to force the Justice Department to prosecute communists. Thomas took the occasion to declare that communists had been given virtual "immunity" from prosecution by the administration and to reiterate his demand for action.[30] The same day Thomas wrote the President a letter published in the press before it was delivered to the White House. He maintained that Truman did not understand the seriousness of the "Communist menace" as did FBI Director Hoover. Thomas asserted that the "fifth column within our midst" might well soon threaten the security of the American people, and he charged the Department of Justice with failure to prosecute these "conspirators."[31] Truman testily replied, "The Attorney General will do his duty as it should be done and in the interest of the welfare of the United States."[32] The President's willingness to go along with the actions of HUAC was now over.

The Attorney General believed it necessary both to prove the Justice Department's determination to act, and to shield the administration from the increasing anticommunist tide. Clark began to accept speaking engagements throughout the country. Wherever he travelled, his theme was the same. The United States was threatened internally by communism, but it must not revert to the methods of Nazism to combat the danger. The latter was an answer to right-wing critics, particularly those in Congress, but increasingly the emphasis was on the former. In April, Clark took advantage of a Jefferson Day dinner to tie the knot between the external and internal dangers which he perceived. He attacked Henry Wallace—the symbolic leader of antiadministration liberals, who was then travelling in Europe—and demanded that Congress pass legislation implementing the Truman Doctrine in order to provide "protection against expanding totalitarianism."[33] Was this to include the "totalitarians" in our midst? Clark did not leave the question open to consideration for long. Within a month he warned that the Department of Justice was studying whether the Communist Party was "the arm of a foreign government" and was "getting up some yardstick for gauging subversive activities."[34] Two days later he said that America must be kept "safe from the Fifth Column and equally safe from the Gestapo." He added: "How many subversives can the United States afford to harbor? Our answer is: Not a single one. It is my purpose to make this a living reality. This can—and it will—be done."[35] The quest for a mythical absolute security from "subversives" could only mean a massive witch hunt, but Clark refused to draw the logical conclusion of his rhetoric.

Clark was now speaking the language of the FBI. His choice of words was deliberately taken from Hoover's statements. The Attorney General did more than just accept Hoover phraseology. In late April 1947, he appointed Vanech as an assistant attorney general.[36] The service

Vanech had done for the President on the Temporary Commission, his identification with a tough loyalty program, and his closeness to Hoover and the FBI were all seemingly important factors in the selection. The appointment symbolized Clark's growing dependence on Hoover.

In June, Clark accepted an FBI recommendation for a new internal security law. The legislation, submitted to the Bureau of the Budget—the administration clearinghouse for all proposals—provided criminal penalties for any person who attempted to give information relating to the national security to any other person not entitled to receive it. The general nature of this provision would have given enormous powers to the Justice Department and particularly the FBI. A second major clause was even more controversial. The Department proposed to "authorize wire-tapping and to ascertain or prevent interference with the national security and defense."[37] The FBI was attempting to gain legislative approval for its long-standing practices.[38]

Clark continued in June with a program to consolidate his alliance with Hoover and at the same time deflect partisan anticommunist attacks against the administration. In what was his most important step, he had a special grand jury empanelled in New York to investigate possible "subversion." Specifically the grand jury would hear the testimony of witnesses such as Elizabeth Bentley and Whittaker Chambers and, although its proceedings were supposed to be held in absolute secrecy, there were as many "leaks" as there were jury sessions.[39] The jury's deliberations led to no indictments for treason or espionage—a fact Clark could undoubtedly have forecast since the Department of Justice had heard all these witnesses in 1945 and had found no indictable offenses at that time or since.[40]

The significance of the grand jury lay more in the personnel assigned to control it than in the specific evidence it initially heard. Clark always believed it necessary to hold weapons in his arsenal, and the grand jury represented just such a threat. It would be there for more than a year, waiting to do the bidding of the Justice Department when and if needed. To take charge of the jury, Clark chose Thomas J. Donegan and T. Vincent Quinn. Donegan had been in the FBI for thirteen years. He had been a trusted adviser and aide to Hoover, and had been in charge of the Newark office of the FBI. He then had acted as an administrative assistant to the Director in Washington. In 1941 he was transferred to the New York office—perhaps considered the most important during the war—as assistant special agent in charge. As such he had been involved in various anti-"subversive" actions and presumably was particularly conversant with the Communist Party, whose national headquarters were a part of his jurisdiction. In March 1946 Donegan resigned from the FBI in order to practice law in New York. Hoover publicly described him at that time as "loyal, industrious and efficient" and praised him for making a "vital contribution to the achievements of the FBI."[41] A year later Donegan was back in the government, but now as a special assistant attorney general in charge of the grand jury.

The former FBI agent was joined by Quinn, a man closely tied to the Queens County Democratic Party machine. As an assistant United States attorney during the war years, he had worked closely with the FBI on black market and other activities and was known as a close friend of the Bureau. Appointed in 1945 as United States attorney for the Eastern District of New York, Quinn had returned to the Justice Department in 1947 in order to be assistant attorney general in charge of the Criminal Division and to share responsibility for the grand jury. The presence of Donegan and Quinn insured the FBI a direct line to and from the jury.

Clark's rhetoric warmed as did the summer weather. Speaking before five thousand religious leaders in the American heartland in July, he warned against the spread of "atheistic communism"—a favorite concept of Hoover.[42] In the fall his warning to "subversives" became even more explicit. "Those who deny freedom to others," he said, "cannot long retain it for themselves—and under a just God they do not deserve it. We must share our freedom—and exchange it—with others, lest we shall lose it entirely."[43]

The FBI-Department of Justice-HUAC connection and its propaganda had a decided impact on the growing anticommunist atmosphere. Concerts by Paul Robeson in such areas as Peoria, Illinois, and Albany, New York, were cancelled by local politicians who believed they had to act in consonance with a growing fear of "procommunist" activity.[44] Bricks were thrown through the windows of Communist Party offices in Richmond, Virginia. In Essex County, New Jersey, local communists were unable to rent a hall for a public meeting, and in Trenton, New Jersey, a riot broke up a meeting featuring Gerhard Eisler as the main speaker.[45] The American Legion's National Convention called for the outlawing of the Communist Party.[46] A short time later Alabama began a wave of state legislation by declaring the Party illegal.[47] At the beginning of November 1947, a rally by the Progressive Citizens of America in Philadelphia's Independence Square was broken up by a mob of several hundred.[48] Violence in the streets—albeit still on a very small scale— was supplementing rhetoric, and the potential for its growth was real. Clark later admitted that the danger he had portrayed in 1947 "was more imagined than real."[49] Many years too late, he reflected, "I was around the country making speeches myself—which maybe I shouldn't have done."[50]

The pressure on the President was growing greater. To some extent, despite the activities of the security agencies of the government, Truman tried to oppose it. Receiving a request in November from the Veterans of Foreign Wars to outlaw the Communist Party and its newspaper, Truman had his secretary reply, "The President has *not* agreed to any request to initiate proceedings to outlaw the Communist Party and the Daily Worker. The President does not contemplate any such action."[51] There is no evidence that this statement of presidential policy was inaccurate, although the federal government had already commenced action to attack the Communist Party. It is very probable that the President had no knowledge of the reality of the internal security measures being taken.

The effects of the Schwellenbach proposal to outlaw the Communist Party, Executive Order 9835, and the rising internal security dialogue was nowhere felt more critically than in the field of labor relations. The inclusion and passage of section 9(h) of the Labor-Management Relations (Taft-Hartley) Act of 1947 came rather directly from all these sources. A legal scholar has suggested that the Executive Order's authorization of dismissal of government employees concerning whom there were "reasonable grounds" to suspect disloyalty led directly to section 9(h) which required labor union officers to file affidavits assuring that they were noncommunist, or have their unions denied the protection of the National Labor Relations Act.[52] There is important evidence to support this view. Shortly after passage of the measure, Ohio's Republican Senator Robert Taft sought to justify it by emphasizing that the federal government had already led the way by barring communists from federal employment. Assuming that "Communist infiltration" in labor represented "a real threat" to the United States, Taft, with some degree of accuracy, suggested that those who had supported the President's Executive Order should do no less with regard to the labor law.[53]

The passage of section 9(h) was critically important in its reflection of the political value of anticommunism, its real effect on communist influence and activity, its evidence of the weakness of liberal opposition, and most important in the coalition formed to gain its passage and implementation. An unusual and surprisingly effective group formed to support 9(h). Its power was demonstrated by its success. The coalition included important business elements, increasingly conservative politicians, right-wing labor leaders, and the internal security establishment of the national administration. The result of the efforts of this strong coalition, in the absence of any countervailing force, was the swift inclusion of the anticommunist clause in the bill prepared by the House Committee on Education and Labor. The provision required that the

National Labor Relations Board not certify a labor union if any of its officers was or ever had been a member of the Communist Party or "believed in" or was in any way associated with any organization teaching the forcible overthrow of the government.[54] The entire Hartley bill passed the House by a 308 to 107 margin on April 17, 1947—little more than a month after the Schwellenbach testimony.

The anticommunist provision was not considered by the Senate until an amendment on the Senate floor by Arkansas Democrat John McClellan added a clause to the bill similar to that adopted earlier by the House.[55] Drafted somewhat more judiciously, the McClellan amendment dropped the concept of past membership in the Communist Party. The two congressional anticommunist provisions were merged into section 9(h) by the Conference Committee at the end of May, at the time the Taft and Hartley bills were combined into an omnibus labor bill.

The formal administration role in connection with section 9(h) was almost nonexistent. There was no effort to oppose the section, no testimony concerning it—other than Schwellenbach's general supporting statements. Administration forces opposed the labor bill created by the Republican majority, but the anticommunist provision was not one of their concerns. An internal analysis of the clause just prior to its being reported out by the Conference Committee concluded that on balance "We favor the provision . . . since it provides a statement of policy which has been sorely missing from national thinking on the subject of industrial relations."[56] The only objection raised to the measure was that it might drive the communists in the labor movement "underground." There was no discussion of civil liberties questions or the possible effects of this anticommunist statement on the national political atmosphere.

Much of the administration appeared little concerned with this effort to rid unions of possible communist officers, but not the FBI, nor the Attorney General, who joined with Schwellenbach to support the provision. Believing it "was necessary for us to have some weapon to use," Clark emphasized the importance of protecting key industries from possible communist influence.[57] But the Taft-Hartley provision dealt with all labor unions, not simply "key" unions. The assumption of a threat to vital industry was highly questionable. The principal source for such suggestions had been and still was the FBI. The Bureau's repeated emphasis since World War II on this labor threat had finally begun to pay dividends.

Director Hoover was not content just to see Congress carry out his legislative wishes. The possibility of a presidential veto of Taft-Hartley was very real. The effective opposition to section 9(h) within the administration appeared to be weak, but if Taft-Hartley was vetoed as an antilabor measure, the anticommunist clause would be lost as well. Hoover dug deep into his sources to provide the President with a series of reports to prove that much of the opposition to Taft-Hartley was communist inspired and, perhaps, even communist controlled.[58] The FBI chief capped his effort with at least three letters to the President in the week before he finally vetoed the measure.[59] In each report he identified exclusively communist opposition to Taft-Hartley, thereby casting a presidential veto as communist inspired.

The fact that the Hoover effort to stop a veto was not successful was probably due more to the realities of the approaching 1948 national election than to a detailed consideration of the communist issue. The latter was never a matter of great concern in the administration's internal analysis of its options. It was viewed simply as one relatively small issue among many. The entire cabinet was polled on its attitude toward the bill and no one dealt with section 9(h). The only cabinet members to oppose Taft-Hartley were Schwellenbach and Postmaster General Robert Hannegan.[60]

The major internal opposition to the Taft-Hartley Act came from Clark Clifford after wide-ranging consultation with political leaders and academics across the country. It was within these groups that some real opposition to 9(h) was manifested on the grounds of "infringement of basic civil liberties" and that it constituted "witch-hunting and thought-policing."[61] The Justice Department disagreed. It found "no fault" in the disclaimer provision and recommended approval of the bill.[62]

The presidential veto of the Taft-Hartley Act was drafted principally by Clifford. His drafts of June 18 and 19 became the presidential veto message of June 20, 1947. While many revisions were made, that portion which dealt with 9(h) was almost unchanged through the various drafts and into the message. The political nature of this portion of the statement is evident. Clifford, and the President, completely ignored the thorny civil liberties questions which had been raised. Truman declared himself to be fully in accord with the objective of ridding labor of all communist officers. Section 9(h) was condemned not for its objective, but because it would not achieve that objective. Instead, the President maintained that only confusion would be sown and that unions would act outside federal law and control, a position taken earlier by the National Labor Relations Board.[63] Unions would be thrown into disarray and confusion—a situation Truman claimed the communists desired.[64] Truman's reasoning was explained in a cabinet meeting just prior to release of the veto message. The President informed the entire cabinet of the veto and indicated his particular dissatisfaction that Congress had not followed his labor proposals. Just as he would later say in his message, he maintained that the bill would "not cure the things we are worried about"—including communism.[65]

The White House made a serious effort to save the veto in the Senate. The House had acted to override within hours of the message. Senate action did not come until three days later. During that period White House and Senate aides made a careful canvass to gain needed votes, but within two days had determined that they would be at least four votes short.[66] At that point administration efforts apparently ceased, and potential Senate supporters were freed to vote as their political needs dictated. The Senate voted sixty-eight to twenty-five to override. Once passed, the law was vigorously enforced. Truman had gained liberal and labor credentials by his veto, but now his administration used the anticommunist weapon which had been provided.

The NLRB, often in apparent cooperation with business and anticommunist union officials, took quick action to obtain disclaimer affidavits from all union officials. Despite the fact that a large grouping of union officers from both the AFL and CIO refused, on principle, to provide such affidavits, the NLRB pushed ahead with its task. It concentrated its attack on alleged left-wing unions. It interpreted the Taft-Hartley Act as a mandate to expedite the congressional objective of "eradicating whatever Communist influences may be present in a few segments of the American labor movement."[67] Within months the Board ruled that Remington-Rand, Inc. had no legal obligation to bargain with the United Electrical Workers—the most powerful and largest of the left-led unions—since its officers had not filed the required affidavits.[68] The fact that other strong unions such as the United Mine Workers and the United Steelworkers had taken a similar position did not stop the assault on leftist unions—those with acknowledged communist officers or with a leadership which worked with the CP. In states such as Missouri the regional boards of the NLRB moved to destroy the influence and power base of alleged communist officials.[69]

The passage of section 9(h) did not provide only the government with a powerful anticommunist weapon. Section 9(h) was also used by business interests to force decertification of militant unions and by anticommunist labor leaders to tear control of entire unions or pieces of unions from longtime leftist dominance. Immediately following passage of Taft-Hartley, CIO President Philip Murray fired his national publicity director, Len DeCaux.[70] The firing of DeCaux, who was considered a symbol of communist influence in the labor movement, was a signal to begin a major campaign to eliminate communists and "fellow travelers" both nationally and locally. During that same year Walter Reuther, the liberal anticommunist president of the United Auto Workers, used compliance with the affidavit provision as a major weapon to help gain control of the Executive Board of his national union from a left-supported coalition.[71]

This government-inspired "house cleaning" by organized labor was part of a growing circle of oppression. Section 9(h) fostered labor's internal anticommunist drive, and this in turn encouraged further government actions. The Department of Justice embarked on a series of deportation proceedings aimed at alien, allegedly communist, labor officials. The proceedings, suddenly begun in September 1947, served the dual purpose of expeditiously removing troublesome leftist leaders from the labor movement and reinforcing the existing images of communist infiltration and the alien nature of the CPUSA.

The deportation proceedings were based on the 1940 Alien Registration Act. Aliens, who at the time of their entry into the United States or subsequently, believed in, taught, advocated, or belonged to any organization which advocated the forcible overthrow of the United States government were made subject to deportation. With a few exceptions—notably that of Harry Bridges—the law had been little used. Attorney General Clark had testified earlier in the year that there were great difficulties involved in prosecuting such cases. The government was required to prove, said Clark, not only membership in a "subversive" organization, but that the group did advocate forcible overthrow of the government and that the alien had a specific belief in the principles of the organization.[72]

Within a few days in September 1947, deportation actions were started against three labor officials. The organizational director of the Transport Workers Union, John Santo, had hearings resumed which had been interrupted in 1941. On the same day, Michael Obermeier, president of Local 6 of the AFL Hotel and Club Employees Union, was arrested, prompting *The Daily Worker* to attack the developing "deportation delirium."[73] Three days later the former business agent of AFL Upholsterers Local 61 in Minneapolis, Peter Warhol, was similarly taken into custody. Following these three actions, Clark, in an appearance before the annual National Conference of United States attorneys, encouraged the wave of alien arrests. "If any alien in your district engaged in Communist activity," he directed, "there is no place for him in the U.S."[74]

On September 30, 1947, Clark spoke with Hoover. They agreed that the FBI would develop additional deportation and denaturalization cases concerning CP members.[75] Clark apparently was unaware that the Bureau had been engaged in such actions at least since the beginning of the year.[76]

The use of deportation statutes was only preliminary to later efforts, but it is an important indication of the FBI search, in cooperation with the Justice Department, for some means of effective prosecution against Communist Party members. Although antialien statutes could only be used against a relatively small minority, they still were a remarkably effective weapon. The alien did not possess the protection of full constitutional rights. Once arrested for violation of deportation laws, the only obligation of the government was to present "reasonable notice, a fair hearing, and an order supported by some evidence."[77] At the same time, considerable anticommunist publicity could be generated, and the concept of communism as an alien philosophy could again be emphasized.

The administration's anticommunist rhetoric and actions, initiated primarily as a result of internal and external right-wing pressure, increasingly took on the character of a response to political pressures from the left. As the election of 1948 approached, the Democratic administration grew fearful of leftist political retribution. The origin of opposition to the Truman administration was a left-liberal coalition developed during World War II, consisting of communists, their supporters, and those liberals willing to tolerate and work with the CP. In 1944 two major organizations had been formed to carry on the popular front program of this left-liberal coalition. These organizations were pledged to support President Roosevelt's program to bring the war to a successful conclusion and create an enduring peace. The Independent Citizens' Committee for the Arts, Sciences and Professions was to act as a cultural center and glittering lobby for liberal policies. The National Citizens Political Action Committee was, according to an observer, "an unofficial outgrowth of the political action wing of the CIO."[78] Its power was to be based on a coalition of forces formed around organized labor.

ICCASP and NCPAC often worked together to further liberal causes. As the Cold War developed, they were subjected to increasing attacks for their continued espousal of a popular front ideology. On November 13, 1946, the two groups merged, presumably to make a united fight for "progressive" objectives. Their unity was an indication of weakness rather than strength; they were forced together by the rising effectiveness of anticommunism. Their weakness perhaps was symbolized by Henry Wallace's ascension to leadership of the liberal community. The former Vice President had been fired from the cabinet in September 1946 as a result of pressures arising from his public criticism of United States foreign policy—criticism which he had been making privately to the President for some time. As a result of his dismissal, the left-liberal coalition apparently gained a champion. Wallace's assumption of this leadership role was not the result of his popular strength but a reflection of his loss of power and influence within the Democratic Party, government, and country, a fact not well understood at the time.

Eight days after Wallace's dismissal from the cabinet, the Conference of Progressives met in Chicago to call upon him to carry on Roosevelt's tradition. Attended by such leaders as Harold Ickes, Henry Morgenthau, James Patton, Philip Murray, and Walter White, the Conference enunciated a comprehensive domestic liberal program together with a call for peace through a continuation of the wartime alliance. It appeared to some that Wallace was now in a position to lead an effective mass movement based on popular front liberalism, but the Conference was not the beginning of such a movement; it was perhaps the end.[79] Elements in the Conference soon began to slip away and to dissociate themselves from the new "progressive" efforts.

The popular front concept was pushed forward by ICCASP-NCPAC which, together with eight minor organizations, created the Progressive Citizens of America in late December 1946. The PCA was to be the combined political striking arm of American liberalism. Some influential figures were already calling for a third party movement led by Wallace; the PCA was to coordinate this sentiment. The question of whether Wallace and the left-liberal forces would challenge Truman within the Democratic Party or without remained tantalizingly in front of the American people for a year. In the interim, Wallace became increasingly critical of the Truman administration, assumed the editorship of the noted liberal journal, *The New Republic*, and made well-covered speaking tours in Latin America, Europe, and the United States.

The anticommunist liberal response to the creation of the PCA—and a very effective one—was the formation of Americans for Democratic Action in early 1947. Arthur Schlesinger, Jr., a founder of ADA and one of its main ideologues, soon referred to its creation as a "watershed" of American liberalism.[80] Its complete identification with administration foreign policy, support for domestic liberalism, and virulent anticommunism became increasingly attractive as the Cold War's intensity grew. It provided a pragmatic opportunity for liberals to stand for the New Deal while not allowing themselves to be buried by anticommunism.

Despite a strong liberal-right-wing attack on Wallace and the PCA, the administration remained concerned by the left vote potential. Democratic National Chairman Gael Sullivan, early in June 1947, assessed the Wallace potential in a memorandum to Clifford and warned that Wallace might play a critical role in the 1948 election. He provided a picture of enthusiastic, and perhaps growing, popular support for Wallace around the country. Ignoring the threat of a third party movement, Sullivan warned of Wallace's potential power in presidential preferential primaries. Calling Wallace a "major consideration in 1948," Sullivan concluded that he should either be appeased or crushed.[81]

The FBI joined with those seeking "to pull the rug" from under Wallace. In the middle of 1947 it began to flood the President with letters detailing the activities of both Wallace and his supporters. Once again, there was no suggestion of illegality. The essence of the American political system is the opportunity for the people to make a free choice at the polling booth, but Hoover's surveillance apparently was intended to limit that choice. Truman was informed of Communist Party discussions concerning the possibility of support for a Wallace-led third party movement.[82] Confidential informants were again used, although much communist discussion of this possibility was going on publicly. Hoover's agents or informants attended meetings of the PCA, and their reports were submitted to the White House. The President was warned that the PCA believed it could gain 40 percent of the delegates to the 1948 Democratic National Nominating Convention, thus gaining sufficient bargaining power to achieve its political and policy objectives, while conceding the presidential nomination to Truman.[83] This purely political intelligence apparently was welcomed by the President and his advisers and no effort was made to impede the flow of Hoover's memoranda.

The impact of the Wallace movement is most clearly seen in the importance which it was given in Truman's electoral battle plan for 1948. Clifford's famous November 1947 memorandum to the President outlined the political strategy to be followed during the next year. Assuming that Wallace and his key advisers were already controlled by the Communist Party, Clifford predicted that Wallace would make a third party race which entailed considerable risks for the President. Clifford's predictions concerning Wallace were far more impressive than his political analysis. His suggestion that the CP would support Wallace as part of a Kremlin plot to bring the Republican Party to power and thus cripple the American economy and destroy American capitalism was an exaggerated stereotypical response to a complex political situation. This view may have deserved to be used on the stump—as it was—but hardly in a confidential memorandum to the President.

Clifford's political judgments, on the other hand, were most impressive. He assumed that the base of presidential support would have to come from the West, the labor movement, liberals, and "progressives." The Wallace threat was seen in key states such as California and New York where a relatively small third party vote could throw those states to the assumed Republican candidate, Thomas Dewey. While seeing the hard core of Wallace's organizational support as being communist, Clifford recognized that the former Vice President had far broader support throughout the United States.

Clifford saw the intensification of the Cold War as a major administration electoral weapon. As the struggle with the Soviet Union grew, as Clifford predicted it would, the American people could be expected to unite behind the President. The Republican assault on domestic communism already had been blunted by the loyalty program, but could be expected to be renewed when it was discovered that no danger within the government existed. Clifford recommended turning the tables on the Republicans and tying them to internal communism. The President would show that in opposing him, domestic communists were deliberately aligning themselves with the Republican Party. The principal "redbaiters" would face a major taste of their own concoction.

Simultaneously, Henry Wallace came under direct and heavy attack designed to discredit him as a tool of the communists. To achieve this, Clifford relied on "prominent liberals and progressives," thus dividing and taking control of the liberal movement. Once this was accomplished, the liberal voter would have nowhere to swing but to the President. To fill the political vacuum created by the destruction of Wallace, the President started to move somewhat "left," at least rhetorically.

Clifford recommended strong Truman stands and programs in the areas of inflation, housing, tax revision, conservation of natural resources in the West, civil rights, and foreign economic aid. Such a comprehensive program, he believed, would cut the ground from beneath Republican efforts to appeal to broader segments of the American people, and would assure broad liberal support for the President. Congressional Republicans either would have to follow the presidential lead in these areas or accept the responsibility for opposing programs perceived to be in the interest of broad masses of the electorate.[84]

While the Clifford strategy was taking shape, Wallace and the PCA were under bitter right-wing attack. Wallace returned from a European tour in November 1947 and received reports of PCA meetings being broken up and increasing verbal assaults from the right, led by HUAC. He reacted angrily at a Pittsburgh meeting by declaring, "We must organize now our resistance movement to preserve democracy or we shall have to organize underground later on to win it back."[85] It was but a short step from there to his candidacy. On December 16, 1947, the Executive Committee of the PCA endorsed the concept of a third party and urged Wallace to lead it. On December 29, on national radio, Wallace declared his candidacy on a third party ticket. The first of Clifford's predictions had now come true.

The cold-blooded Clifford political strategy, with its overtones of "ends justifying means," became the blueprint for the successful presidential campaign of 1948. Just as important, it inevitably would heighten the internal cold war while stiffening United States Cold War policy externally. For political reasons, the administration had nearly reached the point where the internal security establishment had been for some time. Anticommunist statements by publicly chosen government officials began to reflect the concerns of a growing underground government bureaucracy.

Apparently sensing the changing political situation, Director Hoover moved to gain greater authority for his agency. Attorney General Clark again was asked to secure new legislation allowing mass political detention in case of emergency conditions.[86] Increased pressure was exerted to take specific actions against American communists. The administration, as a minimum, was no longer in a political position to oppose such demands, and an admittedly political Attorney General was most sensitive to them.

Within weeks of the FBI's bid for greater power, the President's Committee on Civil Rights issued its report "To Secure These Rights." The document, in the main, was a comprehensive, sharp attack on inequality in the United States. It demanded a national commitment to the protection of civil rights through the passage of legislation and the creation of effective governmental machinery. The report recommended federal action to outlaw police brutality, bar segregation in interstate transportation, abolish the poll tax, make lynching a federal crime, end discrimination in the armed forces, and establish a compulsory Fair Employment Practices Commission. The ultimate objective was a nonsegregated society with an affirmative commitment to a real measure of equality of opportunity.

The President's Committee, heavily weighted with committed anticommunists, also warned that "a state of near-hysteria now threatens to inhibit the freedom of genuine democrats."[87] The warning may well symbolize the coming of "McCarthyism." The Committee was concerned mainly with the freedom of those it perceived to be "genuine democrats." It was a classic statement of what had become the liberal anticommunist position. Together with its warning came a call for federal and state legislation to require the registration of communists. A favorite plan of Committee member Morris Ernst, the proposal later would be adopted fully by the right wing.

Through disclosure of the "real communists," the Committee apparently believed the "real democrats" would be protected. Liberals would again be able to stand for all those positions which communists claimed they favored. As an historian would later complain in describing the atmosphere of 1947: "The American Communist Party did not help matters any, allying themselves with genuine movements for social and economic reform, and opposing foreign policy which had opposition from certain liberal quarters opposed to the 'hard line' of the Truman Administration."[88] The perfect answer seemed to be to isolate the communists so that "real liberals" would no longer face the danger of tainting. But would such a practice not taint the "real democracy" as well? The answer of the President's Committee was that these were people "who would subvert our democracy by revolution or by encouraging disunity and destroying the civil rights of some groups."[89] The Committee made this judgment withouut any real examination of its essential assumptions. In the midst of the political fire, it apparently was willing to risk the destruction of democracy in order to save its perception of democracy—but if its basic assumptions were incorrect, its risks and those of the American people would be for no purpose. To what extent was the relatively small Communist Party of the United States a dangerous "fifth column" and subverter of American democracy? Today there is time, and still a need, to examine the assumption.

NOTES

1. *The New York Times*, February 5, 1947.

2. Susan M. Hartmann, *Truman and the 80th Congress* (Columbia, 1971), 34.

3. J. Edgar Hoover to Harry Vaughan, February 25, 1947, Box 168, Folder L. Hereafter box numbers and folder designations will be cited as 168/L. President's Secretary's Files (PSF), Papers of Harry S. Truman, Harry S. Truman Library, Independence, Missouri. Hereafter cited as HSTL.

4. J. Edgar Hoover to George E. Allen, February 6, 1947, 168/N, PSF, Papers of Harry S. Truman, HSTL.

5. J. Edgar Hoover to Harry Vaughan, February 28, 1947, 167/Atomic Bomb, PSF, Papers of Harry S. Truman, HSTL.

6. J. Edgar Hoover to Secretary of Commerce, May 15, 1947, 167/C, PSF, Papers of Harry S. Truman, HSTL.

7. J. Edgar Hoover to Harry Vaughan, April 3, 1947, 169/P, PSF, Papers of Harry S. Truman, HSTL.

8. Hoover to Vaughan, March 29, 1947, HSTL.

9. U.S. House of Representatives, 80th Cong., 1st sess., Education and Labor Committee, *Hearings . . . on Bills to Amend and Repeal the National Labor Relations Act and for Other Purposes* (Washington, 1947), 3041–3042.

10. Robert J. Donovan, *Conflict and Crisis, the Presidency of Harry S Truman, 1945–1948* (New York, 1977), 282.

11. H. A. Merrick to Lewis B. Schwellenbach, March 13, 1947, Correspon-

dence/K-N, Lewis B. Schwellenbach Papers, Library of Congress, Washington, D.C. Hereafter cited as LC.

12. *San Francisco News*, March 20, 1947.

13. Tom Clark to author, March 28, 1975.

14. Harry S. Truman, *Public Papers of the Presidents of the United States 1947* (Washington, 1963), 187.

15. R. Alton Lee, *Truman and Taft-Hartley: A Question of Mandate* (Lexington, 1966), 22.

16. *Boston Herald*, October 15, 1947.

17. *The Daily Worker*, August 12, 1947.

18. *The New York Times*, February 5, 7, 1947.

19. Ibid., February 11, 1947.

20. Director, FBI, to the Attorney General, March 18, 1947, 1/F.B.I. Loyalty, Papers of A. Devitt Vanech, HSTL.

21. U.S. House of Representatives, 80th Cong., 1st sess., Un-American Activities Committee, *Investigation of Un-American Propaganda Activities in the United States. Hearings . . .* (Washington, 1947), 3. Hereafter cited as *Un-American Propaganda Hearings*.

22. Ibid., 1–3.

23. U.S. House of Representatives, 80th Cong., 1st sess., Un-American Activities Committee, *Menace of Communism* (Washington, 1947), doc. 26.

24. U.S. House of Representatives, 80th Cong., 1st sess., Un-American Activities Committee, *Investigation of Un-American Propaganda Activities in the United States. Hearings . . .* (2 parts, Washington, 1947), II, 43.

25. Ibid.

26. Ibid., 49.

27. *The New York Times*, March 27, 1947.

28. Richard M. Freeland, *The Truman Doctrine and the Origins of McCarthyism, Foreign Policy, Domestic Politics, and Internal Security 1946–1948* (New York, 1972), 147.

29. *The New York Times*, April 2, 1947.

30. Ibid., April 23, 1947.

31. J. Parnell Thomas to Harry S Truman, April 23, 1947, OF 263 (1945–47), Papers of Harry S. Truman, HSTL.

32. Harry S Truman to J. Parnell Thomas, April 25, 1947, OF 263 (1945–47), Papers of Harry S. Truman, HSTL.

33. *The New York Times*, April 16, 1947.

34. Ibid., May 11, 1947.

35. Ibid., May 13, 1947.

36. Ibid., April 25, 1947.

37. Charles Murphy, "Memorandum on internal security legislation," August 18, 1948, 22/Internal Security, Charles Murphy Files, Papers of Harry S. Truman, HSTL.

38. Athan Theoharis, *Spying on Americans: Political Surveillance from Hoover to the Huston Plan* (Philadelphia, 1978), 98–107.

39. Max Lowenthal, *The Federal Bureau of Investigation* (New York, 1950), 432; Freeland, *The Truman Doctrine and the Origins of McCarthyism*, 241–42.

40. Freeland, *The Truman Doctrine and the Origins of McCarthyism*, 133.

41. *The New York Times*, March 2, 1946.

42. Ibid., July 25, 1947.

43. Ibid., September 29, 1947.

44. Ibid., April 19 and 24, 1947.

45. *The Daily Worker*, September 28 and October 31, 1947.

46. *The New York Times*, September 1, 1947.

47. Ibid., October 11, 1947.

48. *The Daily Worker*, November 3, 1947.

49. Francis H. Thompson, "Truman and Congress: The Issue of Loyalty, 1946–1952" (Ph.D. Diss., Texas Tech University, 1970), 248.

50. Tom Clark to author, March 28, 1975.

51. Charles G. Ross to Robert H. Williams, November 20, 1947, OF 263-A, Papers of Harry S. Truman, HSTL.

52. Gerald T. Dunne, *Hugo Black and the Judicial Revolution* (New York, 1977), 279.

53. "Labor Management Relations Act of 1947," Statement by Senator Robert Taft at Panel of State Bar of California, September 12, 1947, 749/Labor–1947, Robert A. Taft Papers, LC.

54. U.S. House of Representatives, 80th Cong., 1st sess., *Labor-Management Relations Acts, 1947. Conference Report* (Washington, 1947), report 510.

55. U.S. Senate, 80th Cong., 1st sess., *Report of Senate Committee on Labor and Public Welfare* (Washington, 1947), report 245.

56. "An Analysis of H.R. 3020," June 2, 1947, 7/Labor (Taft-Hartley Bill), Analysis of Labor Bill, Papers of Clark M. Clifford, HSTL.

57. Tom Clark to author, March 28, 1975.

58. J. Edgar Hoover to Harry Vaughan, June 3, 1947, 167/Communist data, PSF, Papers of Harry S. Truman, HSTL.

59. J. Edgar Hoover to Harry Vaughan, June 17, 1947, 167/Communist data, PSF, Papers of Harry S. Truman, HSTL; J. Edgar Hoover to Harry Vaughan, June 14, 1947, 168/L, PSF, Papers of Harry S. Truman, HSTL; J. Edgar Hoover to Harry Vaughan, June 18, 1947, 169/T, PSF, Papers of Harry S. Truman, HSTL.

60. Margaret Truman, *Harry S. Truman* (New York, 1973), 350.

61. Russell W. Davenport to Robert Hannegan, June 13, 1947, 8/Labor (Taft-Hartley Bill), Correspondence on Labor Bill; Papers of Clark M. Clifford, HSTL; Gael Sullivan, "Memorandum," June 14, 1947, 8/Labor (Taft-Hartley Bill), Correspondence on Labor Bill, Papers of Clark M. Clifford, HSTL.

62. Douglas McGregor, "Justice Department analysis," 8/Labor (Taft-Hartley Bill), Correspondence on Labor Bill 1, Papers of Clark M. Clifford, HSTL.

63. NLRB Analysis of Taft-Hartley Bill, June 12, 1947, 8/Labor (Taft-Hartley Bill), Publications-Labor Bill, Papers of Clark M. Clifford, HSTL.

64. Truman, *Public Papers . . . 1947*, 296–97; "To the House of Representa-

tives," Draft of veto message, June 18, 1947, 8/Labor-H.R. 3020-Taft-Hartley Drafts, Papers of Clark M. Clifford, HSTL.

65. Notes on Cabinet Meetings, June 20, 1947, PPF, Papers of Matthew J. Connelly, HSTL.

66. Ayers Diary, June 22, 1947, Papers of Eban A. Ayers, HSTL.

67. Paul M. Herzog, "The Labor Management Relations Act: The First Two Hundred Days," March 18, 1948, 749/Labor 1947–48, Robert A. Taft Papers, LC.

68. Herzog, "The Labor Management Relations Act"; *The New York Times*, December 5, 1947.

69. Ronald W. Johnson, "The Communist Issue in Missouri: 1946–1956" (Ph.D. Diss., University of Missouri, 1973), 46.

70. Len DeCaux, *Labor Radical From the Wobblies to CIO* (Boston, 1970), 481.

71. Frank Emspak, "The Break-up of the Congress of Industrial Organizations (CIO), 1945–1950" (Ph.D. Diss., University of Wisconsin, 1972), 176–79.

72. U.S. House of Representatives, 80th Cong., 1st sess., Appropriations Committee, *Department of Justice Appropriations Bill for 1948. Hearings . . .* (Washington, 1947), 17.

73. *The Daily Worker*, September 9, 1947.

74. Ibid., September 16, 1947.

75. D. M. Ladd, "Memorandum to Director, FBI," February 2, 1948, copy of document submitted to author by FBI; Director, FBI, "Memorandum to the Attorney General," February 3, 1948, copy of document submitted to author by FBI.

76. Special Agent in Charge, FBI New York Office, "Report on John Williamson," March 20, 1947, copy of document submitted to author by FBI.

77. Milton R. Konvitz, *Civil Rights in Immigration* (Ithaca, N.Y., 1953), 107.

78. Leslie Adler, "The Red Image: American Attitudes Toward Communism in the Cold War Era" (Ph.D. Diss., University of California, Berkeley, 1970), 363.

79. Norman D. Markowitz, *The Rise and Fall of the People's Century: Henry A. Wallace and American Liberalism, 1941–1948* (New York, 1973), 202.

80. Arthur M. Schlesinger, Jr., *The Vital Center, The Politics of Freedom* (Boston, 1962), 166.

81. Gael Sullivan, "Memo Re Wallace Situation," June 2, 1947, 18/Wallace, Henry, Papers of Clark M. Clifford, HSTL.

82. J. Edgar Hoover to Harry Vaughan, June 17 and October 8, 1947, 167/Communist data, PSF, Papers of Harry S. Truman, HSTL.

83. J. Edgar Hoover to Harry Vaughan, June 25, 1947, 169/W, PSF, Papers of Harry S. Truman, HSTL.

84. Clark Clifford, "Memorandum for the President," November 19, 1947, 21/Confidential memo for the Pres., Papers of Clark M. Clifford, HSTL.

85. *The Daily Worker*, November 12, 1947.

86. J. Edgar Hoover, "Memorandum to Attorney General Clark," October 20, 1947, in U.S. Senate, 94th Cong., 2d sess., *Final Report of the Select Committee to Study Governmental Operations with Respect to Intelligence Activities* (6 vols., Washington, 1976), III, 438.

87. The President's Committee on Civil Rights, *To Secure These Rights* (Washington, 1947), 49; Barton J. Bernstein, "The Ambiguous Legacy: The Truman Administration and Civil Rights," in Barton J. Bernstein, ed., *Politics and Policies of the Truman Administration* (Chicago, 1970), 277–81.

88. William R. Tanner, "The Passage of the Internal Security Act of 1950" (2 vols., Ph.D. Diss., University of Kansas, 1971), I, 173–74.

89. The President's Committee, *To Secure These Rights*, 52.

IV

Private Disunity, Public Disaster

The American Communist Party may have been the smallest, least effectual minority ever to take on the proportions of a major enemy in the history of the United States. The paradox of the communist issue during the Cold War was that American communists were almost universally defined as representing no danger to the United States, but their presence was used to fabricate a sufficient hysteria to create an American "mental strait jacket" on both domestic and foreign policy. Few believed that domestic communists could affect American life significantly, much less achieve revolutionary goals or serve as an effective outpost for Soviet penetration of American society. American communists were taken most seriously by themselves, by those on the left most likely to be tarnished by a red smear, and by those who used the fear of communism to achieve their own ends.

The reality of the tactics and goals of the Communist Party of the United States often was submerged by both proponents and opponents in a rush to achieve their own idealized visions of the future. For its part, the CPUSA overemphasized its role, influence, and most particularly its attachment to a world socialist movement with universal rules of social and economic development. The communist emphasis on these aspects of its ideology played into the hands of those seeking to develop the image of an internal "Red Menace" and gravely wounded communist efforts to achieve a place in American society.

J. Edgar Hoover set the tone for the developing paradox when he testified in early 1947: "I do not think for one moment that we are going to have a revolution in this country tomorrow, but I do know that the Communists have penetrated every field of activity in this country."[1]

The lurking danger had to be emphasized for the effect to be created, although Hoover would soon add, "I do not for one moment hold to the opinion that any revolution could be effected by that [Communist] group."[2] Hoover apparently was disturbed by what he perceived as an inadequate response to the external threat of communism and felt "it necessary to activate an internal security threat."[3] Internal fear would be used to strengthen the resolve of the national administration and produce a desired moral and political discipline among the American people.

Hoover readily mixed the reality of a world in dangerous conflict with the unreality of an internal threat. Every personal attack on him or his policies, he maintained, was an assault on American institutions. Every evidence of the diminution of CPUSA membership or public effectiveness was increased proof of the threat of conspiracy in high places. Hoover's efforts to influence national policy through FBI propaganda, direct recommendations to government officials, and the apparent placement of intimates in positions of importance outside the Bureau was based on his belief that elected officials were too subject to the whims of public opinion and the influence of leftist pressure.

There was almost universal agreement with Hoover's public statements that the reality of an immediate serious threat by domestic communists simply was not present. President Truman often discounted the effectiveness of the American Communist Party and suggested, "As far as the United States is concerned, the menace of communism is not the activities of a few foreign agents or the political activities of a few isolated individuals. The menace of communism lies primarily in those areas of American life where the promise of democracy remains unfulfilled . . . ."[4] In developing the philosophical creed of anticommunist liberalism, Arthur M. Schlesinger, Jr. wrote, "It is hard to argue that the CPUSA in peacetime presents much of a threat to American security." He asked, "Does anyone seriously believe that even the Communist Party is absurd enough to contemplate a violent revolution in the United States?"[5]

Conservatives generally followed Hoover's lead in vigorously raising the communist issue, but stopping short of declaring an immediate internal crisis. Even New Jersey Republican J. Parnell Thomas, chairman of the House Un-American Activities Committee, while emphasizing the seriousness of the "Communist menace" in 1947, spoke of it as a possible future danger. "It is a menace that is so serious," he said, "that unless it is dealt with by the law enforcement agencies of the Federal Government, the time may well arrive when the very security of our country will be impared [sic] by this fifth column within our midst."[6]

Most Republicans apparently supported the positions taken in the 1948 presidential election campaign by Ohio Senator Robert A. Taft and presidential candidate Thomas E. Dewey. Taft attacked international communism, but emphasized the right of Americans to remain members of the CPUSA.[7] Dewey supported anticommunist legislation, but opposed the outlawing of the Party, and declared, in a national radio debate, that its influence was "at its lowest ebb in history."[8] Despite this concurrence of views on the lack of a meaningful internal communist threat, hysteria grew and was furthered by some of those who acknowledged that no revolution could succeed or was being planned.

How could an internal threat exist if no possibility of success existed? The answer is in the underlying assumptions of both liberal and conservative analyses of communist weakness. The innate strength of the American politial and economic system made an internal revolution impossible, but this, in itself, did not stop the growth of small, discontented minorities with evil intent. Although they could not succeed, it was assumed that they would make the effort. With the rise of Soviet power, one of these minorities—the Communist Party—could pose a substantial danger as an extension of the external threat. The peril of hostilities with the Soviet Union could substitute for the danger of an internal revolt. The Communist Party would be viewed not as a domestic radical movement, but as the "representative" of Soviet power and the international agent of communism. As such it would be a greater potential security threat than any purely internal organization possibly could be. The acceptance of these assumptions came both from their constant reiteration by various influential sources within the nation and from the activities of a Communist Party which, failing to perceive the importance of the assumptions until it was too late, actually fostered the atmosphere which encouraged them to grow.

The Communist Party of the United States had been viewed, from its founding in 1919, as an appendage of the Soviet Union. It had been closely tied to the international communist movement and had accepted, on a number of occasions, the intervention of that movement in its own affairs. Its adherence to an international communist policy cost it dearly in terms of influence within the United States. The Great Depression of the 1930's gave the Party an unparalleled chance to grow, become active, and influential. It took the opportunity to help build the labor movement, earn respect for a forthright antifascist stand, gain cultural influence beyond its numbers, and achieve a reputation for considerable political expertise. A good deal of all this was thrown away in the late 1930's by the Party's defense of the Moscow purges and particularly by its acceptance of the Nazi-Soviet pact of 1939. The Party's shift to an antiwar position in 1940, and its shift back in the next year with the Nazi attack on the Soviet Union, ruptured its alliances with the noncommunist left. During World War II it began a painful road back to acceptance and a position of some importance. After June 1941 the communists backed the war effort fully. They joined willingly with almost all elements in American society in the formation of a kind of national war front. The meaning of this relatively broad acceptance was not lost on the communists.

Communist influence depended on acceptance within the democratic coalition. The 1943 Teheran Conference of Roosevelt, Stalin, and Churchill provided a seemingly perfect opportunity to harmonize this new acceptance within the democratic coalition with its old international attachments. At Teheran the leaders of capitalist and communist states joined to further their common good. In what appeared a spirit of true harmony, the Allied leaders agreed to the creation of a second front in Western Europe and to a coordinated offense to destroy German power. It seemed that the unremitting warfare between capitalism and communism now could be brought to rest, at least for a time.

Earl Browder, the head of the CPUSA, seized upon the Teheran agreement to develop the beginning of a concept of polycentrism within the communist world which was not to flower fully for another twenty years. As capitalists and communists had cooperated on the international scene, so could they work together domestically. Instead of a period of intensified class warfare, Browder saw a considerable breathing space where worker and owner could join in an effort for their mutual benefit. Such cooperation apparently had existed during the war and possibly could extend into the postwar period. The United States, he believed, would be faced with a serious depression threat as the war machine was dismantled. Increased markets on a massive scale would be needed to meet America's productive capacity. Financial and industrial interests would need a considerable period of international cooperation, particularly with a victorious Soviet Union. Markets would have to be created and shared. Colonial peoples, he said, would be given their independence in order both to further the cause of peace and to create ever growing demand for industrial goods. The American working class fully shared these interests, thereby creating a basis for an internal coalition paralleling the international coalition of the United Nations.

Browder believed the role of the Communist Party in the United States accordingly would change. There would have to be an acceptance of the thesis that socialism could not be an immediate prospect and that American society would be reconstructed in the postwar world, and in the foreseeable future, in a capitalist framework. Communists would join with the democratic majority within the United States—including people of goodwill of all classes—to create progressive policies and to make capitalism work better in the interests of a majority of the people. Browder admitted that his "Teheran thesis" was a considerable departure from orthodox Marxism, but he claimed it was a creative, Marxist response to changing world and national conditions. He proposed that the CPUSA be dissolved to emphasize the Party turn from confrontation politics. It would be replaced by an educational association and political lobby, still with a Marxist perspective, but considerably changed.

Browder's policy departure apparently met an enthusiastic response. Communists seemingly were given theoretical justification for doing what they had wanted to do all along—join the mainstream of American political and economic life. The 1943 dissolution of the Comintern—the international organization of communist parties—apparently had set the stage for national communist goals and policies. Only a few stalwarts, led by Party Chairman William Z. Foster, opposed Browder's new line. Foster vigorously attacked Browder's analysis and asserted that American imperialism was as reactionary as ever and had to be opposed both during and after the war. He rejected any collaboration with "monopoly capital" and suggested that although socialism was not an immediate prospect that the success of the Soviet Union in the war would tend to increase interest in and support for socialism.

Foster was isolated and effectively silenced. Supported by only one other member of the National Committee, apparently unsupported by key communists in other lands, and threatened with disciplinary action, he did not make his views generally known and went along with the 1944 dissolution of the CPUSA. It was replaced by the Communist Political Association with the same leadership and initial membership, but with full acceptance of Browder's "Teheran thesis." The constitution of the CPA said that the organization "looks to the family of free nations, led by the great coalition of democratic capitalist and socialist states, to inaugurate an era of world peace, expanding production and economic well-being, and the liberation and equality of all peoples regardless of race, creed or color."[9] By the time the war in Europe had ended in May 1945, the CPA had grown to approximately eighty thousand—not counting those serving in the armed forces. Although some eventually dropped out of the organization, approximately four thousand a week had been recruited during 1944.[10] The CPA financial situation was solid and it appeared ready to assume a position of some importance.

The approaching end of the war in Europe in 1945 placed an intolerable strain upon the "coalition of democratic states" and, in turn, doomed the CPA—perhaps the first real victim of the Cold War. The Soviet outlook had changed from that of 1943. It foresaw a period of increasing conflict between capitalist and communist nations for control of significant portions of the world. That struggle began in Europe and was reflected in the April 1945 article by French communist leader Jacques Duclos.[11]

While the Duclos article, using a remarkable collection of hitherto secret internal CPUSA documents, was addressed specifically to the American communist movement, it clearly was aimed at similar concepts in other national communist parties. The CPA leadership believed that the decisive influence in the Duclos article came from Joseph Stalin.[12] It was considered to represent the definitive judgments of the international communist movement rather than simply the views of one leader of a major party.

Duclos attacked the decision to "liquidate" the Communist Party. Terming Browder's views a "notorious revision of Marxism," he suggested that instead of class peace, the future would see an all-out struggle against American monopolists. Duclos raised the specter of the rise of fascism again from the expanded trusts created in the war effort.[13] He praised Foster for his internal opposition to Browder's position, but criticized him for failing to raise his voice against the "liquidation" of the Party. The only clear commendation was given to Henry Wallace— interesting in view of future developments—for his statements warning against the trusts and a revived fascism. Throughout the article there was an implicit condemnation of the independent road suggested by the American experience and the fact that apparently it was attractive to other communist parties, notably in Latin America.

The international attack on the American communist movement was a crushing, disabling blow. While Browder had staked out a national road for American communists, he had done so on the basis of seeming concurrence with international events and the views of more experienced communists abroad. The policies of the CPA had opened up new perspectives and opportunities for involvement on the American political scene. A vision of a world at peace and cooperation had been created—one as attractive to American communists as to others. The policies of the growing American communist movement were based, in fact, on the prospects of long-term peace. Whatever else the Duclos article did in attacking the CPA's new organizational concepts, it destroyed the basis of their policies. Duclos had left a stark choice for communists around the world—either fully support the socialist states led by the Soviet Union and the interpretations of Marxism-Leninism as developed by the international communist movement or be relegated to the status of "revisionist" traitors to the cause of socialism and collaborators with capitalism. Alexander Bittelman, a founder of the American Communist Party in 1919 and still a leader in 1945 described the reaction:

To say that we were not prepared for that break-up [of the World War II anti-fascist coalition] and for the consequent arrival of the "Cold War" is to grossly understate the situation. We wanted the coalition to continue, especially the collaboration between the United States and the Soviet Union.[14]

Bittelman added that American communists, not only Browder, had believed that cooperation would in fact continue. The sudden destruction of that vision left them stunned.

There was confusion and uncertainty among CPA leaders when the Duclos article appeared in early May. Most apparently hoped to ride out the storm with minimal changes. They still looked to Browder for leadership and hoped to maintain many of the advances they had achieved without rupturing their position in the international communist movement. Events of that period were moving too quickly for this kind of accommodation. On May 22 the New York *World-Telegram and Sun* published a translation of the Duclos article, the first real notice given to the CPA general membership. Two days later *The Daily Worker* printed its own translation after an inconclusive meeting of the CPA National Board.

Within two weeks the American communist movement made a fateful choice. At a June 2 National Board meeting almost the entire communist leadership turned against Browder and demanded that he accept the Duclos criticism in its entirety in order to maintain his leadership.[15] Browder's explicit refusal to do so led to an intensification and unification of the attack and to the enhancement of the position of his major opponent, Foster.

A meeting of the National Committee was called on June 18, 1945, with a National Convention of the CPA to follow in July. The CPA was to be abandoned, the Communist Party reconstituted, and Browder's vision of internal peace and polycentrism attacked. The decisions, made under foreign instigation and pressure, still were American in origin. There were no "orders" from abroad. There would be no summary executions for refusal to follow Duclos' line. There was free and frank discussion of the issues within the leadership of the CP, but given the history and outlook of the communist movement, the outcome was never in doubt. American communists always had given precedence to the views of international communism. A concept of inferiority, perhaps bred from the relative lack of numbers and influence of American communists or the relative youth of their movement, was clearly evident in their debates. Accepting the reality of the postwar international situation as outlined by Duclos, there seemed no alternative to a return to the militant confrontation tactics of an earlier age. The independent identity of the Communist Party as the "vanguard" of the working class and the identification of "revisionist" traitors to working-class interests were essential once more.

The draft resolution adopted by the National Board in early June, then by the full National Committee and finally by the National Convention, contained a full assault against American capitalism and Marxist-Leninist "revisionism."[16] Browder stood alone in June in opposing the draft resolution as each of his coworkers turned against him with a vengeance. In July he was excluded from the leadership of the reconstituted Communist Party and, despite his protests, was expelled within a year.

The unanimity thus demonstrated to an observant American public proved disastrous. It seemed a repeat of the past and full acknowledgment of the American Party's dependence on the international communist movement. That there was some validity in the view is clear, but it is a simplification. The unity that existed against Browder was more apparent than real. There were those in the leadership, some close associates of Foster, who feared that the Party was swinging too far from its wartime position. Bittelman, who for a quarter of a century had been perhaps Foster's closest ally, believed that Duclos had gone too far in criticizing Browder.[17] He wanted Browder to remain in the leadership and went to him seeking the means to achieve this.[18] Browder would not accept the criticism which had been made and refused. Bittelman, and apparently others, felt too weak to express an independent position and believed unity to be a more important value than principled opposition for its own sake. The result was that the vision of a united Communist Party, completely dependent upon the will of the international movement, was reinforced and projected to the nation.

Browder was condemned not for opposing the Soviet Union—he did not do so—but for tentatively raising the issue of national deviation from international policy. Marxism-Leninism was interpreted to be a universally applicable science of society. Internal Party debates and the testimony of leaders who subsequently left the CP support the view that there was no question of a foreign conspiracy or the operation of foreign agents. Communists fully believed they were serving the interests of the United States within the context of an international commitment.

Strangely, J. Edgar Hoover later recognized this. In writing of those who left the communist movement, Hoover admitted that "some had devoted all of their lives to what they felt was a movement for the betterment of humanity . . . . "[19] There were no "orders from abroad" as part of an intricate international conspiracy. American communists sought the advice and counsel of communists in other lands, and where these could not be gained directly, they did exactly what the State Department and Central Intelligence Agency did—read the foreign press for hints of policy changes. Bittelman, who served during the early Cold War years as the major economic and theoretical adviser to the Communist Party leadership, would often clip American and foreign press articles containing the speeches of influential foreign communists, would underline important passages and pass these on to the leadership. If this was a conspiracy, it was the most inefficient the world had ever seen.

American communists invested the Soviet Union with special qualities born of its status as the first socialist state in the world and reinforced by its role during World War II. Any deviation from support of the Soviet Union or the enunciated principles of Marxism-Leninism was treachery. Bittelman exhibited this view when he wrote: "It is impossible any more for an honest and informed socialist not to know that the innocent looking proposition of the so-called principle or right to discuss 'shortcomings as well as accomplishments' of the Soviet Union links up directly with Wall Street's warmongering incitements 'to criticize Russia.' "[20] The failure to recognize the legitimacy of criticism of the Soviet Union, coupled with disdain for those who would reform capitalism, drove the communists from alliance with their natural friends and served as grist for the propaganda mills of their natural enemies. A former foreign editor of *The Daily Worker*, writing as a disillusioned ex-communist, maintained that "American Communists were neither allies nor agents of the Soviet Communists. In their later years they lived in what can only be called 'a mental Comintern.' "[21] The phrase is apt in that American communists chose to conform to the international communist line in the belief that it was the only real road to social and economic betterment.

It may well be that the American Communist Party would have been isolated and perhaps destroyed during the Cold War no matter what it did. There is a certainty, however, that its choices in 1945 and thereafter made this inevitable and quickened the pace. The Party continued to work for constructive social and economic reforms—civil rights, public works, public housing, higher minimum wages, price controls—but it increasingly emphasized that these were temporary amelioratives which would do little to halt the crisis of American capitalism. The natural result of that crisis was said to be fascism, and those who would not recognize a socialist transformation of society as the ultimate answer were greater enemies than the "fascists." The most bitter communist criticism was reserved for "social democrats"—those such as Walter Reuther, A. Philip Randolph, and Norman Thomas—men who believed in meaningful progress within the system.

The communist movement projected the image of a closed, unified, monolithic agent of a foreign ideology. The fact that the leadership, in reality, represented differing currents within the movement was not known. Foster's early opposition to Browder, and the recognition of this act by Duclos, had left the CP chairman with great prestige within the movement. He was surrounded with a leadership almost intact from the Browder period, with the exception of Browder himself. While communist leaders lined up against Browder and for Soviet policy, they maintained important differences which were neither projected to the membership of the Party nor to the public.

Joining Foster in the top rank of leadership were Eugene Dennis, Robert Thompson, and John Williamson. Dennis had worked in the Comintern in the 1930's as its representative in various areas of the world. He returned to the United States in 1939 to assume a position of importance within the Party. Among Party leaders he was considered closest to the Soviet leadership and regarded as the "fair haired boy of Moscow." [22] Within a year, with the acquiescence of Foster, Dennis was elevated to the position of general secretary, the leading post within the Party. Thompson (who had won the Distinguished Service Cross during World War II) was soon raised to the leadership of the New York state organization, the largest in the CP. Williamson, the Party's organizational secretary, was named labor secretary in 1946 and placed in charge of trade union activities. Thompson, Foster, and Benjamin Davis, communist city councilman from Harlem, joined to form an influential National Board bloc. They were considered the "left" on the Board.

Dennis represented the "center," an apparent majority whose most influential figures were Gil Green and John Gates. Williamson often supported this group. Green had been an international communist youth leader during the 1930's and was a major force during the Browder years. He was considered the most innovative theoretician on the Board. Following Browder's expulsion, Green was moved from the leadership of the New York state organization to that of Illinois. Gates came out of the armed forces and was projected into a developing split within the leadership in 1946. The fact that there was no longer a "right" within the leadership, as a result of the removal of Browder and the campaign against "revisionism," severely limited the available options.

The Foster group demanded strict adherence to the international communist line and a clear demarcation between communists and "reformers." Communists would be encouraged to join in "united front" movements, but only on communist terms and with communist leadership. The "center" sought to soften this position and establish broader areas of contact with the mass of the American people. It was no less devoted to the cause of socialism, both domestically and internationally, but placed greater emphasis on the need to work with nonsocialists on a more equitable basis. The "center" group was constantly placed on the defensive by fear of being branded "Browderite." The division on the Board existed on almost all issues from the maintenance of the five cent fare on New York City subways, to the third party movement, to policy within state and national CIO bodies. The debates often were conducted with great bitterness, but were constantly shielded from the view of even the National Committee, and even more so from the general Party membership and the public.

The split in Party leadership was sometimes mirrored in its public policies, but these were little understood at the time. On September 12, 1946, Henry Wallace delivered an address in Madison Square Garden which led to his removal from the cabinet. The speech, cleared earlier by Truman, was an evenhanded condemnation of both United States and Soviet policies leading to confrontation. The audience, predominantly left wing, cheered his attack upon the United States and hissed his criticism of Soviet policy. *The Daily Worker* responded the next morning with an anti-Wallace editorial which placed him in the company of Secretary of State James Byrnes as a prime cold warrior. Within days, however, Truman was pressured into removing Wallace and the communists felt forced to defend him. Later in the year Dennis criticized the original *Daily Worker* editorial and placed it within the context of the struggle going on in the leadership.

Those tendencies which did exist to regard World War III as imminent, as something that might break out any day or month (a position which, we should note, weakened our generally correct program of action in the struggle for peace) were not sufficiently combatted. From this there developed certain sectarian attitudes toward forces, peoples, and movements, in the labor movement, as well as in the broad democratic camp, and toward certain potential allies in the labor-progressive coalition who, for one or another reason, have been slow in publicly breaking with the Truman administration and its reactionary policies.[23]

The "sectarian" policies—those which tended to isolate the communists from potential allies—originated with Foster, but Dennis could not attack him. Instead, in late September, the leadership expelled four members from the Party for the crime of "left sectarianism" and labeled this as great a danger as "right opportunism," Browder's transgression.[24] Rather than accepting this as a criticism of his policies, Foster joined in the denunciation.

The most vital area of policy change dealt with war and fascism. The "Teheran thesis" had developed the concepts of internal and external peace. The CPUSA turned on this thesis with a vengeance. Even here sharp differences of opinion existed within the leadership, although only subtle hints filtered through to the membership. Foster and his allies emphasized the dangers of war and fascism. Although suggesting, as did the Soviet Union, that these dangers were not inevitable, they strongly implied that there was little to stop them. Foster developed the thesis, in contrast to Browder, that the capitalist drive toward a third world war already had begun during the second world war in secret "anti-Soviet" policies developed at that time. The war drive, he said, became open in the immediate postwar period.[25] Throughout 1946 Foster tied the issues of war and fascism together. In order to open a third world war against the Soviet Union, he maintained, fascism at home would be necessary. The people would have to be controlled and guided along the path of war, and opposition, led by the CP, would have to be crushed. Every anti-Soviet foreign policy action by the administration thus became an internal move toward fascism. Every growth of repression within the nation became a preparation for World War III.

The "center" bloc in the CP leadership attempted to place greater emphasis on the possibility of avoiding war and fascism. It accepted the dangers, but maintained that a coalition of progressive forces could stop the drift towards both war and fascism. Fear of being labeled "Browderite," however, stopped any effective analysis of the reality of American or Soviet policy. Jack Stachel, a member of the National Board who was removed as trade union director in mid–1946, tried to reconcile an acceptance of Foster's assumptions with an attack on their implications. "The system of more open reactionary dictatorship which already exists in this country," he wrote, "is not yet fascism as such. To say otherwise is in reality to underestimate the danger of fascism to the people and also to weaken the fight against it."[26] Stachel bitterly attacked the policies of the Truman administration, as did every Communist leader in 1946, but maintained that as harmful as Truman's antilabor actions were, they did not represent fascism.

The fear of fascism was heightened by economic analyses which stressed a coming crisis in the United States. Bittelman delivered a report to the National Board in September which predicted a major economic disaster within a two-year period.[27] The report was adopted by the Board and, in varying degrees, served as the basic economic outlook of the Party for at least the next five years. The imminence of depression made the development of fascism more plausible. Faced with a growing external challenge and internal economic crisis caused by the limitation of home and foreign markets, monopoly capital could be expected to turn to its most extreme form of power, fascism.

All areas of work now became predicated on what the communists perceived to be an immediate threat of war and fascism. Its allies would be those who would accept the reality of the threat. Its enemies were those who rejected it. Life thus became far simpler and more lonely for the CPUSA. Foster soon claimed: "During the post-war period the Party's main political line has been in favor of building a united front antifascist peace coalition, led by labor. All its individual policies have been based upon and interlocked with the people's general struggle against fascism and war."[28] That united front, and particularly its labor constituent, was to be led by the CP. Foster attacked Browder for having "tailed after" CIO President Philip Murray rather than making Murray follow the Party's positions. At the very time when the CP was to come under greatest attack both within and without the labor movement, it opened its own assault on those who would not accept its line. One observer has suggested, "The party would no longer play the subordinate role that Murray wished. It no longer unequivocally supported Murray within the USW or within the CIO."[29] The key question was not, however, the subordination of the Party role, but its demand for the maintenance of a position of influence within the labor movement.

The Party demanded that the CIO accept its estimate of the international situation and domestic crisis. CIO leaders, led by Murray, became far more receptive, as a result, to the demands of right-wing labor leaders for anticommunist action. In the context of rising Cold War tensions as well as communist pressure, this seemed an attractive alternative. The 1946 Atlantic City convention of the CIO was a clear warning to the Communist Party. Murray's "resent and reject" resolution—expressing the CIO's opposition to communism—told the Party to back off and accept majority views. The fact that communists were forced to accept this resolution was an indication of awareness of their own weakness. Williamson later admitted that "under the circumstances no better alternative action was possible."[30] He maintained that the main resolutions passed by the convention were "progressive." The communists, as early as 1946, were barely holding on to minority influence within the labor movement, but were still projecting a self-image as the prime movers of labor policy. Labor historian Frank Emspak was correct when he noted: "By 1946 it was difficult for the party [within the labor movement] to defend itself,"[31] but his analysis weakened when he suggested that this resulted from its integration into the majority coalition just before and during the war.

It is true that during the Browder years the Party had emphasized the coalition rather than itself. Its members had risen to leadership in various unions not as communists but as militant workers who supported the Murray leadership. Its Party factions had been largely dissolved so that its members could work in coalition with others. All these elements could have provided a source of postwar strength if the communists had accepted the reality of their weakness and had not sought a disproportionate share of influence. The internal Party struggle made this impossible, opening the communists to deadly attack within organized labor.

The Party entered 1947 on the defensive within the labor movement, tied to policies which would repel minorities, identified as an agent of an international communist movement, and internally divided within its top leadership. It was propelled forward by its 1945–46 policies. It did not stop to analyze the realities of conditions in the world and the United States. The basic analysis had already been made with the reconstitution of the Party and Browder's ouster. Party policy in 1947, as a result, would accentuate the damage which already had been done and would make the Party an even more attractive target for those using it as a steppingstone to the creation of a national hysteria.

Williamson welcomed the new year with the painful complaint, "It is necessary to remind the labor movement of the contributions of individual Communists to the building and ideology of CIO and AFL unions."[32] The needs of labor in 1947, however, had little relation to communist contributions in the past. Two weeks later Foster spoke before 20,000 in a Madison Square Garden rally and urged the leaders of the CIO, AFL, and Railroad Brotherhoods to "lay aside their quarrels . . . and join hands in the common cause."[33]

"Join hands" with whom and under whose aegis? Foster's answer lay in the Marxist-Leninist concept of the Communist Party as the "vanguard"—the leader of the working class. The chiefs of organized labor wanted no part of communist leadership. A majority were seeking publicly to sever the communists from the labor movement. The Taft-Hartley Act provided the means for some to achieve this. An important sector of organized labor, led by Murray, was strongly opposed to Taft-Hartley. For this group the communists provided the issues on which the break could be made. The Party increasingly brought its foreign policy dissent into the counsels of organized labor. The reception of this position was generally noncommittal when the Truman Doctrine was the issue, but became extremely hostile when the communists attempted to use organized labor as a major weapon against the Marshall Plan.

The Marshall Plan became a key issue because the communists desired it to become one. The right wing was more than willing to take part in the internal CIO fight on the basis of foreign policy attachments rather than economic issues and strategy. The communists engaged in the struggle on the basis of their perception of the connection between these issues. Few in the labor movement, other than the communists, accepted the connection. Most saw the Communist Party as seeking to use organized labor to further Soviet foreign policy. President Murray, as a consequence, invited Secretary of State George C. Marshall to address the October Boston convention of the CIO, the first time anyone holding that position had been so invited. Marshall, whose June proposal for a vast program of economic assistance to war-damaged Europe had come in the midst of the struggle over the Taft-Hartley Act, was warmly welcomed by a great majority of delegates. Despite this, the communists continued to push their anti-Truman foreign policy program. The delegates responded with a reaffirmation of the "resent and reject" resolution against communist interference within the labor movement. Once again the communists felt compelled to accept this as well as their complete failure to gain support for their foreign policy initiatives.

The Party's policies in 1947 and throughout much of the Cold War were largely reactive. It moved from crisis to crisis, treating each as one further step on the road to fascism and war. Each struggle was fought as if democracy and world peace were in the balance. The Party's decreasing adherents were called upon again and again for massive efforts until, eventually, a pattern of diminishing returns set in. Faced with Secretary of Labor Lewis Schwellenbach's call in March 1947 for outlawing the Party, it appealed for a fighting fund of a quarter of a million dollars. The membership responded within three weeks, whereupon the collection of funds continued as the goal was raised.

The House Un-American Activities Committee hearings on the Communist Party was seen as a public forum which the communists could use to strike back against the growing anticommunist tide, but the struggle within the Party leadership made an effective presentation of its position impossible. The Party demanded the right to appear before HUAC, and the Committee was only too pleased to schedule the Party's representative on the same day as the testimony of J. Edgar Hoover. A bitter debate occurred within the Party leadership to determine its spokesman. Dennis seemed the logical choice but knew that if he appeared he would be subject to a series of questions which would prove embarrassing . His years as a Comintern representative would be opened to public view as well as his use of various surnames during his career. The Committee might even be aware that he had left a young son in the Soviet Union when he returned to the United States in the late 1930's. The boy, who had a heavy Russian accent, would have proven an embarrassment to a leader of the *American* Communist Party.

Dennis' hesitancy to testify was sharply attacked within the National Board. Benjamin Davis reportedly accused Dennis of being a "coward" and of being "afraid to go into these hostile situations."[34] Faced with this challenge, and defended by none of the Board members, Dennis accepted the responsibility to testify, although he had no intention of answering Committee questions. He would have no opportunity, as a result, to set forth the Party position. The resulting HUAC hearing was a farce accentuated by nationwide newspaper photographs showing Dennis being led from the Committee room. Not only had the Party missed an opportunity, but it had contributed to the growing atmosphere of repression. Within months Dennis was indicted for contempt of Congress as a result of his refusal to testify before HUAC, tried, convicted, and sentenced to a year in prison. The Party leadership had played an influential role in sending its own general secretary to prison.

Just as the Party reacted to domestic threats and crises, it reacted to news from abroad with great sensitivity. During the first few months of 1947 three major trips to Europe were made by leading communists, and the results of their reports were to be instrumental in determining the tone of Party policy for years to come. Paul Novick, editor of the Yiddish communist newspaper *Morning Freiheit*, travelled to Europe in 1946 and returned in late January 1947. He spent a good deal of time in the Soviet Union and reportedly had conversations with leaders high in the Soviet and other communist parties. He returned with the first news that serious discussions were taking place with regard to the establishment of an international coordinating committee of communist parties.

The emphasis on the need for greater centralization of the international communist movement could only mean that a perspective of deepening Cold War had been accepted. This would be confirmed in September with the creation of the Communist Information Bureau (Cominform). The Novick report strengthened Foster's internal position. Novick also brought back severe criticism of the American Party from abroad. The Party was accused of having failed to grow sufficiently or to have significantly increased its influence in the postwar period. It was urged to step up its recruitment policies and to seek to play a leading role in national affairs.[35]

Armed with Novick's report, Foster set sail for Europe on February 5, 1947. He held conversations with leading European communists, but apparently did not travel to the Soviet Union. The next month, *Daily Worker* editor Morris Childs was sent to Moscow, ostensibly to cover the meeting of foreign ministers, but in reality to have important conversations with leaders of the Soviet Communist Party. No "instructions" were sought in these conversations, according to those involved. The leadership of the American Party was seeking an assessment of the world situation from which it could develop its policies. Childs returned in early May after having held most of his talks with Solomon Lozovsky. An old friend of Browder, Lozovsky was secretary general of the Red International of Labor Unions, vice commissar of foreign affairs, director of the Soviet Information Bureau, a member of the Soviet Politburo, and a former leader of the Comintern. The American Party could only see his views as definitive in terms of the Soviet outlook.

Childs reported the Soviet view that a third world war was not an immediate prospect. He said that Lozovsky had criticized the American Party for a variety of sectarian activities. These included the development of the concept of a third party which might lead to a Republican victory in 1948 and the failure to maintain a left-center coalition within the labor movement. A third party without strong labor support, Lozovsky suggested, would be isolated and become a small left-wing party without influence.[36]

The Childs report was a severe indictment of Party policy since the reconstitution of the CP. As early as 1945 the communists had proposed the creation of a third party. Throughout 1946 the issue had been discussed within and without communist circles. Support for a third party had been greatly strengthened as the Truman administration took what appeared to be antilabor positions. Various leaders of the labor movement had spoken of the possibility of an independent ticket in opposition to Truman and the Republicans in the 1948 election. The same month he left for Europe, an article by Foster in *Political Affairs* presented a clear call for a third party led by the communists. "We must," he said, "make the question of building the new party our major task and leave no stone unturned for its realization."[37] Foster called for the CP to provide the party with its ideological content as well as its organizational backbone. He predicted that with the communists' "broad mass contacts" and "strength" the new party would receive many times more votes than had the La Follette Progressive candidacy in 1924.[38] LaFollette had gained close to five million votes and had received the unwanted support of Foster and the Workers Party, the Communist Party at that time.

Foster's apparent position in favor of an independent candidacy in

1948 did not yet have the backing of the Party leadership. While there was almost unanimous agreement that a third party movement would be valuable, there was great disagreement over whether the thrust of its activity should be an independent challenge or come from within the Democratic Party. Dennis, in the same month as the appearance of the Foster article, indicated that both those who wanted to work within the Democratic Party and those seeking an independent candidacy were "progressives" and equally acceptable. The CP was yet to determine its approach.[39]

The Childs report strengthened Dennis' position and was strongly criticized by the Foster faction. Childs was accused of providing a false summary. Under great attack, he was removed as editor of *The Daily Worker* in June and replaced by John Gates.[40] The newspaper announced that "Childs' doctors ordered him to take a badly needed rest."[41] Gates later saw his appointment as a "clever move on Dennis' part." As a result of his war service, Gates had not been involved in the internal struggles of those years and was one of the few members of the reconstituted National Board who could not easily be tarnished with the "Browderite" brush.[42] The only criticism which could be made of him was that he had no journalistic background, but that had never been a criterion for the editorship of the paper, an essentially political position. The removal of Childs did not detract from the significance of his report. There was some independent evidence to support its content. Stalin, in an interview with former Republican Minnesota Governor Harold Stassen, had rejected the inevitability of war and projected at least a period of coexistence between the Soviet Union and "the capitalist powers."[43]

Foster returned from Europe with a somewhat grimmer assessment of the future than the one Childs had brought back. Foster reported in late June to an extremely important Party plenum—an enlarged National Committee meeting, including district organizers, key members from mass organizations, and trade unionists. At that meeting Foster said that the "forces of monopoly capital on a world scale" had been weakened since the end of World War II as a result of the growing strength of the "democratic forces"—the Soviet Union and its allies.[44] Rather than taking comfort in this alleged weakness, Foster saw even greater dangers. His thesis was based on the belief that a capitalist world which faced the prospect of diminishing power would strike out before it was too late. "Behind these immediate purposes of American warmongering," he warned, "there lies a real war danger."[45] Since the end of World War II, Foster said, big business had been seeking to establish a fascist regime in the United States and to precipitate war with the

Soviet Union. Now it would feel forced to do both. Although theoretically granting that war was not inevitable, he placed all his emphasis on its likelihood. He said that an "acute" war danger would arise if there developed "a serious weakness of the democratic forces in the country" through losses caused by major strikes, the enactment of repressive legislation, such as the Taft-Hartley Act, or through a Republican victory in 1948.[46] By the time the speech was printed, the Taft-Hartley Act had been enacted over the President's veto, hence, according to Foster, an imminent danger of war already existed. Foster added that it would be an "ostrich policy" to ignore it. "The only tenable conclusions we can draw from the whole situation," he said, "is [sic] that the Truman foreign policy, if unchecked, will lead to war: and that, therefore, we must combat it as essentially a war policy."[47]

The imminence of war automatically meant the almost immediate development of a fascist regime—the first victim of which would be the Communist Party. Foster emphasized, in a portion of his report not made public, that Party survival was at stake in the immediate period ahead.[48] The CP had to be prepared to go "underground." Going "underground" was not a new concept in Party history. "Whenever the Party entered a period of militancy as against popular front government," Gates maintained, "whenever it felt the direct threat of government persecution or prosecution, it went 'underground.' "[49] This response did not necessarily mean the development of illegal activities. It was essentially a defensive measure to insure its continued existence by protecting its leading members from arrest or imprisonment. The Party had used such a procedure during the "Red Scare" following World War I, also in local situations in the 1920's and 1930's, and again in 1940 when it had turned against United States involvement in the war. In each of these cases some members and leaders had hidden in order to protect themselves from government prosecution. They had emerged during calmer times when the Party perceived the threat to have diminished.

Foster's proposal for an "underground" during the Cold War period went considerably beyond anything which had existed in the past. He had brought back from Europe knowledge of underground structures established under Nazi rule during the war, and he proposed the creation of a comprehensive new apparatus designed to protect the continued existence of the Party and its ability to maintain an antifascist struggle. The Party organization would be scrapped, and a new system established that would be directed entirely from top down. Three leaders at the top would each name three others to serve on a secondary level. The plan, labeled the "system of 3's," called for each of the three to know the other two and the leader who had appointed them. In turn, they would appoint three others to a third level of Party leadership, and these would know only two others on their level plus the leader who had appointed them. This system would go down to a fourth level and beyond. The concept was that each person would know and have contact with a maximum of six other members. Informers within the Party and government agents, even if successful in penetrating Party security, would be able to identify only a small group at any one time, with the bulk of the "underground" structure able to continue to function. The apparatus would accommodate only some 10 percent of the Party membership and its institution would mean a drastic curtailment of membership.[50]

The Foster outline of a full-scale "underground" structure was considered preliminary and "not taken too seriously" at that time.[51] The concept of an "underground" was taken very seriously. Those at the Party plenum spread Foster's words throughout the membership, and Party fear of impending disaster rose.[52] On the national level, key CP leaders were ordered to change their daily routines from time to time. Some Party leaders were to be unavailable at all times so that all could not be arrested in a swift government operation.[53] Within several months Party members in New York were being given training in the use of electric mimeograph machines and in writing and printing just in case *The Daily Worker* was suppressed.[54] The effect was a greatly heightened sense of fear among Party members and a greater willingness to accept Foster's thesis on the imminence of war and fascism. These moves gave an appearance of sinister maneuverings and dangerous conspiratorial actions, which the FBI, fully conversant with the steps being taken, was anxious to spread.

The majority of the Party's National Board attempted to limit the effect of Foster's report to the June plenum. The Board was reorganized to include Gates and the state leaders of Illinois, Michigan, and Ohio—Green, Carl Winter, and Gus Hall. Foster and Dennis were to serve jointly as the new "secretariat," the highest leaders in the Party. Gates, who had replaced Davis in January as the chairman of the National Legislative Bureau, the CP's political action arm, delivered the main report on the development of the third party movement. While acknowledging the need for a third party, Gates declined to endorse an independent ticket in 1948. There would have to be broad support for the third party, including unions such as the United Auto Workers and the Amalgamated Clothing Workers, large sections of the Democratic Party, and farmers before a third party could be effective. None of these elements was as yet in support of a third party, according to Gates, and the outlook appeared questionable.[55] A major pro-Wallace effort was to be made within the Democratic Party while the prospects of forming a broadly based third party continued to be explored. Dennis endorsed this policy and suggested that "the Wallace-For-President movement is the key for bringing about a certain realignment in sections of the Democratic party."[56]

Dennis sounded the same theme throughout the summer and into September. Speaking at a Madison Square Garden meeting on September 18, 1947, celebrating the twenty-eighth anniversary of the Party, Dennis again called for a "new political alignment" and the building of an "independent people's party," but he said that the new President, "a man of the Roosevelt stamp," could come from either the Democratic Party or an "independent ticket."[57] Four days after Dennis' speech an historic meeting began in an obscure Polish town. This, along with other events in the United States, was to have decisive effects on CPUSA policies.

From September 22 to 27 representatives of the communist parties of the Soviet Union, Yugoslavia, Bulgaria, Rumania, Hungary, Poland, Czechoslovakia, France, and Italy met to organize the Cominform. In announcing its creation, these major and influential parties declared that the United States had fought World War II principally to secure additional major markets around the world and to rid itself of its principal competitors, Japan and Germany. The Cold War split was thus traced back to allied war aims and the entire blame for its inception placed on the United States and, to a lesser extent, Britain. The division of the world had been forced by capitalist imperialism, they said, which was now threatening war to destroy the rising "socialist democracies."

The Cominform statement called upon all communist parties to "take the lead in resisting the plans of imperialist expansion and aggression in all spheres—state, political, economic, and ideological." The leaders of these parties were asked to "close their ranks, unite their efforts on the basis of a common anti-imperialist and democratic platform, and rally around themselves all the democratic and patriotic forces of the nation."[58] The militant call for confrontation was heightened by the injunction that "the principal danger for the working class today lies in underestimating their own strength and overestimating the strength of the imperialist camp."

The details of the Cominform meeting were not published for a month, but when they appeared they had an electrifying effect on the CPUSA. Foster's line apparently had been endorsed by the international communist movement. Dennis, always attuned to Soviet policy, quickly changed his emphasis and policy, and the rest of the National Board followed suit. The formation of the Cominform and the apparent turn to the left by other communist parties had set a pattern which American communists did not wish to resist.

Events within the United States also seemed to reinforce the Cominform analysis. Early in November Dennis allegedly received a "tip" that mass arrests of communist leaders could be expected within two weeks.[59] The source of the information was O. John Rogge, a former special assistant to the Attorney General who had been dismissed by Tom Clark in 1946 apparently for his insistence on releasing a report concerning fascist activity in the United States. Rogge subsequently took on various left-wing causes. As others, he had become increasingly disturbed by the constant "leaks" coming from the special espionage grand jury meeting in New York. Receiving information that this jury would be used to indict dozens of communist leaders and "fellow-travelers" on various charges, he apparently hurried to Dennis with the information and then announced it in a November 8 press conference in Los Angeles.

There is some evidence that Rogge's information was planted by the FBI as part of its pre-COINTELPRO operations to disrupt the Communist Party. In a November 12 letter to the President, J. Edgar Hoover stated that the FBI was well aware of the Communist Party's "system of 3's" and had Party leaders under close surveillance.[60] The letter reported that these leaders were holding meetings throughout the country and were warning of possible mass arrests within thirty days. Party documents were ordered destroyed and select leaders told to go into temporary hiding. The FBI, meanwhile, monitored the entire operation and gained valuable information concerning the Party's reaction in an emergency.

At his press conference and in subsequent speeches, Rogge charged that the Department of Justice had been attempting to create pressure on the grand jury to come out with indictments for espionage and treason. He said that the arrest of dozens of communists probably would be timed to coincide with the November 17 opening of the special meeting of Congress. Comparing the arrests to the "Reichstag fire," Rogge warned of the development of a modern "witch-hunt."[61] Foster and Dennis, claiming to have learned of the Rogge charges in *The New York Times*, immediately sent a telegram to President Truman. Using the same analogy to the Reichstag fire, they demanded Attorney General Clark's removal from the cabinet.[62]

During the following week, the Party quickened its security measures. Almost everyone in a leadership position was ordered to disappear.[63] National Committee members from New York flew to other parts of the nation to spread the word personally. In their haste to give the signal, the telephone was often used with code words to order Party leaders to disappear for a time. The FBI, apparently through extensive wiretapping, monitored the calls and understood the messages. On the afternoon of November 11 a CP messenger, a member of the National Committee, arrived by plane in Detroit. He stopped long enough to telephone National Board member Winter and to meet him briefly on a Detroit street corner. Winter called his wife and told her "to get ready, start to get going." Later in the day, Winter was called at home and told that a cousin was ill and that he should spend a few days with him—the code message to leave. On the same day similar calls were made to Party officials in Indianapolis, Minneapolis, Milwaukee, Gary, and St. Louis. On November 12 the FBI reported the details of all this activity, and more, to the President.[64]

The grand jury was considering no indictments at that time, although it would be used later for such a purpose. The scare apparently was manufactured deliberately, but it had a telling effect on the Communist Party. It encouraged a swiftly growing feeling of persecution among members and bolstered the Cominform statement's conclusions. In the midst of the Rogge scare, the National Board declared that the Party would not join the Cominform—although it had never been asked to do so. The Party's statement was revealing.

The present political situation in the United States is such that the Communist Party should not affiliate. The reactionary and pro-fascist forces now whipping up anti-Communist hysteria and war incitement in our country would undoubtedly seize upon such action by the American Communist Party as a pretext for new provocations and repressions against the Communists and all other sections of the American labor and progressive movement.[65]

In early December 1947 the Attorney General's list of "subversive" organizations was published. Dennis and Foster issued a public statement saying, "This purge list takes the U.S. a long way toward fascism and police state totalitarianism."[66] Internal events seemed again to justify the international communist analysis.

The Party moved swiftly to place itself within the orbit of the new international militancy. The concept of a third party movement was transformed quickly into the necessity for a third party ticket. Dennis sought and received assurances that Henry Wallace would run for the presidency on a third party line. "Wallace knew very well the Party was his greatest ally," said Gates. "It was a mutual decision."[67] The CP would use the Wallace candidacy to show that the American working class, as its counterparts in other lands, was ready to struggle against the power of the imperialists. Wallace would use the organizational strength of the Communist Party. It was a bad bargain for both, ignoring completely the more thoughtful analyses each had made earlier in the year.

Dennis had moved all the way to Foster's position. As Foster had done in June, Dennis, in December, defined the two major parties as being essentially the same—neither representing a "lesser evil" for the people to choose. The support of organized labor's leaders, considered so valuable only a short time before, was no longer sought after. The tactic of "united front from below," which had been enunciated by Andrei Zhdanov, the Soviet delegate to the founding of the Cominform, was to be the tactic employed. The leaders were no longer necessary. The workers would ignore them and act in their own best interests. "Substantial sections of the workers support the Roosevelt-Wallace program and favor independent political action," said Dennis.[68]

Acceptance of the communist position on the third party was made the basis for continued cooperation with other groups. The failure to achieve such acceptance resulted in Party isolation from almost all influential noncommunist groups.[69] The CP went its own way at a time when its growing weakness already was apparent. Under severe and growing attack, its membership had begun to decline. The Party's organizational secretary reported to the June plenum that the attacks on the Party were having a "degree of success" and that the CP was having great difficulty in gaining members.[70] The FBI had received information earlier in the year that Party membership had fallen to 60,000,[71] although, interestingly, both it and the Party continued publicly to claim that membership numbered 74,000.[72]

It is fitting that 1947 closed and the new year began with a four-part series in *The Daily Worker* attacking Browder's "Progressive Imperialism." Written by Jack Stachel, the Party's national education director who had been drawn reluctantly to a pro-Foster position, it disclosed a party looking backward rather than forward. Its greatest challenges were imminent, but the Party was totally unprepared for them. It had severed alliances with potential supporters, projected a dangerous image of foreign attachment, and reacted hysterically to the deliberate provocations of its enemies. The Party had become, in fact, its own worst enemy.

NOTES

1. U.S. House of Representatives, 80th Cong., 1st sess., Appropriations Commmittee, *Department of Justice Appropriations Bill for 1948. Hearings . . .* (Washington, 1947), 147.

2. U.S. House of Representatives, 80th Cong., 1st sess., Un-American Activities Committee, *Investigation of Un-American Propaganda Activities in the United States. Hearings . . . on H.R. 1884 and H.R. 2122* (2 parts, Washington, 1947), II, 47.

3. Tom Clark to author, March 28, 1975.

4. Harry S. Truman, *Public Papers of the Presidents of the United States 1948* (Washington, 1964), 289.

5. Arthur M. Schlesinger, Jr., *The Vital Center: The Politics of Freedom* (Boston, 1962), 129.

6. J. Parnell Thomas to Harry S Truman, April 23, 1947, Official File 263 (1945–47), Papers of Harry S. Truman, Harry S. Truman Library, Independence, Missouri. Hereafter cited as HSTL.

7. *The New York Times*, April 25, 1948.

8. Ibid., May 18, 1948.

9. "Constitution of the Communist Political Association" [1944], Folder 17, Papers of Alexander Bittelman, Bittelman Home Library, Croton, New York. Hereafter cited as BHL.

10. David A. Shannon, *The Decline of American Communism, A History of the Communist Party of the United States Since 1945* (New York, 1959), 3.

11. Jacques Duclos, "On the Dissolution of the Communist Party of the United States," *Political Affairs* XXIV (July 1945), 656–72. Reprinted from April 1945 *Cahiers du Communisme*.

12. Alexander Bittelman, "Autobiography" (Unpublished Typescript, 1963, Tamiment Library, New York University), 718.

13. Duclos, "On the Dissolution . . . ," 670–72.

14. Bittelman, "Autobiography," 713.

15. Joseph R. Starobin, *American Communism in Crisis, 1943–1957* (Cambridge, 1972), 92.

16. "The Present Situation and the Next Tasks," 1945, Folder 20, Papers of Alexander Bittelman, BHL.

17. Bittelman, "Autobiography," 718–19.

18. Alexander Bittelman to author, May 1, 1978.

19. J. Edgar Hoover, *On Communism* (New York, 1969), 9.

20. Alexander Bittelman, "Where is 'Monthly Review' Going?" April 10, 1951, Folder 2, Papers of Alexander Bittelman, BHL.

21. Starobin, *American Communism in Crisis*, 231–32.

22. John Gates to author, March 5, 1978.

23. Eugene Dennis, "Concluding Remarks on the Plenum Discussion," *Political Affairs* XXVI (January 1947), 15.

24. "Statement of National Board," September 29, 1946, Folder 8, Papers of Alexander Bittelman, BHL.

25. William Z. Foster, *History of the Communist Party of the United States* (New York, 1968), 459.

26. Jack Stachel, "Highlights of the Recent Labor Developments," *Political Affairs* XXV (July 1946), 581.

27. Alexander Bittelman, "Report on the Economic Situation," September 18, 1946, Folder 19, Papers of Alexander Bittelman, BHL.

28. Foster, *History of the Communist Party of the United States*, 469.

29. Frank Emspak, "The Break-up of the Congress of Industrial Organizations (CIO), 1945–1950" (Ph.D. Diss., University of Wisconsin, 1972), 50.

30. John Williamson, *Dangerous Scot: The Life and Work of an American "Undesirable"* (New York, 1969), 151.

31. Emspak, "The Break-up of the Congress of Industrial Organizations," 49.

32. *The Daily Worker*, January 7, 1947.

33. Ibid., January 23, 1947.

34. Peggy Dennis, *The Autobiography of an American Communist, A Personal View of a Political Life 1925–1975* (Westport, 1977), 170.

35. J. Edgar Hoover to George E. Allen, February 24, 1947, Box 168, Folder N. Hereafter box numbers and folder designations will be cited as 168/N. President's Secretary's Files (PSF), Papers of Harry S. Truman, HSTL.

36. Philip E. Jaffe, *The Rise and Fall of American Communism* (New York, 1975), 88–90.

37. William Z. Foster, "On Building a People's Party," *Political Affairs* XXVI (February 1947), 120.

38. Ibid., 114.

39. *The Worker*, February 23, 1947.

40. John Gates to author, March 5, 1978.

41. *The Daily Worker*, July 13, 1947.

42. John Gates to author, March 5, 1978.

43. *The Daily Worker*, May 6, 1947.

44. William Z. Foster, "American Imperialism and the War Danger," *Political Affairs* XXVI (August 1947), 676–77.

45. Ibid., 680.

46. Ibid., 684.

47. Ibid., 681.

48. Sidney Steinberg (then CP district organizer for New Jersey) to author, December 25, 1974.

49. John Gates to author, March 5, 1978.

50. *United States v. Flynn, et al.*, "Transcript of Trial," Testimony of John Lautner (June 10, 1952), 4443–44.

51. John Gates to author, March 5, 1978.

52. *United States v. Trachtenberg, et al.*, "Transcript of Trial," Testimony of Barbara Hartle (May 17, 1956), 3158.

53. Sidney Steinberg to author, December 25, 1974.

54. Angela Calomiris, *Red Masquerade, Undercover for the F.B.I.* (Philadelphia, 1950), 168.

55. John Gates, "The 80th Congress and Perspectives for 1948," *Political Affairs* XXVI (August 1947), 728.

56. *The Daily Worker*, July 27, 1947.

57. Ibid., September 19, 1947.

58. "Announcement of Establishment of the Cominform," in Robert H. McNeal, ed., *International Relations Among Communists* (Englewood Cliffs, N.J., 1967), 55.

59. George Watt to author, June 29, 1975.

60. J. Edgar Hoover to Harry Vaughan, November 12, 1947, 167/Communist data, PSF, Papers of Harry S. Truman, HSTL.

61. *The New York Times*, November 8, 1947.

62. William Z. Foster and Eugene Dennis, Telegram to the President, November 9, 1947, 10 Justice Department Investigation 10 Misc. (1950), 10-Misc. (1947), Papers of Harry S. Truman, HSTL.

63. George Watt to author, June 29, 1975.

64. Hoover to Vaughan, November 12, 1947, HSTL.

65. "Statement on the Question of Affiliation to the Information Bureau of the Nine Communist Parties," *Political Affairs* XXVI (December 1947), 1141.

66. *The Daily Worker*, December 7, 1947.

67. John Gates to author, March 5, 1978.

68. *The Worker*, December 21, 1947.

69. Peggy Dennis, *The Autobiography of an American Communist*, 174.

70. Henry Winston, "Not Against But With the Stream," *Political Affairs* XXVI (August 1947), 730–38.

71. J. Edgar Hoover to Harry Vaughan, March 15, 1947, 167/Communist data, PSF, Papers of Harry S. Truman, HSTL.

72. *The Daily Worker*, January 9, 1947; U.S. House of Representatives, 80th Cong., 1st sess., Appropriations Committee, *Department of Justice Appropriations Bill for 1948. Hearings . . .* (Washington, 1947), 146.

V

An Indictment of Democracy

Instead of building bridges to possible coalition partners, the American Communist Party deliberately "burned its bridges" in 1948. Following a classic Soviet "scorched earth" policy, the Party attacked its "enemies" by retreating from any possible contact with them. The leaders of organized labor and liberalism were written out of the "progressive" movement. Only the few who accepted communist positions on foreign policy and the third party were acceptable "coalition" partners.

Leaders of both the CIO and AFL were criticized sharply in the Party's theoretical organ, *Political Affairs*. They were blamed, as the year began, for having been responsible for passage of the Taft-Hartley Act and, in large measure, "for the advance of reaction." Organized labor's support for the Truman Doctrine and the Marshall Plan was cited as evidence of its treachery.[1] Shortly after the appearance of this attack, the CIO Executive Board met to determine its attitude toward the third party. The Board voted thirty-three to eleven against supporting Henry Wallace's new party. The CP used all its influence, but even its adherents' disciplined support for Wallace meant little in the highest councils of organized labor. The Communist Party's weakness was demonstrated again and, more important, the left-leaning unions were isolated within the labor movement. The road to virtual extinction of the left forces within the CIO clearly was marked, but the Communist Party refused to see it. Some leaders within the Party desired an accommodation with organized labor and manifested a willingness to recognize labor autonomy in the areas of foreign and political policy. The majority of the CP's National Board was unwilling to follow such a policy.

A three-day meeting of the National Committee in early February exacerbated the communist split from a majority of the labor movement. In his report to the meeting, Dennis termed the leaders of organized labor "treacherous" and decried the tendency of Party district chiefs and trade union officials to seek an accommodation. He demanded that Party leaders accept the thesis that organized labor's officials had little relation to the position of "the rank and file of labor."[2] The brunt of the communist attack on organized labor was left to Labor Secretary John Williamson. He labeled anticommunist labor leaders, such as Walter Reuther, David Dubinsky, and Emil Rieve, as "the real watch-dogs and stool-pigeons of American imperialism," and as the main obstacles to the progressive movement.[3] Rather than accepting the need for some kind of compromise with the heads of organized labor, Williamson further isolated the Party by declaring that the CP had not been sufficiently militant in pressing for its own positions within the CIO. He condemned agreements with labor's "center," the forces of President Philip Murray, and suggested that those within the Party who supported such compromises were guilty of "Browderism."[4]

The communist position caused the more rapid creation of a center-right coalition within the CIO. The barriers to anticommunist action within the labor federation quickly came down. The left was stripped of all its positions of importance. Within a week of the CP's National Committee meeting, CIO Counsel Lee Pressman was forced to resign. He subsequently went into an important position within the Wallace campaign, but soon lost all real influence. Murray invited Minneapolis' then mayor, Hubert Humphrey, to address the national convention of the United Steel Workers Union. Humphrey, a leader of Americans for Democratic Action, received a rising, stamping, shouting ovation when he declared: "The sooner the labor movement gets itself scot-clean of this raggedy taggedy outfit [the CPUSA], the better off the labor movement will be."[5] The union thereupon repudiated the third party on the basis of alleged communist influence. By October the national CIO convention was ready to support fully Truman and his domestic and foreign policies. The left was routed in its desperate effort to maintain its position and limit the CIO's move to the right. Not only did the CIO establish an anticommunist policy, but it created an organizational and ideological framework which would soon lead to the raiding of left-wing unions and their expulsion from the CIO.[6]

Foster's report to the February National Committee meeting reemphasized the dangers of war and fascism, although claiming that they were not yet inevitable. Admitting that the attack on the Party and its supporters had been the most severe in its history and that the danger of war was "greatly increased," Foster said that the "drive of reaction" actually offered the Party "a magnificent opportunity to grow in numbers and mass influence."[7] The third party apparently was the cause of his optimism which, as events would show, proved to be misguided.

The Party's organizational secretary reported at the same meeting that the recruitment drive had completely stalled, particularly among workers and Negroes.[8] Foster's emphasis on the imminence of war and fascism and the need for a complex underground structure, as well as the Rogge incident, had created a deep trauma within the ranks of the Party. CP members of all positions were developing an "underground" mentality. Tragedy, both nationally and internationally, was expected at almost any time. A feeling developed that the Party should retrench rather than seek to grow. The sentiment was so prevalent that Dennis found it necessary to caution Party leaders:

I call upon the members of the National Committee decisively to reject those capitulatory concepts and "theories" which claim that under present conditions the Party cannot grow, that its organized base is doomed to decline, and that now a loss in membership is even "desirable" because today we need "quality and not quantity."[9]

The same day the National Committee meeting ended, Attorney General Tom Clark received an FBI "brief" which was to serve as the basis for prosecution of the leaders of the American Communist Party and was to go a long way toward conditioning the American people to accept the reality of what J. Edgar Hoover perceived to be an internal "Red Menace."

The internal and external pressure for government action against the Communist Party had accelerated throughout 1947. The tentative use of deportation statutes against minor labor officials, as well as the quick enforcement of congressional contempt citations, had been the beginning of a Department of Justice response. In an election year, with growing political stakes to supplement the rising anticommunist fear, the Department determined to act with greater forcefulness and effect. Using the earlier deportation efforts as a base, the Department acted against high Communist Party and trade union officials in a blaze of national publicity. On January 17, 1948, the new deportation drive began as Alexander Bittelman, identified in the press as a communist national committeeman, was arrested and held for deportation while on vacation in Florida. The Bittelman case served as the pattern for a series of arrests over the next two years. The press was informed that he had been taken into custody on a warrant issued by personal direction of Attorney General Clark. The Attorney General later claimed, "I never issued a warrant in my life" and "I didn't have anything to do with it."[10] He suggested that the announcement was "a technique that Edgar [Hoover] had I suppose" for gaining publicity.

The warrant for Bittelman's arrest was executed by the FBI. The government claimed he was subject to deportation on the same basis as those similarly arrested in 1947—that subsequent to his arrival in the United States he had joined an organization that "believes in, advises, advocates, and teaches" the necessity for violent overthrow of the United States government.[11] Clark testified that the Bittelman case had come to the attention of the Department of Justice in 1940 after the passage of the Alien Registration Act.[12] The Department took no action for eight years. The Attorney General could offer no explanation for this delay, other than United States involvement in World War II during a portion of that time. Appearing before a congressional committee, Clark said he had asked the Department for a list of "all aliens who are active in subversive activities" and promised to deport them. Bittelman, fifty-eight years old in 1948, had come to the United States in 1912. He had been a founder of the American Communist Party in 1919 and, during the intervening years, had served in a variety of influential positions, both in the American Party and in the international movement. At the time of his arrest he was secretary of the Morning Freiheit Association, the publisher of the Yiddish communist newspaper, in charge of the Jewish Nationalities Division, and an influential party theoretician. He seemed a perfect symbol for government deportation efforts. He had been born in the Ukraine. He still had a partial accent from his youth and, despite his residence of thirty-six years in the United States, had not become a citizen. During the 1930's Bittelman had made frequent trips to the Soviet Union—some, it was charged, with the use of fraudulently obtained passports—and he also had been associated with the Comintern.

Clark later defended the deportation efforts. "Those who had been here a long time and had not become citizens obviously did not identify with this nation."[13] The charge became a familiar one, but at least in the case of Bittelman it lacked substance. Bittelman had applied on several occasions for citizenship, but had been denied, apparently on the basis of his Party activities. His arrest provided the government with an opportunity to emphasize its opposition to "alien" influences and ideologies. He was initially held without bail in Miami until his attorneys were able to gain a shift of the case to his home area of New York.

The Communist Party reacted swiftly to Bittelman's arrest. *The Daily Worker* editorialized: "President Truman's political police move another step closer toward the police state repression they are planning for the whole country. The witch-hunt is growing."[14]

Three days after Bittelman's arrest, the FBI took Claudia Jones into custody in New York on the same deportation charge. Jones, born in Trinidad in 1915, had come to the United States at the age of nine. She was a member of the National Committee and executive secretary of the National Women's Commission of the Communist Party. She, too, had applied for citizenship in 1940, but had received no reply to her application. The communist press now recalled the days of A. Mitchell Palmer's raids and warned: "No American is safe. If J. Edgar Hoover's police can't 'get' this or that progressive on one 'charge' they'll trump up another. The frame-up system is steadily wiping out democracy in our land."[15] The deportation drive was gaining force, and the Communist Party's reaction brought the effort more publicity. Returned to New York at the end of January, Bittelman held a press conference to denounce his arrest and other deportation efforts. Questioned by reporters on his attitude toward the Soviet Union and war, he replied: "I would not fight against the Soviet Union in any war. Any war against the Soviet Union would be an unjust war."[16] The unequivocal nature of the statement was a propaganda gift for the government, yet the substance of his remarks was repeated by Communist spokesmen on other occasions.

Attorney General Clark apparently was disturbed by Bittelman's relatively quick release from custody and was determined to use the alien issue to its full effect. Testifying before the House Un-American Activities Committee, he promised to use "the deportation statutes to remove from among us those aliens who believe in a foreign ideology."[17] Deportation seemed to be taking on the appearance of a major Cold War weapon for the Department of Justice. Clark recommended Congress pass new legislation giving his Department the authority to hold a deportable alien in custody when his native country refused to accept his return.[18] This proposal had been introduced in Congress for several years but had made little progress since it would allow indefinite imprisonment for aliens who had not necessarily committed any crimes. For the first time, and without general consultation within the government, the Department of Justice seemingly had committed the administration to such a measure. The proposal was made as part of a package of Department internal security legislation which almost certainly originated within the FBI.

On the morning of February 10 Communist Labor Secretary Williamson, a native of Scotland, was arrested on a New York street by five FBI and Immigration Service agents. During 1947 Williamson had been actively considered as a possible Bureau informant. The FBI's New York office had recommended strongly that its agents be given the authority "to interview him under the pretext of his questionable citizenship status." Special Agent in Charge Edward Scheidt requested permission to offer the CP officer five thousand dollars per year, or a higher sum if necessary, to secure his services as an "invaluable" informant.[19] Scheidt's proposal was considered by the FBI Executive Conference—the Bureau's highest ranking body. It recommended: "No such approach should be made at this time, it not being believed that there was sufficient information to indicate that Williamson was approachable and in the absence of any workable means of contacting him." Hoover concurred in the judgment.[20] On January 8, 1948, Hoover denied a second request by the New York office for permission to contact Williamson directly.[21]

With the rejection of the proposal for an overture to the Communist leader, the Bureau concentrated its efforts on preparing a deportation case against him. It used its agents across the country, on an "urgent" basis, to prove that the CP National Board member was, indeed, an alien. Williamson had claimed for many years that he had been born in San Francisco prior to the 1906 fire which had destroyed the city's birth records. Agents in San Francisco, Seattle, Chicago, Cleveland, New York, Baltimore, and Norfolk, Virginia, were ordered to examine official records and to contact anyone who might have dealt with Williamson's family. The Bureau developed considerable evidence to dispute Williamson's claim that he had been born in the United States.[22]

Despite the Bureau's efforts, the Immigration and Naturalization Service (INS) advised the FBI in late January 1948 that it did not have "definite proof" that Williamson was an alien and would not execute a requested warrant of arrest at that time.[23] The Bureau actively opposed the INS position. In a February 3, 1948, memorandum, J. Patrick Coyne, head of the FBI's Internal Security Section, strongly recommended deportation action against Williamson on the grounds that it would "unquestionably do irreparable damage to the Communist Party." Coyne added that Williamson's arrest "should result in excellent publicity for the Bureau."[24]

Hoover went over the head of the INS to secure Williamson's arrest. On the same day as the Coyne memorandum, he wrote to Attorney General Clark to request the initiation of deportation proceedings against the CP's labor officer. The FBI Director emphasized that his major purpose was to harass the Communist Party. He wrote: "In view of Williamson's prominence in the Communist Party, USA, that group would undoubtedly have to devote a considerable amount of their energies and funds to his defense to the detriment of other important projects in which they are interested."[25]

Three days later the Justice Department told the FBI that Williamson's arrest would be "expedited." Informed by internal memorandum of the decision to initiate proceedings against Williamson, Hoover wrote: "I believe this is the 'rock-ribbed' American who heads labor section of Com. Party. It will or should jolt the comrades when they learn he is not even a citizen."[26] Disruption of the CPUSA apparently was the FBI's primary objective.

On the night of February 9, 1948, agents of the FBI and INS placed themselves in the vicinity of Williamson's home to await his return. When he did not arrive home by 11:00 P.M., it was decided to postpone the arrest until the following morning. The decision was based primarily on a desire to "get a better 'spread' in the papers than could be gotten if the apprehension were made" late at night.[27]

After his arrest the following morning, Williamson was taken to Ellis Island to await deportation proceedings. Gerhard Eisler was there already. In the same month three major labor leaders were arrested on similar charges. Alex Balint, regional director of the Mine, Mill, and Smelter Workers Union was taken into custody in Cleveland. Ferdinand Smith, national secretary of the National Maritime Union, and Charles Doyle, vice president of the Gas, Coke, and Chemical Workers Union, were arrested in New York. Smith and Doyle joined Williamson and Eisler on Ellis Island, where all were held without bail.

The government maintained that in deportation proceedings it had no obligation to grant bail and in these cases did not intend to do so. While their attorneys brought *habeas corpus* actions in court, the four Ellis Island prisoners went on a hunger strike beginning March 1 to protest the refusal to allow bail. The Communist Party sought to use the strike as a nationwide rallying point, with mass demonstrations planned from one coast to the other. Although the hunger strike generated some press interest, it failed to precipitate the widespread protest the Party expected. Instead, the arrests went on. The day after the strike began, a fifth participant was incarcerated. Irving Potash, a vice president of the International Fur and Leather Workers Union and a major figure in both New York City and state CIO organizations, was arrested. Potash was one of the few open communist labor leaders and a member of the National Board of the Party. He immediately joined the hunger strike, but was released on bail the next day.

Appearing on March 5, 1948, at a federal court hearing before Judge William Bondy, Williamson declared: "We are fighting against the first signs of fascism in the United States."[28] His words were not simply propagandistic. The Party believed a major legal attack was underway. Bittelman recalled: "We perceived the deportation proceedings as a beginning of a general attack on the Party."[29]

The Department of Justice attempted to avoid an adverse precedent in the setting of bail in political deportation cases by announcing it would hold hearings within the next week,[30] but it was too late to stop the judicial process. Judge Bondy ruled on March 6 that the imprisoned Party and labor leaders were entitled to bond, and they were released. Williamson later claimed that the popular support given to the hunger strike was responsible for setting him and his imprisoned colleagues free. The strike, he said, had "defeated Tom Clark's efforts to establish a concentration camp for left-wing aliens."[31]

The CP emphasized its propaganda theme that mass popular action could reverse any judicial or political decision, but in actuality this claim had little substance. It was the judicial process which temporarily had set the communist leaders free. In the midst of a growing self-imposed hysteria over the development of fascism, the Party was unable to credit the reality of an available judicial process. The CP already had created the mental image of a fascist regime in the United States, making its use of normal political and judicial channels difficult. The Party believed it necessary to rely upon "mass action," although the masses were rarely there. The resulting public image of the CP was of an "alien" political grouping which preferred to go to the streets rather than use democratic institutions of protest.

The court's action temporarily slowed the deportation drive, but it did not end it. Increasingly, the administration used its antialien actions to buttress its anticommunist credentials. In a nation shaken by the fear of war, generated in large part by the Soviet blockade of Berlin in June and the Western response to it, not much was needed to develop an antialien atmosphere. Clark deliberately used this climate during the election campaign. In a set speech delivered in various parts of the United States during the late summer and early autumn, he took credit for the arrest of alien communists. He proudly read the communist press attacks on him and declared: "Like President Truman, I, too, believe there is no room in this country for even one alien Communist or one Communist in the Government service."[32] America's chief legal officer did not claim that these aliens had committed any illegal or dangerous act. A *New York Post* editorial struck at the heart of the administration's actions: "The men have been imprisoned not because they have committed any hostile act against the United States, but because they hold what the Justice Dept. believes to be 'dangerous thoughts.' "[33] The *Post* was one of the few newspapers to criticize the government's actions.

In June, in the midst of developing tension over Berlin, National Board member Jack Stachel was arrested on deportation charges. While hearings for those arrested did not immediately take place, the image of an internal alien menace had been created. Historian Richard Freeland has suggested that the deportation arrests were deliberate administration efforts to silence the voices of those opposed to its foreign policies and to force popular acceptance of the Marshall Plan. "The arrests," he wrote, "played a major role in preparing the country psychologically for the war scare of 1948."[34] But the deportation arrests were only the public tip of the iceberg. A much more serious anticommunist campaign was being mounted secretly by a small group within the government.

Confronted by the growing responsibility being given the FBI in loyalty investigations, *The Daily Worker* warned on January 2: "The police state which is wiping out the United States Constitution is advancing swiftly. This police state dictatorship is being carried out by the FBI, and most notoriously by its sinister chief, J. Edgar Hoover."[35] There seemed no supporting evidence for the emotional statement and most civil libertarians put it in the category of continuing communist propaganda. Morris Ernst, for instance, defended the FBI in testimony before HUAC the following month. He criticized anti-FBI rumors from the left and said that as long as the Bureau continued its present investigatory practices, no danger existed.[36] Unfortunately, the FBI and its close colleagues within the Justice Department already had gone beyond mere investigation of specific criminal acts.

On April 14, 1947, Hoover ordered all Bureau offices to compile a list of the Communist Party's "top functionaries." These leaders were to be the subjects of "continuous, active and vigorous investigation." Their "cases" were to "remain pending at all times" and reports were to be "submitted to the Bureau on a periodic basis."[37] There is no indication that the Justice Department was informed of the FBI's extraordinary measures concerning a group of people who had not been accused of violating federal statutes.

At approximately the same time as the January 2, 1948, *Daily Worker* warning was printed, a "blind memorandum"—one not attributable to a specific source—was prepared in the Justice Department in answer to continuing FBI pressure for new legislation to establish an emergency detention program. Internal evidence indicates that the memorandum may have originated from T. Vincent Quinn, the head of the Criminal Division. At the time he and his Internal Security Section were working closely with the FBI's Domestic Intelligence Division on the espionage grand jury. The memorandum, it appears, was the product of a joint effort. It repeated the Attorney General's rejection of the request for additional legislation, suggesting, "The present is no time to seek legislation. To ask for it would only bring on a loud and acrimonious discussion . . . . " The political cost of such a drastic proposal at a time when the administration was seeking to win liberal support from the Wallace camp seemed far too much and needless. The memorandum noted that in an emergency the President could suspend the use of *habeas corpus*, thereby opening the way immediately to mass detention. Congress could then be asked to ratify the presidential action if it "is in a position to assemble—and if not, then the situation has obviously become so desperate that the President's action will not be questioned." The only threat to such a procedure could come from the courts. The memorandum, supposedly from the nation's chief legal office, said that what was needed was "sufficient courage to withstand the courts . . . if they should act."

While the request for detention legislation was considered unnecessary and politically unwise, the FBI anticommunist campaign was endorsed and encouraged. The authors of this memorandum recommended a "campaign of education directed to the proposition that Communism is dangerous." The proposal was remarkably similar to one advanced secretly within the FBI two years earlier by Domestic Intelligence Division head D. Milton Ladd. The similarity is so close as to suggest that Ladd may have been the real author of the memorandum and may have used friendly Justice Department attorneys as a "front" to endorse already existing FBI programs and open up new jurisdictional areas for the Bureau.

The "blind memorandum" further proposed the prosecution of communist leaders under the Smith Act as part of the campaign to educate the American people to the real dangers of communism.[38] The FBI used the memorandum almost as a charter giving it a free hand in its anticommunist war. The Domestic Intelligence Division recommended a program to prepare for mass arrests in case of an emergency. The Director of the Division wrote to J. Edgar Hoover suggesting an examination of the Bureau's Security Index to bring it up to date. He proposed the development of a "plan of action" for an emergency situation so that "dangerous" persons might be apprehended quickly, and he urged careful study of those who might be considered dangerous in such a situation.

The proposal for prosecutions under the Smith Act was at the very heart of the FBI plan. The Bureau welcomed the suggestion (supposedly from the Department of Justice) and took as its own the responsibility of assuring such prosecutions. In an internal memorandum to Hoover on January 22, Ladd wrote:

. . . it is felt that as a broad but an immediate objective of the Bureau that it work earnestly to urge prosecution of important officials and functionaries of the Communist Party, particularly under Sections 10–13 of Title 18, United States Code [the Smith Act]. Prosecution of Party officials and responsible functionaries would, in turn, result in a judicial precedent being set that the Communist Party as an organization is illegal; that it advocates the overthrow of the government by force and violence; and finally that the patriotism of Communists is not directed toward the United States but towards the Soviet Union and world Communism. Once this precedent is set then individual members and close adherents or sympathizers can be readily dealt with as substantive violators. This in turn has an important bearing on the Bureau's position should there be no legislative or administrative authority available at the time of the outbreak of hostilities which would permit the immediate apprehension of both aliens and citizens of the dangerous category.[39]

The Bureau obviously was playing for higher stakes than simply the "education" of the American people. The Ladd memorandum reveals the FBI purpose as being the destruction of the Communist Party and the detention of any persons whom the Bureau considered "sympathetic" to communism, quite possibly an impressive number. The FBI was seeking a precedent which would allow the arrest of large numbers of left-wingers in peacetime and masses of people in wartime. Once employed against the Communist Party, the Smith Act would serve as a judicial mandate for the Bureau to act without any further legislative or executive authority.

The Ladd memorandum clearly projects the role of the FBI not as a disinterested investigatory agency, but as a major protagonist in the unfolding domestic cold war. This role was not statutory and, indeed, had always been denied by the FBI and its supporters.[40] The FBI role in developing Smith Act prosecutions was known only to a few within the Department of Justice. Assistant Attorney General Lawrence Bailey, brought into the Smith Act case within the first few months, maintains that the FBI had no role in proposing Smith Act prosecutions and was in no way responsible for them.[41]

The Bureau's role in securing Smith Act prosecutions, however, was direct, persistent, and persuasive. Within days of receiving the Ladd memorandum, Hoover wrote to Attorney General Clark, again disagreeing with the decision not to seek emergency detention legislation and predicting that such a proposal would "be adopted readily by Congress." Hoover suggested that the Attorney General "might wish to consider the prosecution well in advance of such an emergency of the Communist Party under [the Smith Act] . . . thereby obtaining judicial recognition of the aims and purposes of the Communist Party."[42]

It would appear that the Attorney General had no knowledge of the "blind memorandum"; nor was he aware of the FBI's effort to use the Smith Act in order to circumvent the failure to gain detention legislation. Hoover's memorandum implied the use of the Smith Act as an alternative to the Department's plan to suspend the writ of *habeas corpus* in time of emergency. The FBI Director's position was that if the Department would not propose emergency detention legislation, for political or other reasons, it had to give the FBI the latitude to accomplish the same purpose through use of the Smith Act. Attorney General Clark did not agree, nor was he aware of the secret plans being worked out by his subordinates.

Clark stated publicly that the Smith Act was an inadequate prosecutorial tool and one which the Department of Justice had no plans to use. Testifying before HUAC on February 5, he said:

This [Smith] act is aimed at the individual rather than the group or party. Adequate proof against the individual in this regard is most difficult to adduce. In fact, the dignitaries of the American Communist Party have each denied that they have any aim or purpose to overthrow the Government by force and violence. Because of the shifting program and character of the party line, which can adjust itself to suit almost any limitation, we have found it more practical, effective, and much more speedy to proceed under other Federal statutes.[43]

Later in the same testimony, Clark recommended as part of his legislative package "re-study of the Smith Act with relation to proof of individual activity in the light of present-day techniques of subversive groups."[44] Clark's testimony ignored the proposed use of the Smith Act either as an educational tool or as precedent for mass detention. The evidence that Clark had no intention of employing the law is strengthened by the fact that a month later Deputy Attorney General Peyton Ford indicated that the Department was still seeking changes in the Smith Act. In objecting to a proposal to bar the Communist Party from the ballot in state and local elections, Ford argued that such a law would be unconstitutional. He suggested, instead, that changes in the Smith Act might include a provision that those convicted of subversive activities could be excluded from public office.[45] Later Clark stated: "I was opposed to use of the Smith Act" for any purposes.[46]

Although Clark had no intention of using the Smith Act as an alternative to emergency detention legislation, he had no objection to increased FBI powers in this area. He fully accepted the two-year-old Department of Justice policy on suspension of the writ of *habeas corpus* in time of emergency. He reiterated his support for such a procedure in his testimony before HUAC, providing for *ex post facto* approval by Congress of such a suspension. The Attorney General also agreed that in an emergency the powers of the FBI would be expanded greatly. In time of war, he said, "the FBI could pick up such persons as they thought

were inimical to the safety of the United States."[47] Through this for-
mula he attempted to satisfy the FBI. A proclaimed national emergency
would allow the Bureau to determine, by itself, the nation's internal
enemies and bring them into custody without any effective check.

Appearing before the House committee for the Communist Party,
Benjamin Davis challenged the Department of Justice to take action and
declared: "The Attorney General has no real case against the Communist Party, for the simple reason that my party, in principle and practice, is not the advocate of force and violence."[48]

The FBI was not satisfied with the Department of Justice position as
expressed in the Attorney General's testimony; the Bureau wanted to
take up Davis' challenge. The HUAC hearings had not reflected the sense
of urgency which the Bureau believed was needed, nor had the FBI
gained the jurisdictional control over a war on communism which J.
Edgar Hoover was seeking. As a result, the Bureau felt compelled to
take matters into its own hands and to act with forcefulness on the basis of the previous month's Ladd memorandum.

On the same date as Clark testified before HUAC, the Bureau delivered to his office eight heavy black cardboard folders containing 1,350
pages and 546 exhibits. Within months two supplemental briefs added
some five hundred pages and three hundred exhibits to the huge collection. The FBI had assembled a massive legal brief to be used in the
prosecution of the Communist Party. The semi-official biographer of the
FBI described the document as "a giant new edition of the brief which
Hoover had drawn against the same Communist Party twenty-seven
years earlier."[49] Much of the brief consisted of a history of the CPUSA,
and many of the witnesses quoted and documents used dealt with events
which had occurred twenty to forty years earlier.[50] There is no evidence that the brief was requested by the Attorney General. It was intended as the major weapon of the FBI to force prosecution of the
Communist Party under the Smith Act.

Hoover did not try to disguise his objective in presenting the massive document to the Attorney General. In an accompanying memorandum to Clark, he wrote: "There is forwarded herewith a copy of a brief
to establish the illegal status of the Communist Party of the United States
of America."[51] There was no effort to provide evidence that any individual communist had committed an illegal act. The FBI Director said:
"This brief relates to the Party rather than to its members and officers.
It does not purport to present and it does not present detailed and
complete evidence of specific violations of Federal law within the Statute of Limitations on the part of an individual officer or member of the
Party."[52]

Despite previous requirements that the Bureau limit investigations to specific, individual violations of federal law, Hoover now apparently intended to seek the indictment of an entire political organization. He claimed that the brief provided evidence

that through its advocacy and teaching of these [Marxist-Leninist] doctrines the Communist Party of the United States of America had advocated and taught and advocates and teaches today the duty, necessity, desirability, and propriety of overthrowing and destroying the Government of the United States by force or violence.[53]

The language chosen paralleled that of the Smith Act.

Two copies of the brief were given to the Attorney General. Clark gave both to his deputy, Peyton Ford. He, in turn, consulted with Criminal Division head Quinn. Ford kept one copy of the brief and gave the other to Thomas Donegan, then in charge of the espionage grand jury in New York. The Department had been beset for many years with FBI communications concerning communism, and although this was the most massive, Clark apparently felt no great sense of urgency. Ford, and perhaps Clark, initially believed that it would be best to give the brief to a prominent anticommunist liberal, such as Morris Ernst, to determine if it contained any basis for prosecution. Aware of Hoover's many efforts over the years to bring action against the Communist Party, and perhaps fearful of a liberal reaction to prosecution, the more independent judgment of a man considered a prominent civil libertarian was desired. The FBI vigorously objected to such a procedure and killed it. It claimed Ernst might turn over the brief to junior assistants, which would spread knowledge of a "Very Top Secret" document.[54] The FBI may well have been more concerned with keeping control of the brief and its uses than with any possible "leaks." Those in the Department of Justice who were aware of the brief were closely associated with the Bureau and could be depended upon to accept the FBI's conclusions. Outsiders, even those considered sympathetic, would be much less reliable and less easily controlled.

The FBI assumed its efforts to gain prosecution of the Communist Party finally had been successful. More important, it seemed that through indirect means the Bureau's jurisdiction in an emergency situation would be expanded greatly. In March 1948, FBI field offices were instructed, as a priority matter, to intensify their investigation of "Security Index subjects." A new, separate "Communist Index" also was created. It was to "contain information on all known Communist Party members."[55] There is no indication that the Attorney General had any knowledge of the new index. FBI field offices, in addition, were asked to suggest the best means to implement an emergency detention program, although no such program had been approved.[56] The FBI had acted quickly in accordance with the Ladd memorandum.

For three months little action was taken on the FBI brief. The intelligence establishment became impatient with the delay and began to put pressure on the Department of Justice. On March 26, 1948, Secretary of Defense James V. Forrestal requested the National Security Council to consider the problem of internal security and the need for establishing effective coordination of the intelligence establishment.[57] The NSC had been established by the 1947 National Security Act and consisted of four statutory members, the President, Vice President, secretary of defense, secretary of state, and others as appointed by the President. The chief executive acted as NSC chairman. The Forrestal emphasis on greater coordination and vigilance within the area of internal security was to be a continuing one and to become a matter of some dispute within the White House. The NSC considered Forrestal's proposal, and on April 2, 1948, directed its executive secretary, Admiral Sidney W. Souers, to commission an internal security survey.

Admiral Souers chose J. Patrick Coyne to conduct the NSC survey.[58] Coyne had been director of the Internal Security Branch of the FBI. It is certain that he had already played a role in formulating FBI policy with regard to the Communist Party and, more specifically, its use of the Smith Act. Coyne's placement in this key NSC role, and his later service for the NSC, provided another vital link for Hoover in his effort to influence government policy.

The Forrestal request and NSC action, together with the appointment of Coyne, apparently pushed the Department of Justice to take action on the FBI brief. On April 8 Assistant Attorney General Quinn telephoned John F.X. McGohey, the United States attorney for the Southern District of New York. Quinn informed McGohey of the existence of the FBI brief and said that it had been decided that McGohey should study the brief to determine if a sufficient case had been made to present to a grand jury. Quinn suggested that McGohey discuss the case with Donegan, who already had a copy of the brief, and that if McGohey agreed to take on the prosecution, Peyton Ford's copy would be sent to him.

McGohey spoke to Donegan that afternoon. The latter informed him that he had skimmed through only a portion of the massive brief and, at Quinn's suggestion, was also examining the case of *U.S. v. Dunne, et al.*, a Smith Act case successfully concluded during World War II against members of the Socialist Workers Party. Quinn had not read the FBI brief, yet his intervention had placed it within the context of the Smith Act.[59] In taking this position, Quinn seemingly was working as an agent of the FBI since the Attorney General and Deputy Attorney General had indicated recently that the law would not be used.

Quinn also chose the forum in which the indictments should take place. Donegan informed McGohey, in their first conversation on April 8, that Quinn wanted the espionage grand jury to hear the case. This choice would serve the FBI purpose of identifying the Communist Party with treason and espionage, although no such charge would be placed against it. McGohey dissented from the proposal to use a grand jury which had been in session for ten months and continued to be a center of both publicity and political controversy. In accepting the case in a telephone conversation with Quinn on April 12, McGohey made clear his objection to use of the sitting grand jury and said that he did not want "to be identified with [the] case presented during [the] last 10 months."[60] Quinn replied that he would send him the Peyton Ford copy of the brief and talk to him further at a later date.

Quinn brought the FBI brief to New York on April 15, 1948, for a conference with McGohey and Donegan. He informed them that the Attorney General wished the brief studied with the greatest speed and wanted the case presented to the espionage grand jury. Clark later said that he believed calling a new grand jury could not be kept secret, but if the case was presented to a sitting jury, it could be handled "without any notice."[61] In view of the record of "leaks" from that grand jury, the explanation is highly suspect.

McGohey spent two nights and a day at his office reading the brief, but could only get through a small portion. He had to ask Quinn to delay further meetings on the subject, but he made it clear that he was studying the brief in conjunction with the Dunne Smith Act case. McGohey and Donegan were called to Washington on April 29 to meet with the highest officials of the Department of Justice. In a five hour afternoon meeting, they discussed the FBI brief with Clark, Ford, Quinn, and H. Bergson. The latter may have been an FBI representative and took no active part in the meeting. Clark opened the session with the remark: "What are you going to do about Commies?"[62] McGohey informed him that he still had read only a portion of the brief but believed "it was possible to support charge of violation of [the] Smith Act and Voorhis Act . . . . " While Clark remained for almost the entire meeting, he made little contribution to it except to urge that the procedure be speeded up so that the case could be presented to the grand jury as quickly as possible.

Most of the discussion was left to Donegan, Quinn, and McGohey.

The latter, supported by Ford, insisted a great deal more work on the case was required before it could be presented. Indicating concern with the nature of the evidence gathered, he said that additional evidence might well be necessary and different witnesses, more current than those in the brief, would have to be interviewed. Although Donegan admitted he had not completed a reading of the brief, he believed the case made by the FBI was adequate and urged the presentation of evidence to the grand jury immediately. Quinn, who had read none of the brief, pushed hard for action. He said the Bureau "undoubtedly" had proven its case and wanted to proceed to the grand jury at once.

Only McGohey's threat to withdraw from the case, if required to proceed immediately, brought a further delay. He demanded at least two months to prepare the case. Quinn and Donegan complained it would be difficult to hold the grand jury for that long, particularly since its members were anxious to take some dramatic action either by voting indictments or, at least, making a presentment. It had been partially as a result of fear of a "runaway grand jury" that Clark agreed to present this new case to it.[63] It was finally agreed that George Kneip, an attorney in the appeals section of the Criminal Division who had previously been involved in communist deportation cases, would be asked to draw up an indictment. Quinn wanted him to do so without examining the brief—simply to put the indictment in the language of the Smith Act. McGohey and Ford insisted that Kneip would need an opportunity to read the brief.[64]

In order to get the case under way, Clark suggested that McGohey interview Louis Budenz. Budenz was to serve as the government's most important witness in the case. He had come out of the left-wing movement to join the Communist Party in the early 1930's. He rose to the National Committee and served into 1945 as managing editor of *The Daily Worker*. Although Budenz had never served in the top rank of leadership, his position had been sufficiently high to qualify him as an "expert" on Party affairs and doctrine. In 1945 he suddenly left the Party to join the Catholic Church and become a major anticommunist spokesman and witness. Aware that Budenz recently had indicated irritation at being constantly asked to testify and provide interviews, McGohey put off contacting him until after the indictments were drawn.

The pressure to proceed under the Smith Act, much of it orchestrated by the FBI, was becoming overwhelming. The FBI directly pressured the Attorney General. "Mr. Hoover," Clark recalled, "recommended strongly that we have the prosecutions," and "I usually followed the recommendations." Clark added that Hoover "had spent so much of his money on communist prosecutions, I guess he wanted to see some fruits." Hoover "handed [this case] to us on a silver platter."[65] Much of the FBI activity to force prosecution was indirect.

Legislative pressure was exerted through the introduction of the Mundt-Nixon "Subversive Activities Control Act of 1948." HUAC concluded its hearings in February 1948 and came out with its new proposal in April. The measure included the requirement that communist and "front" organizations and their members must register, but it went far beyond this obligation.

The Mundt-Nixon bill contained a legislative finding that communist organizations "seek the overthrow of existing governments and are organized conspiratorially" with members having an allegiance to a foreign power. The bill found the existence of a "clear and present danger" to the United States as a result of communist success around the world and the nature of the communist movement. Membership in communist political organizations was made illegal and members of such organizations were required to register—a rather clear violation of the Fifth Amendment's guarantee against self-incrimination. Any effort to establish or aid in the establishment of a "totalitarian dictatorship" was prohibited and violators were subject to ten years in prison, with no statute of limitations on the crime. Members of prohibited organizations were liable to denaturalization, a loss of passport privileges, and denial of government positions.[66] There is little wonder that *The Daily Worker* termed the bill a "conspiracy to turn the United States into a terrorized police-state—where all independent thought will be a crime . . . ."[67]

Communist fear of the bill was real and vigorously expressed. By the end of April 1948, HUAC had passed it and sent it to the House Rules Committee. House passage was achieved on May 19 by a vote of 319 to 58. Before Rules Committee action, Foster and Dennis warned against the consequences of the new Mundt bill:

Overnight a free country can become a police state. The "little" steps by which a people is robbed of its freedom carry a nation to the brink of the precipice. Then comes the last big step—the step into fascism.

Today our country is being pushed to that last big step.[68]

The reference to a nation on "the brink of the precipice" would be repeated for three years, until it was finally implied that the United States had fallen to fascism.

Senate hearings on the Mundt-Nixon bill provided an opportunity to increase pressure for use of the Smith Act against the CP. The FBI apparently leaked its plan for use of the sedition law to Republican Senator Homer Ferguson of Michigan. Attorney General Clark always was convinced that Ferguson "had a direct line to the F.B.I. No question in my mind about that."[69] He specifically believed the FBI briefed Ferguson on its desire to use the Smith Act in an effort to bring increased pressure on the Department of Justice.[70] On April 26, 1948, Ferguson called for prosecution of some sixty-four CP leaders under the Smith Act as a "test case," exactly the same position taken by the FBI. He attacked the Attorney General for simply collecting evidence, rather than taking action.[71]

As a member of the Senate Judiciary Committee, Ferguson used its hearings to bring pressure to force use of the Smith Act rather than gain passage of the new bill. The Senate hearings provided the first full-scale public debate on the merits of the Mundt-Nixon bill. Richard Nixon, then a freshman Republican representative from California, apparently was not yet the direct recipient of FBI information as was his more highly publicized congressional senior, Senator Ferguson. Testifying in support of his bill, Nixon said the Smith Act would be of no value since "the Communists have developed techniques for taking over governments without using force and violence." He added that it was "because of the inadequacies of existing legislation that this bill did pass the Congress [the House] by an overwhelming majority."[72]

Ferguson closely questioned witness after witness who appeared to oppose the Mundt-Nixon bill. Acting under the assumption that use of the Smith Act had been ruled out by the Attorney General, several witnesses hypothetically agreed that if an effort to overthrow the government by force and violence could be proven, the government should prosecute the case. Henry Wallace, Paul Robeson, Professor Thomas I. Emerson, and O. John Rogge all gave support to use of the Smith Act on this basis. Rogge, under questioning by Ferguson, said:

You have a law on the statute books which makes it a crime to overthrow the Government by force and violence . . . .

Now, if it is true, as alleged, which I doubt, that the Communists are out to overthrow this Government by force and violence, there are statutes under which they could have been prosecuted; and in my opinion the FBI, which is the best detective agency in the world, would long ago have found those facts, and they would long ago have been prosecuted . . . . [73]

Ferguson specifically suggested use of the Smith Act to Robeson when the latter spoke of "laws to take care of any people who would attempt to overthrow this Government." Robeson gave him the positive response he was seeking.[74]

The Communist Party, on its own, challenged the government to use the Smith Act. William Z. Foster, in a statement read to the Committee by John Gates, declared: "The director of the FBI and the Attorney General have long tried in vain to prosecute the American Communist Party under these laws."[75]

Both Ferguson's questions and the reality of the Mundt-Nixon bill set the stage for a final push for use of the Smith Act. The Senate committee sought the advice of Clark, Charles Evans Hughes, and Seth Richardson, head of the Loyalty Review Board. Each gave his opinion that the proposed law was unconstitutional. Clark said the measure probably would be found to "deny freedom of speech, of the press, and of assembly, and even to compel self-incrimination." In addition, he objected to the bill on grounds set forth previously by Hoover—that the Communist Party would be forced underground.[76] Indeed, the Party had warned continuously that a major purpose of the bill was to drive it underground.[77]

Clark's opposition to the bill, although expressed only in a letter to the Committee after the conclusion of public testimony, reinforced the need to find a means to prosecute the CP under existing law. An administration which opposed an anticommunist measure passed by overwhelming vote in the House of Representatives needed new anticommunist credentials. Admiral Souers later claimed that the Senate hearings established the public atmosphere which made possible the Smith Act prosecutions.[78] Clark believed if new and dangerously unconstitutional legislation were to be avoided, positive anticommunist steps had to be taken. "There is much to be said about a program that meets repressive legislation head on" and tries to use selective prosecutions to alleviate the pressures on Congress to pass more stringent laws, said Clark.[79]

The pressure to bring a Smith Act case against leaders of the Communist Party was heightened by Coyne's NSC report. Souers claimed it was Coyne who "made up the cases against all these leaders of the Communist Party based on his feeling that we could get a conviction under it." It is not clear whether Souers meant Coyne had done this while in the FBI or as a part of his NSC survey report. It is clear that Coyne's report included a recommendation for use of the Smith Act against the CPUSA and that it came at a critical time. Although Coyne's report was not delivered to the NSC until late June 1948, it is fair to assume that the essence of the report was communicated to high administration officials in May. President Truman, at a May 13 press conference, was asked to comment on the Mundt-Nixon bill. He said:

I never make comments on bills that are pending until they come before me, but as to outlawing political parties in the United States, I think that is entirely contrary to our principles. I don't think the splinter parties do any harm, and if there is conspiracy to overthrow the Government of the United States, we have laws to cover that.[80]

Souers believed the Smith Act "prosecution took place on the instructions of the President."[81] While Souers is undoubtedly correct in the sense that the President as chairman of the NSC approved of the proposed action, it appears certain the decision to use the Smith Act already had been made. Coyne's report, although received in late June, was not adopted by the NSC until August 5.[82] The NSC, the nation's highest ranking security and intelligence body, apparently was not involved in the earlier decisions. Coyne's real importance was in the pressure he was able to exert on the Department of Justice in April and May to take swift action. Clark maintained that neither President Truman nor the White House staff ever was involved in the decision to use the Smith Act.[83] It appears that this is correct and that, in fact, Clark, as well, played a minor role.

Justice Department attorney Kneip travelled from Washington to New York on the morning of May 6, 1948, to meet with McGohey, Donegan, and Justice lawyer Tom Murphy. He carried with him a fourteen-page memorandum analyzing the possibilities of prosecuting leaders of the CPUSA, as well as drafts of two short indictments to be used. He also brought a demand from Quinn for speedy submission of the case to the grand jury.[84] The Kneip memorandum highlighted both the weakness of the case to be prosecuted and its political nature. Although concentrating on use of the Smith Act, Kneip considered three other measures, the seditious conspiracy statute, the Voorhis Act, and the Foreign Agents Registration Act. Seditious conspiracy was rejected since it required proof of an actual conspiracy to act against the government— conspiracy to "overthrow, put down, or to destroy by force the Government of the United States." It would have to be proven, according to Kneip, that "the conspirators were definitely contemplating the forcible overthrow of the Government in the fairly near future." Kneip concluded, "Evidence of the above character is entirely lacking with respect to the officers and leaders of the Communist Party."[85]

Kneip considered both the Voorhis Act and the Foreign Agents Registration Act as inadequate vehicles for prosecution. The Voorhis Act required the registration of organizations "whose aim or purpose is . . . seizure or overthrow of a government . . . by use of force, violence, military measures, or threats of any of the foregoing." Not only would proof be difficult, but the penalties for individual officers were few and a defense under the Fifth Amendment to the Constitution might destroy the law. The Foreign Agents Registration Act was quickly discarded as inapplicable. There was no evidence to prove that leaders of the Communist Party had acted as agents "of foreign principals" during the previous three years.[86]

Kneip recommended use of the Smith Act although cautioning that "a reading of this [FBI] report makes one realize that the Government will be faced with a difficult task in seeking to prove beyond a reasonable doubt, in a criminal prosecution, that the Communist Party advocates revolution by violence."[87] Section 11 of the Smith Act, however, contained a conspiracy provision. It would not be necessary to prove that the Communist Party or its officers actually had taken steps to overthrow the government or had even advocated the use of force and violence. Under section 11 it would be necessary simply to prove that communists had conspired—criminally joined "knowingly or willfully to advocate, aid, abet, or teach the duty, necessity, desirability or propriety of overthrowing or destroying the Government of the United States by force or violence," or published literature to that effect, or had organized a group to accomplish this result. Even with use of the conspiracy weapon, Kneip suggested proof against individual defendants would be difficult to produce and recommended that they be charged with organizing the Communist Party rather than individual acts.[88]

The Kneip memorandum again made clear that the government's purpose was not the prosecution of individual criminal activities, but the destruction of the Communist Party. Kneip wrote: "Since the primary purpose of the contemplated prosecutions is to seek to establish that the Communist Party, through its officers and members, advocates, teaches and encourages the overthrow and destruction of the Government of the United States by force and violence, the *Smith Act* appears to be a fairly satisfactory vehicle for that purpose."[89] The FBI and the Justice Department were seeking a "vehicle" for prosecution. This search became all the more apparent in the conference held in McGohey's office. The Communist Party was the target. Government attorneys did not even have the names of the Party's leaders—those who would be subject to indictment. After determining to go ahead under the Smith Act, the conferees decided to request from the FBI the names of the CP's current leaders.[90]

Although there was some disagreement over the specific provisions of the Smith Act to be used, there was no discussion of alternative laws. McGohey made clear his view that the "clear and present danger" doctrine would have to be used—a concept which would play an important role in the trial and later court decisions. He agreed with Kneip that it would be impossible to provide "proof of actual personal teaching and advocacy of forceful overthrow," hence making necessary the use of the far more vague conspiracy provision.

The next day McGohey and Donegan met with three FBI agents to request additional evidence regarding "teaching, advocating and distributing literature by top officials of the party." The FBI representatives suggested that Bureau files on officers and National Committee members be provided. McGohey requested additional files on the head of Party publications in New York and the director of the Party school.[91] Within a week the Bureau provided McGohey with a list of seventeen possible defendants.[92] The decision to indict leaders of the Communist Party had been made conclusively. By early May 1948 the process of securing indictments already was well under way, but the highest officials of the Department of Justice were not involved. Relatively minor Department officials and the highest officers of the FBI jointly determined the procedure to be followed, and they carried it out.

Quinn and the FBI constantly pressured McGohey to hurry his work. Their efforts were not known to Attorney General Clark or Deputy Attorney General Ford. In mid-May McGohey requested additional evidence from the FBI to prove his case against each of the proposed defendants. The Bureau began to betray impatience with McGohey and strongly suggested that sufficient evidence already existed in the Department of Justice. Kneip reported in early June that Hoover's principal assistants, D. Milton Ladd and Edward A. Tamm, feared that McGohey's continued requests for more evidence would delay the indictments for as long as forty-five days—too long from their viewpoint.[93] The Bureau declined to comply with the Department's requests and demanded action. Quinn provided McGohey with a staff of five assistants from Washington to hurry the case and work was ordered for weekends. McGohey interviewed Budenz to prepare him to testify before the grand jury, while Quinn called the jury into session for June 22. With a great sense of urgency, final preparations were made to secure indictments.

Four days before the grand jury was scheduled to meet, McGohey had a telephone conversation with Ford on other matters. Ford inquired as to McGohey's progress on the communist case and was surprised to learn that indictments were about to be sought. Quinn had provided him with no information. Ford asked McGohey to come to Washington the next day to meet with the Attorney General. The meeting must have been an uncomfortable experience for McGohey. Clark told him immediately that he had not been informed of the proposed action. More important, both he and Ford objected to the planned indictments and expressed their opinions that a case against the communist leaders could not be made. Clark stated his view that evidence of specific actions was necessary, such as the formation of military groups or at least statements by the defendants to the effect that "we ought to take up arms." Since these were lacking, he did not believe the prosecutions should proceed.[94] He was concerned, in addition, that the proposed action would be at variance with his testimony before HUAC on February 5, and he asked McGohey to study his statement at that time.

Significantly, Clark did not order the prosecutions to stop. The pressure, despite his strong reservations, apparently was too great for that. Clark did request that the indictments be delayed until after the Democratic convention had ended on July 20. McGohey objected to such a procedure, claiming it would bring aspects of the case outside the three year statute of limitations. Clark then asked that the indictments at least be sealed until after the convention so that a possible charge of bringing the indictments for political purposes could be avoided. McGohey again refused.

McGohey went ahead with the June 22 meeting of the grand jury. For two hours on that day he and his assistant presented evidence, continuing their presentation the following day. After the June 23 session, the jury was adjourned until June 28 when it was to hear Budenz' testimony. It would then vote on and file the indictments. Justice Department personnel looked forward to the publicity which would answer their congressional critics.[95] McGohey requested that the FBI prepare to arrest the twelve members of the CP National Board on July 6. The Bureau reported on June 28 that, though three of them were out of town, it had the proposed defendants under surveillance.

Clark and Ford called McGohey on June 28 to express surprise that he was going ahead with the indictments instead of, as requested, holding them up until after the Democratic convention. Clark said that he "had told someone" this would be done, and he would be embarrassed if it were not. Clark later recalled it was probably Clark Clifford who had been informed that the indictments would not be filed until after the convention.[96] McGohey continued to insist on the necessity for an immediate filing and rapid arrests, although he agreed to delay the next grand jury session until June 29. On the same day, Kneip informed McGohey that Quinn, despite the opinions of his superiors, was still pressing for quick indictments and arrests.

The following morning Clark sent Quinn to New York to instruct McGohey to delay filing indictments until the appeals division and the solicitor general had an opportunity to review them in order to make certain they contained no "technical defect." Given no choice, McGohey acceded to his instructions.[97] The grand jury voted the indictments, but agreed to return to file them on July 20. In a June 29 letter to Clark, McGohey requested the FBI be instructed to make the arrests in the case.[98]

Clark had gained a small victory through the delay, but the FBI and the Internal Security Section of the Department of Justice's Criminal Division won the war. Indictments of the Communist leaders under the Smith Act had been voted and only remained to be served. They were based on an FBI effort to enlarge its powers and cripple a movement its Director had been fighting for thirty years. The results of the FBI war would charge the internal atmosphere in the United States dramatically and contribute to a deepening Cold War climate, consequences which the FBI must have anticipated eagerly.

NOTES

1. "Editorial Comment, Outlook for 1948 and the Third Party," *Political Affairs* XXVII (January 1948), 8.

2. *The Daily Worker*, February 11, 1948.

3. John Williamson, "Trade Union Problems and the Third-Party Movement," *Political Affairs* XXVII (March 1948), 225.

4. Ibid., 234.

5. *The New York Times*, May 13, 1948.

6. Frank Emspak, "The Break-up of the Congress of Industrial Organizations (CIO), 1945–1950" (Ph.D. Diss., University of Wisconsin, 1972), 272.

7. "The February Plenary Meeting National Committee, C.P.U.S.A.," *Political Affairs* XXVII (March 1948), 205.

8. Ibid., 244.

9. Ibid., 214.

10. Tom Clark to author, March 28, 1975.

11. *The New York Times*, January 17, 1948.

12. U.S. House of Representatives, 80th Cong., 2d sess., Un-American Activities Committee, *Hearings on Proposed Legislation to Curb or Control the Communist Party of the United States* (Washington, 1948), 33. Hereafter cited as *Communist Control Hearings*.

13. Tom Clark to author, March 28, 1975.

14. *The Daily Worker*, January 19, 1948.

15. Ibid., January 21, 1948.

16. *The New York Times*, January 31, 1948.

17. *Communist Control Hearings*, 17.

18. Ibid., 23–24.

19. FBI New York office to Director and SACs, FBI Teletype, May 18, 1947, copy of document submitted to author by FBI; Edward Scheidt, Special Agent in Charge, to Director, FBI, June 19, 1947, copy of document submitted to author by FBI.

20. The Executive Conference, "Memorandum to the Director," July 9, 1947, copy of document submitted to author by FBI.

21. Director, FBI, to SAC, New York, January 8, 1948, copy of document submitted to author by FBI.

22. G. R. McSwait, Chicago SAC, "Report on John Blake Williamson," September 2, 1947; SAC Seattle, "Memorandum to Director, FBI," September 4, 1947; Edward Scheidt, New York SAC, "Report on John Williamson," October 28, 1947; J. A. Rohey, Norfolk SAC, "Report on John Williamson," November 12, 1947; Fred Hanford, Baltimore SAC, "Report on John Williamson," December 22, 1947; FBI Cleveland to Director, FBI, Teletype, January 19, 1948, copies of documents submitted to author by FBI.

23. SAC, New York, "Memorandum to Director, FBI," January 23, 1948, copy of document submitted to author by FBI.

24. J. P. Coyne to D. M. Ladd, February 3, 1948, copy of document submitted to author by FBI.

25. Director, FBI, to the Attorney General, February 3, 1948, copy of document submitted to author by FBI.

26. D. M. Ladd, "Memorandum to E. A. Tamm," February 6, 1948, copy of document submitted to author by FBI.

27. J. E. Milnes, "Memorandum to Mr. Ladd," February 10, 1948, copy of document submitted to author by FBI.

28. *The Worker*, March 7, 1948.

29. Alexander Bittelman to author, May 1, 1978.

30. *The New York Times*, March 5, 1948.

31. John Williamson, *Dangerous Scot: The Life and Work of an American "Undesirable"* (New York, 1969), 179.

32. Tom C. Clark, "An Address by Tom C. Clark, Prepared for Delivery Before the Jewish War Veterans of the U.S.," September 18, 1948, Box 30, White House Assignment, Miscellaneous Previous Speeches Folder. Hereafter box numbers and folder designations will be cited as 30/White House Assignment . . . . Papers of Stephen J. Spingarn, Harry S. Truman Library, Independence, Missouri. Hereafter cited as HSTL.

33. *The Daily Worker*, March 5, 1948.

34. Richard M. Freeland, *The Truman Doctrine and the Origins of McCarthyism, Foreign Policy, Domestic Politics, and Internal Security 1946–1948* (New York, 1972), 297.

35. *The Daily Worker*, January 2, 1948.

36. *Communist Control Hearings*, 295.

37. SAC, New York, "Memorandum to Director, FBI," April 29, 1947; Director, FBI, "Memorandum to SAC, New York," May 12, 1947, copies of documents submitted to author by FBI.

38. Summarized and quoted in memorandum from D. M. Ladd to J. Edgar

Hoover, January 22, 1948, in U.S. Senate, 94th Cong., 2d sess., *Final Report of the Select Committee to Study Governmental Operations With Respect to Intelligence Activities* (6 vols., Washington, 1976), III, 438. Hereafter cited as *Final Report*.

39. D. M. Ladd to J. Edgar Hoover, January 22, 1948, in *Final Report*, III, 438.

40. J. Edgar Hoover, Foreword, in Don Whitehead, *The FBI Story, A Report to the People* (New York, 1956).

41. Lawrence Bailey to author, July 24, 1974.

42. FBI Director, "Memorandum to the Attorney General," January 27, 1948, in *Final Report*, III, 439.

43. *Communist Control Hearings*, 21.

44. Ibid., 23–24.

45. *The Worker*, March 14, 1948.

46. Tom Clark to author, March 28, 1975.

47. *Communist Control Hearings*, 33.

48. Ibid., 452.

49. Whitehead, *The FBI Story*, 295.

50. John F.X. McGohey, handwritten "Memo of Conferences on F.B.I. Brief," 4,1/Correspondence, memoranda, Note, Smith Act cases, 1948–49, Papers of John F.X. McGohey. Hereafter cited as "McGohey Memo." HSTL; Federal Bureau of Investigation, "Brief to Establish the Illegal Status of the Communist Party of the United States of America" (10 vols.), copy of document submitted to author by FBI.

51. Director, FBI, "Memorandum to the Attorney General," February 5, 1948, copy of document submitted to author by FBI.

52. Ibid.

53. Ibid.

54. "McGohey Memo," 1.

55. "Memorandum from FBI Headquarters to all SACs," March 15, 1948, in *Final Report*, III, 439.

56. SAC Letter No. 57, Series 1948, April 10, 1948, in *Final Report*, III, 439.

57. J. Patrick Coyne, "Major Chronological Developments on the Subject of Internal Security," 31/National Defense-Internal Security 2, Papers of Stephen J. Spingarn, HSTL.

58. Ibid.

59. "McGohey Memo," 5.

60. Ibid., 2.

61. Tom Clark to author, March 28, 1975.

62. "McGohey Memo," 3.

63. Tom Clark to author, March 28, 1975.

64. "McGohey Memo," 4–6.

65. Tom Clark to author, March 28, 1975.

66. U.S. Senate, 80th Cong., 2d sess., Judiciary Committee, *Control of Subversive Activities. Hearings . . .* (Washington, 1948), 1–9. Hereafter cited as *Subversive Activities Hearings*.

67. *The Daily Worker*, April 29, 1948.

68. Ibid., April 30, 1948.

69. Tom Clark, Oral History Interview, 210, HSTL.

70. Tom Clark to author, March 28, 1975.

71. *The Daily Worker*, April 27, 1948; *The New York Times*, April 27, 1948.

72. *Subversive Activities Hearings*, 42–43.

73. Ibid., 373.

74. Ibid., 318.

75. Ibid., 99.

76. Ibid., 423–24.

77. *The Daily Worker*, May 3, 1948; "Draft Resolution for the National Convention, C.P.U.S.A.," *Political Affairs* XXVII (June 1948), 490.

78. Sidney W. Souers, Post-Presidential Conversations Memoirs 2, December 16, 1954, Post-Presidential File (PPF), HSTL.

79. Tom Clark to author, March 28, 1975.

80. Harry S. Truman, *Public Papers of the Presidents of the United States 1948* (Washington, 1964), 255.

81. Souers, Post-Presidential Conversations Memoirs 2, December 16, 1954, HSTL.

82. Coyne, "Major Chronological Developments . . . ," HSTL.

83. Tom Clark to author, March 28, 1975.

84. "McGohey Memo," 8–11.

85. George F. Kneip, "The Communist Party of the United States of America," 1–2, 1/Correspondence, memoranda, Note, Smith Act cases, 1948–49, Papers of John F.X. McGohey, HSTL.

86. Ibid., 7–10.

87. Ibid., 11.

88. Ibid., 3–6.

89. Ibid., 3–4.

90. "McGohey Memo," 11.

91. Ibid., 12.

92. "Proposed Defendants Preliminary Statement," 1/Correspondence, memoranda, Note, Smith Act cases, 1948–49, Papers of John F.X. McGohey, HSTL.

93. "McGohey Memo," 14.

94. Ibid., 20.

95. Attorney General to Honorable John E. Rankin, June 14, 1948, Papers of Tom C. Clark, HSTL. June 23, 1948, handwritten comment at bottom.

96. Tom Clark to author, March 28, 1975.

97. "McGohey Memo," 23–25.

98. John F.X. McGohey to Tom C. Clark, June 29, 1948, 1/Correspondence, memoranda, Note, Smith Act cases, 1948–49, Papers of John F.X. McGohey, HSTL.

VI

A Freezing of the Internal Cold War

The Communist Party was busily destroying itself as the Smith Act indictments were drawn and voted. It had delayed its fourteenth national convention, originally scheduled for 1947, to August 1948. The Party expected to use the convention to mobilize its forces for the final months of the Wallace campaign. In preparation for the convention, a draft political resolution was circulated among Party leaders during the spring. It was published in June to allow comments by CP members. The statement was a centerpiece of the convention and provided the main Party line for years to come.

The initial draft of the resolution's section on "The General Political Situation," apparently written by Alexander Bittelman, was given to Party head William Z. Foster for his comments. Foster, sixty-seven years old, ill with severe heart problems, and not directly involved in daily Party decisions, remained the single most influential leader in the movement. The document given Foster strongly attacked the Truman administration for its "betrayal" of the policies of Franklin Roosevelt and noted "the growing danger of a new world war." The emphasis was not sufficient for Foster. In comments written in the margins of the draft, he demanded the resolution be made "stronger on [the] war danger" and suggested dealing with the question of the "inevitability of war." Foster also emphasized the necessity of building the Party.[1] The failure to enlarge the CPUSA in the postwar years had been a major criticism from abroad.

Foster's comments were incorporated in the draft resolution before its June publication. The political section now began: "The great and decisive issues facing . . . the American people are the crucial issues of peace or war . . . . ." The statement went on to declare:

The American people want peace. Therefore the monopolistic warmakers seek to induce in the American people a fatalistic idea that war has become inevitable. Hence, the crucial importance of the most intense struggle against the ideological war offensive of the imperialists and their agents. It is necessary to demonstrate daily that a new world war is not inevitable, that the masses of the people are already unfolding many struggles for peace against the warmakers, as is demonstrated by the spectacular growth of the Wallace-for-President movement.[2]

Those who believed a small Party would be necessary during the period of attack were criticized severely, as Foster had suggested, and the resolution concluded: "We must demonstrate further that only a strong mass Communist Party, recognized by the masses as its vanguard, will be able to lead the fight against war and fascism . . . . "[3]

The Party's assessment was published at the beginning of the Berlin crisis. International events thus heightened its lack of reality and further pushed the communists into political isolation. The "masses of the people" whom Foster was waiting to lead were travelling in the opposite direction. The Wallace movement was growing weaker. The inelastic and narrow view of American society and international events Foster had forced on the CPUSA was making it an object of scorn. This view of the Party was increased by its reaction to the ouster of Yugoslavia from the Communist Information Bureau (Cominform).

The CPUSA had no advance notice of the split in the international communist movement. It was as surprised as the rest of the world when Yugoslavia was expelled from the Cominform in June 1948. The Party's initial reaction was tentative. The columns of *The Daily Worker* contained articles expressing the hope that the differences were minor and soon would be resolved. When this hope was not realized, the Party swiftly and disastrously fell into line with the international movement. Although the American communist press had heaped praise on Tito's regime from World War II up to the split, it and the Party leadership quickly turned against the Yugoslavs. The day after the Smith Act indictments secretly were voted, Foster and Dennis issued a statement fully supporting the international communist movement against Yugoslavia. The Cominform was praised for having "rendered an outstanding service to the cause of world peace, the independence of nations, and the fight for Socialism," and Yugoslavia was condemned for its "betrayal of that cause." The two leaders implicitly admitted that the CPUSA had no knowledge of the split prior to the Cominform communiqué.[4]

Foster used Tito's split from the international movement to consolidate his own position. Tito soon was accused of the crime of "Browderism" and, in turn, Browder was accused of having been an early exponent of "Titoism." Foster took credit for having exposed this "right deviation" three years before the international communist movement took action. The resultant strengthening of his position within the CPUSA was in sharp contrast to the party's general loss of influence. The CP again had demonstrated its attachment to international communism. Its sudden reversal of policy on Yugoslavia generally was taken as proof of its part in an international communist conspiracy, rather than as evidence of a lack of close contact with the international communist movement. From the Party's viewpoint, there could not have been worse timing.

Rumors already had begun to circulate concerning the possible indictment of Party leaders. There had been numerous leaks from both the Department of Justice and the grand jury, despite an official policy of absolute secrecy. Most of the reports were only partially factual, but some were strikingly accurate. The Daily Worker on July 6, 1948, printed a summary of the many stories which had appeared in metropolitan New York newspapers during the previous week. All the stories involved possible indictments and The World-Telegram and Sun printed an accurate story concerning use of the Smith Act against Party leaders. The communist newspaper editorially commented that "a frame-up is on the way," but there was no sense of panic. Stories concerning indictments had circulated for at least a year, and the Party press continually warned of impending disaster, yet nothing had happened. Perhaps the Rogge scare of the previous November had cast some doubt among Party members and leaders as to the accuracy of such reports. This time some of the accounts were accurate.

United States Attorney John F.X. McGohey remained active while the solicitor's office considered the Smith Act indictments. By the middle of July he had received no response to his proposal for FBI arrests of the twelve communist leaders. He telephoned Assistant Attorney General T. Vincent Quinn on July 14, 1948. Quirn said he had received no information, but would check and call McGohey back. Later in the afternoon he informed McGohey that the FBI did not want to execute the warrants. The Bureau believed deputy marshals should make the arrests and claimed this was the usual procedure. The FBI suggested, in addition, that the defendants' "intense hatred" of the Bureau could cause difficulties. It was anticipated that claims of a denial of civil rights would be made if the FBI was required to take the defendants into custody.[5]

McGohey was amazed by the FBI refusal to execute the warrants. His surprise deepened the following day when he received a letter from Raymond Whearty, head of the Internal Security Section of the Justice Department's Criminal Division. Whearty's letter, dated July 13, stated that the Department had decided the arrests should be made in a routine way by the marshals rather than the FBI. He added that if "the Marshal desires any information as to the appearance or whereabouts of these subjects, the local Bureau field office will be glad to cooperate with his office." The FBI was maintaining its involvement in the case and continued to provide surveillance of the prospective defendants, but did not wish to be involved publicly with their arrests. The Bureau's connection with the Internal Security Section was shown once more by the Whearty letter. McGohey could not understand why both were opposed to his request.

In correspondence to Attorney General Tom Clark, the United States Attorney protested the plan to use marshals. He stressed that neither he nor the FBI had treated this as a "routine case," and that traditionally "where the FBI conducts the investigation and produces the evidence it insists on executing the warrants." McGohey emphasized that the FBI was the most competent agency to make the arrests and was most familiar with the defendants. He strongly suggested that proper secrecy and synchronization in this matter could be achieved only by a highly disciplined, centralized group such as the Bureau.[6]

Clark accepted McGohey's arguments, and the FBI was directed to execute the warrants. The Bureau's sudden reluctance to be involved publicly in the arrests of the communist defendants is curious after all its efforts to achieve that goal. It may be that Hoover was seeking to reduce the glare of publicity so that the FBI's real role would not be brought into the open. The chance that this exposure would have occurred, however, was remote. In view of the Bureau's attitudes and previous policies, it is more likely that the FBI did not wish all the arrests to be made on July 20, and that it did not want to be associated with failure to apprehend all the defendants. If responsibility for the arrests were left in the hands of federal marshals, they would be blamed for any defendants who could not be found.

While McGohey was seeking to force the FBI's acceptance of responsibility for taking the communist leaders into custody, the Democratic Party convention proceeded as scheduled. The renomination of Truman and adoption of a platform which extolled administration foreign and domestic policies formalized the split with the left wing. Seeking to protect the Party from conservative charges, the platform stated: "We reiterate our pledge to expose and prosecute treasonable activities of anti-democratic and un-American organizations which would sap our strength, paralyze our will to defend ourselves, and destroy our unity, inciting race against race, class against class, and the people against free institutions."[7]

Clark Clifford, who had major responsibility for the platform, may well have had the Smith act prosecutions in mind as he inserted these sentences. With its political flank now protected, the administration was ready to go ahead with the FBI's bidding.

On the morning of July 20, 1948, the grand jury reassembled in the federal courthouse at Foley Square, New York. Its work had been done a month before, and little time was needed to complete its task. The indictments, as originally drawn a month earlier, were filed within an hour. The jury adjourned before noon.

The FBI was given the arrest warrants to execute. Presumably it would make the arrests in one secret, swift stroke, apprehending those indicted at various places in New York and other parts of the United States. The twelve members of the National Board had been under close FBI surveillance for more than a month. Each defendant was well known to the Bureau and had been the subject of intense investigation for years. Agents familiar with each defendant were to be dispatched to make the arrests.

Despite the planning involved in the procedure to be used, there was an almost immediate breakdown. By early afternoon full accounts of the indictments went out over news wires into newspaper offices around the United States. In his *Daily Worker* office in the Communist Party building on Twelfth Street, in Manhattan, John Gates picked up the news ticker to read of his impending arrest. He hurried up the stairs to the ninth-floor offices of the national Communist Party. There he informed several members of the National Board, including Foster and Dennis, that they were about to be taken into custody.

Why had advance notice of the arrests been given—particularly when the FBI was aware of communist plans to go underground if threatened? The Communist leaders did not stop to ask themselves that question. They were too busy considering their next steps. Much later Gates would reflect that perhaps the FBI deliberately had leaked news of the impending arrests to give the Communist leadership an opportunity to go into hiding.[8] Any CP action similar to that which had occurred at the time of the Rogge scare would be interpreted by the American people as an admission of guilt and would be viewed as part of a dangerous conspiracy. If that were the FBI intention, the communists fell into the trap.

The CP leaders could not be certain of the depth of the threat. They knew the National Board faced immediate arrest but did not know if the government effort would go deeper. The New York leadership decided that at least four members of the National Board should seek to escape immediate apprehension. There was time to advise Gil Green in Chicago and Gus Hall in Cleveland to go into hiding. Among the New York leaders, it was decided that Gates and Robert Thompson should go underground.[9] Another CP chief, Irving Potash, was on vacation in New England. The nucleus of four or five leaders would remain underground if it appeared the government purpose was to strip the Party of its entire leadership.

Henry Winston, Jack Stachel, and John Williamson joined Dennis and Foster in the national office to await arrest. They had time to write and mimeograph a statement before the FBI arrived. The Party's attorney, Abraham Unger, was summoned to be present. Gates left the Party building, which must have been under intense surveillance, and went into hiding. At 5:55 P.M. the FBI arrived at Party headquarters, together with a full complement of the press. The five CP heads quickly were arrested. The FBI special agent in charge asked Foster the whereabouts of Gates and Thompson. Not surprisingly, the veteran communist refused to provide any information. The Party's prepared statement was distributed to the press as the five leaders were taken away.[10]

The CP statement bitterly attacked the Truman administration for staging the arrests just before the opening of the convention of the new third party in Philadelphia three days hence. Truman was accused of an "effort to win the election by hook or by crook." The CP leaders claimed that their arrest represented a direct attack on the new party, thus more closely identifying the coming Wallace campaign with the communists. The statement added:

Terrified of the growing support for the Wallace-Taylor ticket, the Democratic high command is seeking to brand the new party as "criminal" because among the opponents of Wall Street's two old parties and their candidates are the Communists, who also join with all other progressives in supporting the new people's anti-war party.[11]

The communist statement was incorrect. The "Democratic high command" had not ordered the arrests, nor had they been timed to come just before the convention of the Progressive Party, the new third party. The only political element in the timing was to insure that they came after the Democrats had concluded their meeting. The arrests represented a much more dangerous threat to the Communist Party and challenge to the democratic system than the statement suggested.

Benjamin Davis was picked up by FBI agents in the evening, and Carl

Winter, Michigan head of the Party, was arrested at the same time in Detroit. Gates unilaterally decided that the editor of the Party newspaper should not go "underground." He turned himself in to federal authorities on the following day. Although this was a breach of Party discipline—those not arrested were to remain underground "until they got instructions to come back"—Gates received surprisingly little criticism. Davis was among the few to criticize Gates' personal decision.[12] On the same day Gates surrendered, Potash notified the United States attorney that he would return to New York City the following morning to give himself up. To have remained a fugitive would have destroyed his leadership role in organized labor.

Thompson, Green, and Hall remained at large more than a week. Those in custody in New York were granted bail and freed despite the failure to apprehend the three fugitives. There was considerable debate within the CP leadership whether the three who remained at liberty should surrender. It was decided finally that with the granting of bail it would be "ridiculous" to remain underground. The Party and its leaders were still able to operate publicly, and the arrests had not gone beyond the highest echelon.[13]

Surprisingly, there was little publicity about the missing leaders. Nor did the FBI apparently make extensive efforts to locate them. Within days the Bureau had received informants' reports that the three leaders would surrender voluntarily and that the Party had decided not to go underground.[14] On July 19, 1948, Thompson surrendered in New York and refused to answer questions concerning his whereabouts during the preceding week.[15] The following day Green turned himself in to federal officials in Chicago. Hall was the last to give up. Described in the press as "well-tanned," he surrendered to authorities in Cleveland.[16] The three soon were released on bail to join their colleagues.

Although little publicity surrounded the missing Party leaders, those defendants taken into custody were the subjects of great press interest. Foster used the federal court press chamber the day after the arrests to claim that "This frame-up is one more of the steps being taken by the Government and Wall Street to force the United States into fascism as part of their program of war."[17]

Few shared Foster's belief that the indictment of twelve leaders of the CPUSA was part of a deliberate government effort to establish fascism and bring war. If Foster and the Party had appealed simply on the basis of a destruction of essential civil liberties, the response might have been better. Despite the Party's ideological reaction, there were groups willing to oppose the government's actions. The American Civil Liberties Union sent a letter to Attorney General Clark which reflected both the fear of being forced to defend communists and a determined response to what was perceived as an attack on basic freedoms.[18] Henry Wallace accused the administration of a violation of the First Amendment's guarantees and said that this new "Red scare" was a deliberate effort to create sufficient fear among the American people to keep the administration in power.[19] Perhaps the most typical and colorful reaction of those opposed both to the Party and the government's action was expressed by Transport Workers Union head Michael Quill. The union leader earlier had broken with the Party and the Wallace movement. He had moved a long way towards occupying a significant anticommunist position within the labor movement. He reacted to the arrests by accusing the administration of making "martyrs out of harmless crackpots." Quill claimed that the use of the Smith Act "apes the Palmer raids of 1920 and it creates in New York the first step in a reign of terror similar only to Hitler's Reichstag fire scare."[20]

Through statements, its press, and public demonstrations, the CP interpreted the attack upon itself as a general attack upon the Progressive Party. In so doing the CP benefited neither itself nor the new party. When questioned at a July 22 news conference on communist charges of an effort "to smear their party," President Truman denied any prior knowledge of the arrests.[21] Despite the denial, *The Daily Worker* headlined the charge that the President had approved plans to arrest the CP leaders several months before.[22]

The Party's effort to tie Truman to an anticommunist plot actually played into the hands of Clark Clifford's strategy. There was no way the communist arrests could have avoided entanglement in a political web, coming as they did in the midst of Democratic and Progressive Party conventions. The Smith Act's use at the height of the political season inevitably coupled the CP with Wallace's party and insured an anticommunist reaction against both. The rising heat of the election campaign already had created an anticommunist political environment. The arrests and the reaction to them intensified this political atmosphere.

The electoral strategy planned by Clifford in 1947 was carried out almost exactly as he had proposed, and it achieved the predicted results. From the beginning of the year events and planned strategy came together to make the anticommunist issue work for Truman rather than against him. In January the President received a copy of an electoral poll which placed him considerably ahead of any of his possible Republican opponents. In examining the poll at a staff conference, Clifford observed that if Wallace ran as a radical left-winger "we would not expect him to draw enough Democratic votes to cause Mr. Truman's defeat."[23] As Clifford had earlier recommended, the Democratic strategy was to push Wallace further left and build a public perception of his party as a captive of the communists.

The FBI was anxious to help the President in his anti-Wallace efforts. Many reports were supplied to the chief executive detailing communist actions on behalf of the Wallace candidacy. In an early January letter to the President, Hoover warned of CP efforts to place the third party on the ballot in California. He carefully detailed Party plans to organize its members to collect the 280,000 signatures needed to place Wallace on the ballot in that key western state. Fearing that mobilization of the entire California CP for this task would curtail its normal operations and organizational activities, he reported, the Party considered hiring professional signature collectors.[24] Political intelligence apparently had become an accepted practice for the Bureau, and again the Truman administration welcomed it.

Hoover's reports indicated the CPUSA had mobilized all its nationwide resources and cadre in the third party campaign. Truman was informed that an unnamed CP National Committee member had said the Party's major objective was to obtain "just enough votes to defeat Truman and prepare the way for the election of a progressive president in 1952."[25]

The high degree of FBI involvement in the campaign is shown also by its production of a massive document entitled "Communists and Pro-Communists for Wallace." The pamphlet, apparently written by the FBI, made extensive use of supposedly secret Bureau files. No author was listed, and there is no indication of the extent to which it was distributed. At least one copy was sent to the President. The document consisted of an all-out attack on the third party and its backers. Wallace was termed "Stalin's candidate—nothing more, nothing less." Included were profiles of such supporters as Lee Pressman, Senator Glen Taylor, and Representative Leo Isaacson. Some of the biographical sketches went back as far as twenty years to examine alleged procommunist activities.[26] It is possible the document was circulated only in government circles, although this is doubtful in view of the FBI's expressed purposes. Even if it remained solely within the government, it provides damaging evidence of the seeming development of a political police, one tolerated, perhaps encouraged, by the administration.

Truman apparently was not as concerned by the rise of the Wallace movement as was Hoover or high Democratic officials. The President seemed confident he could isolate the new party by pinning a communist label on it. A sense of alarm had spread through the Democratic Party in mid-February as the result of a special election in the

Bronx's twenty-fourth congressional district. In a three-cornered race, Leo Isaacson, the American Labor Party candidate, easily defeated his Democratic and Republican opponents. Isaacson received Wallace's active support and the Communist Party's open, energetic assistance. The Democrats also sent influential national figures to campaign, including Eleanor Roosevelt, but they were unsuccessful in swaying the very liberal, predominantly Jewish constituency. The issue of administration policy toward Palestine was considered by most observers as a key to the Isaacson election victory. Shortly after the election, Democratic National Chairman Senator J. Howard McGrath "all but invited Wallace to return to the Democratic fold."[27]

The President was not alarmed by the Isaacson victory. In an important sense, he welcomed it. At a staff conference on the day following the election, Truman brought up the results himself and seemed pleased by them. He suggested this might be a "year of decision" in bringing about a liberal-conservative realignment of the major parties. Confident of his own ability to control the Democratic Party, the chief executive saw himself as the leader of the liberal forces and believed he would fall heir to the rising popular militancy reflected in Isaacson's victory.[28] Rather than seeking a personal accommodation with Wallace, Truman's comments and actions concerning the new party sharpened.[29]

Much of the early attack on Wallace was left to identifiable liberals. Clifford's strategy of using left of center people to attack the Wallace movement was carried out with great success. One observer later suggested that groups such as the ADA had "contributed greatly to the creation of the Communist issue in 1948."[30] Criticism by anticommunist liberals, together with the CP's avowed support for the third party, attached a communist label to Wallace long before his official nomination in July.

The use of the communist issue by the Republican Party was of much greater concern to the President than the CP's political activities. The Republican speaker of the House of Representatives, Joseph Martin, Jr., of Massachusetts, went so far as to warn against a possible coup d'état by communist "saboteurs" if they succeeded in their effort to discredit Congress.[31] While the Martin warning was extreme, it did represent a groping effort by some influential members of the opposition to find a means to use the communist issue effectively in a national election year. The issue flamed briefly during the spring in a series of primary battles.

Harold Stassen, considered a representative of the more liberal wing of the Republican Party, introduced the issue into the campaign. In attempting to win delegates from his major opponents, New York's

Thomas Dewey and Ohio Senator Robert A. Taft, Stassen assailed domestic communists and demanded that the CP be outlawed.[32] Taft and Dewey rejected Stassen's call. Taft's position may have been critical in killing the Mundt-Nixon bill in the Senate. He reminded Stassen that "under our Constitution a man can be a Communist if he desires."[33] Campaigning in the critical Oregon primary, Dewey attacked Stassen's "hysterical suggestions for handling communism," but agreed that communism would be a major issue in the campaign.[34]

There were dangers for the Truman administration in the Republican controversy concerning internal communism. At some point each of the Republican candidates individually or the Party as a whole could be expected to use the same issue against the Democrats. It did not take long for this to occur. In the midst of the primary campaign a vital Republican supporter of a bipartisan foreign policy, Michigan Senator Arthur H. Vandenberg, linked foreign and domestic communist threats. In a warning aimed at Joseph Stalin, he said: "Underlying everything else we shall not surrender to Communist conspiracies in the United States." Vandenberg added significantly: "We are suicidal fools if we do not root out any treason at home which may dream of bringing world revolution to the United States."[35] Dewey made the implied criticism of the Truman administration more concrete in Oregon the following week. He charged: "If we had a national administration that wanted to move, it could and would move today to convict them [communists] and get rid of them."[36]

Truman handled the issue with caution and generally attempted to ignore it. Attacked by the House Un-American Activities Committee for refusing to open loyalty investigation files to the congressional committee, he responded by directing the Attorney General to write a presidential order prohibiting the release of investigatory information without the express approval of the President.[37]

In seeking to turn the disclosure question to one of executive authority, rather than emphasizing the limited and slanted nature of FBI reports, the chief executive succeeded only in postponing the issue and raising the American people's level of anxiety. Similar efforts to play down the communist issue in public comments had little positive effect. In a cross-country "non-political" train trip in June, the President spoke little of communism. His only extensive reference emphasized that the way to defeat any internal threat was to build "more and better democracy."[38] At another stop he charged that the Soviet Union had used communist parties in various nations to intervene in their internal affairs, but saw no threat from this in the United States.[39] While Truman was attempting to quiet the fears of communism and reduce its value as a campaign issue, his Attorney General was doing the opposite.

In March Clark said that communism was still a "serious threat" in the United States, although the FBI had the situation "pretty well in hand."[40] In early May he was characterizing communists as people who "feed on human weaknesses . . . distort facts . . . flaunt constituted authority . . . vilify every act of the government, and every hour of the day and night . . . try to bring about chaos and confusion."[41] Later in the month he notified the Loyalty Review Board that the Communist Party came within the purview of the Hatch Act. Any member of the CP was to be discharged immediately from federal employment. As part of this administrative ruling, Clark stated that the CP advocated the overthrow of the government by force and violence. This conclusion came in the midst of Justice Department consideration of Smith Act prosecutions which might establish a judicial determination of this question. The President claimed he knew nothing of the Attorney General's action.[42]

The combination of congressional pressure, government action, and administration rhetoric intensified the anticommunist atmosphere. The potential for a dangerous reaction was exemplified by several violent incidents. A local communist effort in Columbus, Ohio, on March 19, 1948, to distribute a pamphlet criticizing a presidential address was broken up by a crowd of several hundred. The leaflets were torn out of the hands of the three Party workers and thrown to the ground.[43] In late May, in the same city, what was described as a "mob" attacked the home of a communist labor leader, Frank Hashmall. The reaction of the Republican governor of Ohio was to suggest that "Hashmall should go back to Russia."[44] Walter Reuther, president of the United Automobile Workers, was outraged by the attack and wrote to both the President and the Attorney General requesting federal action. He suggested that the President make a national broadcast condemning such violence.[45] Attorney General Clark assured the President that the matter was being given "appropriate consideration."[46] Clark later suggested there were great difficulties in handling such cases.

The FBI had little interest in local outbreaks of anticommunist violence. Clark said Hoover was "allergic" to interfering in local affairs, and particularly so where civil liberties were concerned. "I rather doubt that Hoover was interested in protecting the rights of radicals," Clark reflected. "He was dragging his feet." To involve the FBI in any such instance required a specific letter from the Attorney General. "It was like pulling eye-teeth to get anything done."[47]

Questioned at a press conference about the Reuther request for intervention, President Truman agreed that the attack on Hashmall was not "a proper thing that happened," but emphasized it was a local matter not under his control.[48] The federal government's reluctance to act led to further incidents. A few days after the Columbus attack, a communist organizer in Alabama was arrested on a charge of "disorderly conduct" for distributing a pamphlet containing answers by CP head Foster to questions submitted by the *Herald-Tribune*. The distributor was sentenced to 180 days at hard labor and a $100 fine.[49] Six days later a group in Rochester broke up a CP meeting and burned communist books in the street.[50] In the beginning of May Senator Glen Taylor was arrested and treated roughly by Birmingham, Alabama, police. The Senator had challenged a local segregation statute by seeking to speak at a racially integrated meeting of the Southern Negro Youth Congress.[51] In July a communist effort to distribute leaflets at a Houston factory was brought to an end by force. The Party distributors were taken away physically from a plant of the Hughes Tool Corporation, and their leaflets were destroyed. The incident was mentioned in an FBI letter to the President which concerned various examples of CP activity. The FBI's informant apparently had watched without intervening, and Hoover predicted that similar incidents would occur again.[52]

The administration had to find a means to quiet the violent emotions growing out of the anticommunist atmosphere. The White House staff undertook this task, but was faced with constant opposition from the Justice Department. The Department continued to push for administration acceptance of its 1947 internal security bill. In its enhanced definition of espionage, it included almost any communication of government information to nongovernmental personnel, and provided for the legalization of wiretapping by government intelligence agencies. Attorney General Clark continued to insist on the need for the legislation despite the objections expressed in 1947 by the Department of State and the Federal Communications Commission. The Bureau of the Budget requested guidance on the subject from the White House staff. The President's administrative aides recommended seeking an evaluation of the proposed measure from the Treasury Department—traditionally opposed to extensions of Justice Department investigatory powers.[53]

New internal security legislation would have exacerbated the growing fear of communism. The Treasury Department report, written at the end of March 1948, harshly criticized the Department of Justice bill. Drafted by Secret Service counsel Stephen J. Spingarn and signed by Secretary of the Treasury John Snyder, it stated that the bill did not "provide safeguards for adequate protection of civil rights of the people of the United States from infringement or abuse in the name of security."[54] The President informed the Bureau of the Budget that he agreed with the criticisms of the bill, and the Justice Department was told, in turn, that changes would be necessary. But Justice refused to compromise. The dispute remained quiet until mid-August, when contents of the governmental exchanges concerning it were leaked to the press.[55] The leak came at a particularly critical time for the administration. It had been put on the defensive earlier in the month by two major congressional investigations.

The Smith Act indictments (and subsequent arrests) of communist leaders on July 20, 1948, had not quieted congressional critics of the administration. The issue of communism seemed more alive than ever and the President more vulnerable. Both Senate and House investigating committees seized the initiative on the issue. HUAC resumed hearings on communist infiltration into government. Its first witness was Elizabeth Bentley, who recounted the tales she had told the FBI in 1945 and, more recently, had given to the grand jury. A far more damaging witness was called on August 3. Whittaker Chambers appeared to provide an impressive list of government employees, including Alger Hiss, who, he said, had operated as part of an organized communist ring during the 1930's. The Chambers testimony, particularly as enlarged in the days to come, was considered a damaging attack on the Democratic administrations of both Roosevelt and Truman.

More immediately threatening to President Truman were new hearings opened by Senator Homer Ferguson, chairman of the Senate Investigations Subcommittee of the Committee on Expenditures in the Executive Department. Claiming to be concerned with the loyalty program, the Senator opened his examination on July 29 by calling Bentley as his first witness. Greater publicity was gained when Ferguson demanded investigatory files concerning William Remington, an alleged communist who was employed in the Department of Commerce.

Ferguson's August 2 request for confidential government information created a difficult political situation for the administration. The Smith Act indictments had intensified the public's fear of communism, and a refusal to give congressional investigating bodies requested information concerning alleged CP members could be dangerous. The President asked that a high-level interdepartmental meeting informally consider the problem. The gathering took place on the morning of August 4, 1948, and included Tom Clark, Peyton Ford, Clark Clifford, and the secretaries of Army, Navy, and Air, and seven other high-ranking government officials. Meeting in the cabinet room, they determined to recommend continued refusal to divulge investigative information. A counterattack against the congressional hearings was proposed, with particular emphasis on the idea that they were simply a "red herring" serving no positive good and "doing irreparable harm."[56]

The Department of Justice considered the hearings "a completely political effort on the part of the Republican leadership." The Department submitted a memorandum to the President on the morning of August 5 suggesting that "the Republican leadership seem entirely willing to smear anyone mentioned by any former communist."[57] With the administration under what it perceived to be political attack, the President held a press conference that afternoon. In answer to an apparently planted question as to whether he believed the spy scare on Capitol Hill to be a "red herring," the President said, "yes, I do," and added that the hearings were doing "irreparable harm."[58] Truman also attacked the HUAC hearings and was asked, "If there wasn't ever anything to it [charges of a communist spy ring], why did the FBI start the investigation?" "To be on the safe side," he replied. "They got a lot of indictments on these people in New York . . . . That was the reason for it. Everything has been presented to the grand jury that they wanted to know about, and if it was possible to indict these people, they would have been indicted."[59] The President's comments succeeded in confusing the Smith Act indictments with the grand jury espionage investigation.

The cabinet discussed the Ferguson demands on August 13,[60] and the following day the Attorney General wrote to the Senator to reject his requests for confidential information. Clark and Ferguson exchanged mutually recriminatory letters, with Clark accusing Ferguson of failing to distinguish between the Smith Act indictments and the espionage examination—an exercise in which the President already had succeeded.[61]

Clark and Peyton Ford met with the President's three top administrative aides. They joined in recommending a counterattack against the hearings. The Justice Department was to "make every effort to ascertain if Whittaker Chambers is guilty of perjury." The Bentley testimony was to be discredited by showing that information she had supposedly provided to the Soviet Union already was in its possession.[62]

The FBI chose this moment of political controversy to advance its own objectives. It may have been responsible for leaking to the press the file on the Department of Justice's internal security legislation. The proposed legislation had originated in the Bureau.

Within the privacy of the government, J. Edgar Hoover pressured the Attorney General to enlarge the FBI's jurisdiction. President Roosevelt had issued public directives in 1939 and 1943 giving the Bureau the authority to investigate matters related to espionage and sabotage. Efforts by the FBI at that time to include formal authorization of investigations in "subversive activities" had not been successful.

The FBI's director suggested to the Attorney General that it was time to issue a new presidential directive.[63] This time the FBI was to be given the authority to "take charge of investigative work in matters relating to espionage, sabotage, subversive activities, and in similar matters." The Bureau was to be the "single central agency" with the power to deal with matters "relating to the internal security of the United States."

Clark sent a draft of this statement to the President on August 17, 1948, and recommended he sign it. Although the Attorney General included copies of Roosevelt's two previous statements, he did not call to Truman's attention the great increase in FBI power the new statement would authorize.[64] Fearing the proposed statement would "confuse the 'Spy' issue," George Elsey, Clifford's assistant, temporarily stopped it from being issued.[65] The FBI was disturbed by this temporary setback.

The administration was clearly on the political defensive and needed some means of providing a coordinated defense of its internal security policies. Elsey believed the spy-communism controversy had become "a major Republican issue." A series of events had made "the *Red Menace* real," observed the administrative assistant. "The Administration's most vulnerable point is 'Communism.'" If the election were to be won, "effective counteraction" would be necessary. Elsey suggested the appointment of one man to coordinate all administration activities in the area of domestic communism.[66]

President Truman apparently agreed with Elsey, and Clifford was assigned the task of filling the job. His choice was Stephen Spingarn. Spingarn had served as a counterintelligence officer during World War II. After the war he went into the Treasury Department and had been appointed as its alternate member on the President's Temporary Loyalty Commission. He had been instrumental in developing the Treasury Department's position on the proposed new internal security law. Springarn seemed a logical choice both in terms of a security background and a commitment to individual rights.

Clifford was given information that Springarn had been too liberal on security matters. Spingarn believed that this "loose smear" came from A. Devitt Vanech who, he said, was acting as a "sort of spokesman for the FBI."[67] Admiral Souers recalled later that Hoover had opposed Clifford's choice because of a belief that Spingarn opposed the FBI's security efforts.[68] After discussing these matters with Springarn, Clifford was satisfied and recommended that the President appoint him to the White House staff.

On September 8, 1948, Spingarn was summoned to the President's office. He met with Truman, Clark, Clifford, and presidential assistants Charles Murphy and Donald Dawson. The President told him he was being brought into the White House to coordinate "loyalty and security matters."[69] His specific responsibilities were not defined, although a memorandum on that date indicated he was to keep "the record . . . clear and the facts developed in proper perspective" with regard to "employee loyalty, communism and the like."[70] Spingarn believed his role was "to put the lid on the repercussions of the Alger Hiss case and other related cases and try to dehydrate it before the election."[71] There is no question that his role was primarily political, at least in the months leading to the election.

It was inevitable that the Smith Act prosecutions would play a part in the 1948 election campaign. Administration sources pushed for the trial to begin at an early date to provide a partial answer to Republican attacks. Two days after assuming his White House position, Spingarn recommended bringing the Smith Act case to court either in September or October. He spoke with the Attorney General concerning the case and was pleased to hear that the trial was scheduled for October 15. In the same memorandum Spingarn suggested that Hoover appear before Ferguson's subcommittee to defend the decision to deny loyalty files to congressional committees.[72]

The Justice Department used its considerable power to limit the effectiveness of the communist issue. Clark continued to travel around the country, and declared: "We have the fifth column on the run in the United States."[73] He felt a particularly heavy political burden since he considered Truman a personal friend. In addition, the secretaries of Defense and State had declined to take an active part in the campaign. Clark would later admit: "Whatever rhetoric I used may have" helped spread needless fear. Some of his statements, he said, represented a political response to the attacks on the administration.[74]

Legal action against communists intensified. The deportation hearings of communist leaders Alexander Bittelman and Claudia Jones were scheduled for September. The communists responded by charging that these hearings were being used to establish "a super-charged atmosphere" around the Smith Act trial. "Today's deportations are worse [than in the 1920's], they are the signals of advancing fascism," asserted *The Daily Worker*.[75] The administration's words and actions did not satisfy the congressional right wing. Ferguson chided Clark for having failed to gain additional indictments from the espionage grand jury. The Senator demanded publicly that additional grand juries be formed in various cities to investigate communist infiltration of the government. Ferguson's "suggestion" for more investigations was, once again, apparently the result of a leak. The Justice Department already had planned such a tactic to emphasize its commitment to anticommunist action.[76]

A few days after Ferguson's criticism, the administration empanelled a new grand jury in Denver and subpoenaed leading Colorado communists. The CP leaders were asked to name Communist Party members in government employment. When the communists refused to provide names, they were cited for contempt and imprisoned.[77] Although there was no suggestion that Colorado communists, in or out of government, had committed any illegal acts, the administration had found a means to jail them—it had taken the action demanded by congressional critics. The precedent of the Denver grand jury was followed the next month, shortly before the election, in Cleveland and Los Angeles.[78]

The FBI used the increasing tension over communism to press for issuance of the presidential statement giving it more authority. Assistant Director D. Milton Ladd called presidential assistant Dawson, circumventing the Justice Department, to urge the President to issue the directive. Dawson passed the call on to Spingarn who had already received the file on the matter and discussed it with Elsey and Admiral Souers. Spingarn pointed out that the new statement would "go further than the statements on this subject made by President Roosevelt in 1939 and 1943." He had Admiral Souers redraft the directive to bring it into accord with the earlier presidential orders, but recommended that it be held up at least until after the election.[79] Faced with only a restatement of previous policy, the FBI temporarily ceased to press the matter.

Despite the highly publicized anticommunist actions taken by the Department of Justice, the administration continued to be subject to heavy criticism. Richard Nixon, now gaining some fame through the Chambers-Hiss hearings, charged that the indictment of the twelve communist leaders was "a blind by the Attorney General to cover up his failure to prosecute the spy ring."[80] National Republican leaders began their attack on the administration immediately after Nixon's comment. Dewey, now a presidential nominee, accused the administration of allowing "Communists and fellow-travelers" to gain high positions in "Government, in some labor unions, in some places in our arts, sciences and professions." Although continuing to oppose outlawing the Party, he promised to give communists "traitors' treatment" if they "break our law against treason" and, if necessary, to seek new legislation.[81]

Republican National Chairman Hugh Scott, Jr., continued the attack, claiming on September 25 that the President showed "indifference to Communist penetration at home." He said this resulted from communist support of Truman for the vice presidency in 1944. The President's "red herring" remark was attributed to a history of communist support.[82] Democratic strategists now believed that only a sustained response by the President could neutralize the impact of the communist issue.

The first assignment given Spingarn was to prepare a major presidential address on internal communism. It was decided the speech should be given in Oklahoma City since the charges of communism were having their greatest impact in the Middle West. Spingarn asked for contributions to the speech from the departments of Justice and State, the Loyalty Review Board, the Civil Service Commission, and other government personnel. The first rough draft of the speech was ready on September 13, 1948, and began to be circulated on the fifteenth.[83] Six major drafts of the speech were prepared before its delivery on September 28. Throughout the shaping process, Spingarn's original draft remained largely intact.

The Oklahoma speech was preceded by a sharpening of the President's tone with regard to the third party. "The fact that the Communists are guiding and using the third party shows that this party does not represent American ideals," he declared in a Los Angeles speech.[84] The Clifford strategy of linking the third party with communism and alleging communist support for the Republican Party was continued in the Oklahoma address. "The Communists feel that by backing the third party they will take votes away from the Democratic ticket and thus elect a Republican President," Truman said. "The Communists want a Republican administration, because they think that its reactionary policies will lead to the confusion and strife on which communism thrives."[85] The chief executive recited his administration's anticommunist record. Great emphasis was placed on the espionage grand jury's investigation, the Smith Act indictments, and the deportation drive. The President criticized Congress for failing to give the Department of Justice an alien detention bill and promised, "We shall prosecute subversive activities wherever we find them."[86]

Truman carefully praised the FBI as the "greatest counterespionage organization in the world, headed by J. Edgar Hoover [who] is alert, vigorous, and skillful." The Bureau would protect the people if only left alone by the administration's critics, he implied. "This is the United States of America. We are the oldest major democracy on earth. Our democratic values are deep and sound. They cannot be destroyed by a few Communists. We must protect ourselves against communism, but we must not abandon the fundamental ideals of our democracy."[87]

The speech was an effective political counterattack, although not totally accurate. The charge that the CP was seeking a Republican victory, while an excellent political ploy, was not correct. The communist position was that neither Dewey nor Truman could be considered a "lesser evil." The Wallace movement was seen as crucial in the development of a new "people's coalition" with the CP acting as the "vanguard."[88] The Party did not believe Wallace could win the election, but expected him to receive a significant vote. In the late spring Bittelman considered it possible for Wallace to receive between 20 and 30 percent of the total ballots. This support, he thought, would be sufficient to destroy the existing two-party system, split the Democratic Party, and cause the creation of a new labor-based party. Bittelman believed that a "small Wallace vote" would be between 8 and 12 percent and even this would be sufficient to prove an important progressive influence.[89]

The communist position reflected "the illusion," according to a veteran communist, that the Wallace movement "represented a major realignment in American politics."[90] The CP was sufficiently certain of its position to demand support for the third party as the price for continued cooperation with others. Transport Workers Union head Michael Quill asserted that in December 1947 Dennis, Thompson, and Williamson had demanded he support Wallace "even if it split labor right down the middle."[91] Quill claimed that his final split with the Party resulted from this issue. In April 1948 he wrote to a foreign communist unionist to complain that Foster had threatened to brand "as agents of the enemy camp" those labor leaders who would not obey Party orders in the campaign.[92]

The CP did not recognize that it had isolated itself and destroyed the third party by its insistence on a "vanguard" role in the Wallace campaign. It viewed the campaign, opposition to the Marshall Plan, and support for the Soviet Union as part of the same struggle.

Foster continually stressed the dangers of war and fascism. He demanded "total and unqualified opposition" to the Marshall Plan. Communist leaders such as Gilbert Green and Dennis "saw and appreciated the danger of the growing isolation" of the Party, but did not propose policy alternatives. Communist trade unionists wanted to "go along" with the rest of the trade union movement in endorsing the Marshall Plan. Bittelman proposed "qualified" opposition or support for the Plan in order to minimize CP isolation.[93] Foster's antagonism forced withdrawal of the Bittelman suggestion and resulted in leaving leftist trade unionists in a difficult position. Some, such as Harry Bridges, gave only nominal support to the Wallace candidacy, while others moved away from the Party, further adding to its lack of influence. The Communist Party, which Truman accused in September of helping the Republicans, had lost much of its capacity even to aid itself. The Party held what was intended to be a giant anniversary rally on September 23 in Madison Square Garden. It was unable to fill the arena for the first time in many years.[94]

GOP candidates rarely mentioned the communist issue in the latter stages of the campaign. One observer has written that "it was not an issue between Truman and Dewey."[95] It was certainly not a Republican weapon as Election Day approached, but it became a positive Democratic point. The Democratic National Committee's research division, under the direction of ADA member William L. Batt, Jr., printed a sixty-page document entitled "Loyalty and Subversive Activities." Spingarn sent pages of material, much of it dealing with the Smith Act case, to the President's campaign train.

In the last few weeks of the campaign, Truman used the communist issue to his advantage. In Ohio he gloried in Soviet radio attacks against him.[96] In Indiana on the morning of October 25 he linked the Republicans again with the extreme left. "The Communists are doing everything in their power to beat me. They have taken over the Third Party and are using it in a vain attempt to split the Democratic Party. The Republicans have joined up with the Communist-inspired Third Party to beat the Democrats." He claimed the Republicans had aided third party efforts to get on the ballot in Indiana and Illinois.[97] The next day in Toledo he stated: "The Communists want a Republican victory."[98] "As the Democratic rhetoric would have it, a vote against Truman was a vote for Communist domination of the world," one observer noted.[99]

On October 27 in Boston Truman warned that "the free peoples of the world are threatened by the red menace of communism." Again he claimed that the communists were seeking to bring about a Republican victory. Communists had achieved their "maximum strength," he reminded his audience, "in 1932, under a Republican President."[100] Within days he made the same claims in other stops in Massachusetts and in a major speech in New York City.

"On the morning of November 3," according to one historian, "the Communist issue no longer menaced the Truman administration; indeed, it seemed to have been turned to the President's account."[101] The President successfully had employed the rhetoric of the right wing to crush the left. He had aligned himself with the prevailing anticommunist sentiment in the United States. Although temporarily defeated, the right wing was ultimately strengthened by this presidential action. Its anticommunist campaign was legitimized and the opposition to it largely crushed.

The campaign left the Communist Party isolated and bereft of influence. The events of the preceding three months had been far more damaging to the CP than the fact that Wallace received only 2 percent of the popular vote. The fate of the Party's indicted leaders already had been determined. The trial drama was played out in an atmosphere of hostility which was to embitter the political climate for years to come.

NOTES

1. "The General Political Situation" [1948], Folder 8, Papers of Alexander Bittelman, Alexander Bittelman Home Library, Croton, New York. Hereafter cited as BHL.

2. "Draft Resolution for the National Convention C.P.U.S.A.," *Political Affairs* XXVII (June 1948), 487.

3. Ibid., 512.

4. *The Daily Worker*, June 30, 1948.

5. John F.X. McGohey, "Memo of Conferences on F.B.I. Brief," Box 1, Correspondence, memoranda, Note, Smith Act cases, 1948–49 Folder. Hereafter box and folder designations will be cited as 1/Correspondence . . . . Papers of John F.X. McGohey, Harry S. Truman Library, Independence, Missouri. Hereafter cited as HSTL; John F.X. McGohey to Tom C. Clark, July 15, 1948, 1/Correspondence, memoranda, Note . . . . Papers of John F.X. McGohey, HSTL.

6. McGohey to Clark, July 15, 1948, HSTL.

7. *The New York Times*, July 14, 1948.

8. John Gates to author, March 5, 1978.

9. Ibid.

10. *The Daily Worker*, July 21, 1948.

11. *The New York Times*, July 21, 1948.

12. John Gates to author, March 5, 1978.

13. Ibid.

14. J. Edgar Hoover to Harry Vaughan, July 26, 1948, 167/Communist data, President's Secretary's Files (PSF), Papers of Harry S. Truman, HSTL.

15. *The New York Times*, July 30, 1948.

16. *The Daily Worker*, July 31, 1948, August 5, 1948.

17. *The New York Times*, July 22, 1948.

18. Ibid.

19. Ibid.

20. Ibid.

21. Harry S. Truman, *Public Papers of the Presidents of the United States 1948* (Washington, 1964), 414.

22. *The Daily Worker*, July 23, 1948.

23. Eben A. Ayers, "Diary," January 20, 1948, Box 16, Papers of Eben A. Ayers, HSTL.

24. J. Edgar Hoover to Harry Vaughan, January 19, 1948, 167/Communist data, PSF, Papers of Harry S. Truman, HSTL.

25. J. Edgar Hoover to Harry Vaughan, January 27, 1948, 167/Communist data, PSF, Papers of Harry S. Truman, HSTL.

26. "Communists and Pro-Communists for Wallace" [1948], 168/FBI, PSF, Papers of Harry S. Truman, HSTL.

27. David A. Shannon, *The Decline of American Communism, A History of the Communist Party of the United States Since 1945* (New York, 1959), 158.

28. Eben A. Ayers, "Diary," February 18, 1948, Box 16, Papers of Eben A. Ayers, HSTL.

29. Mary T. Norton to Harry S Truman, March 18, 1948, President's Personal File 957, Papers of Harry S. Truman, HSTL.

30. Leslie Adler, "The Red Image: American Attitudes Toward Communism in the Cold War Era" (Ph.D. Diss., University of California, Berkeley, 1970), 392.

31. *The New York Times*, February 1, 1948.

32. Ibid., April 3, 1948.

33. Ibid., April 25, 1948.

34. Ibid., May 2, 1948.

35. Ibid., April 27, 1948.

36. Ibid., May 4, 1948.

37. "Notes on Cabinet Meetings," March 12, 1948, Post-Presidential File, Papers of Matthew J. Connelly, HSTL.

38. "Address Delivered by HST June 4, 1948, Before the Swedish Pioneer Centennial Association in Chicago," President's Personal File 200, Papers of Harry S. Truman, HSTL.

39. Truman, *Public Papers . . . 1948*, 338.

40. *The New York Times*, March 28, 1948.

41. Ibid., May 2, 1948.

42. Ibid., May 28, 1948; Truman, *Public Papers . . . 1948*, 280.

43. *The New York Times*, March 20, 1948.

44. *The Daily Worker*, April 5, 1948.

45. William D. Hassett, Memorandum to the Attorney General, April 8, 1948, Official File (OF) 136A, Papers of Harry S. Truman, HSTL.

46. Tom Clark to William D. Hassett, April 9, 1948, OF 136A, Papers of Harry S. Truman, HSTL.

47. Tom Clark to author, March 28, 1975.

48. Truman, *Public Papers . . . 1948*, 210.

49. *The Daily Worker*, April 6, 1948.

50. Ibid., April 12, 1948.

51. Ibid., May 3, 1948; *The New York Times*, May 2, 3, 1948.

52. J. Edgar Hoover to Harry Vaughan, July 26, 1948, 167/Communist data, PSF, Papers of Harry S. Truman, HSTL.

53. Charles S. Murphy, "Memorandum on Internal Security Legislation," August 18, 1948, 22/Internal Security, Files of Charles S. Murphy, Papers of Harry S. Truman, HSTL.

54. John W. Snyder to the Director, Bureau of the Budget, March 23, 1948,

31/National Defense-Internal Security and Individual Rights 2, Papers of Stephen J. Spingarn, HSTL.

55. Murphy, "Memorandum on Internal Security Legislation," August 18, 1948, HSTL.

56. Clark Clifford, "Memorandum for the President," August 4, 1948, 68/Internal Security-Congressional Loyalty Investigations (2), Papers of George Elsey, HSTL.

57. "Department of Justice Suggestions," August 5, 1948, 68/Internal Security-Congressional Loyalty Investigations (2), Papers of George Elsey, HSTL.

58. Truman, *Public Papers . . . 1948*, 432–33.

59. Ibid., 434.

60. "Notes on Cabinet Meetings," August 13, 1948, Post-Presidential File, Papers of Matthew J. Connelly, HSTL.

61. Homer Ferguson to Tom Clark, August 16, 1948; Tom Clark to Homer Ferguson, August 17, 1948, 68/Internal Security-Congressional Loyalty Investigations (2), Papers of George Elsey, HSTL.

62. George M. Elsey, "Memorandum for Mr. Clifford," August 16, 1948, 68/Internal Security-Congressional Loyalty Investigations (2), Papers of George Elsey, HSTL.

63. Tom Clark to author, March 28, 1975.

64. Tom C. Clark, "Memorandum for the President," August 17, 1948, 85/Federal Bureau of Investigation, OF 10-B, Papers of Harry S. Truman, HSTL.

65. "Suggested Statement for the Pres. from Justice Reaffirming Role of FBI in Investigative Matters," August 19, 1948, 68/Internal Security-Congressional Loyalty Investigations (2), Papers of George Elsey, HSTL.

66. George M. Elsey, "Random Thoughts 26 August," August 26, 1948, 68/Internal Security-Congressional Loyalty Investigations (2), Papers of George Elsey, HSTL.

67. Stephen J. Spingarn, Oral History Interview, 59, HSTL.

68. Sidney W. Souers, Post-Presidential Conversations Memoirs 2, December 16, 1954, Post-Presidential File, HSTL.

69. Spingarn, Oral History Interview, 42, HSTL.

70. "Memorandum," September 8, 1948, OF 1730, Papers of Harry S. Truman, HSTL.

71. Spingarn, Oral History Interview, 43, HSTL.

72. Stephen J. Spingarn, "Memorandum for the SJS White House Assignment File," September 10, 1948, 30/White House Assignment, Memos, letters, telegrams, Papers of Stephen J. Spingarn, HSTL.

73. *The New York Times*, September 19, 1948.

74. Tom Clark to author, March 28, 1975.

75. *The Daily Worker*, September 13, 1948, September 15, 1948.

76. *The New York Times*, September 18, 1948.

77. Ibid., September 24, 1948.

78. *The Daily Worker*, October 21, 1948, October 27, 1948.

79. Stephen J. Spingarn, "Memorandum for Mr. Clifford," September 21, 1948, 30/White House Assignments, Memos, letters, telegrams, Papers of Stephen J. Spingarn, HSTL.

80. *The New York Times*, September 23, 1948.

81. Ibid., September 25, 1948.

82. Ibid., September 26, 1948.

83. Stephen J. Spingarn, "First Rough Draft of Communism Speech," September 15, 1948, 30/White House Assignment, Communism speech, 1948, 2, Papers of Stephen J. Spingarn, HSTL.

84. Truman, *Public Papers . . . 1948*, 559.

85. Ibid., 610.

86. Ibid., 612–13.

87. Ibid., 613.

88. "Draft Resolution for the National Convention, C.P.U.S.A.," *Political Affairs* XXVII (June 1948), 488.

89. Alexander Bittelman, "Notes for July Article," May 21, 1948, Folder 8, BHL.

90. Al Richmond, *A Long View from the Left, Memoirs of an American Revolutionary* (Boston, 1967), 293.

91. *The New York Times*, September 12, 1948.

92. Mike Quill to Luigi Longo, April 16, 1948, in Philip J. Jaffe, *The Rise and Fall of American Communism* (New York, 1975), 144–47.

93. Alexander Bittelman, "Autobiography" (Unpublished Typescript, 1963, Tamiment Library, New York University), 728.

94. *The New York Times*, September 24, 1948.

95. Earl Latham, *The Communist Controversy in Washington from the New Deal to McCarthy* (Cambridge, 1966), 398.

96. Truman, *Public Papers . . . 1948*, 729.

97. Ibid., 845.

98. Ibid., 860.

99. Adler, "The Red Image," 391.

100. Truman, *Public Papers . . . 1948*, 883–86.

101. Alan D. Harper, *The Politics of Loyalty: The White House and the Communist Issue, 1946–1952* (Westport, 1969), 82–83.

VII

Reacting to the Past, Preparing for the Future

A suspicion existed within the Communist Party and other political groups that once the 1948 election was over, the Smith Act prosecutions would be dropped quietly. The fact that court proceedings were postponed several times and the trial had not yet begun as the year's end approached seemed to lend credence to this view. President Truman was asked at a December press conference if the case would be discontinued. The reporter might better question the Attorney General on that subject, he replied, but he had given "instructions to go ahead and prosecute all the lawbreakers of that sort."[1] It might well have been more productive for the newsman to have asked J. Edgar Hoover. The FBI was determined that the prosecutions would go forward.

The Bureau had continued an unprecedented interest in the case after the indictments and arrests of the twelve Communist leaders. Not only did the FBI monitor CP activities, but it also followed closely the actions of the Department of Justice.

Without authorization or request, Hoover ordered his agents to prepare extensive reports on legal proceedings involving the twelve defendants. Some of these accounts were submitted to a "surprised" Attorney General.[2] The FBI's director was concerned particularly with the defendants' efforts to enlarge their bail jurisdiction. On September 1, 1948, attorneys for William Z. Foster, Eugene Dennis, and Henry Winston asked the court to allow them to travel throughout the United States instead of being restricted to the Southern District of New York. They cited the necessity of actively working on their defense, as well as continuing normal Party activities. The United States attorney opposed the application on the grounds that further CP activity would mean a continuation of their criminal acts. The motion was denied, but the Party's lawyers announced they would seek to enlarge the bail jurisdiction of all defendants in a future action. Hoover reported all this to the Attorney General in a September 3 memorandum.

On September 8 attorney Abraham Unger requested that Judge Simon J. Rifkind permit nine of the communist leaders to travel throughout the United States in order to further their defense. The government opposed the effort again, arguing it was not done in good faith since the defense had not included its previous suggestion that the defendants wished to continue Party activities. The Judge took the case under advisement, but shortly granted the application and in a written opinion said: "It is not so much as intimated in the answering affidavits that the teachings which the defendants are alleged to have conspired to promote are about to be crowned with success."[3] Hoover was outraged by the judge's decision.

The FBI chief wrote to the Attorney General advising him of the court hearing and of Rifkind's opinion. Tom Clark later observed: "I don't remember any [other] case Hoover ever did this in."[4] The Director informed his superior that the Judge had "stated that since there is no evidence that the defendants' teachings are about to become successful and since the purpose of bail, to make the defendants available, appears to be met and admission to bail is never judicial license to continue the commission of a crime, the application was being granted."[5] Hoover apparently expected the Justice Department to take action as a result of his reports, but no steps followed.

Disturbed by the lack of response to his memorandum, Hoover wrote an angry letter a week later. He charged that the United States attorney had erred seriously in failing to take exception to Judge Rifkind's remarks concerning a lack of evidence that "the defendants' teachings were about to become successful." The Director suggested that the court ruling "might be interpreted to mean that the court has admitted that the Communist Party does not constitute a 'clear and present danger' in this country." Hoover suggested that the government's entire case might have been prejudiced. "The extreme importance of this case to future investigations" was emphasized.[6]

Clark sent Hoover's letter to United States Attorney John McGohey and asked to be "advised" on the matter. McGohey was surprised by the Director's comments and answered that Hoover had misinterpreted the legal situation. He intimated that "Edgar's" recent illness, which had "incapacitated him," might have hampered his judgment. McGohey defended his own actions and said that even though he had been on weak legal grounds, he had opposed the defendants' motions. He noted that the Judge's decision was legally unassailable and that Rifkind's opinion never mentioned the word "evidence" as alleged by Hoover.

The government's attorney told Clark that he had no grounds to believe communist efforts "were about to become successful." He asked that if the FBI had such evidence, it be submitted to him immediately. McGohey assumed that no such material existed. Although there was no immediate danger to the United States, the government expected to "urge" the "clear and present danger" doctrine.[7]

The bail question was settled, but heavy FBI involvement remained. Other than FBI agents, Louis Budenz was one of the few witnesses available to McGohey. While the Bureau's massive brief quoted many potential witnesses, it had identified most by letters rather than names.[8] Only after the indictments were secured did the FBI agree to make selected informants available. Bureau agents arranged some sixty interviews between its witnesses and Justice Department attorneys from August 1948 through January 1949.[9] One witness met several times with two government lawyers in November and December, but they were never given her name.[10] While this process continued, McGohey was having unexpected difficulties with Budenz, his most important witness.

The former communist, now a Fordham University professor, wrote to McGohey claiming he was ill and, on doctor's advice, would be unable to appear as a witness until February.[11] With the case scheduled to begin on October 15, the United States attorney was disturbed. After vigorous efforts to contact Budenz, he was able to arrange a meeting for September 30, 1948. Budenz seemed healthy, and McGohey informed him that "under no circumstances would I agree to excuse him as a witness." To emphasize the point, he served the reluctant witness with a subpoena to appear on the trial's scheduled first day. McGohey than met with the dean and president of Fordham University to gain their cooperation in dealing with Budenz.[12] Other government attorneys had no knowledge of Budenz' reluctance to testify and there is no indication as to his reasons for apparently seeking to avoid the witness stand.[13]

The FBI used the additional prestige it had gained within the government to increase pressure for its favorite projects. Beginning in October 1948 lists of the names of persons on the Bureau's Security Index—its compilation of people considered "dangerous"—were forwarded to the Internal Security Section of the Justice Department's Criminal Division.[14] Although no plan for an emergency detention program had been approved, it was clear that the lists were to be used as the basis for mass arrests in a crisis. The Internal Security Section prepared many draft proclamations and orders to be employed in such an emergency. These plans were compiled in an "Attorney General's Portfolio" for use when needed.[15]

The demand for special measures to meet the perceived domestic threat was accentuated by an apparent alliance between the FBI and the Department of Defense. A recommendation to correct serious weaknesses in the United States' internal security was sent to the President by Secretary of Defense James Forrestal early in October 1948. Forrestal's memorandum coincided with the Department of Justice's drawing of contingency plans for emergency detention.

The Defense Secretary claimed the existence of a serious espionage, sabotage, and subversion threat. He intended to submit a comprehensive proposal to the National Security Council to remedy the problem, but desired action by the President before this was done. Forrestal suggested the appointment of one individual or an agency with complete authority in the area of internal security. This security "czar" would receive his authority directly from the President.[16]

Some members of the White House staff considered the Forrestal proposal "an outrageous suggestion."[17] Presidential assistant Charles Murphy sent the memorandum to Stephen Spingarn for a full analysis and recommendation. Other important members of the President's staff and the cabinet also were asked for comments.

Spingarn's analysis of Forrestal's proposals was remarkable in view of the public atmosphere created by the arrest of the twelve Communist leaders. The President's aide rejected the dark picture of internal security painted by the Defense Secretary. He noted that "loud shouts from some quarters" had influenced people to believe "that Communism is the major menace confronting the country today, that Communists have infiltrated every area of American life, and that the Communists are ready at a moment's notice to take over the country." Spingarn considered these suggestions a "political smoke-screen" and a "serious distortion of the facts." Commmunists might be "bothersome," he said, but they were not an internal danger.

The real internal security problem, said Spingarn, was that the FBI had been given total investigative authority in this area. There had been no "external scrutiny" of its activities, even by the Department of Justice, for fifteen years. The administrative assistant questioned the capabilities of the Bureau in dealing with internal communism. He asked that a task force be sent to the FBI with complete authority to examine its operations and with full access to the Bureau's records and information.

Spingarn recommended that the NSC establish a small, full-time organization to "survey the whole internal security picture," and that it be granted the authority to act as an internal investigative unit to examine the practices of security agencies such as the FBI. He emphasized that democratic controls in the area of internal security were essential. The dangers of being "stampeded into drastic action" were real and should be avoided.[18]

President Truman placed the subject of internal security on the agenda of the NSC's next meeting. Spingarn's warning concerning the FBI was ignored. Supporting the essence of Forrestal's proposal, Attorney General Clark suggested that centralized authority in internal security matters be placed in the hands of the NSC's Interdepartmental Intelligence Conference. The IIC was chaired by J. Edgar Hoover and included the heads of the army, navy, and air force intelligence services.[19]

Pressure on the administration mounted to support additional domestic security measures. The Justice Department pushed hard for permission to introduce its legislation broadening the definition of espionage and authorizing the use of wiretapping. It used the same grand jury which had indicted the communist leaders to put the administration in an untenable position.

The jurors made a presentment on December 16, 1948. Unable to find grounds for further indictments, they recommended the passage of legislation remarkably similar to that proposed earlier by the Department of Justice. The presentment was not made public immediately, but its existence hung heavy over the President.[20] The implied criticism of the administration for its failure to introduce new legislation to Congress was powerful, particularly since it came from the jury which had been investigating espionage for a year and a half and had successfully indicted Alger Hiss and the CP's leaders.

The administration began to accede to the urgings of the internal security establishment. The President authorized the Justice Department to submit to Congress a slightly changed version of its legislation. Spingarn, who had not been consulted on the matter, observed that "considerable mystery" surrounded the reversal of the President's position.[21] Earlier opponents of the proposals were not consulted. The bill was to be submitted as a Justice Department measure without official administration support.

Clark introduced his department's bill with considerable fanfare and failed to mention that it was not a part of the administration's program. In letters to Speaker of the House of Representatives Sam Rayburn and Nevada Democrat, Pat McCarran, chairman of the Senate Judiciary Committee, he wrote: "The swift and more effective weapons of modern warfare, coupled with the treacherous operations of those who would weaken our country internally, preliminary and in conjunction with external attack, have made it imperative that we strengthen and maintain an alert and effective peacetime vigilance."[22] The proposals were endorsed by the FBI.

The Smith Act case subsequently gained greater importance for the Justice Department. A nationally syndicated columnist, Marquis Childs, reported after an interview with Clark that the Attorney General believed "the case now being tried in New York and its outcome may well determine how far Congress will go in granting further powers."[23]

Efforts also continued to establish an emergency detention program without congressional authorization. From the latter part of 1948 into early 1949 negotiations to work out a suitable plan proceeded between the departments of Justice and Defense. These efforts succeeded on February 11, 1949, when Clark and Forrestal signed a classified agreement providing " . . . maximum security with respect to the apprehension and detention of those persons who, in the event of war or other occasions upon which Presidential Proclamations, Executive Orders, and applicable statutes come into operation, are to be taken into custody and held pending further disposition."

The Attorney General was given the entire responsibility for "apprehending and detaining civilians in such an emergency." The FBI, in turn, gained its long sought objective. It was charged "with the complete responsibility of investigating and apprehending the persons to be detained."[24] The Bureau officially had been seeking such authority for three years and preparing itself for the exercise of this power for nine.

Forrestal's proposal for centralizing internal security controls came before the NSC within a month of the agreement to establish the detention program. The momentum towards such a plan had become unstoppable. A separate organization, the Interdepartmental Committee on Internal Security, was created on March 23, 1949, to coordinate "all non-investigatory, internal security activities which are not within the purview" of the IIC. It was assigned the task of developing a comprehensive policy against subversive activity in the United States. ICIS consisted of members from the military establishment, and the departments of State, Treasury, and Justice. The first Justice representative was Raymond P. Whearty, an assistant attorney general who headed the Internal Security Section.[25]

The Interdepartmental Intelligence Conference, headed by Hoover, was given a confidential directive granting it the authority to investigate subversive activities.[26] With former FBI official J. Patrick Coyne as the coordinator of the activities of ICIS and IIC, the Bureau had gained the preeminent position of authority it had been seeking. Spingarn's effort to limit the FBI's power was useless in the aftermath of the Smith Act indictments. The internal security establishment had taken advantage of the legitimization of a domestic communist threat.

While the government centralized its internal security machinery, the CPUSA sought to regroup. The communists had been surprised by the timing of the arrests. Important functionaries were on vacation, and the Party organization had to be geared for immediate action. All vacations were cancelled immediately, and personnel from the national office were ordered to return. Plans were made for demonstrations in various parts of the nation.[27] The Party went ahead with the organization of its fourteenth national convention, scheduled to open August 2. A mass "fight back" meeting was scheduled for Madison Square Garden on the gathering's opening day.

A heavy sense of pessimism permeated the Party's convention. Dennis' main report placed great emphasis on the rise of fascism in the United States. The arrests of the CP's leaders made dictatorial control seem imminent. "The development of fascism in the United States now appears as a serious and threatening menace," the General Secretary maintained.[28] Although claiming that fascism had not as yet triumphed, Dennis asserted: "The reactionary and warmongering policies and measures of the trusts and their bipartisan political agents are facilitating and promoting the drive toward world war and the internal process of militarization and fascization now under way."[29]

The CP's national leadership was restructured to prepare the Party for inevitable future difficulties. The National Board was eliminated, and the National Committee, the Party's leading body, was reduced to thirteen members. The twelve indicted leaders were to constitute the National Committee, and Elizabeth Gurley Flynn, a veteran labor organizer, was added as the thirteenth member.[30] If the twelve indicted leaders went to prison, one national figure would be left to rally the Party. At the same time, reducing the size of the CP's top echelon had eliminated easy targets for the government.

Dennis warned the Party's delegates: "Many of our brother Communist parties have passed through the fires of fascist trial, and their heroism imbues us with determination to prove equally worthy in the face of whatever trials may be ahead."[31] The implication of a coming underground struggle seemed clear.

Foster had no doubt that the government purpose was to outlaw the CP.

The meaning of the arrest of our 12 leaders is that it is an attempt to outlaw our Party. The reactionaries aim to do this by wholesale convictions and by securing hostile legal interpretations of the Constitution that in the hope that this would drive our Party underground and would lay the basis for the further condemnation of the Party by legislative action.[32]

Dennis agreed fully.[33] Throughout the year the Party's membership already had been falling. It was reportedly 60,000 at the time of the convention, probably an exaggerated figure.[34] Legal attack seemed certain to weaken the Party even more. Drastic measures would be needed if the CP was to survive.

The developing of an organization structure for the underground was ordered within weeks after the convention. In New York State, Robert Thompson asked a Party member to draw up a plan based on the concept of "threes" which Foster had brought back from Europe a year earlier. Some 3,000 New York members of the Party were to be integrated into the system eventually. Preference would be given to trade unionists and people in "mass organizations," while much of the remainder of the Party would be cut adrift. The state was to be divided into three areas, each having a separate underground structure—all controlled by a directorate of three leaders at the top. Instructions were given to acquire printing apparatus and to find places which could be used for hiding purposes, contact areas, and meeting centers.[35]

Thompson described the purpose of the underground structure as to "enable the Party to function under any and all conditions. If the Party is declared illegal, then this organization will function in an organized fashion and carry on Party organizational work in a limited way."[36] The preliminary steps for establishing an underground were carried out across the country, but the formal structure was not to come into existence until additional leaders were indicted or a general war with the Soviet Union developed. In the latter eventuality, it was anticipated that wholesale arrests of Party leaders and perhaps of members would take place. The CP's decision to establish the skeletal framework of an underground was communicated to district organizers, district committees, and as far down as section committees.[37] Future testimony revealed that FBI informants at the various Party levels were among those integrated into the system.

The National Committee established a separate security system for itself. Dennis called in George Watt, a trusted Party member, and asked him to go underground immediately in order to organize a secret apparatus for the top leaders. The General Secretary told him that mass arrests could be expected and that the Party would be forced below the surface. Watt's U.S. Air Force plane had been shot down over Europe during World War II, and he had been passed through the Belgian and

French undergrounds to freedom. This war experience seemed to qualify him for his new role.

John Williamson instructed Watt on the "system of threes." A small group in New York was recruited to work with the national leadership in an emergency situation. Watt claimed he was ill in order to stay out of his normal Party work. In January 1949 he was instructed to go to Mexico to establish an apparatus for the National Committee should it become necessary to go into exile. Taking his family with him on a vacation pretense, Watt built a small undercover organization. He was given one contact, a businessman, whose knowledge was used to gather a group of some six people who would be willing to receive the CP's leaders. All six had come from the United States, but were not well known party members. Watt left within a month after establishing the nucleus of a Mexican underground connection. Those who remained were to build the apparatus into an efficient organization.[38]

The Party then turned to securing its membership against both physical and prosecutorial attack. Increasing acts of violence against Party members made open operation of the CP difficult. On the night of September 21, 1948, New York State Chairman Thompson was beaten and stabbed as he walked near his home in Queens.[39] The assailant was not found. An FBI informant in the CP, who would soon testify against the Party's leaders, feared she might become a victim of anticommunist violence before her true role was revealed.[40]

CP security measures were instituted. Party cards were destroyed. Membership lists no longer were kept. Dues were collected, but receipts with names were not given.[41] Despite acts of violence against it, the Party did not contemplate reciprocation. The security measures were defensive in nature. FBI informants in the Party testified at later trials that there never was any consideration of the use of force by the Party— only efforts to defend itself.[42] The CP's national leaders had to prepare their trial strategy in the midst of what they perceived to be a deteriorating national and international situation.

Trial preparation was made more difficult by the political and theoretical split among the CP's leaders. This division manifested itself over trial strategy. The internal debate concerned what Marxist concepts would be defended, the length of the trial, the constitutional issues to be raised, and the personalities who would play leading roles. The Party's heads believed the case against them was essentially political. Their response, as a result, leaned most heavily on political rather than legal judgments. The twelve intended to make all the basic trial decisions themselves, rather than rely upon their lawyers.

Foster and Dennis clashed over important trial issues. The Party's chairman, Foster, supported by most of the other defendants, demanded that Dennis play the leading role in the case. As the CP's general secretary, Dennis was its highest official. He should be the Party's chief spokesman and most important witness, said Foster. Benjamin Davis and Thompson, sometimes joined by Alexander Bittelman in the secondary leadership, also urged the Party's secretary to take the lead. Dennis refused to accept this role. Again he feared that his past international involvements and the son he had left behind in the Soviet Union would be used against him. Although unwilling to take the witness stand, he formally discharged his attorney and assumed his own defense. In this role he would be able to speak extensively to the jury without facing the danger of cross-examination. A majority of the National Committee defended this decision, "but were very embarrassed by it." They had little respect for a man who would lead while refusing to place himself in jeopardy.[43]

Some of the defendants wanted the case argued on a civil liberties basis with emphasis on the lack of a "clear and present danger" to justify the limitation of freedom of speech. Their belief was that such a defense had a chance of success and would receive the widest possible support in the United States. Dennis proposed that the trial be delayed so that the "masses" could be rallied in support of the CP's position. Foster sharply criticized such a tactic and called for a short trial with a full exposition of the Party's program—seemingly a contradiction.

The decision was to seek a lengthy trial with a full development of both the Party's ideology and its immediate program. The judiciary would be attacked as representative of a class system of injustice.[44] The time gained through dilatory trial tactics would be used to bring massive pressure to free the defendants and halt the increasing attacks against the CP.

On October 16, 1948, attorneys for the twelve applied in federal court for a ninety-day extension to allow the preparation of various motions. As a result of regular rotation, they appeared before Judge Harold R. Medina. The jurist had been appointed to the court a year before after a long career as a law professor and a period of impressive private practice. He had been the choice of many influential figures in the legal community. In naming him, President Truman had ignored the various political efforts on behalf of others by the New York Democratic organization, and the nomination had been approved by the Republican-controlled Senate with unusual speed.[45]

Despite great legal expertise, Medina had personality traits which sometimes encouraged confrontation. One historian has described his work on the bench as "abrasive, demonstrating a flippant attitude, a fondness for wisecracking with and at attorneys, and a readiness to use language that was often caustic and sometimes downright rude. Although often lashing others with a biting tongue, he was extremely sensitive and reacted strongly against what he interpreted as insults from the bar."[46] Some of these qualities were demonstrated in his handling of the first motion in the Smith Act case.

Judge Medina blocked the defendants' effort to gain a ninety-day extension and suggested it was "absurd" in a case of this nature.[47] "It seems to me," he said, "that the interests of the Government, as of the people, are a little bit more imporant here than the interests of the defendants. It is a public question of great importance and it is important that it be determined very soon."[48]

Attorney Abraham Unger argued that the issues in the case were complex. Difficult matters relating to basic constitutional guarantees would be raised, he said, and these would require considerable legal exploration. After examining the indictment, Medina responded: "Of course, if the difficulty and complexity has to do with this idea of overthrowing the Government by force I should think that public policy might require that the matter be given prompt attention and not just held off indefinitely when perhaps there may be some more of these fellows up to that sort of thing."[49] In response to the observation that the indictments alleged no acts of force or violence, the Judge asserted: "No, they want to wait until they get everything set and then the acts will come."[50] He granted only a thirty-day delay for the defense.

Medina's tone and comments led the defendants' attorneys to submit an affidavit of "bias and prejudice" when the Judge was appointed to try the case in early November. Medina quickly denied the motion, claiming that his earlier court discussion had been "necessarily based upon the assumption that the facts as alleged in the indictment were true."[51] These events set a pattern of antagonism which carried on through the entire trial.

In early October the defense counsel went before Judge Murray Hulbert in an effort both to have the indictments dismissed and to require a bill of particulars listing specific overt acts charged against the defendants. The lawyers argued that the Smith Act was an unconstitutional infringement on freedom of speech and that the indictments were essentially political in character. After considering the motions for more than two weeks, Judge Hulbert denied both. He relied on the earlier Court of Appeals decision in the Smith Act case of the Socialist Workers Party leaders and said: "If there be merit in the charges contained in the indictment, the Smith Act is as essential to the attainment of these ends [maintenance of domestic tranquility and a republican form of government] now as it ever was."[52]

The attack on the Smith Act's constitutionality was supported by many civil libertarians, but the communists' position was inconsistent. The CP had supported use of the law against the SWP during World War II. It apparently even had provided evidence for the government's use.[53] When criticized for its contradictory position during the 1949 trial of its own leaders, the CP continued to maintain that its earlier actions had been correct. Liberal columnist I. F. Stone was taken to task for suggesting that all Smith Act prosecutions should be opposed.[54]

The original trial date of October 15, 1948, repeatedly was set back. Some communists assumed the delays meant there would not be a serious government effort. *The Daily Worker* complained in a front page editorial that many believed the case would be won easily. "To fall for this and to sit back and watch the frame-up," it claimed, "is the same tragic mistake that millions of Germans made in 1933."[55] In late December, defendant Carl Winter still noted a sense of apathy among Party workers and asked their active involvement.[56] Winter knew it was the defendants who had sought to delay the trial. In court action they had contended that a long continuance was made necessary by the Department of Justice's deliberate creation of a prejudicial atmosphere. These defense efforts soon faced a major roadblock when Judge Medina was appointed to serve during the trial. The chief judge, John C. Knox, apparently believed he should assign the case to a non-Catholic who had played some role in the earlier proceedings and was physically able to stand the rigors of a long trial. Medina seemed the only judge to meet the criteria.[57]

Judge Medina denied each of the defendants' motions with the exception of those dealing with the illness of Foster. Eventually the case was scheduled to begin on January 17, 1949, and Medina made clear that no delays beyond that date would be allowed. Defense efforts to have Medina removed from the case were rejected by higher courts.

About to face their greatest legal challenge, the Communist Party leaders were fearful and divided. Elizabeth Gurley Flynn, the only unindicted member of the National Committee, publicly voiced the belief that extreme political repression was inevitable. "This trial follows the pattern which introduced fascism in other lands," she said. "Can it be brushed aside on the grounds of differences of political opinions? That's what was done in Germany."[58]

Flynn's observations accurately mirrored the private thoughts of the heads of her party. In his private notebook, almost on the eve of the beginning of the trial, Bittelman expressed the view that the recent elections had shown that there must be "no extravagant hopes about our importance." He believed that in the future the Truman administration would move toward closer ties with labor, farmers, and the middle class, and would couple this with "mounting persecution" of the CP and other left-wingers. Fascism was the probable outcome of such policies, he confided to himself.

Tied to the probability of fascism, Bittelman wrote, was the inevitability of war. Despite the Party's position for the trial that peaceful coexistence could be achieved, the veteran communist predicted that an economic and political crisis would bring the world to war. He foresaw the "general crisis of capitalism deepening." The struggle for international markets among capitalist nations would grow "more acute." The United States, he reasoned, would become more desperate. "Wall Street feels it must press harder and faster for world domination before it gets too late. It must prepare to make war to achieve it."

The only possible check on the move toward a general war, Bittelman believed, must come from the working class. A campaign of masses of people "may effect a lessening of the tempo and urgency of the expansionist drive *and not otherwise*," he wrote.[59] In reality, there was no mass movement in opposition to administration policies—just the reverse situation existed.

The communists adopted a strategy of using their trial to spark a massive popular movement against the policies of the United States government. In a quasi-fascist state, which they believed had arrived already, there was little possibility of justice for dissenters. Out of a sense of pessimism and defeatism, they decided to defend themselves by attacking American capitalism. The Party's press proclaimed: "The accused have become the accusers in the New York District Federal courtroom."[60] The Communist leaders soon learned that they could not bend the judicial system to their will.

NOTES

1. Harry S. Truman, *Public Papers of the Presidents of the United States 1948* (Washington, 1964), 960.

2. Tom Clark to author, March 28, 1975.

3. John F.X. McGohey to Tom C. Clark, September 27, 1948, Box 1, Correspondence, memoranda, Note, Smith Act cases 1948–49 Folder. Hereafter box and folder designations will be cited as 1/Correspondence . . . . Papers of John F.X. McGohey, Harry S. Truman Library, Independence, Missouri. Hereafter cited as HSTL.

4. Tom Clark to author, March 28, 1975.

5. Director, FBI, to the Attorney General, September 10, 1948, copy of document submitted to author by FBI.

6. Director, FBI, to the Attorney General, September 17, 1948, 1/Correspondence, memoranda, Note . . . . Papers of John F.X. McGohey, HSTL.

7. McGohey to Clark, September 27, 1948, HSTL.

8. Lawrence Bailey (Special assistant to the Attorney General in 1948) to author, July 24, 1974; Federal Bureau of Investigation, "Brief to Establish the Illegal Status of the Communist Party of the United States of America" (10 vols.), copy of document submitted to author by FBI.

9. Don Whitehead, *The FBI Story, A Report to the People* (New York, 1956), 295.

10. Angela Calomiris, *Red Masquerade, Undercover for the F.B.I.* (Philadelphia, 1950), 237.

11. Louis Budenz to John F.X. McGohey, September 27, 1948, 1/Correspondence, memoranda, Note . . . . Papers of John F.X. McGohey, HSTL.

12. John F.X. McGohey, "Memorandum for the file," September 30, 1948, 1/Correspondence, memoranda, Note . . . . Papers of John F.X. McGohey, HSTL.

13. Lawrence Bailey to author, July 24, 1974.

14. Memorandum from H. B. Fletcher to D. M. Ladd, August 26, 1949, in U.S. Senate, 94th Cong., 2d sess., *Final Report of the Select Committee to Study Governmental Operations With Respect to Intelligence Activities* (6 vols., Washington, 1976), III, 439. Hereafter cited as *Final Report*.

15. Memorandum from F. J. Baumgardner to D. M. Ladd, June 28, 1949, in *Final Report*, III, 439.

16. Stephen J. Spingarn, "Memorandum for the President," October 15, 1948, 31/White House Assignment 1, Papers of Stephen J. Spingarn, HSTL.

17. Stephen J. Spingarn, Oral History Interview, 48, HSTL.

18. Spingarn, "Memorandum for the President," October 15, 1948, HSTL.

19. "Memo to the President . . . ," n.d., White House Central Files, Confidential File, Justice Department/2, Papers of Harry S. Truman, HSTL.

20. *The New York Times*, April 27, 1949.

21. Stephen Spingarn to Tom Lynch, January 26, 1949, 31/National Defense-Internal Security 2, Papers of Stephen J. Spingarn, HSTL.

22. *The New York Times*, January 15, 1949.

23. *The Daily Worker*, February 1, 1949.

24. "Joint Agreement of the Secretary of Defense and the Attorney General Respecting the Temporary Detention of Dangerous Persons in Event of Emergency," February 11, 1949, in *Final Report*, III, 440.

25. *The New York Times*, May 11, 1949; Mr. Lay (NSC) to Stephen Spingarn, April 14, 1949, 31/National Defense-Internal Security 2, Papers of Stephen J. Spingarn, HSTL.

26. *Final Report*, II, 45.

27. J. Edgar Hoover to Harry Vaughan, July 26, 1948, 167/Communist data, President's Secretary's Files (PSF), Papers of Harry S. Truman, HSTL.

28. Eugene Dennis, "The Fascist Danger and How to Combat It," *Political Affairs* XXVII (September 1948), 778–79.

29. Ibid., 786.

30. J. Edgar Hoover to Harry Vaughan, August 10, 1948, 167/Communist data, PSF, Papers of Harry S. Truman, HSTL.

31. Dennis, "The Fascist Danger and How to Combat It," 811–12.

32. *The Daily Worker*, August 16, 1948.

33. *The Worker*, September 26, 1948.

34. David A. Shannon, *The Decline of American Communism, A History of the Communist Party of the United States since 1945* (New York, 1959), 97.

35. *United States v. Flynn, et al.*, "Transcript of Trial," Testimony of John Lautner (June 10, 1952), 4443–54.

36. Ibid., 4454.

37. Sidney Steinberg (CP assistant labor secretary in 1948) to author, December 25, 1974.

38. George Watt to author, June 29, 1975.

39. *The New York Times*, September 22, 1948.

40. Calomiris, *Red Masquerade*, 245–46.

41. Ibid.

42. *United States v. Flynn, et al.*, "Transcript of Trial," Testimony of John Lautner (July 14, 1952), 6123.

43. John Gates to author, March 5, 1978.

44. Ibid.

45. *The New York Times*, July 1, 1947; Hawthorne Daniel, *Judge Medina* (New York, 1952), 207–13.

46. Michal R. Belknap, *Cold War Political Justice, The Smith Act, the Communist Party, and American Civil Liberties* (Westport, 1977), 68.

47. Daniel, *Judge Medina*, 218.

48. *United States v. Dennis, et al.*, "Joint Appendix on Appeal from Judgments of Conviction of the United States District Court for the Southern District of New York." Hereafter cited as "Joint Appendix." Colloquy Annexed to Opinion Striking Affidavit of Prejudice (November 5, 1948), 12877.

49. *United States v. Dennis, et al.*, "Joint Appendix," Affidavit of William Z. Foster, et al. of Personal Bias and Prejudice (November 4, 1948), 12860.

50. Ibid., 12862.

51. *United States v. Dennis, et al.*, "Joint Appendix," Opinion Striking Affidavit of Prejudice (November 5, 1948), 12866.

52. *United States v. Dennis, et al.*, "Joint Appendix," Opinion on Motion to Dismiss the Indictments (October 22, 1948), 12834.

53. Philip J. Jaffe, *The Rise and Fall of American Communism* (New York, 1975), 50–51.

54. *The Daily Worker*, May 31, 1949.

55. Ibid., October 6, 1948.

56. Ibid., December 20, 1948.

57. Daniel, *Judge Medina*, 218–19.

58. Elizabeth Gurley Flynn, "They Must Go Free," *Political Affairs* XXVII (December 1948), 1078.

59. Alexander Bittelman, Notebook, January 11, 1949, Papers of Alexander Bittelman, BHL.

60. "The Defense Prosecutes," *Political Affairs* XXVIII (February 1949), 5.

VIII

A Trial of Ideas

The "largest detail in police history" to be assigned to a judicial proceeding converged on Foley Square in New York City on the morning of January 17, 1949. The trial of the twelve leaders of the American Communist Party finally was about to begin. Some 400 policemen were assigned to the area for what was expected to be massive demonstrations. They were to remain, newspapers reported, during the entire trial.

A lunch hour picket line involving an estimated 500 people was all that occurred to occupy the law enforcement officers on the first day. Although the crowd was noisy, it was orderly. The massive police presence had proven unnecessary, but it had helped to further the feeling of tension already present.[1]

Judge Harold R. Medina quickly moved to take control of his first-floor courtroom. Despite the defendants' objections, he granted a government motion to sever Party Chairman William Z. Foster from the case. Doctors from both sides had agreed that Foster's heart ailment made his active participation in the trial impossible. The defense had hoped his illness could be used as a means to delay the proceedings, but Medina would not allow this. After six months of preliminaries, eleven of the top twelve CPUSA leaders were to be tried for violation of the Smith Act.

During the first six weeks of the trial the defense challenged the system of choosing jurors. It alleged that "the poor, slum dwellers, manual laborers, wage workers, blacks, members of other racial and national minorities, and persons affiliated with the Communist and American Labor Parties" had been excluded illegally. The grand jury which had indicted the eleven did not represent a cross-section of the population, the attorneys argued, and the indictments should be dismissed.[2] Perhaps in an effort to impede the trial's progress, the defense called dozens of witnesses to support its allegations. The middle- or upper-class status of many jurors was shown through routine questioning. Judge Medina was increasingly angered by what he considered deliberate delay and eventually forced an end to the challenges. With the last testimony on the subject heard on March 1, 1949, the Judge ruled three days later that the defense had shown no systematic or deliberate exclusion of any groups. Higher courts were to uphold his ruling.

International events once again intervened just as the jury challenge ended. The heads of the communist parties of France and Italy, Maurice Thorez and Palmiro Togliatti, issued a statement relating to the deteriorating situation in Europe. They said their parties would aid the Soviet Union in repulsing aggression even if it meant assisting Soviet troops within the borders of their own nations. The American press asked the CPUSA immediately for its position.

With their trial just days away, there was a fierce, private struggle over the response to questions concerning the French-Italian declaration. Foster, Benjamin Davis, Robert Thompson, and Alexander Bittelman demanded that the CPUSA issue precisely the same statement as its foreign colleagues. A majority of the National Committee "fought like hell against that."[3] The result was a "compromise" in which Foster and Dennis publicly asserted: "If, despite the efforts of the peace forces of America and the world, Wall Street should succeed in plunging the world into war, we would oppose it as an unjust, aggressive, imperialist war, as an undemocratic and anti-Socialist war."[4] The "compromise" was "terrible," Gates said, "but we thought we had gained a victory by stopping the most extreme statement."[5]

The CP's position provided an easy political target. The Democratic Senate majority leader, Scott Lucas of Illinois, said: "It is not surprising that these men who are under indictment and being tried for crimes against the Government would support the Communist government instead of our own."[6] President Truman's comment was even more direct and prejudicial to the upcoming trial. Asked about the statement at a March 3 press conference, he replied: "I have no comment on a statement made by traitors."[7]

Despite the disastrous effects of the declaration, the Party continued to restate it. *The Daily Worker* strongly defended it in its issues of March 4, 6, and 7. The National Committee voted its formal endorsement at an April 23–24 meeting.[8] Later testimony would reveal that the Dennis-Foster view was spread throughout the Party in schools and club meetings.[9] The CP itself had helped to create an even more prejudicial atmosphere.

By the time the jury challenge was over and the trial was ready to begin on March 7, 1949, the Judge and the defense attorneys already were bitter antagonists. Medina expected difficulties in the courtroom and his attitude, together with the defendants' determined effort to challenge the judicial system, may have precipitated conflict. Almost immediately upon being assigned to the case, the jurist gathered all the material he could find on a trial of Nazi sympathizers during World War II.[10] That prosecutive effort had involved thirty-one "neo-fascists" who were accused of seditious conduct. Their trial had lasted eight months. It ended in a mistrial due to the death of the presiding judge, apparently from exhaustion, after constant disruption in the courtroom.[11]

Medina believed the communists similarly would seek to wear him down. He viewed any delay in the proceedings as a direct provocation and, perhaps, even a threat. Every vociferous objection was seen as disruptive behavior. Every delay was considered an effort to exhaust him. The Judge's consequent emotional reactions were demonstrated on numerous occasions during the trial. The communists considered Medina to have a "violent class bias" and believed he had been assigned to assure a guilty verdict.[12] Gates later lamented: "We permitted the trial to become a duel between judge and defense; it is difficult enough to get a federal jury to vote against the government prosecutor, it will never vote against the judge."[13]

Mutual irritation was shown between judge and attorneys during the week a jury was chosen. When defense attorney Louis McCabe pointed out that a prospective juror accidentally had admitted prejudice, despite numerous warnings concerning the need for no bias, Medina responded: "You don't think you are going to provoke me into any hasty action? You are not going to do it. You should know it by this time, and there is no use continuing these efforts."[14] He warned a second attorney, Richard Gladstein, not to argue defense objections and implied, at this early date, that some form of discipline might be forthcoming.[15]

Jury selection was completed on March 17, 1949. Seven women were selected and there were three blacks among the jurors. Among those empanelled were three housewives, "two secretaries, a department store clerk, a beauty operator, an industrial engineer, and a retired beer salesman." The last juror chosen, after exhaustion of the defense's peremptory challenges, was Russell Janney, a writer and theatrical producer known for his authorship of *The Miracle of the Bells*.[16] *The New York Times* reported:

As a whole the jury appears to be a representative cross-section of the New York melting pot. It is the kind of jury that defense counsel, in their futile seven-week attack on the Federal jury system here, said could not be obtained because of discrimination against Negroes, Jews, women, manual workers and poor people in favor of the "rich, propertied and well-to-do."[17]

The emphasis on defense failures and prosecution successes became a continuing feature of the newspaper's coverage.

The Judge cautioned the jury that the defendants were not charged with being communists in general or members of the Communist Party. "The charge is specific and refers to a conspiracy to organize an assembly of persons who teach and advocate the overthrow and destruction of the Government of the United States."[18] The fact that this "assembly" was the CPUSA made the Judge's distinction of little value. The prosecuting attorney intended to indict the Communist Party. That had been the FBI's objective in urging the prosecution, and the government had adopted this position.

John F.X. McGohey's opening remarks traced the history of the CPUSA. He placed great emphasis on Jacques Duclos' article as the major impetus for the 1945 change from the Communist Political Association to the CP. Indeed, the indictment alleged that the communist leaders had turned in 1945 from peaceful protest to a conspiracy to overthrow the government violently. The United States attorney charged that Marxism-Leninism included the teaching that socialism "cannot be established by peaceful evolution but, on the contrary, can be established only by violent revolution."[19] This would be proven, he said, by a reading of Marxist classics such as the 1848 *Communist Manifesto* and *The History of the C.P.S.U.* The organizational structure of the CP was carefully described by the prosecutor. There could be no doubt what was on trial—the economic and political theories of Marx and Lenin were to be used to convict the communist leaders.

Dennis defended "the immortal classics," but said they contained neither "blueprints nor directives."[20] His efforts to outline the program of the CP were stopped constantly by Medina whose comments became more caustic as Dennis continued. The jurist ruled that all the Party could introduce was evidence to show that it had not advocated or intended to advocate the use of force and violence. The defense believed it could rebut the charges only by showing what it had believed in, rather than proving a negative. Medina maintained: "You see, you may have done a lot of good things, and that is true in criminal cases generally, but a man who is charged with crime does not have a defense to him to show that in many other respects he was very good and obeyed the law in other respects continually."[21] When Dennis later continued his remarks and claimed: "We Communists will show that when we taught and advocated . . . " Medina interrupted him, saying, "You mean you think you will show. I don't believe you are going to get around to that."[22] The six-month trial was to be marked with controversy over this central issue, with Medina successfully reiterating his ruling.

The Judge was attempting to treat the trial as an ordinary criminal case, but it was not. Beliefs, not acts, were being judged. In reality, a political party was on trial. Defense advocate Abraham Isserman pointed this out in his opening remarks. He told the court that these eleven individuals were accused only because they constituted most of the National Board of the CP at the time of the indictments. If they had not happened to hold these positions, he said, they would not have been on trial.[23] The government had in its possession documents to prove that he was correct, although they were not offered to the court. A noncommunist observer of the Smith Act proceedings concluded: "Legal fact-finding processes simply are not equal to the demands placed upon them by these proceedings," and "the trial process is simply not equal to the demands being made of it."[24] The complex theoretical questions to be placed before the jury could not be fit into neat packages of factual evidence, but Medina continued to insist that this could be done.

The impossibility of reconciling Medina's views with those of the defense was demonstrated as the opening statements ended. The defendants' attorneys demanded a mistrial on the basis of Medina's prejudicial conduct as demonstrated by his tone of voice, gestures, and comments. The Judge quickly denied the motion, and the trial was ready for its first witness.[25]

The testimony of Louis F. Budenz was the high point of the government's case. Budenz had ranked higher in the communist hierarchy than any other prosecution witness. Already a well-known left-winger when he joined the Party in 1935, he was immediately given positions of responsibility. He served as labor and managing editor of *The Daily Worker* and, for a short time, headed the Party's Chicago newspaper, the *Midwest Daily Record*. He was elected to the National Committee at various times, but never achieved the top rank of leadership. Apparently his career in the communist movement had passed its peak by 1945 when he suddenly left the CP to join the Catholic Church and become a professional anticommunist. Following his public split with the Party, he was hired to teach economics at Notre Dame and then went to Fordham University.

A veteran witness, Budenz presented the image of a calm, sophisti-

cated, knowledgeable interpreter of Marxist jargon. As a former inti-
mate of most of those on trial he was invaluable to the prosecution. In
the years to come Budenz' reliability and truthfulness would be questioned severely,[26] but he was an effective witness in the first communist trial.

Budenz read to the jury the CP's 1945 constitution to prove what was
never disputed—that the Communist Party accepted the philosophy of
"Marxism-Leninism." Using this concept as a basis, he served as a vehicle for the introduction of a series of books by Lenin, Stalin, and other
Marxist authors. The government's theory was that since the American
communists had accepted a Marxist philosophy, they were bound by
the statements in these classics, many of which were used in their schools
and discussion groups. Budenz read portions of Stalin's *Foundations of
Leninism*, Lenin's *Imperialism, The Highest Stage of Capitalism*, and *State
and Revolution*, the *History of the C.P.S.U. (Bolsheviks)*, and similar works.
Carefully chosen were sections dealing with the need to smash the
bourgeois state and establish a dictatorship of the proletariat.

Despite defense objections, Budenz interpreted the first sentence of
the preamble to the CP's constitution: "The Commmunist Party of the
United States is the political part of the American working class basing
itself upon the principles of scientific socialism, Marxism-Leninism."
Budenz said:

This sentence as is historically meant throughout the Communist movement,
is that the Communist Party bases itself upon so-called scientific socialism, as
appears in the writings of Marx, Engels, Lenin and Stalin, therefore as interpreted by Lenin and Stalin who have specifically interpreted scientific socialism
to mean that socialism can only be attained by the violent shattering of the capitalist state, and the setting up of a dictatorship of the proletariat by force and
violence in place of that state. In the United States this would mean that the
Communist Party of the United States is basically committed to the overthrow
of the Government of the United States as set up by the Constitution of the
United States.[27]

Defense attorneys attempted to stop Budenz' definition, maintaining
that it represented only his understanding and could not be binding on
the defendants. They repeatedly objected when Medina suggested a
rephrasing of McGohey's question to make it legally acceptable. Faced
with continued objections, the Judge remarked: "When I hear these objections one after the other, after having been in this sort of thing for
some months, I begin to get a pretty good idea of what you are up to."[28]

The government faced a problem in explaining a segment of the CP's
constitution which provided for the immediate expulsion of any mem-

ber who advocated the use of violence. The provision appeared to strike at the heart of the prosecution's case. Budenz ingeniously solved the difficulty. The CP's dedication to "Marxism-Leninism" took precedence over anything else that might appear in the constitution. "It implies," he said, "that those portions of this constitution which are in conflict with Marxism-Leninism are null in effect. They are merely window dressing asserted for protective purposes, the Aesopian language of V. I. Lenin."[29] Through this interpretation, any communist literature which supported the government's position on the use of force and violence by the CP was to be accepted literally, but anything in conflict with this thesis was to be rejected as "Aesopian language"—deliberately inserted to provide a security cover and to be interpreted as the opposite of its literal meaning. If the communists claimed the capitalist state had to be smashed, they were to be believed. If they said they favored a peaceful transition to socialism, this was to be interpreted as meaning the opposite.

During his two weeks of testimony, Budenz identified each of the defendants and his party positions. He dealt extensively with the reconstitution of the CP in 1945, although he had not been directly involved in most of the events of the period. He attributed the decision to end the Communist Political Association to the considerable influence of foreign communists.

The performance of the government's star witness, on the whole, was impressive, but not very convincing. He succeeded in presenting an aura of conspiracy, but provided little hard evidence. He had little knowledge of the period from 1945 to 1948, although these were the specific years covered in the indictment. Aspects of his testimony actually supported the defendants' claims. He said Stachel had been present during a 1945 *Daily Worker* staff discussion at which the statement was made that "Soviet power [in the United States] could be established only with the aid of the Red Army." Stachel opposed this position, although Budenz said he agreed later it was "permissible for discussion."[30]

Budenz testified that Foster had withdrawn a proposal to call and "politicalize" strikes in 1945 after opposition was expressed by communist trade union leaders.[31] He agreed that there had been nothing published in communist literary organs which advocated violent overthrow of the government.[32] An attempt to introduce Budenz' own writings between 1941 and 1945 on the meaning of socialism was blocked by Medina.

The judge added significantly to the first witness' effectiveness. He agreed with Budenz that "the fact that the Communist Party changed its line from supporting the People's Front to attacking President

Roosevelt is certainly material."[33] Medina provided credence to the thesis of a conspiracy. "I also notice a, what strikes me as a curious way of expressing themselves [communists] in these articles and resolutions . . . . There are a lot of words that don't mean very much to me. It seems to me like a special jargon that, maybe is used in this particular subject matter."[34]

The defense's argument that books were on trial in the case was rejected by the Judge, and he added significant gratuitous comments. "I charge you," Medina instructed the jury, "that no books are on trial here. These individual defendants, that you see here, who once in a while seem to enjoy the proceedings so much, are the one's [sic] on trial, not any books . . . ."[35] By the time the first witness left the stand, the jury could not have lacked an understanding of the Judge's attitude toward the defense.

The dramatic appearance of the second prosecution witness was far more impressive than the substance of his evidence. Herbert A. Philbrick had joined the Young Communist League in 1942 and the Communist Party in 1944 at the urging of the FBI. He was still active in the CP when he appeared to testify on April 6, 1949. During the period of five years of CP membership, he had made reports to the Bureau continually. His exploits were soon publicized in his book, *I led 3 Lives*, and later in a television series of the same name.

While Philbrick had been in the Party during the entire period covered by the indictment, his position, unlike Budenz', had been so low level as to give relatively little weight to his evidence. He identified many of the same books as had the previous witness, and said they continued to be used. *The Communist Manifesto*, written a century before, was introduced through his testimony.

Philbrick was a member of the professional group of district 1 of the Massachusetts CP. He had risen to the position of literature director of his local cell, which consisted of five members. He testified that a teacher in a 1945 training course had "defined revolution as a violent revolution to be carried out by bands of armed workers against the existing state government."[36] He said he had been taught that a revolution could not be expected until two major conditions were met. There had to be a "heavy depression" and a major war.[37]

Philbrick clearly lacked the theoretical understanding of Budenz. He said that at a local club meeting they had discussed "turning a war into a civil war through the medium of civil disobedience, and I recall that Martha said that we must arm the workers for the struggle against the capitalists."[38] The relationship of "civil disobedience" to armed struggle was not explained.

Under cross-examination Philbrick testified that he had used his reports to the FBI in preparation for his appearance. The defense requested copies of the reports, but Medina refused. "It is my ruling," he said, "that the defense counsel has no right to look through the Government's files and the FBI files and seek what they may find later to be to their advantage. It would be a queer state of affairs to have, in a criminal prosecution, the Government suddenly put on trial, and that is not going to happen here."[39] Eight years later, in a changed political climate, the Supreme Court reversed a conviction on the basis of the government's refusal to make informants' reports available to the defense as a check on the reliability and truthfulness of their testimony.[40]

As had the government's initial witness, Philbrick admitted that he had never reported "any act of force or violence on the part of any member of the Communist party."[41] He added little to the government's case, but maintained the concept of conspiracy through his description of the Party group to which he belonged as being "underground"—composed of professionals whose Party memberships were secret.[42]

As an assistant advertising director for a theatre chain in Boston, Philbrick may have been aware of the lucrative opportunities which his testimony would open for him. His book and the television series based on it became very popular. Tom Clark later observed: "I thought Philbrick's book was a bunch of trash," and had no real value.[43]

The next three government witnesses testified in a day and a half. Frank S. Meyer had been a Party member from 1934 to 1942 and then a member of the CPA in 1944 and 1945. He had held some educational posts within the Party and identified certain of the texts used in various courses. All had been previously introduced into evidence.

Eugene H. Stewart and Fred G. Cook were special agents of the FBI. Both had attended a meeting addressed by Carl Winter in Detroit on January 31, 1946. Stewart claimed that Winter had said: "the time was soon to come when Lenin's teachings would be put into action,"[44] and a Canadian communist had added: "the time was soon coming when the Communists would smash their way to victory." The special agent claimed Winter had made no objection to the remark.[45]

Cook said Winter had spoken beneath a picture of Lenin—it was a Lenin memorial meeting—and had criticized Walter Reuther for striking one auto company instead of all. He admitted, under cross-examination, that he had been instructed only to record statements which "indicate that the Party was advocating the overthrow of the Government . . . by force and violence."[46]

The sixth government witness, William Nowell, had left the CP thirteen years earlier. He had known Stachel, Irving Potash, and Gus Hall. He was apparently asked to testify principally about his attendance at the International Lenin School in Moscow during 1931 and 1932. He claimed to have attended a course conducted by a Red Army officer on the "science of civil warfare." He said that various books, most of which had been identified already, had been used at the school, and he was taught that the dictatorship of the proletariat "would be established by the violent overthrow of the capitalist state."[47]

Nowell had been removed from Party positions in 1934 for opposing CP policy and had resigned in 1936. Beginning in 1939 he became a familiar witness at various trials and hearings. Four months before appearing at the trial of the eleven, he was hired by the Department of Justice as a clerk in the Immigration and Naturalization Service.

The next witness had been a Party member from 1937 to 1940 and again from 1944 to 1946. Charles W. Nicodemus' major purpose apparently was to describe a statement allegedly made by a maritime leader of the CP in 1945. He claimed that Al Lannon had said the only way a revolution could occur in the near future would be for the Red Army to come in from Siberia, through Alaska, through Canada, to the United States where "they could even destroy Detroit."[48] The story was embellished at later trials when Nicodemus claimed that the plan was for the Soviet air force to establish bases in Alaska from which "they could attack Canada and bomb Detroit."[49]

The last six government witnesses had been placed in the CP by the FBI. With one exception, they had joined during World War II. None had held a high position, and their testimony was similar. All described the Party schools and classes they had attended, and they continued to identify the books and outlines used. Most of the defendants were named as having given lectures or written articles based on Marxism. Each witness cited a remark by one or more Party members—but none of the defendants—that a violent revolution would be needed in order to achieve socialism. No testimony suggested any CP official ever had advocated a specific act of violence. The witnesses indicated a widespread ideological assumption within the Party that at some point violence would be necessary to offset the concentrated power of the ruling class.

The prosecution asked most of these witnesses to describe various security measures put into effect by the Party during 1947 and 1948. There was an obvious effort to develop the image of a secret, conspiratorial communist grouping. Considerable testimony was introduced to show that Party membership cards had been destroyed in 1948. William Cummings, the government's eleventh witness, said that his local

Cleveland club had been told in 1947 not to use telephones and to tighten security in preparation for the possibility of going underground.[50] The last witness, Balmes Hidalgo, Jr., recalled that his Party club had been broken up into smaller groups in 1947 to protect itself against government infiltration. In April 1948 he was informed that the Party might be forced underground if the Mundt bill was passed.[51]

The key nature of classic books and Party outlines was constantly a source of friction. Judge Medina attempted to clarify the government's purposes in using these materials.

I suppose it will be the Government's claim that taken as a whole and in its various parts and these other books [sic] that were shown or given to the students from time to time constitute an integrated scheme . . . in support of the charge in the indictment . . . . But you could not prove all of that at one time, but that you have taken it according as it appeared in these outlines as it was given to the students by the defendants or those acting with them.[52]

McGohey agreed with the Judge. Medina also lectured Dennis when he objected to the use of these materials.

Let us suppose, for the purposes of argument, that a group of individuals have decided that they will organize a larger group to overthrow or to teach and to advocate the overthrow of the United States Government by force and violence, and they get some pamphlets and books that were written years ago, but they show just how a violent revolution was brought about, how to do it, how to have persons get uniforms of soldiers and put them on, and make out that they are part of the army and navy, they show them just how to get in charge of the railroads by violent means, and to do all the various other things that will, if the teaching and advocating goes on to its ultimate conclusion, bring about the overthrow of the Government by force and violence. Now, how can it be that those books and pamphlets are being tried when the charge is that the individuals of such a group used those books and pamphlets and papers, of one kind or another, as mere instruments for the perpetration of a conspiracy? How can it be a trial of books?[53]

The government rested its case on May 19, 1949, after thirteen witnesses and two months of testimony. Its strongest witness had been its first, and the case had become, in the final weeks of direct prosecution testimony, a dreary repetition of the contents of books and pamphlets. Most of the government's witnesses had received some financial rewards from their testimony, and some would receive considerably more in the future. Many had been planted in the Communist Party by the FBI. Those who had waited for the calling of a highly placed informant to expose the communist conspiracy had been disappointed. An historian, Alonzo Hamby, concluded:

The government evidence amounted to little more than proof that the defendants had reestablished the Communist Party of the United States in 1945 and had disseminated Communist propaganda. The trial was a sedition trial based on a questionable sedition statute, no less distasteful because of the totalitarian attitudes of the defendants.[54]

Judge Medina ordered that the defense begin the presentation of its case on the next court date, May 23. He denied all defense motions and refused to grant any adjournment.

The defense presented thirty-four witnesses over the period of four months. Their testimony was marked by a constant battle with Medina. The Party sought to present a full exposition of its program, while the Judge increasingly limited the areas in which he would allow defense witnesses to testify.

John Gates was the first witness for the defendants. He had been mentioned rarely in the government's testimony. The only evidence produced against him was his editorship of the Party's newspaper. He had not even been present when the CP had been reconstituted in 1945 and could not be tied to the Duclos article or its immediate aftermath. Gates attempted to outline Party policies from the period of the Great Depression. The Judge sustained many objections to questions concerning his beliefs outside the specific area of the use of force and violence.

An exchange between Medina and Gates set the pattern for the next four months.

The Witness: We advocated the winning of a majority of the American people for the establishment of socialism. We sought a peaceful means of doing that and the only way that force and violence would come into the picture would be if the big corporations and financial interests of the United States would attempt to prevent the American people from instituting socialism when they so desired.

The Court: Maybe that is the catch in it.

The Witness: The catch in what, sir?

The Court: As to how you figured that out. Do you say that you would wait until they did use the force and violence first before you would try to overcome it?[55]

The Judge then sustained an objection to his own question, but the jury had heard it. In an important sense, he had joined the prosecution team.

Two days later the courtroom exploded. Gates was asked by McGohey to state the Party office held by Dennis in January 1946. He refused, claiming he would not identify the positions held by others. Medina directed him to answer the question. After a conference with attorneys and fellow defendants, the defense agreed to stipulate all offices held by the defendants during the period of the indictment. McGohey would not accept this, and Medina agreed with him. The government's attorney asked Gates to name the members of the Party's national veterans committee. He refused, and the case adjourned to the next morning to allow the defense time to submit a memorandum on the subject.[56]

Medina described the morning of June 3:

It was Friday the third of June, 1949. I shall never forget it. When I went in there that morning you could just feel something in the atmosphere. You know when you feel the hair on the back of your neck going up a little bit, you know there is something going on. You don't know just what it is. And all day in the courtroom the place was full of these Commie sympathizers.[57]

The Judge quickly disposed of all efforts to block McGohey's questions.

Gates again was asked to identify fellow Party members. He refused to name any other than the defendants, claiming: "It would degrade me in the eyes of my associates and the labor movement, in the eyes of the public, and in the eyes of the jury to act as a commmon stool pigeon to give you such other information as you desire."[58] Medina adjudged Gates to be in contempt of court and sentenced him to a maximum of thirty days in prison. The courtroom erupted.

The Judge heard Henry Winston shout: "More than five thousand Negroes have been lynched in this country for such . . . and the government of the United States should be ashamed for bringing in this monstrosity." Medina immediately remanded him to prison for the remainder of the trial. Hall was on his feet screaming: "It sounds more like a kangaroo court than a court in the United States. I have heard more law and more constitutional rights in kangaroo courts." He was sent to prison for the balance of the proceedings. The Judge then threatened to take action against Dennis.[59] Medina later recalled: "All this time this shouting and yelling and hullabalooing was going on, and I picked off about four of them."[60]

The New York Times provided a clearly biased version of the day's events. It reported that Gates had been given "thirty days for refusal to answer questions that would have laid bare part of the secret Communist underground among war veterans," and added, according to the evidence, "party members were taught how to infiltrate the armed forces, get possession of soldiers' and sailors' uniforms, and use force and violence with the aid of the Red Army, when the time is ripe, to destroy the United States Constitution and its guarantees of freedom and democracy."[61] The story was an incredible exaggeration of bits and pieces from the previous two months of government testimony.

Although the names of other Party members had little relation to the case, higher courts upheld Medina's action as a proper exercise of a judge's plenary powers. The contempt citations damaged what remained of the defense. Defendants were aware of what would happen to them if they took the stand. Two of the eleven partially were separated from the defense team for the trial's duration.

Despite the obvious danger, two other defendants immediately followed Gates to the stand. Gil Green emphasized the CP's commitment to majority acceptance of socialism and a rejection of the use of force, unless fascism came to exist. He denied that the experiences of the Soviet Communist Party could be "mechanically applied" to the United States since conditions were so vastly different. He read those portions of the *History of the C.P.S.U.* which supported his viewpoint. Course outlines emphasizing the concept of peaceful change were introduced. Green had used these materials to teach classes in Illinois.

Despite a relatively calm exposition of Party policy, Green soon found himself in difficulty with the Judge. On June 20 Medina refused to admit into evidence a 1938 article on democracy authored by Green and Dennis. Green responded: "I thought we were going to be given a chance to prove our case." The Judge ordered him to prison for the remainder of the trial.[62]

Benjamin Davis was the third defense witness and avoided imprisonment through the forbearance of the United States attorney who did not press him for names of Party members. Davis outlined his reasons for joining the Communist Party and concentrated on its struggle for winning black rights. He cited campaign speeches rejecting the use of force and violence which he had delivered during his races for the New York City Council.[63]

The next three witnesses were Party officials from Massachusetts who, while refuting aspects of Philbrick's testimony, emphasized the democratic nature of CP proceedings. Fanny Hartman and Frances Hood testified that the 1945 CPA state conventions had been run democratically and said that the decisions reached had resulted from open discussion. Hartman denied any use of "Aesopian language" and claimed the CP had never discussed the use of violence in relation to revolutionary change with the United States. Hood attempted to dispel the mystery surrounding Party clubs by describing their general, positive activities.

Daniel Boone Schirmer, Harvard graduate and New England CP official, noted that he had taught in Party schools that socialism would be achieved through majority choice. He emphasized that the CP in the Boston area had not gone underground.[64] The sixth witness, Frank Hashmall from Ohio, contradicted the testimony of Cummings and a second prosecution witness, and denied that the CP ever had taught the necessity of violent overthrow of the government. He said that instead of precipitating violence, he had been a 1948 victim of a series of acts of violence.[65]

Herbert Phillips, a college philosophy professor who had been fired recently from the University of Washington as a result of CP membership, took the stand on July 21, 1949. He had taught a course in Marxism-Leninism at a Party school in Seattle in 1946, but the Judge would not permit him to testify as an "expert witness" unless some connection between the Seattle school and the defendants was shown.[66] The same restriction had not been used during the presentation of the prosecution's case. Phillips was withdrawn as a witness.

During the next three weeks a succession of eight defense witnesses took the stand to describe communist activities and theoretical concepts, as well as to dispute specific aspects of prosecution testimony. Three attempted to quiet fears created by the government which had implied sinister purposes in the Party policy of "concentration"—placing members in key industries, groups, and activities. Efforts to gain influence among miners, steelworkers, veterans, blacks, and others were described as a natural consequence of the CP's theoretical and practical commitment to mass activity and to those most likely to lead the march toward socialism. Similarly, the aura created by the prosecution concerning Party education was attacked as all eight answered questions concerning schools they had attended or in which they had taught. Anthony Krchmarak, Party leader in Cleveland, described a 1945 Chicago educational program intended to raise the socialist consciousness of workers. He detailed lectures he had given in Youngstown, Ohio, for the purpose of teaching socialism's historical development. Edward Chaka summarized a Gus Hall lecture at a Party school. Hall, he said, had emphasized that socialism would be achieved as part of a process of educating the working class and that any violence would be initiated by the ruling class. Robert Manewitz, the 1946 Missouri state education director of the CP, said he had taught the necessity of establishing a "people's front government" to reflect the will of the majority.[67]

A fourth defendant, Thompson, testified from August 9 to 12. He described his winning of the Distinguished Service Cross in the Pacific during World War II, and defended Marxist-Leninist theory. There were few disturbances during this testimony.[68]

A group of thirteen additional witnesses was heard during the balance of August. Most were Party functionaries who continued the process of seeking to put forward the CP program and to defend its activities. Party schools were described as being open to the public and to democratic discussion, rather than secretive means of indoctrination. Simon Gerson, who had been a 1948 candidate for the New York City Council, read a portion of his platform into the record, while another witness served as a vehicle for the introduction of the CP's 1948 draft resolution. The defense seemed to be seeking to educate the jury. The most impressive of these witnesses was Max Weiss who had been a member of the National Committee until it was radically changed in 1948, and also had been an editor of *Political Affairs*. He was permitted to give a one-hour lecture on the theory of proletarian revolution and disputed most of Budenz' claims. Weiss emphasized the possibility and desirability of a peaceful transition to socialism and said he had never heard of "Aesopian language" until Budenz had used the phrase in court. None of the defendants, according to Weiss, had ever advocated the use of force or violence.[69]

Carl Winter, a fifth defendant, began his testimony on August 31. For two days he answered questions with little disruption. The court then adjourned for the Labor Day weekend. That Sunday night a benefit outdoor concert was to take place in Peekskill, New York, with Paul Robeson scheduled to perform. Despite the presence of a large detail of state police, a mob attacked the audience as it was leaving. Clubs and stones were used to injure hundreds of people. Irving Potash was among those hurt. The windshield of the car in which he was travelling was smashed sending shattered glass into his eyes. Potash was in the hospital when court reconvened on Tuesday. After receiving a medical report, the Judge reluctantly recessed the case for two days.[70]

Medina believed communists had precipitated the riot in order to force an end to the judicial proceedings. He later said: "No one else, so far as I know, saw at the time or has since commented on the connection between the so-called 'Peekskill Riot' and the trial. Doubtless, others realized what the Communists were up to. But I was powerless to prevent it."[71]

The defense did apply for a mistrial as a result of the riot. Attorney Harry Sacher termed the Peekskill events "a manifestation of the bias and prejudice engendered by the Government agencies . . . against the

Communist Party and its members and against these defendants in particular."[72] The Judge denied the motion.

Winter continued the Party's defense against Budenz' definitions and sought to put the CP's program into the record. His testimony was relatively uneventful until September 12, 1949, when he refused to answer questions concerning the alleged presence of his father-in-law at the 1945 Party convention. Medina found him in contempt and sentenced him to a maximum of thirty days.[73]

The quietest part of the trial followed Winter's testimony. Gates took the stand to read a long deposition from Foster who was too ill to testify. Gates later described the Foster statement as a "terrible thing" which caused "the jury to fall asleep."[74] Those who were awake heard a qualitative change in Foster's previous beliefs. He argued that "theory grows out of practice," and that the ideas of the past could not be "applied in any mechanical sense." Marxism-Leninism was described as a "guide to action" and not a "dogma."[75] Socialism was not seen as an immediate objective, but one which would come when the majority accepted its necessity. Foster specifically denied any use or advocacy of force and violence.[76]

The trial finally was winding down to its end. The defense called Paul Robeson to the stand. He formerly had been a law student in a class taught at Columbia University by Judge Medina. Robeson's former teacher would not allow him to testify concerning conversations with the defendants, all of whom he knew.[77] An effective vignette was presented by the next witness, the director of the New York Public Library. He testified that all the Marxist classics introduced by the government were available for general circulation in his library.[78]

The final witness was Winston, the sixth defendant to testify. He said he had joined the CP in 1931, and had studied in the Soviet Union for a year and a half. He had held many responsible positions in the Young Communist League and then the Party. Winston defended the structure of the CPUSA as "democratic" and denied any teaching or advocacy of force or violence. He claimed that security measures which he had helped to initiate were necessary. The CP's members, he said, had to be protected "against hoodlum attack, against snooping, against the activities of the FBI, which was trying to cripple the activities of the Party."[79] Much of the government's cross-examination, as with other defense witnesses, was concerned with minor inaccuracies concerning dates, and claims that Winston had supplied false data on official forms such as passport applications and voter registration cards.

On September 23, 1949, the defense rested, and the government quickly followed suit. The evidence for the past six months often had been confusing, complex, and presented in such a contentious atmosphere as to be severely tainted.

The defense's motions at the end of testimony to provide a directed verdict of acquittal brought the case to the vital civil liberties questions which were inherent in the proceedings. Attorney Isserman presented the essential consideration for the defense:

If I stand in the courtroom or in a classroom and do advocate the overthrow of the Government, or put it in a resolution, or make it a platform of a party, if I do that and nothing more, I may do no more than project an idea for discussion, for consideration, for thinking, in the market place of ideas, which is precisely what the First Amendment says you can do. We don't reach your Honor's question, Does the Government have to wait until, because this is so far removed from any clear and present danger of incitement to overthrow or of overthrow itself, or of conspiracy to overthrow, that it is placed exactly where the First Amendment allows it to be placed, and that is the realm of discussion and thinking.[80]

The defense's argument rested on the Supreme Court's 1919 *Schenck* decision. Isserman asked that the free speech standard stated by Justice Oliver Wendell Holmes in that earlier case be applied now: "The question in every case is whether the words used are used in such circumstances and are of such a nature as to create a clear and present danger that they will bring about the substantive evils that Congress has a right to prevent. It is a question of proximity and degree."[81]

The prosecution had made no showing of such a danger. Indeed, it indicated privately that it had no evidence to support such a charge. Instead, McGohey relied upon the 1925 *Gitlow* decision, from which Holmes had dissented. This ruling, which had dealt with a New York State law, had given the legislature great latitude in restricting freedom of speech. The court had said: "The general provisions of the statute may be constitutionally applied to the specific utterance of the defendant if its natural tendency and probable effect were to bring about substantive evil which the legislative body might prevent."[82]

The government did not intend to rely on the "clear and present danger" test. McGohey stated that he believed "the Gitlow case is still law."[83] Judge Medina was not as certain. He led McGohey to agree that even if the *Gitlow* decision were not applicable, the restriction of freedom of speech could still be upheld.[84] The Judge then denied the motions for acquittal.

The defense team took three days to present its summation to the jury. Its arguments covered a wide range of issues. Attorney Isserman contended that the disagreement between Browder and Foster over the dissolution of the CPA had involved differing interpretations of Marxism-Leninism. Their conflict, Isserman asserted, had not been connected with any question of "the teaching or advocacy or with the conspiracy to teach and advocate the overthrow of the United States Government by force and violence."[85] Sacher alleged that the prosecution had been brought for political purposes.

Dennis presented a far-ranging defense of Marxism-Leninism, and maintained that if the jury convicted the defendants, "every member of our organization and the friends of our organization also would be subject to indictment, persecution and harassment."[86] He said that socialism would be created by the working class "in accord with the majority will." The Party's general secretary reiterated the concept of the CP as the "vanguard" of the workers, supported the principle of a dictatorship of the proletariat with a need "to smash the old state machinery of the exploiters," and defended opposition to "unjust wars."[87] It seemed that Dennis was speaking more directly to his Party's members than to the jury.

The government's case was outlined fully by McGohey in a summation of more than a day. He alleged that the CP's reconstitution in 1945 had meant a return to the teaching and advocacy of the Marxist-Leninist doctrine of violent overthrow of the government. The CP, he said, had used the Russian Revolution as its model and classic works by Marx and Lenin as its guides. It had attempted to concentrate its membership in key industries for the "sinister purpose" of endangering the United States' military security through political strikes.[88] He particularly stressed the "underground" nature of some Party clubs and the existence of "secret schools and classes."

Both the defense and prosecution realized that the Judge's charge to the jury could be critical in a case as complex as this. Medina indicated he would consider proposals from both sides for inclusion in his charge, and each responded with recommendations. The defense placed greatest emphasis on the "clear and present danger" concept. It asked that the jury be instructed to decide if such a danger existed. Without the existence of immediate peril, the defendants should be found innocent.[89] The government made no reference either to the First Amendment or a "clear and present danger" in its proposals.

Medina's instructions to the jury left little room for an acquittal. He rejected almost all the defense's suggestions. The Judge himself determined the applicability of the First Amendment. "I find as a matter of law," he said, "that there is sufficient danger of a substantive evil that the Congress has a right to prevent to justify the application of the statute under the First Amendment of the Constitution."[90] Medina had stated, in effect, that a "clear and present danger" existed. A government attorney active in Smith Act cases later recalled that if Medina had relied upon the *Gitlow* decision, as urged by McGohey, the verdicts would have been reversed on appeal.[91] To find the defendants guilty, the jury had to find simply an intent to overthrow "by force and violence as speedily as circumstances would permit it to be achieved."

The Judge destroyed much of the defense's case in a few sentences. He said that positive actions by the defendants were not proof of a lack of a criminal conspiracy. A conspiracy exists "if two or more persons, in any manner, or through any contrivance, impliedly or tacitly, come to a mutual understanding to accomplish a common and unlawful design knowing its object." Additional conspirators could join later. "Words may be the instruments by which crimes are committed," the Judge charged. Abstract advocacy was not punishable, but it was illegal if "such teaching and advocacy be of a rule or principle of action and by language reasonably and ordinarily calculated to incite persons . . . with the intent to cause the overthrow or destruction" of the government.[92]

The jury received the case at 3:55 P.M. on October 13, 1949. Within an hour it was back in the courtroom asking to see various documents dealing primarily with the reconstitution of the CP in 1945 and with teaching materials for Party classes. Apparently the jurors had accepted the government's thesis. At 10:20 P.M. the jury retired for the evening. A little after eleven the next morning, the jurors had reached their verdict—a surprisingly short period of deliberation in view of the length of the trial and the complexity of the issues involved.

Mrs. Thelma Dial, forelady of the jury, read the verdicts. Each defendant was found guilty.[93] Almost fifteen months after the indictments had been filed, the national leaders of the American Communist Party were to be imprisoned for what one observer said was "disseminating revolutionary ideas."[94] Judge Medina immediately remanded the eleven to prison. He would not consider bail.

The Judge then turned to the legal antagonists with whom he had done battle during the previous year. He accused the defense attorneys of engaging in a deliberate conspiracy against him and the proceedings, including an effort to impair his health. Medina cited thirty-nine instances of contempt by the battery of lawyers and proceeded to impose sentences. Sacher, Gladstein, and Dennis were each given six months. Isserman and George W. Crockett, Jr., were to be imprisoned for four months, and McCabe was to face thirty days.[95] Protests were of no avail—Medina finally had been able to strike back at the "communist conspiracy" which apparently he had come to accept.

Little was understood of the meaning or future effects of the verdict but congratulations poured in on Medina and McGohey. *The New York Times'* page one story reported the eleven had been "convicted of secretly teaching and advocating, on secret orders from Moscow, overthrow of the United States Government and destruction of American democracy by force and violence."[96] The fact that this was not even the charge did not seem to concern the *Times'* reporter. The public's perception of an internal "Red Menace" had been increased immeasurably.

One week later the eleven communist leaders appeared before Judge Medina for sentencing. Each was given a five-year prison term and a $10,000 fine, with the exception of Thompson. In recognition of the latter's DSC, his sentence was set at three years. Despite the certainty of a long, legally controversial appeal, the Judge continued to deny bail. He said the jury had determined the eleven had a specific intent to overthrow the government, and added: "It seems to me absurd on its face to say, as you do, that there must be a clear and present danger of immediate overthrow to justify prosecution. By any such test the Government would be overthrown before it could protect itself and the very important right of freedom of speech would be gone with all the other freedoms."[97]

Those who believed the prosecution of the top leaders of the American communist movement would end the gathering political hysteria were mistaken. Those who had worked so hard for this prosecution as a first step toward stringent political limitations were encouraged. A more restrictive political atmosphere had grown concurrent with the trial proceedings. The verdict could only foster this trend.

NOTES

1. *The New York Times*, January 17, 1949.
2. Michal R. Belknap, *Cold War Political Justice, The Smith Act, the Communist Party, and American Civil Liberties* (Westport, 1977), 71.
3. John Gates to author, March 5, 1978.
4. *The New York Times*, March 3, 1949.
5. John Gates to author, March 5, 1978.
6. *The New York Times*, March 3, 1949.
7. Harry S. Truman, *Public Papers of the Presidents of the United States 1949* (Washington, 1964), 158.
8. *The Worker*, May 8, 1949.
9. J. Howard McGrath, *Attorney General of the United States v. The Communist Party of the United States of America*, "Official Report of Proceedings Before the Subversive Activities Control Board," Testimony of Mary Markward (Septem-

ber 27, 1959), 5891, Testimony of Herbert A. Philbrick (October 16, 1951), 6186–87.

10. Harold R. Medina, *The Anatomy of Freedom* (New York, 1959), 2.

11. Belknap, *Cold War Political Justice*, 40.

12. John Gates to author, March 5, 1978; John Williamson, *Dangerous Scot: The Life and Work of an American "Undesirable"* (New York, 1969), 180.

13. John Gates, *The Story of an American Communist* (New York, 1958), 124.

14. *United States v. Dennis, et al.*, "Joint Appendix on Appeal from Judgments of Conviction of the United States District Court for the Southern District of New York." Hereafter cited as "Joint Appendix." *Voir Dire* (March 10, 1949), 2806.

15. Ibid., 2808.

16. *The New York Times*, March 17, 1949.

17. Belknap, *Cold War Political Justice*, 78.

18. *United States v. Dennis, et al.*, "Joint Appendix," Opening Statement by the Court (March 21, 1949), 3202–03.

19. Ibid., Opening Statement on Behalf of the Government (March 21, 1949), 3209.

20. Ibid., Opening Statements on Behalf of Defendants (March 21, 1949), 3245.

21. Ibid., 3231.

22. Ibid., 3240.

23. Ibid. (March 22, 1949), 3287.

24. Herbert L. Packer, *Ex-Communist Witnesses, Four Studies in Fact Finding* (Stanford, 1962), 220, 230.

25. *United States v. Dennis, et al.*, "Joint Appendix," Colloquy of Court and Counsel After Openings (March 22, 1949), 3315–17.

26. Joseph Alsop, "The Strange Case of Louis Budenz," *Atlantic Monthly* CLXXXIX (April 1952), 29–33; Len De Caux, *Labor Radical From the Wobblies to CIO* (Boston, 1970), 319.

27. *United States v. Dennis, et al.*, "Joint Appendix," Testimony of Louis Budenz (March 29, 1949), 3638.

28. Ibid., 3636.

29. Ibid., 3639.

30. Ibid. (March 25, 1949), 3557.

31. Ibid., 3574–75.

32. Ibid. (March 31, April 4, 1949), 3852, 3964.

33. Ibid. (March 23, 1949), 3401.

34. Ibid. (March 25, 1949), 3553.

35. Ibid. (March 30, 1949), 3768.

36. Ibid., Testimony of Herbert A. Philbrick (April 7, 1949), 4188.

37. Ibid., 4220.

38. Ibid. (April 8, 1949), 4282.

39. Ibid., 4315.

40. *Jencks v. United States*, 353 U.S. 657 (1957).

41. *United States v. Dennis, et al.*, "Joint Appendix," Testimony of Herbert A. Philbrick (April 11, 1949), 4341.

42. Ibid. (April 7, 1949), 4262.

43. Tom Clark to author, March 28, 1975.

44. *United States v. Dennis, et al.*, "Joint Appendix," Testimony of Eugene H. Stewart (April 13, 1949), 4569.

45. Ibid., 4572–74.

46. Ibid., Testimony of Fred G. Cook (April 18, 1949), 4591.

47. Ibid., Testimony of William O. Nowell (April 18, 1949), 4659.

48. Ibid., Testimony of Charles W. Nicodemus (April 22, 1949), 4803–4.

49. *United States v. Flynn, et al.*, "Transcript of Trial," Testimony of Charles W. Nicodemus (August 4, 1952), 7612.

50. *United States v. Dennis, et al.*, "Joint Apppendix," Testimony of William Cummings (May 11, 1949), 5834.

51. Ibid., Testimony of Balmes Hidalgo, Jr. (May 18, 1949), 6117–6249.

52. Ibid., Testimony of Thomas A. Younglove (May 5, 1949), 5531–32.

53. Ibid., 5534–35.

54. Alonzo Hamby, *Beyond the New Deal: Harry S. Truman and American Liberalism* (New York, 1973), 387.

55. *United States v. Dennis, et al.*, "Joint Appendix," Testimony of John Gates (June 1, 1949), 6702.

56. Ibid. (June 2 and 3, 1949), 6807–31.

57. Medina, *The Anatomy of Freedom*, 7.

58. *United States v. Dennis, et al.*, "Joint Appendix," Testimony of John Gates (June 3, 1949), 6838.

59. Ibid., Colloquy of Court and Counsel (June 3, 1949), 6845.

60. Medina, *The Anatomy of Freedom*, 8.

61. *The New York Times*, June 4, 1949.

62. *United States v. Dennis, et al.*, "Joint Appendix," Testimony of Gil Green (June 20, 1949), 7456.

63. Ibid., Testimony of Benjamin Davis (July 8, 1949), 8377.

64. Ibid., Testimony of Fanny Hartman, Daniel Boone Schirmer, Frances A. Hood (July 13–July 20, 1949), 8563–8911.

65. Ibid., Testimony of Frank Hashmall (July 21, 1949), 8912–76.

66. Ibid., Testimony of Herbert Phillips (July 21, 1949), 8976.

67. Ibid., Testimony of Anthony Krchmarak, Yolanda Hall, Edward Joseph Chaka, Geraldyne Lightfoot, Samuel J. Hall, Jr., Robert Manewitz, Helen Musil, Florence Hall (July 22–August 9, 1949), 9004–841.

68. Ibid., Testimony of Robert Thompson (August 9–August 12, 1949), 9841–10073.

69. Ibid., Testimony of Howard Johnson, Wilbur S. Broms, Alan Max, Joseph Starobin, Herbert Aptheker, Abner Berry, Simon W. Gerson, George C. Squier, Jr., Samuel Sillen, Edward E. Strong, Max Weiss, Arthur Schusterman, Boyd Coleman (August 12–August 31, 1949), 10075–980.

70. Ibid., Colloquy of Court and Counsel (September 6, 1949), 11087.

71. Medina, *The Anatomy of Freedom*, 89.

72. *United States v. Dennis, et al.*, "Joint Appendix," Application for Mistrial and for Investigation of Violation of Constitutional Rights (September 8, 1949), 11091.

73. Ibid., Colloquy of Court and Counsel (September 12, 1949), 11310.

74. John Gates to author, March 5, 1978.

75. *United States v. Dennis, et al.*, "Joint Appendix," Deposition of William Z. Foster (September 16, 1949), 11536.

76. Ibid., 11541.

77. Ibid., Testimony of Paul Robeson (September 20, 1949), 11680–87.

78. Ibid., Testimony of Ralph A. Beals (September 20, 1949), 11688–700.

79. Ibid., Testimony of Henry Winston (September 22, 1949), 11827.

80. Ibid., Motion for Directed Verdict of Acquittal (September 28, 1949), 11955.

81. *Schenck v. United States*, 249 U.S. 47 (1919).

82. *Gitlow v. New York*, 268 U.S. 652 (1925).

83. United States v. Dennis, et al., "Joint Appendix," Motion for Directed Verdict of Acquittal (September 29, 1949), 12037.

84. Ibid., 12038.

85. Ibid., Summation for the Defense (October 6, 1949), 12086.

86. Ibid. (October 11, 1949), 12332.

87. Ibid. (October 12, 1949), 12338–39.

88. Ibid., Summation for the Government (October 13, 1949), 12451.

89. Ibid., Defendants' Proposed Jury Instructions (October 13, 1949), 12556.

90. Ibid., Judge's Charge to the Jury (October 13, 1949), 12488.

91. Kevin Maroney (assistant to the Attorney General) to author, July 24, 1974.

92. *United States v. Dennis, et al.*, "Joint Appendix," Judge's Charge to the Jury (October 13, 1949), 12459–86.

93. Ibid., Jury Deliberations (October 13 and 14, 1949), 12506–22.

94. I. F. Stone, *The Truman Era* (New York, 1972), 94.

95. *United States v. Dennis, et al.*, "Joint Appendix," Adjudications of Contempt (October 14, 1949), 12522.

96. *The New York Times*, October 15, 1949.

97. Ibid., October 22, 1949.

IX

"Right Thinking Americans"

"The thought of a Soviet United States is at once revolting to every right thinking American," declared the federal government's chief police-man to a national radio audience on May 2, 1950. J. Edgar Hoover, who had played such a vital, often hidden, role in bringing the country to the brink of political hysteria, appeared to be pushing the United States into the abyss. Together with a select few, he sought to determine the identity of the "right thinkers" who were to inherit control of political institutions built over a period of close to two centuries. Hoover sym-bolized a right-wing grouping which seized its opportunity to establish and demand the enforcement of ideological norms for the American people. Abetted by a deep and widespread fear among their most in-fluential opponents, these conservative forces established the reality of political repression.

Hoover set the scene for many actors to follow:

Communists have been and are today at work within the very gates of Amer-ica. There are few walks in American life which they do not traverse. Their allegiance is to Moscow; their hopes are spurred by the writings of Marx and Lenin, not Jefferson, Madison and Lincoln; their enthusiasm is whetted by ex-pediency and deceit, not tolerance and brotherhood. Atheistic materialism is their idol; the destruction of the God of our fathers their goal. Wherever they may be, they have in common one diabolic ambition: to weaken and to even-tually destroy American democracy by stealth and cunning. Theirs is an orga-nization built and supported by dishonor, deceit and tyranny and a deliberate policy of falsehood.

Hoover told his audience that "Western civilization was at stake."[1]

The government's internal security establishment fully agreed with the FBI Director's analysis. Hoover and his colleagues carried their message to Congress and through that legislative body to the American people. Months before the Korean War began, they used the mass media and governmental power to create a sense of panic among the people and their legislative representatives. The extreme left wing feared that it was about to be destroyed through direct suppression, while much of the remainder of the country believed that internal enemies on the left were readying a crushing blow against democracy.

While encouraging congressional action on its legislation to enlarge the definition of espionage, sanction wiretapping, and increase federal powers in time of national emergency, Justice Department officials set the stage for political hysteria in testimony before the House and Senate appropriations committees in January and February 1950. Department representatives sought to justify requests for budget increases by portraying an increasing internal danger. They promised vast new actions to protect the United States.

Raymond P. Whearty, acting assistant attorney general in charge of the Criminal Division, termed the Smith Act case of the eleven Communist leaders "the most important" matter before his department and predicted a final Supreme Court decision in 1951. He said that the Department had received FBI reports on 21,105 people who were regarded as possible prosecutorial subjects under the Smith Act. Whearty estimated that "roughly 12,000" would face indictment if the law's constitutionality was upheld.[2] A month later, James J. McInerney, head of the Internal Security Section, increased this estimate to 15,000 persons.[3]

The Whearty and McInerney estimates of 12,000 to 15,000 more Smith Act prosecutions were neither haphazard nor intended simply to frighten the CP. Both attorneys had been associated closely with the FBI for several years. In an effort to gain support for its emergency detention program, the Bureau had informed the Attorney General in 1946 of the existence of the Security Index. In July 1950 the FBI reported that the list contained the names of 11,930 people—including 11,491 CP members—and that its size was increasing.[4] Justice was not informed of three new lists of Americans. If an individual did not appear to be sufficiently disloyal to merit inclusion on the security listing, he was placed on the Communist Index, which was "a comprehensive compilation of individuals of interest to the internal security."

"Comsab" and "Detcom" were designations reserved for those considered most dangerous by the FBI. The former was for those communists considered to have a potential for sabotage "either because of their training or because of their position relative to vital or strategic installations or industry." The "Detcom" program referred to "all top functionaries, all key figures, all individuals tabbed under the Comsab program," and "any other individual who, though he does not fall in the above groups, should be given priority arrest because of some peculiar circumstances."[5] Names for the indexes could be gathered in any kind of FBI investigation. Agents were warned to make no reference to the various lists in any investigative reports.[6]

The appropriations hearings provided an effective forum for a fresh portrayal of the internal "Red Menace." Whearty claimed that "the Smith Act has in effect outlawed" the CPUSA.[7] Hoover said the trial of the Party's eleven leaders had proven that the CP "has as its aim and program an objective to bring about the forcible overthrow of the United States Government." The FBI had to increase its ability to meet this threat, said the Director. Its involvement in the internal security field already was "heavier than it was at the peak of World War II."[8]

Hoover used the February Senate hearings to castigate both philosophical Marxism and those who claimed to see a diminishing internal threat. There were no shadings in the FBI chief's views. It is not surprising that by the end of the year an estimated 200,000 people were included on the Bureau's Communist Index, although the size of the CP was approximately a quarter of that number.[9]

Hoover insisted that the size of the Communist Party made little difference. It was a "branch of a world-wide underground movement," he said, and the threat it represented had "increased proportionately" to the world spread of communism. For every member of the Party, Hoover estimated there were "10 others who follow the party line and who are ready, willing, and able to do the party's work. In other words, there is a potential fifth column of 540,000 people dedicated to this philosophy."[10] When the testimony was released to the press three months later, the President's administrative assistant complained: "Nowhere in Mr. Hoover's statement . . . is there any suggestion that we are licking or even hurting the CPUSA. On the contrary, the whole suggestion is that they are getting more and more dangerous." Stephen Spingarn said that the Director's testimony "should be required for all Government officials who wish to get their appropriations through Congress unscathed." He did not consider Hoover's approach to be entirely honest, but admired its effectiveness.[11]

The hearings were used to put pressure on Congress to pass the Hobbs bill which empowered the Justice Department indefinitely to detain deportees whose native countries refused their return and removed requirements for fair administrative hearings. Hoover decried the "travesty upon our democratic processes" which allowed "subversive aliens" to remain in the United States without being held in custody. He strongly supported new legislation to correct this,[12] as had Attorney General Clark in previous testimony.[13] Immigration and Naturalization Service officials endorsed their position while noting that more than a hundred "political aliens" already were under order of deportation, another hundred were ready for hearings, and more than a thousand were in the process of or being considered for denaturalization proceedings "on subversive grounds."[14]

The Justice Department and its internal security branches were for the Hobbs bill, but the administration was not. Truman was informed, apparently in early January 1950, of the continuing efforts to push the bill. He attempted to take strong action. The President's secretary, Matt Connelly, called the assistant to the Attorney General to tell him of Truman's concern and to direct the Justice Department to halt its actions.[15] The chairman of the House Rules Committee was told on January 25, 1950, of the official administration opposition to the bill, and was asked to hold it up.[16]

Five days later, Truman, with the advice of Spingarn and Special Counsel Charles Murphy, decided to ask the Attorney General to take steps to stop the bill's progress. In a memorandum concerning the meeting, Spingarn expressed his apprehension that a series of events—such as Alger Hiss' conviction and the announcement of construction of the hydrogen bomb—had given "impetus to the passage of increasingly more repressive internal security legislation." He feared a concentration on security to the exclusion of "the protection of individual rights."[17]

Despite the efforts of the President and the White House staff, support for an alien control law did not lessen. Within days of Truman's intervention, the Justice Department again backed the Hobbs bill before the Senate Appropriations Committee. In early May the White House was told that Justice still supported the bill, and that pressure for its passage had grown greatly. Spingarn called Peyton Ford, the Department's second-ranking man, to remind him of the President's strong opposition. Ford said he knew Truman's views, but hoped that the President might change his mind.[18]

Spingarn proposed that stronger action be taken on the Hobbs bill and on the failure to control Justice Department actions. Truman agreed and directed him to meet immediately with Attorney General J. Howard McGrath who had been appointed in mid–1949 upon Clark's elevation to the Supreme Court.[19] The President gave Spingarn a memorandum to take to Justice's chief warning against the dangers of "excessive security" which "encroaches on the individual rights and freedoms which distinguish a democracy from a totalitarian country."

Spingarn was empowered to work out a means of "improving Executive Branch policy formulation in the field of internal security legislation."[20]

Truman's aide had what he considered a "very satisfactory and worthwhile discussion" with McGrath. Claiming that Tom Clark had initiated the Hobbs bill two years earlier, the Attorney General said he had not known of the President's opposition. He promised to "take prompt action to correct this situation."[21] Subsequently the Department prepared a noncommittal letter to the House Rules Committee chairman indicating that "the whole problem involving subversives and undesirable aliens" was being given "further consideration."[22]

On July 17, 1950, the House of Representatives, with debate limited to forty minutes, passed the Hobbs bill by a vote of 326 to 15.[23] The Democratic majority leader, John McCormack of Massachusetts, called the White House that afternoon to inform the President's advisers that the measure had passed. McCormack was "startled" to learn that the President opposed the bill, and said he had understood the President favored it.[24] Administration efforts to control the government's internal security agencies had failed again.

The administration's ineffectiveness in dealing with the Hobbs bill added to a growing feeling of desperation among the President's closest advisers. Spingarn, Clark Clifford, and Max Lowenthal, a former associate, close personal friend, and unofficial adviser to the President, had written a series of confidential memoranda in 1949 to bolster Truman's opposition to the curtailment of civil liberties. They had attacked the use of sedition statutes, such as the Smith Act and the proposed Mundt-Nixon bill, and warned that the greatest internal danger had arisen from "the consuming fear of communism."[25] Truman was urged to speak out and did so at a June 16, 1949, press conference. Asked by a reporter for a "word of counsel" on the fact that "an awful lot of fine people are apparently being branded as reds, unemployables, subversives, and whatnot, these days, and there are any number of trials, hearings, employment situations in the Army, and whatnot," the President replied: "I am going to suggest that you read the history of the Alien and Sedition laws in 1790 under almost exactly the same circumstances, and you will be surprised at the parallel; and then also read how they came out." In answer to further questions, the chief executive added: "Continue to read your history through Jefferson's administration, and you will find what the remedy was. Hysteria finally died down, and things straightened out, and the country didn't go to hell, and it isn't going to now."

When faced with a question as to whether he was "confident that no part of your executive branch is gripped by this hysteria," Truman answered: "I am. I will clean them out if they are."[26] The words, taken almost entirely from the advisory memoranda, were impressive, but there was little change in the administration's actions. The President's comments came in the midst of the communist sedition trial. The contradiction hopelessly compromised the administration's position. Either there was or there was not a sufficient internal threat to justify the use of sedition statutes. Administration actions continued to provide evidence to the American people and Congress of the existence of a domestic danger. The executive branch seemed unable to control the movement toward political hysteria. Subsequent right-wing attacks would not be limited to communists and their allies, but increasingly would come close to Truman himself.

In search of a popular issue which would help keep his senatorial seat two years hence, Wisconsin's Republican Senator Joseph R. McCarthy opened the oratorical assault on February 9, 1950. Speaking before the Women's Republican Club of Wheeling, West Virginia, he patched together from various sources a general attack on the administration's security policies, and declared: "In my opinion the State Department, which is one of the most important government departments, is thoroughly infested with Communists." The Senator claimed he had a list of 205 or 57 names—how many remains a matter of dispute—of Communist Party members who were still State Department employees.[27] In the atmosphere of the period, McCarthy's attack caught on, and he pursued it for all its political value. Spingarn later recalled that McCarthy's charges "caused special trepidations through the entire Government of the United States."[28]

Others were quick to jump on the anticommunist, antiadministration bandwagon. Virginia's Democratic Senator Harry F. Byrd declared that Truman was leading the nation down "a super, non-stop, high-speed, no-turn highway, straight to socialism." He was joined by Massachusetts Republican Representative Joseph W. Martin, who added that the administration "is a prisoner of socialistic advisers, thinkers and planners."[29]

The President's staff attempted to develop a campaign against the right-wing assault. Lowenthal was given space in the White House basement from which he was to organize a counterattack against Senator McCarthy. Lowenthal, who had predicted accurately the hysteria of 1950, was to answer immediately every charge emanating from Wisconsin's junior senator.[30] Truman quietly encouraged liberal opposition to the pressure from the right. In early March he congratulated West Virginia Democratic Senator Harley M. Kilgore for opposing an omnibus anticommunist bill. Kilgore had written Senate Judiciary Committee Chairman Pat McCarran of Nevada that the final committee draft was "fundamentally a sedition bill" which might have dangerous consequences "in the hands of a prejudiced prosecutor or national administration." The President told Kilgore that he had read his letter "with a lot of interest," and was "certainly most happy that you wrote it."[31]

The next month the President commended well-known civil libertarian Zechariah Chafee, Jr., for his opposition to the latest version of the Mundt-Nixon bill. Truman said: "In our early history we had an unfortunate experience under John Adam's [sic] Alien and Sedition Acts, an experience that we do not want repeated in the mid-period of the twentieth century."[32] The chief executive promised to give careful consideration to Chafee's views if the bill reached the White House.

More than private encouragement and basement White House operations were needed if the growing spirit of "McCarthyism" was to be stopped. The President scheduled a major address for April 24, 1950, before the Federal Bar Association. The speech went through at least six drafts within a month before its delivery. Truman challenged the right wing:

Now I am going to tell you how we are not going to fight communism. We are not going to transform our fine FBI into a Gestapo secret police. That is what some people would like to do. We are not going to try to control what our people read and say and think. We are not going to turn the United States into a rightwing totalitarian country in order to deal with a leftwing totalitarian threat.

In short we are not going to end democracy. We are going to keep the Bill of Rights on the books . . . . We know that the greatest threat to us does not come from the communists in this country where they are a noisy but small and universally despised group.[33]

The President had defined the real threat as he viewed it, but he was not about to allow himself to be labeled a procommunist. He promised to strike "hard blows at communist subversion wherever it is found." Truman reminded the right wing that his administration was responsible for the conviction of the eleven Communist leaders, and that 138 "persons are under orders of deportation on grounds involving communism." More than a thousand people were being investigated, the President added, to determine whether their naturalization should be revoked.[34]

It appears that Truman's approach validated right-wing anxieties. If no internal security threat existed, why make such extensive efforts to prosecute domestic communists? Why contemplate a difficult denaturalization procedure when the United States was perfectly safe? The

President wanted to stop the growing political hysteria but had no desire to protect the communist minority. Without protection of the apparently despised minority, the growth of fear would be unavoidable.

Attorney General McGrath added to the confusion through a series of speeches around the country. Using the same tactics as his predecessor, he attempted to defend the administration by attacking the CPUSA. On March 17, 1950, he termed communism a "pagan . . . philosophy" and said: "We must know that its threat to us is real, and probably imminent. We must make our own sacrifices to destroy Communist fanaticism."[35] The next month he called communists "rodents," and asked the American people for greater "vigilance" against this internal enemy. Private citizens were requested to provide the FBI with any information on those persons they suspected. "The most insignificant and seemingly irrelevant bit of information may be of the utmost value when integrated with other data," he said.[36]

In May the Attorney General attacked McCarthy and said that the FBI knew "every Communist in the United States," and none was employed by the federal government.[37] He warned against adopting the "secret police tactics of the Nazis," but promised to push the effort to revoke the citizenship of hundreds of people for involvement in subversive activities.[38] Administration actions seemed to indicate the presence of an internal threat, while the government's rhetoric denied its existence.

The White House staff grew concerned with the administration's image. They, too, attempted to follow the contradictory policy of attacking the right wing while imitating some of its methods. In late May 1950 Spingarn received a letter from a group known as the National Council Against Conscription. It included the names of several prominent members of Americans for Democratic Action. The administrative assistant sent a memorandum to four staff members, saying:

This is quite an impressive list with quite a collection of well-known *anti*-commy liberals on it plus a few *non*-commy liberals who have sometimes let their names be used on letterheads rather indiscriminately (examples: Albert Einstein & John Dewey). Does anyone note any known fellow-travellers on the list (I don't)?[39]

The substance of the letter apparently was less important than the names of those involved in the organization. Conservatives seemingly already had won a considerable victory over the liberal White House staff.

While the administration increasingly felt the right-wing heat, the Communist Party felt the fire. On March 27, 1950, the Supreme Court upheld, by a five to two vote, the contempt of Congress conviction of the CP's general secretary, Eugene Dennis.[40] The case, arising out of Dennis' defiance of the House Un-American Activities Committee, had taken three years to reach the high court.

Four days before Dennis' imprisonment on May 12, an even more devastating legal blow was struck against the Communist Party. The Supreme Court upheld the noncommunist affidavit provision of the Taft-Hartley Act.[41] Strong labor-administration efforts to modify the law, including a tentative attempt to eliminate the affidavit provision, had been futile.[42] This failure added significance to the finding by a majority of the Court that Congress had sufficient evidence to conclude that communists "had infiltrated union organizations not to support and further trade union objectives, including the advocacy of change by democratic methods, but to make them a device by which commerce and industry might be disrupted when the dictates of political policy required such action."[43] Congress had concluded that the CP was unlike other political parties, and the Court agreed. "The right of the public to be protected from evils of conduct" was placed above the exercise of First Amendment freedoms.[44] Under the Constitution's interstate commerce clause, said the Court, Congress had a right to protect the United States from communist-instigated "political strikes."

Justice Robert Jackson's concurring opinion was even more harsh than the Court's decision. Considered a "swing vote" on civil liberties questions, Jackson's position directly threatened the future liberty of the CP leaders. The Justice asserted that Congress had a rational basis for determining that the CP "is a conspiratorial and revolutionary junta, organized to reach ends and to use methods which are incompatible with our constitutional system."[45] He agreed that Congress had sufficient evidence to conclude: "The goal of the Communist Party is to seize powers of government by and for a minority rather than to acquire power through the vote of a free electorate;" the CP "alone among American parties past or present is dominated and controlled by a foreign government;" and "violent and undemocratic means are the calculated and indispensable methods to attain the Communist Party's goal."[46]

With Justices Tom Clark, William Douglas, and Sherman Minton not participating in the decision, Hugo Black was left as the sole dissenter. The Justice attempted to defend his concept of the First Amendment's absolute guarantees, declaring: "Whether religious, political, or both, test oaths are implacable foes of free thought. By approving their imposition, the Court had injected compromise into a field where the First Amendment forbids compromise." Black reminded the Court that "not the least of the virtues of the First Amendment is its protection of each member of the smallest and most unorthodox minority."[47] He recalled that "fears of alien ideologies have frequently agitated the nation and inspired legislation aimed at suppressing advocacy of those ideologies." Black said it was at such times that the Bill of Rights required the Court's most careful protection.[48]

The dissenting Justice understood the significance of the Court's decision and the opinions expressed. Shortly afterwards, he received a letter from a former Supreme Court law clerk congratulating him on his dissent, commenting: "The cause of Civil Liberties seems to be falling pretty low under the majority opinions this year."[49] The Justice responded: "I particularly regretted to have to be in dissent there."[50]

The Court's decision came a month before the Court of Appeals heard arguments concerning the Smith Act convictions of the CP leaders. The opinion of the Supreme Court's justices inevitably would weigh heavily with the lower court. The high court had found that Congress had a right to conclude that the CP was an internal danger. It also had indicated a willingness to restrict freedom of speech and association. The Court's attitude played a significant role in heightening both the anti-communist climate and the fears of American communists.

The CPUSA was beset by a mounting, effective attack from the outside amidst a continuing internal ideological struggle among its top leaders. Increasing international tension, together with domestic threats against the CP, were pushing the Party towards William Z. Foster's "leftist" position. As the CP moved in this direction, it gave more ammunition to its enemies.

A combination of government action and CIO pressure lessened the already depleted CP influence in organized labor. Philip Murray and other CIO leaders had determined it was necessary to drive communists from the labor movement. One observer believed the decision to expel the left-wing unions from the CIO resulted from a desire to limit the effectiveness of a right-wing attack against the labor movement.[51] Other historians suggested that the expulsions came as the result of an effort "to end political opposition to the Democratic Party within the CIO."[52]

One of the few remaining communists in a leadership position, Max Perlow, president of the United Furniture Workers Union, resigned in June 1949 so that he could sign the Taft-Hartley affidavit and maintain his union position. Communist Labor Secretary John Williamson implicitly criticized Perlow's decision and said that it should not be a precedent. He maintained that communist labor leaders had an obligation to win the workers over to an anti-Taft-Hartley position, rather than capitulating before the law's requirements.[53]

The CIO leadership was unwilling to accept any accommodation with communist union heads. At the October 1949 convention of the labor organization, the United Electrical Workers, the largest of the unions alleged to have a procommunist leadership, was expelled and a charter given to establish an anticommunist electrical union. Other expulsions followed soon after. The Committee on the Constitution recommended an amendment to bar from the Executive Board members of the CP or those who pursue "policies and activities directed toward the achievement of the program or the purposes of the Communist Party . . . rather than the objectives and policies set forth in the constitution of the CIO."[54]

There was little the CP could have done to save its union allies by the time of the eleven's trial. The CIO's leadership had much to gain by the expulsions and nothing but civil libertarian principles to lose— the latter apparently not very imporant in the political context of the period. John Gates has argued that although anticommunist action apparently was inevitable, communist actions "made it easier for the expulsion policy to be carried through."[55]

There were tentative efforts within the CP to develop a more independent analysis of the world situation, but these were cut short again by internal and external developments. At his deportation hearing in September 1949, Alexander Bittelman used the theoretical line developed for the trial of the Party's leaders. He said that although he considered "the law of violent proletarian revolution . . . is a general, universal law of social change from capitalism to Socialism," this did not preclude the possibility of an individual road to socialism within a particular country. "There is a fundamental difference between teaching the Marxist-Leninist theory of social change, including the law of violent proletarian revolution," he said, "and teaching the overthrow of a particular government by violence."

Bittelman rejected the inevitability of war and asserted that the strengths of the socialist nations, together with "the forces of democracy," would be sufficient to "impose peace upon the imperialist war makers." He conceded that government success in its anticommunist actions would intensify the dangers of war and fascism, but assumed that these efforts would fail.[56]

As the Smith Act trial drew to a close, the confidence of the CP's leaders began to wane. The Peekskill riot of early September 1949 played a significant part in the change of attitude. A Party leader referred to the events at Peekskill as proving that "the Trial itself has already let loose a wave of fascist violence." It appeared that a guilty verdict had become inevitable, prompting a warning: "If the authors of this frame-up trial are allowed to go through with their pro-fascist intent, this will let loose new dangers for the entire American people."[57]

Although long expected, the verdict of the jury badly shook the Party. The trial judge's refusal to grant bail seemed to justify the belief that legal avenues quickly were being closed off. The Party reacted with some confusion. The CP's newspaper declared: "The press is already saying that this verdict outlaws the Communist Party, which is not true; all such talk is intended to frighten people."[58] On the same day as the appearance of that editorial, William Z. Foster, Elizabeth Gurley Flynn, and the heads of major CP state and district organizations made a statement with a radically different emphasis.

This verdict gives aid and comfort to the pro-fascist forces that threaten peace and democracy in America and throughout the world.

Its aim is to try to outlaw the Communist Party, in violation of the constitutional guarantees of the Bill of Rights, as the first step toward new and more drastic measures of repression against the civil liberties of the American people.[59]

The international situation seemed to fall in with national events. The Communist Information Bureau issued a statement in Moscow at the end of November 1949. This coordinating agency of major communist parties declared: "It would be mistaken and harmful to underestimate the danger of a new war prepared by the imperialist powers headed by the United States and Great Britain."[60] Domestic fascism and world war seemed imminent to the leaders of the CPUSA. For a year the Party had emphasized the possibilities of avoiding both. The conviction of its leaders and the comments of international authorities destroyed the bases of its policy. Bittelman received a Party document in December dealing with the 1950 election outlook. He wrote at the end: "We should . . . consider making a restatement of our main line and sharper emphasis on the war danger which is not diminishing but growing."[61]

The Party's course of action in the event of war or fascism already had been planned. It hurried its efforts to organize an underground structure. In September 1949 Eugene Dennis publicly said: "We declare here tonight that if the executioners' legal axe falls on the twelve leaders of the Communist party—our party, although crippled, will survive." His comment was interpreted correctly to be a threat to go underground.[62]

The effort to find hiding places was accelerated. Portable mimeographing machines were obtained, and district organizers were given instruction in their use. A communications network, using high-frequency radio equipment, was inaugurated, although still on a limited basis.[63] Each national leader of the Party was instructed to provide himself with a temporary place to stay and a means of contacting the national office "in case of attack."[64]

Following the Smith Act case verdict, George Watt, head of the National Committee's underground apparatus, returned to Mexico to enlarge the security structure he had established earlier in the year. He brought with him three important figures in the CP who were to take up local residence. They were to serve as a part of the CP's reserve leadership in case a massive legal assault wiped out the Party's leaders in the United States. All were trained in the use of a secret communications system, including the use of invisible ink and coded messages.[65]

A few in the Party's leadership protested that plans for the underground inevitably would undermine the CP's open, legal activities and would lead to further isolation. National Committee member Flynn observed that "this is 1949, not 1919." Gates told her she was an "old lady" and did not understand the existing situation.[66]

In January 1950 the National Committee again accepted an economic analysis which predicted "an economic crash of catastrophic proportions."[67] New York State Party Chairman Robert Thompson, aligned with Foster, predicted "the rapid maturing of a cyclical economic crisis of vast proportions."[68] He said that Truman administration efforts to halt this process would lead to war abroad and fascism at home.[69]

In a letter to the National Committee on February 21, 1950, Foster defended himself against internal Party criticism. He cautioned that "there might possibly be among our comrades a tendency towards an underestimation of the fascist danger," and warned: "These dangerous signs of fascism are increasing, rather than decreasing." The Party National Chairman dissociated himself from the deposition he had given at the trial of the CP's leaders. His previous emphasis on a peaceful transition to socialism was rejected. "We have learned from Lenin's teachings and from all the practical revolutionary experience of the international working class," he said, "that the bourgeoisie will always fight arms in hand when it feels that the life of capitalism is at stake."[70]

Foster's "left" position was opposed by a group centering around Illinois State Chairman Gil Green. In an article published in March 1950, which Green had started the previous October while in prison, he rejected the inevitability of war and fascism. He said that a mass movement could be created to stop these two perils. Accepting the thesis that economic crisis and class conflict had accelerated the movement toward these dangers, Green maintained that these conditions also had weakened "American capitalism in the eyes of the masses" and had made possible its defeat.[71]

Green's more moderate position was made difficult by events which seemed to support Foster's analysis. *The Daily Worker* began a campaign against the Mundt-Nixon bill, declaring: "If the . . . bill becomes law, the Constitution of the United States will be dead and buried. There will be nothing left of it but a fond memory. America will have entered the portals over which are written POLICE STATE FASCISM AND WAR."[72] An enlarged meeting of the National Committee from March 23 to 25, 1950, demonstrated a changed Party emphasis.

Dennis accepted Foster's privately expressed opinion that "there exists a gross underestimation of the process of fascization now going on in the country."[73] Anticommunist legislation in Congress provided the Party's leaders with evidence they could not ignore. Alexander Bittelman advised Dennis to include in his report the concept that "increasing fascisation in all spheres plus more intensified attacks upon the economic standards are part of war preparations."[74] Dennis followed the advice, and declared that passage of the Mundt-Nixon bill "would constitute a major victory for the war camp."[75]

The CP general secretary accepted criticism of the "party line" during the eleven's trial. "We did not sufficiently defend the historic democratic rights of the people, of the majority, to revolution" he said, and added that the concept of the "dictatorship of the proletariat" also should have been upheld more forcefully.[76]

The entire CP leadership supported Dennis' conclusions. Gus Hall warned: "Each additional step toward war is prepared by a step toward fascism at home," and said the CP would not comply with the new anticommunist legislation if it was passed.[77] Henry Winston, the Party's organizational secretary, asserted that the public threat to arrest 12,000 additional communists was a portent of the coming "fascist offensive."[78] Green contributed to the meeting's general tenor by calling for greater vigilance by Party adherents. He demanded that the personal and political activities of each member be investigated to discover "government spies and provocateurs."[79] The Illinois State Chairman called for a "Leninist party" which would have "no united front approach to theoretical and ideological questions."[80]

The CP's quest for ideological purity led to another attack on its potential allies. Henry Wallace and the remnants of the Progressive Party were criticized harshly for writing a plank in their party's 1950 platform which blamed both the United States and the Soviet Union for the Cold War's development. CP members were instructed never to vote for resolutions which condemned the Soviets.[81] The National Association for the Advancement of Colored People—to which the CP had appealed during its leaders' trial—was berated for a "policy of pseudo-liberalism" which tied the organization to the Truman administration and the "Social-Democratic" leadership of organized labor.[82] These labor leaders were described as "class-collaborationist" and were said to be working "to make it easier for Wall Street to hurl humanity into the bloody holocaust of World War III and to impose upon the American people a regime of fascist oppression and slavery."[83]

Dennis' imprisonment exacerbated the CP's feelings of isolation and internal disunity. Hall was chosen as a compromise candidate to act temporarily as the Party's general secretary. Foster supported Thompson for the position, while Dennis reportedly wanted Green.[84] On the eve of his imprisonment, Dennis cautioned Party members: "We must guard against fatalistic notions that it is impossible in the United States in this period of rampant imperialist reaction to reverse an outrageous court decision or to check the advocates of a fascist police state and a third world war."[85] Hall's emphasis was different. He told the Party: "Today the forces of peace are not yet strongly enough organized to be able to stop any war." Hall described recent Supreme Court decisions as "wartime rulings and findings" which were part of a "desperate war drive" by the ruling class.[86]

A few members of the CP leadership attempted to retard the Party's leftward movement, but were unsuccessful. Bittelman privately criticized an initial draft of Foster's new book, *An Outline History of the Americas*. He wrote to Foster suggesting that his treatment of war and fascism were inadequate. Bittelman believed that Foster had portrayed both as imminent. He asked that the draft be changed to indicate that only "a process of fascisation" was taking place and that *"war is not inevitable*—the war danger is growing but so are the opportunities for licking it."[87] The advice was rejected. In June 1950 an article by Foster appeared which reversed his previous suggestion of a peaceful road to socialism.[88] Even the most optimistic National Committee member, Elizabeth Gurley Flynn, wrote: "No one can have illusions today as to favorable court actions."[89]

With little confidence, the Party's attorneys faced the Court of Appeals on June 21, 1950, to argue for reversal of the convictions of eleven of the CPUSA's leaders. Their arguments were familiar. They had been made before in the District Court. The three-judge panel was asked to apply the "clear and present danger" standard and to determine that the 1925 *Gitlow* decision was not applicable. The appellants argued that the trial had been conducted in a prejudiced atmosphere, and that the Judge had added to the climate of bias through his actions and attitudes. Lawyers for the communist leaders reminded the Court of the Justice Department's threat to bring 12,000 additional prosecutions if the

Smith Act was upheld, and asked that this threat of political repression be stopped.[90]

The government's written brief relied heavily on the *Gitlow* decision's concept that a legislative body has a right to determine and restrict specific kinds of speech which lead to a "substantive evil." It denied the necessity of proving a "clear and present danger," but said such a peril could be shown.[91] Chief Judge Learned Hand sharply questioned the government's attorney during oral arguments on June 23. He interrupted Robert W. Ginnane to comment: "Anyone who undertakes to overthrow the government by force and violence undoubtedly falls within the condemnation of numberless statutes, but we are here concerned with whether the teaching and advocacy of the propriety of doing so shall be unlawful." Hand wondered whether Thomas Jefferson's advocacy of revolt against "utterly offensive" governments would be circumscribed by the Smith Act, and indicated doubt concerning the existence of a "clear and present danger."[92]

It appears that two of the three judges, Thomas Swan and Harrie Chase, were "ill disposed" toward the defendants even before the hearings began. Their private memoranda indicated a predisposition to rule against the communist leaders.[93] The position of Judge Hand was considered far more important. He was perhaps the most widely respected appellate judge in the United States. Although the CP might lose the case at the circuit court level, a dissent by Hand would carry great weight with the Supreme Court. Once again, outside events intervened to block this communist hope.

On June 25, 1950, the Korean War began. The possibility of a favorable Court of Appeals dissent or of stopping comprehensive anticommunist legislation faded quickly. Many observers have noted the critical part played by the war in furthering internal hysteria and setting the stage for passage of repressive laws.[94] Events in Korea certainly created a new emotional plateau, but the essential elements of a right-wing-initiated panic had been growing steadily for some time.

More than thirty bills involving internal security were working their way through Congress before the war began.[95] The most important of these measures had been under consideration for several years. They included seven versions of the Mundt-Nixon bill to control "subversive activities." The Hobbs bill was still very much alive in the House, and the Department of Justice's espionage legislation had passed the House earlier in the year and was before the Senate.

The White House staff had consistently opposed all these proposals. The war did not change the attitude of the President's advisers immediately, but Spingarn informed the President that "the current version of the Mundt-Nixon bill . . . is gaining strength as a result of the tensions created by the Korean situation." He said that unless the administration developed alternatives—"it is usually difficult to lick something with nothing"—drastic internal security legislation was likely to pass. Under these circumstances, Spingarn proposed approval of Justice's bill to enlarge the definition of espionage and increase federal powers in time of national emergency.[96]

On July 20 Spingarn outlined three steps to meet the threat of extreme legislation. He suggested the establishment of an independent group to study the problems of security and individual rights, a presidential message to Congress, and the drafting of new alternative legislation.[97] The administration sought a more direct means of reassuring the American people than Spingarn's proposals. At the Justice Department's urging, it turned to the FBI again as a symbol of national protection against domestic threats. The restatement of FBI preeminence in the field of internal security, which had been stopped by the White House staff two years earlier, was issued, although somewhat weakened.

On July 24, 1950, Truman made a public statement reiterating 1939 and 1943 presidential directives providing for FBI control of investigative work in "matters relating to espionage, sabotage, subversive activities, and related matters." The President gave his support to this continuing directive and said: "I suggest that all patriotic organizations and individuals likewise report all such information relating to" these areas to the FBI.[98] There was no recognition of the significant difference between the 1950 statement and the previous two. The 1943 directive had not mentioned "subversive activities," and that of 1939 had not authorized investigation of such matters.[99]

Hoover issued his own statement two days later. He asked the citizenry to "be alert" and to report even "a small bit of information" which might indicate the possibility of subversion or sabotage. Decrying "hysteria, witch-hunts and vigilantes," the FBI Director warned:

The forces which are most anxious to weaken our internal security are not always easy to identify. Communists have been trained in deceit and secretly work toward the day when they hope to replace our American way of life with a Communist dictatorship. They utilize cleverly camouflaged movements, such as some peace groups and civil rights organizations, to achieve their sinister purposes. While they as individuals are difficult to identify, the Communist Party line is clear. Its first concern is the advancement of Soviet Russia and the godless Communist cause. It is important to learn to know the enemies of the American way of life.[100]

The administration's effort to reassure the people once again apparently led to a heightening of fear.

The President did consider Spingarn's proposal for a "Presidential Commission on Internal Security and Individual Rights," and accepted the suggestions for a message and alternative legislation. Work on both began immediately. Truman told his advisers that he was concerned that the kind of legislation Congress seemed prepared to pass was dangerous. "The situation in this respect," he was quoted as saying, "was the worst it had been since the Alien and Sedition laws of 1798."[101]

The August 1, 1950, decision on the communists' appeal of their Smith Act convictions made work on the presidential message more difficult. Written by Chief Judge Hand, the unanimous opinion appeared to be a product of the hysteria and, in turn, increased the general sense of fear in the United States.

Hand emphasized that the phrase "clear and present danger" required interpretation and that competing interests had to be weighed.[102] He rejected the concept that a "present danger" need be immediate. To maintain this position, he believed, would be to allow future evils which we would not permit for ourselves. "In each case," the jurist declared, the courts "must ask whether the gravity of the 'evil,' discounted by its improbability, justified such invasion of free speech as is necessary to avoid the danger."[103] A probable danger exists if the conspirators intend to "strike as soon as success seems possible," and Hand added, "no one in his senses would strike sooner." Within the Communist Party, Hand found thousands of "rigidly and ruthlessly disciplined" members for whom "the violent capture of all existing governments is one article of the creed of that faith" and who are committed to illegal means. Either American democracy "must meet that faith and that creed on the merits, or it will perish," he warned.[104] The world situation, he said, created a condition of "the utmost gravity" with crises such as the Berlin airlift creating the possibility of world war. "We do not understand how one could ask for a more probable danger, unless we must wait till the actual eve of hostilities." Revolutionary success had been achieved in other nations during the past thirty years under similar circumstances, he declared, and that lesson must not be forgotten by the United States.[105]

The decision added impetus to the drive for restrictive legislation. The court appeared to have verified the existence of an internal danger. Attorney General McGrath sought to use the decision to the administration's advantage. He informed the cabinet that he would ask for revocation of the eleven convicted leaders' bail since the "Court has held that they are a danger to national security."[106]

With no objection from the President, the United States attorney was directed to ask the Court of Appeals to cancel the CP leaders' bonds on the grounds that they "are continuing the same course of conduct which led to their conviction." He said that the communists had criticized American policy regarding the war in Korea and warned against the dangers of fascism in the United States. "They should not be at large in this hour of national crisis," argued the Justice Department attorney.[107] The court, by a two-to-one vote, sustained the government's position, but stayed its decision pending possible Supreme Court action on the issue.

The pressure for extreme congressional action was becoming irresistible. At a July 27 press conference, Truman again attempted to use words to hold back the threatening flood. He warned against creating an "alien and sedition mood" as had occurred in 1798.[108] His effort was little more effective than putting a finger in one hole of a dam filled with fissures. The dam was ready to break.

Spingarn reported on August 1, the same day as the Court of Appeals' decision, that there was little possibility of stopping the Mundt-Nixon bill. Heavy pressure for passage was being exerted by the American Legion and the Chamber of Commerce, and the Senate's Democratic Policy Committee was about to consider it favorably.[109] Spingarn proposed rushing the President's internal security message.

Truman delivered his special message on August 8, 1950. It was an effort to project an administration concerned with the needs of real security but determined to maintain constitutional guarantees. The President again warned against the excesses of the alien and sedition period, but promised "to keep our freedom secure against internal as well as external attack, without at the same time unduly limiting individual rights and liberties."[110] Much of the first part of the speech was an exposition of the communist danger. He accused communists of engaging in "espionage, sabotage, and other acts subversive of our national safety." They had sought to "infiltrate and gain control" of mass organizations, he said, but had been unsuccessful in the United States.[111]

The President claimed that existing laws had proven adequate to meet the real threat. He pointed to the Smith Act convictions of the communist leaders and the appellate court's affirmation of that decision. Other laws to deal with specific acts of sabotage or espionage—by citizens or aliens—were in existence and ready for use where needed, he said.[112]

Accepting the advice that alternative legislation was necessary, Truman gave support to two additional measures. He recommended that Congress "remedy certain defects in the present laws concerning espionage, the registration of foreign agents, and the security of national defense installations"—essentially the Justice Department's internal security bill. He gave his support also to a modified version of the Hobbs bill. The President said the Attorney General needed greater supervisory powers over deportable aliens, but continued to oppose the detention provision of the earlier bill.[113]

The chief executive ended by defending the Bill of Rights. He attacked "extremists who urge us to adopt police state measures," and added: "Laws forbidding dissent do not prevent subversive activities; they merely drive them into more secret and more dangerous channels."[114]

Instead of serving as a signal for reflection, as the President hoped, the speech inflamed the political atmosphere. Truman's public endorsement of additional legislation apparently was a sign for many that a real internal danger existed. Democrats seemingly were free to support both the President and the new domestic laws increasingly demanded by the public.

Two days after the President's message, Senator McCarran combined several of the internal security measures into what Spingarn described as "a blockbuster bill."[115] Included in the new omnibus proposal was the latest version of the Mundt-Nixon bill, the Hobbs bill, the Justice Department's internal security measure, and McCarran's own legislation to control more closely the entry and deportation of aliens.

Introduction of the McCarran Internal Security Act encouraged a desperate administration search for an effective alternative. The Justice Department already had its own proposal. Acting on a suggestion made a month earlier by Spingarn, the department had prepared a new substitute for Congress' internal security bills. It was given to Democratic Majority Leader Scott Lucas of Illinois who was in a close race to keep his Senate seat. The measure included a legislative finding, patterned after the Mundt-Nixon bill, that "communist" and "communist front" organizations "present a clear and present danger to the security of the United States and to the existence of free American institutions."

The substantive portion of Justice's proposal provided an amendment to the 1938 Foreign Agents Registration Act. "Foreign aid organizations"—groups formed to seek the overthrow of the government— were to be required to register with the Attorney General, and to provide full membership lists, organizational data, and disclosure of financial resources and disbursements. The Attorney General was given the power to determine subject organizations, with the proviso that his decision be "supported by any evidence constituting reasonable ground."

The Justice Department gave Lucas the impression that the proposal had White House approval. When the President learned of the measure on August 8, he asked his staff for an analysis.[116] Spingarn and presidential aide David D. Lloyd agreed the measure was a "dangerous bill" which should not be supported. The proposal was so broadly drawn, and the evidential standards so loosely written, they believed, that many "innocent" organizations would be trapped in it.[117] On August 10 Spingarn attempted to convince staff members of the Senate Democratic Policy Committee to ignore the Justice Department draft. He emphasized that the President would not support any measure beyond those recommended on August 8. Spingarn called the Justice Department on August 11 and 12 to make the same point.[118]

Despite intervention by the White House staff and the chief executive, Justice continued to push a slightly changed version of its substitute bill. A five-page accompanying explanation described the measure as a simple financial disclosure statute.[119] The President's assistants intensified their opposition. Lloyd commented: "The substitute is worse than the Mundt bill." He particularly objected to the powers given the Attorney General.[120]

The administration attempted to block McCarran's internal security legislation by supporting an amended version of the Hobbs bill and Justice's original espionage measure.[121] After a week's effort it seemed more practical to offer a separate proposal. The new bill, embodying the President's recommendations, was introduced into Congress on the same day as the Senate Judiciary Committee reported favorably on the McCarran Act.

The administration sought to rally support for its proposal. The White House staff sent out numerous letters. Spingarn asked for Hoover's endorsement of the administration's "professional counter intelligence bill . . . in opposition to the amateurish internal security legislation embodied in the Mundt-Ferguson bill and 5/6ths of the McCarran bill."[122] The Attorney General provided Senator Lucas with a long analysis questioning the wisdom and constitutionality of McCarran's proposals.[123] There was little positive response to these efforts.

Liberal Senate Democrats were certain that the President's proposal would not stop the McCarran Act's passage. On the morning of September 6, 1950, eight senators met with the President to discuss an "emergency detention" amendment which they were prepared to introduce as a substitute for McCarran's bill. Truman told them to go ahead if they believed it necessary, but reserved judgment on their proposal.[124]

Later that day the bill was introduced into the Senate by Kilgore, Paul Douglas of Illinois, Minnesota's Hubert Humphrey, New York's Herbert Lehman, Frank Graham of North Carolina, and Estes Kefauver of Tennessee. The "Kilgore amendment" provided for mass detention of civilians during a presidentially proclaimed internal security emergency. The Attorney General was delegated the authority to apprehend persons by issuing individual warrants based on suspicion of possible disloyalty. Administrative review of detention would be provided by the Justice Department, a special Detention Review Board, and ultimately by the courts. Imprisonment of Communist Party members was specified, as well as any other person about whom there was "reasonable ground to conclude that such person may engage in, or conspire with others to engage in, espionage or sabotage."

South Dakota Republican Senator Karl Mundt described the Kilgore amendment as "police state legislation,"[125] but the President apparently disagreed. At a September 7 press conference he said he would veto the McCarran Act if it were passed, but would not comment on the Democrats' substitute measure.[126] Two months earlier, Spingarn had described a proposal similar to Kilgore's as "maybe worse than the Mundt-Nixon bill," of doubtful constitutionality, and certain to be labeled by liberals as a "concentration camp bill."[127] He had been proven wrong. Liberals introduced the measure, and conservatives attacked it.

Within a few days the Senate refused to consider the "liberal Democratic substitute," and the McCarran Act was scheduled for a vote. The House already had approved a somewhat different companion measure. Democratic congressional leaders informed Truman that the bill would pass and unanimously recommended that he sign it. The President did not give them a commitment, but significantly did agree that if the bill were vetoed, it would be done quickly enough to allow Congress an opportunity to override before adjournment.[128]

The Senate passed the McCarran Act with seven opposing votes on September 12, 1950. The action was taken only after the Kilgore substitute was added to the measure through an amendment offered by the Democratic majority leader. The efforts to block the bill thus disintegrated in a series of actions which inflamed the political climate and ultimately led to even more restrictive legislation than proposed by the right wing.

The President ordered his staff to analyze the law intensively as it was being considered in conference committee. Within days of the Senate's action, five separate drafts of a possible veto message were prepared as well as a signing statement. On September 19 the conference committee filed its report, and the President decided a veto would be necessary.[129] Spingarn strongly supported the decision. In a memorandum the next day, he wrote: "The signing of the bill would represent an action of moral appeasement on a matter of highest principle." Truman's assistant said that the bill which came out of conference was even "worse" than the original McCarran Act, and warned: "Before we finished [sic] with this business we might well go through a period that would make the Alien and Sedition Laws look like one of moderation."[130]

The departments of Justice, Defense, and State, along with the Central Intelligence Agency advised a veto. Attorney General McGrath personally brought his written recommendation to a cabinet meeting.[131] The agencies most concerned with internal security investigations particularly objected to the Kilgore amendment. They had pressed for the concept of mass detention for many years, but believed Kilgore's approach would not guarantee the absolute security they were seeking. They feared *habeas corpus* proceedings might be used to free detained persons. The requirements for issuance of warrants and various appeals procedures were "entirely impractical" in an emergency, argued an internal Justice Department memorandum. An approach providing complete administrative control of the entire procedure was preferred.[132]

On September 20 Congress passed the final version of the Internal Security Act. In accordance with Truman's instructions, the White House staff worked feverishly, through four more drafts and endless changes, to complete a veto message in time for an almost certain override. The message was delivered to Congress on the afternoon of September 22, along with an unprecedented note from the President to each congressman urging careful consideration of the veto before a vote.

The President said that much of the new law would be ineffective and would weaken rather than strengthen the fight against internal communism. He claimed the measure would require the FBI "to waste immense amounts of time and energy attempting to carry out its unworkable registration provisions."[133] Registration of the CP was favored by Truman, but he feared that applying these provisions to "communist front organizations" would endanger basic freedoms.[134] The chief executive endorsed six provisions of the law, mainly those he had recommended, and said he would sign a measure which included only these. The message, as a whole, was not nearly as critical of the law as had been internal administration memoranda. Its recognition of the existence of a domestic danger—albeit a relatively minor one—would do nothing to hold back the growth of hysteria.

The House almost immediately overrode the presidential veto by a vote of 186 to 48. The Senate began debate that same evening. A small band of liberals, encouraged by telephone calls from the President, decided to keep discussing the issue at least until the following day in order to bring their case before the public. They took the floor in shifts throughout the night. Led by North Dakota Republican Senator William Langer, who spoke for five hours until collapsing in a diabetic coma, the small group of liberals talked until the next morning. At 9:30 A.M. Humphrey's legislative assistant called to ask the President if they should continue the debate. They did not want to appear to be carrying on a filibuster. The President said that if they were not strong enough to stop Senate action entirely, they might as well allow a vote that afternoon. Truman encouraged the White House staff to call wavering senators, but there was little hope. At 4:30 P.M. the Senate voted fifty-seven to ten to override the veto.[135] Perhaps the most repressive legislation in the history of the United States had become law.

The Korean War, the Court of Appeals decision in the Smith Act case, and the events leading to passage of the McCarran Act caused Communist Party members to develop a virtual siege mentality. The worst of their fears had been realized—just as their leaders had been predicting for three years. As each new disaster unfolded, the Party's leaders reacted with a sense of panic that was transmitted quickly to the general membership. Truman's decision to send troops to Korea meant, said CP leaders, that "atomic war threatens the people of the world."[136] "Operation Dictatorship" had begun in the United States, wrote the Party's temporary chief, Gus Hall, and the "zero hour" had been reached.[137] He told a National Committee meeting in September: "As our country is being pushed to the precipice of world war it is being pushed at great speed toward fascism."[138]

Upon passage of the McCarran Act, a communist statement claimed: "No, all is not lost. No, fascism has not come to power."[139] The tone of leadership comments and the reality of Party actions belied this assessment. Foster warned: "The new anti-communist law is a long step towards the establishment of a police state and fascism in the United States."[140] Hall demanded that the CP "Bolshevize" its ranks—a call for a smaller, more security conscious, largely underground party. "If we had always kept in mind that under the best of conditions, legality of a Communist party under capitalism means in reality only semi-legality," he complained, "we would not be facing some of the problems that we face today."[141]

The Party further disrupted its structure and the remaining opportunities to operate legally by ordering elements of the underground into operation. CP members in various sections of the country were told to drop out of all Party work so that they might become part of the "reserve leadership" which would function once higher leaders were arrested. They were expected to move from their homes, change their names, and maintain only the most minimal contact with the CP.[142]

Communists were required to write autobiographies of their Party and personal lives to help in ferreting out possible government agents. All members were ordered to register—apply for CP membership again—in the hope of weeding out weak or suspected elements. The Party's organizational secretary soon complained that many clubs were decimated in the process. A large unit in a steel plant dropped 86 percent of its members, while only 5 percent of the rubber workers in another area were registered. He reported that only one percent of the membership in an industrial plant was permitted to remain in the Party.[143]

Following passage of the Internal Security Act, the CP began preparations for a December national convention. The first draft of a convention resolution was written in early October 1950. The document bitterly attacked the Truman administration and attributed passage of the McCarran Act totally to the atmosphere created by presidential actions. A "rapid movement" toward a new world war and fascism in the United States was emphasized. Party members were asked to beware of both "right opportunism" and "left sectarianism."[144]

In a letter to the National Committee, Foster approved the main outline of the draft resolution, but criticized it for not being sufficiently militant. The Truman administration and the heads of organized labor had to be exposed, he said, as "the main war instrument of American imperialism" and "the war agents of imperialism." The major internal danger to the Party came from rightists, he said, who wished to differentiate international from domestic issues. The Party chairman demanded that the resolution "stress the general correctness of the Party's political line since the [1945] Emergency Convention."[145]

The resolution was changed to conform to Foster's criticisms. A new draft on October 22 declared that "a police state" already had come into existence, and the United States was "in transition to the open and terroristic dictatorship of the most reactionary and warlike circles of American finance capital—to fascism." Rightist "illusions" of legal victories were attacked. The Party could only succeed through "political struggles of the masses," the new draft said.[146]

Selective enforcement of the McCarran Act began as the CP's resolution was being framed. Three days after the passage of the law, the Attorney General informed the cabinet that he was proceeding as quickly as possible to implement "the iniquities of the bill."[147] McGrath assured the press that he was "taking every necessary step to enforce the law" and would "scrupulously enforce the Act as written."[148] The

President continued to criticize the law, but said: "I expect to enforce it to the letter."[149]

On October 19, 1950, the Attorney General issued regulations for enforcement of the McCarran Act's provisions concerning registration by "communist" organizations and immigration procedures.[150] Four days later he appointed a five-member Subversive Activities Control Board which was to hold hearings prior to the designation of organizations which were to register.[151] McGrath also received a 660-page report from the FBI to be used in proving that the CP was a group coming within the law's purview.[152]

At 3:00 A.M. on the morning of October 23, Immigration and Naturalization Service personnel began the apprehension of eighty-six aliens who had been on bail pending deportation proceedings. The arrests went on until midnight.[153] In court action, the government argued that the McCarran Act gave it the right to hold aliens in custody without bail at the discretion of the Attorney General pending final determination of deportability. The Department of Justice attorney said: "Those aliens who threaten our defenses and our national security are enemies."[154]

The courts did not uphold the government's position. On November 17 Judge Sylvester J. Ryan freed sixteen aliens from detention on Ellis Island and held that the denial of bail "was arbitrary and an abuse of discretion on the part of the Attorney General." He added that there was "not a scintilla" of evidence that these people were seeking to overthrow the government or presented a "security peril." Included among the group of freed prisoners were communist leaders Bittelman, Claudia Jones, and Betty Gannett.[155] Despite this setback, the INS moved in December for final deportation orders against each of these leaders.

Only government agencies sometimes were exempted from strict adherence to the McCarran Act's provisions. McGrath informed the FBI that it could disregard the detention provisions of the law and "proceed with the program as previously outlined." Justice Department officials were quoted in internal memoranda as saying that the law was "undoubtedly in conflict with the Department's proposed detention program" and that the act's provisions were "unworkable."[156]

The deputy Attorney General told the FBI that all persons listed on its Security Index "should be considered subjects for immediate apprehension" in an emergency.[157] The Index included the names of individuals considered potentially dangerous by the Bureau, while the McCarran Act required individual warrants based on "reasonable grounds" to believe the subject would conspire to or engage in espionage or sabotage.

The letter of the law was to be enforced for communists, but apparently partially to be circumvented with regard to the law enforcement agencies' legal responsibilities.

Lawyers for the CP leaders argued before the Supreme Court on December 4, 1950, in an effort to overturn the Smith convictions, but the Party had no "illusions" of victory. The Court had limited its review to the question of the constitutionality of the Smith Act. The defendants' attorneys repeatedly warned that mass arrests would follow if the law were upheld, and a brief for the American Civil Liberties Union supported this contention.[158] The government did not dispute this claim.

The defense lawyers maintained that a "clear and present danger" within the United States had never been shown. Judge Hand had used his own opinion of the international situation in 1948, they said, to justify the view that a domestic "Red Menace" existed.[159] The attorneys said the government had rejected use of the "clear and present danger" test at the trial stage, and that the Court of Appeals had used a different standard for restriction of free speech than that used by Judge Medina.[160]

The government insisted that the more restrictive *Gitlow* decision could have been used, but willingly accepted Hand's standard for restricting freedom of speech. The United States attorney said: "Utterances . . . like the petitioner's advocacy of political violence, are inherently evil and are as devoid of the values protected by the First Amendment as obscene and fraudulent utterances."[161] The Smith Act was constitutional, the government claimed, and could be applied "to the American leaders of a worldwide totalitarian political movement which employs freely the methods of military aggression, civil war, espionage, sabotage and mendacious propaganda to overthrow non-Communist governments."[162]

The Supreme Court's decision would take several months, but only Elizabeth Gurley Flynn among CP leaders had any hope. "I do believe there will be a carefully considered and not a speedy snap judgment," she wrote after viewing the Court's proceedings. "I am not a fatalist, nor do I have legislative illusions. But I am convinced, it's not all cut and dried and that the American people can influence events, even here. I believe we have a fighting chance to win it."[163]

The CP's fifteenth national convention, meeting in the last four days of 1950, was a somber affair. There were constant references to the Party's growing weakness and its inability to attract new people.[164] The thirteen members of the National Committee were reelected, and nine "alternative members" were chosen. No one was aware that it would be more than six years before another general meeting of the Party would take place, but a heavy sense of foreboding penetrated the convention hall.

Three months later, at 8:00 A.M. on March 12, 1951, CP general secretary Eugene Dennis was set free after spending ten months in prison for "contempt of Congress." The FBI gave impressive attention to the Party's head. Two days prior to Dennis' scheduled release, special agent Edward Scheidt "urgently" teletyped FBI Director Hoover to inform him of CP plans to greet their leader. There was to be a reception at Communist Party headquarters, and the FBI man reported that roast turkey and scotch whiskey would be served. The Bureau's agents were assigned to cover the day's events.[165]

Dennis' emergence from the Federal House of Detention in New York City occasioned another "urgent" FBI wire describing the circumstances of the release, including the presence of Dennis' wife and son.[166] The Bureau's New York office followed the next day with an elaboration of its report.[167] The agent in charge also recommended that Dennis' name immediately be restored to the Security Index. Dennis was to be included in the "Detcom" category.[168]

Apparently the attention given to Dennis had no relation to the commission of a crime, and the "Detcom" listing was unknown to the Attorney General. Both steps were a continuation of the FBI's war against internal communism.

The Department of Justice was placing even greater reliance on the Bureau as a result of the McCarran Act. The Criminal Division was "in constant consultation" with the FBI "concerning problems of enforcement, the use of investigative material and informants, and preparing memoranda analyzing and interpreting the Act." Hoover apparently played a vital role in speeding proceedings against the Communist Party. On November 22, 1950, only days after the formation of the Subversive Activities Control Board, Justice had filed a petition to force the CP to register as a "Communist-action organization."[169]

By the end of January 1951, the Department had added more than thirty staff attorneys to aid in these proceedings, and an additional thirty were being processed. The formal hearings in the case—conducted as if the Communist Party were on trial—began on April 23, 1951, before a three-member SACB panel consisting of Charles La Follette, Peter Campbell Brown, and Kathryn McHale.[170] The government's attorney opened the case by declaring that the legitimate political activities in which the CP had engaged were "but a window dressing to conceal its real purposes, which have been to overthrow the government, and to supplant it by what they call a dictatorship of the proletariat."[171] Tes-

timony continued for more than a year, with the prosecution presenting twenty witnesses, most of whom had appeared at the communists'
Smith Act trial.

The atmosphere in which the SACB hearings began was prejudiced
by the almost simultaneous public release of testimony given two months
earlier by Justice Department officials.[172] Appearing before the House
Appropriations Committee on February 15, 1951, Hoover asserted that
the CP's "subversive activities" represented a greater threat than "Nazi
fifth column" actions during World War II. Describing the communists
as a "more fanatical group" than the Nazis, Hoover outlined the underground structure established after the CP leaders' convictions in 1949.
He claimed that a secret "alternate committee" had been formed to operate the Party if "their top functionaries are arrested and sent to prison."
In "off the record" testimony, Hoover apparently supplied the names
of the "underground" leaders to the committee—names which had been
printed in the communist press more than a month earlier.[173]

Assistant Attorney General James M. McInerney said that 14,000
communists would be taken into custody immediately in the event of
a national emergency.[174] He claimed that all these people had been
identified as CP members and had been "thoroughly investigated."
McInerney added: "They have been found by reason of their positions
or other activities to be dangerous." The Attorney General's assistant
threatened to disclose publicly the names of the 14,000 rather than wait
for a "national emergency." "Why can we not flush them out and put
the Communist Party out of business overnight?" he asked.[175]

The government's deportation weapon also was to be used with
greater frequency. The Immigration and Naturalization Service was
considering the arrest of 5,000 communists during the following year,
McInerney said.[176] He "personally agreed" that the CP simply should
be made illegal.[177] The official's testimony seemed to threaten that the
Department of Justice was prepared to go far beyond the requirements
of the McCarran Act.

Attorney General McGrath promised to enforce the internal security
law fully. He declared himself "in agreement with the objectives of the
act."[178] The Attorney General presumably was aware that McInerney's
figure for numbers of communists to be arrested in an emergency paralleled the FBI's Security Index. In May 1951 the Bureau informed the
Department that more than 14,000 CP members were included on the
list. The FBI asked the Department to examine each name so that "the
Bureau would not be open to an allegation of using Police State tactics."[179]

The Criminal Division agreed to review the names on the Index under the supervision of a former FBI agent and four other officials. Although the FBI had suggested the examination, it was fearful it would get out of control. Hoover demanded the names of the five attorneys making the review and directed examination of the Bureau's files on each lawyer.[180]

Despite McInerney's assurances, the list of persons to be apprehended in the event of a national emergency had not necessarily been compiled by "careful investigation." Names had been added on the basis of a one-page document completed by an agent in any of the Bureau's offices acting on his own concept of "dangerousness." It was not until June 1951 that the Justice Department undertook to review Security Index standards "so as to conform more closely" to the McCarran Act's provisions.[181] The FBI objected to a proposed new set of criteria based on the law since it would eliminate many of those persons whom the Bureau considered "dangerous." The internal FBI analysis indicated that the Justice Department still had no knowledge of Bureau listings other than the Security Index, nor of various programs to disrupt groups considered a peril by the FBI.[182]

Hoover wrote to the deputy Attorney General to inform him of the wide disparity between the FBI's criteria and those proposed by the Department. He said that the Bureau still wished to list individuals who were not affiliated with proscribed groups, but whose "anarchist or revolutionary beliefs" might make them dangerous. In addition, it wished to maintain the names of individuals who had been designated many years before and about whom there was no "positive indication of disaffection or cessation of the activities which caused them to be placed on the index." They might be communist "sleepers," said the Director. Hoover asked continued use of the FBI's standards.[183]

The Justice Department made no decision on detention criteria for more than a year. The FBI remained the sole judge of the detention list during that time. In 1952 the Department finally acceded to the Bureau's request and specifically agreed to return to the "pre–1950" standards— the criteria which ignored the McCarran Act's provisions.[184]

The President's actions contributed to the growing sense of national insecurity. In late March 1951 he asked Congress for an appropriation of $775,000 to finance the Federal Bureau of Prisons' establishment of "detention centers" as provided by the emergency provisions of the McCarran Act.[185]

On April 28 Truman issued an executive order to change the government's standard for hiring or removing employees, as recommended by the Loyalty Review Board.[186] While the President apparently thought the change to "reasonable doubt" of loyalty rather than "reasonable grounds" to prove disloyalty was a small one, it caused the Review Board to reopen many cases which previously had been closed—a result which Truman had not anticipated.[187]

A month after the President's action on the loyalty standard, he wrote his special counsel to complain about the activities of various loyalty boards. Prompted by the complaints of members of Americans for Democratic Action, Truman said: "I want to find some way to put a stop to their [loyalty boards'] un-American activities." Later he complained: "There is an outrageous condition in connection with loyalty investigations. People are being persecuted without cause."[188] The President asked for staff recommendations to deal with the situation, but did not recognize that it was his loyalty program and subsequent actions which had allowed inequities to occur.

The anticommunist fever, which touched virtually all elements in the political life of the United States, most sharply affected the CPUSA. Hoover reported that as 1951 began, communist membership had fallen to 43,217 and was declining rapidly.[189] In January 1951 *The Daily Worker* noted that its circulation had decreased to the point "where the existence of the paper is definitely menaced." Fewer than 14,000 copies of the newspaper were being sold daily. Subscriptions for its Sunday edition had fallen below 50,000, and more than half that number were scheduled to expire soon.[190] The West Coast Party newspaper, the *People's World*, had lost more than a third of its readership during the previous four years and was forced to reduce the size of its issues.[191]

CP members' apprehensions grew as each new legal attack occurred. On February 9, 1951, five heads of a group known as the Peace Information Center—including famed black leader W.E.B. Du Bois—were arrested for failing to register as foreign agents. Their "crime" was circulation during the previous year of a communist-sponsored international peace petition, the Stockholm Peace Appeal.[192] Two months later, Ethel and Julius Rosenberg were sentenced to die for what the jury considered involvement in World War II espionage activities.[193] On May 23 the only liberal member of the SACB abruptly resigned from the panel hearing evidence against the Communist Party. La Follette, a former ADA national director, criticized what he viewed as collusion among the Justice Department, board members, and anticommunist witnesses.[194]

An intensive debate began within the Communist Party to determine its future policies. The key factor in the discussions remained the imminence of war and fascism. William Z. Foster continued to emphasize the possibility of approaching disaster.[195] The Party's other leaders were less certain. In early February they agreed to send an emissary to the Soviet Union to determine the views of Soviet leaders.

Hall and Gilbert Green briefed Party staff member Joseph Starobin on the areas to be covered in his Moscow discussions. Starobin determined on his own to seek a full exploration of the war danger and of the Soviet theoretical attitude toward a peaceful transition to socialism.[196]

During Starobin's absence, Joseph Stalin was quoted in a *Pravda* interview as saying that "at the present time" war "is not inevitable." The story was headlined the next day in the American communist press.[197] Starobin returned in late February to emphasize the same point.

In conversations with top members of the Soviet Politburo, including Georgi Malenkov, Starobin was assured that the Soviet Party had not accepted the position that war was inevitable. He was told also that the Soviets supported the concept of a peaceful road to socialism.[198] "There were no orders" from Moscow sought or given in Starobin's conversations.[199] Starobin simply conveyed contemporary Soviet attitudes to the CPUSA's leadership.

Neither Foster nor FBI chief Hoover accepted the view that the Soviet Union believed war to be avoidable. Two weeks after Stalin's interview, Hoover widely disseminated a report that an informant had determined: "Stalin's remark that a new world war is not inevitable 'at least at the present time,' will be interpreted by Communists to mean that war is inevitable!"[200]

George Watt, secretary of the Party's National Review Commission—a body entrusted with protecting Party security—served as the National Committee liaison with Foster who was recuperating in California. He twice made trips to the Party's chairman in the early part of 1951. In the spring he met with Foster to determine his views on the most vital questions facing the CP. Fearing that his room was "bugged," Foster took out a pencil and paper to jot down his definitive answers. He wrote: "illegality—inevitable; fascism—not inevitable; war—inevitable."[201]

By the spring of 1951 there was widespread communist acceptance of the immediate danger of world war, the CP's illegality, and the rise of fascism within the United States. As a result, the CP's leaders agreed to activate their underground structure.

The specific impetus for the decision to submerge was provided by the upcoming Supreme Court ruling on the appeal from the eleven Communist leaders' Smith Act convictions. Alexander Bittelman prepared a memorandum for the National Committee at the end of May

1951 which assumed that the convictions would be upheld. Bittelman wrote: "The Bill of Rights is being discarded and a police state is coming into existence in the United States dominated by a war-time dictatorship of the Wall Street monopolies. The decision marks a new and major step in the direction of fascism and of the unleashing of a new world war." He urged the Party to continue to fight for "the rights and opportunities of . . . an open and legal political party" and warned against self-imposed isolation. Bittelman also urged that the Party protect its members from "reactionary persecutions"—a reference to the decision to go underground.[202]

The agreement among the CP heads to utilize their secret apparatus only sharpened their differences. Bitter daily debate took place over whether convicted leaders should surrender once the Smith Act convictions were upheld, and who should lead the Party in the approaching critical period.

A strong group led by Robert Thompson and Benjamin Davis, and including Hall, Henry Winston, John Williamson, John Gates, and Foster supported the concept that at least some of the convicted leaders should join the underground. Elizabeth Gurley Flynn, Carl Winter, Jack Stachel, Irving Potash, and probably Gilbert Green opposed this position. They argued there was still a possibility of maintaining the Party's legal existence, which would be lost if some leaders "jumped bail." Dennis' position was ambivalent.[203] He reportedly proposed sending another mission to Moscow to determine whether the Soviets believed the American leadership should go into hiding. Other Party chiefs unanimously opposed this suggestion.[204] In the inner councils of the Party, Foster supported a refusal to surrender, but he displayed "some contempt for the whole underground operation" to Party members.[205]

Contingency plans were made while the debate over the "bail jumping" issue continued. Possible escape routes out of the United States were explored. Teams were sent to Canada and Mexico to determine if suitable arrangements could be made for handling fugitive communist leaders. Contact was made with Soviet and Polish authorities to gain needed assistance in moving the Party heads to "safe" nations. It was decided initially that Canada would be the best route to use, but Soviet authorities, through an intermediary, insisted that Mexico was "the only way to go." They agreed to provide detailed arrangements, including rendezvous areas, code words, and documents.[206]

The government's internal security establishment had finally achieved its major goal. The heads of the American Communist Party were consumed by the planning of their own organizational destruction. The "right thinkers" had won.

NOTES

1. J. Edgar Hoover, "Address at the Dinner of the Grand Lodge of New York," May 2, 1950, Box 12, Speeches Folder. Hereafter box number and folder designations will be cited as 12/Speeches. Papers of Eleanor Bontecou. Harry S. Truman Library, Independence, Missouri. Hereafter cited as HSTL.

2. U.S. House of Representatives, 81st Cong., 2d sess., Appropriations Committee, *Department of Justice Appropriations for 1951. Hearings . . .* (Washington, 1950), 85–86, 91. Hereafter cited as *House Appropriations Hearings*.

3. U.S. Senate, 81st Cong., 2d sess., Appropriations Committee, *Department of State, Justice, Commerce and the Judiciary Appropriations for 1951. Hearings . . .* (Washington, 1950), 167. Hereafter cited as *Senate Appropriations Hearings*.

4. FBI Director, "Memorandum to the Attorney General," July 27, 1950, in U.S. Senate, 94th Cong., 2d sess., *Final Report of the Select Committee to Study Governmental Operations With Respect to Intelligence Activities* (6 vols., Washington, 1976), III, 441. Hereafter cited as *Final Report*.

5. SAC Letter No. 97, Series 1949, October 19, 1949, in *Final Report*, III, 440–41.

6. Ibid., 441.

7. *House Appropriations Hearings*, 92.

8. Ibid., 229.

9. D. M. Ladd, "Memorandum to the FBI Director," January 12, 1951, in *Final Report*, III, 442.

10. *Senate Appropriations Hearings*, 141, 143.

11. Stephen J. Spingarn, "Subject: J. Edgar Hoover Article in the *U.S. News & World Report*, issue of June 23, 1950 (pp. 11–13)," June 28, 1950, 31/National Defense-Internal Security and Individual Rights 2, Papers of Stephen J. Spingarn, HSTL.

12. *Senate Appropriations Hearings*, 144.

13. *The New York Times*, May 21, 1949.

14. *Senate Appropriations Hearings*, 220, 247.

15. Stephen J. Spingarn, "Memorandum for Mr. Murphy," February 1, 1950, 13/Assistant to the President File, Chronological File January-April 1950, Papers of Stephen J. Spingarn, HSTL; Stephen J. Spingarn, Oral History Interview, 781–82, HSTL.

16. Stephen J. Spingarn, "Memo," January 27, 1950, 34/National Defense-Internal Security, Deportation and Exclusion of Aliens, Papers of Stephen J. Spingarn, HSTL.

17. Spingarn, "Memorandum for Mr. Murphy," February 1, 1950, HSTL.

18. Stephen J. Spingarn, "Memorandum for the Files," May 6, 1950, 34/National Defense-Internal Security, Deportation and Exclusion of Aliens, Papers of Stephen J. Spingarn, HSTL.

19. Stephen J. Spingarn, "Memorandum for the Files," May 20, 1950, 31/National Defense-Internal Security and Individual Rights 2, Papers of Stephen J. Spingarn, HSTL.

20. Harry Truman, "Memorandum for Attorney General McGrath," May 19,

1950, 31/National Defense-Internal Security and Individual Rights 2, Papers of Stephen J. Spingarn, HSTL.

21. Spingarn, "Memorandum for the Files," May 20, 1950, HSTL.

22. Peyton Ford to Adolph J. Sabath, May 23, 1950, 34/National Defense-Internal Security, Deportation and Exclusion of Aliens, Papers of Stephen J. Spingarn, HSTL.

23. *Congressional Record*, 81st Cong., 2d sess., July 17, 1950 (Vol. 96, Washington, 1950), 10460; *The New York Times*, July 18, 1950.

24. Stephen J. Spingarn, "Memorandum for the Record," July 17, 1950, 31/National Defense-Internal Security and Individual Rights 1, Vol. 1, Papers of Stephen J. Spingarn, HSTL.

25. "Memorandum on Your Bill of Rights Record," January 25, 1949, and Max Lowenthal, "The Sedition Bills of 1949," 15/Sedition Bills of 1949, Papers of Clark M. Clifford, HSTL; Stephen J. Spingarn, "Memorandum for Mr. Clifford," April 6, 1949, 31/White House Assignment 2, Papers of Stephen J. Spingarn, HSTL.

26. Harry S. Truman, *Public Papers of the Presidents of the United States 1949* (Washington, 1964), 294.

27. Eric F. Goldman, *The Crucial Decade-And After, America, 1945–1960* (New York, 1966), 139–45; Robert Griffith, *The Politics of Fear, Joseph R. McCarthy and the Senate* (Rochelle Park, 1978), 48–51.

28. Spingarn, Oral History Interview, 135.

29. *The New York Times*, February 21, 1950.

30. Spingarn, Oral History Interview, 125–26.

31. Harry S Truman to Senator Harley M. Kilgore, March 7, 1950, Official File (OF) 482, Papers of Harry S. Truman, HSTL.

32. Harry S Truman to Dr. Zechariah Chafee, Jr., April 19, 1950, OF 482, Papers of Harry S. Truman, HSTL.

33. Harry S. Truman, *Public Papers of the Presidents of the United States 1950* (Washington, 1965), 272.

34. "Speech Before the Federal Bar Association in Wash., D.C.," April 24, 1950, 6/Federal Bar Association Speech, April 24, 1950, Charles S. Murphy Files, Papers of Harry S. Truman, HSTL.

35. *The New York Times*, March 18, 1950.

36. Ibid., April 20, 1950.

37. Ibid., May 24, 1950.

38. Ibid., May 28, 1950.

39. Stephen J. Spingarn, "Memorandum to Elsey, Bell, Lloyd, Hechler," June 26, 1950, 31/National Defense-Internal Security and Individual Rights 2, Papers of Stephen J. Spingarn, HSTL.

40. *Dennis v. United States*, 339 U.S. 162 (1950); *The Daily Worker*, March 28, 1950.

41. *American Communications Assn., C.I.O. et al. v. Douds, Regional Director of the National Labor Relations Board*, 339 U.S. 382 (1950).

42. "Alternate Drafts of Provisions Dealing With Communist Influence in Unions," [December 2, 1948], 22/Taft-Hartley law material, and "Questions for

Consideration in Connection with 'One Package' Legislation to Repeal the Taft-Hartley Act, Re-enact the Wagner Act, and Amend the Wagner Act," January 10, 1949, 22/Labor Disputes P-W, Taft-Hartley Law Material, Papers of John W. Gibson, HSTL; U.S. Senate, 81st Cong., 1st sess., Commmittee on Labor and Public Welfare, Hearings . . . on S. 249 (Washington, 1949), 19–52, 203–406; *Congressional Record*, 81st Cong., 1st sess., June 28, 1949 (Vol. 95, Washington, 1949), Part 7, 8505.

43. *American Communications Assn. v. Douds*, 389.

44. Ibid., 398.

45. Ibid., 424.

46. Ibid., 425–29.

47. Ibid., 448.

48. Ibid., 453.

49. Eugene Nickerson to Hugo Black, May 26, 1950, 303/*American Communications v. Douds, U. Steelworkers v. NLRB*, Papers of Hugo Black, Library of Congress, Washington, D.C. Hereafter cited as LC.

50. Hugo Black to Eugene Nickerson, June 7, 1950, 303/*American Communications v. Douds, U. Steelworkers v. NLRB*, Papers of Hugo Black, LC.

51. Mary S. McAuliffe, *Crisis on the Left, Cold War Politics and American Liberals, 1947–1954* (Amherst, 1978), 58–59.

52. Frank Emspak, "The Break-up of the Congress of Industrial Organizations (CIO), 1945–1950" (Ph.D. Diss., University of Wisconsin, 1972), 380; Harvey A. Levenstein, *Communism, Anticommunism, and the CIO* (Westport, 1981), 226.

53. *The Daily Worker*, June 23, 1949; Levenstein, *Communism, Anticommunism, and the CIO*, 218.

54. McAuliffe, *Crisis on the Left*, 56.

55. John Gates, *The Story of an American Communist* (New York, 1958), 116.

56. Alexander Bittelman, "My Statement," 1949, Folder 4, Papers of Alexander Bittelman, Alexander Bittelman Home Library, Croton, New York. Hereafter cited as BHL.

57. William Schneiderman, "The Defense of the Party," *Political Affairs* XXVIII (October 1949), 20.

58. *The Worker*, October 16, 1949.

59. *The Daily Worker*, October 17, 1949.

60. Ibid., November 30, 1949.

61. Alexander Bittelman, "A Criticism," December 19, 1949, Papers of Alexander Bittelman, BHL.

62. *The New York Times*, September 16, 1949.

63. J. Howard McGrath, *Attorney General of the United States v. The Communist Party of the United States of America*, "Official Report of Proceedings Before the Subversive Activities Control Board," Testimony of John Lautner (January 22–23, 1952), 9363, 9421.

64. Sidney Steinberg (assistant CP labor secretary in 1949) to author, December 25, 1974.

65. George Watt to author, June 29, 1975.

66. John Gates to author, March 5, 1978.

67. "Economic Notes & Perspectives," January 11, 1950, Papers of Alexander Bittelman, BHL.

68. Robert Thompson, "Truman's 'Perspective' and American Reality," *Political Affairs* XXIX (February 1950), 5.

69. Ibid., 4.

70. William Z. Foster to the National Committee, February 21, 1950, Folder 6, Papers of Alexander Bittelman, BHL.

71. Gilbert Green, "Capitalism's Crisis—and Mr. Browder's," *Political Affairs* XXIX (March 1950), 71.

72. *The Daily Worker*, March 6, 1950.

73. Eugene Dennis, "For Communist Clarity and Resoluteness to Forge Working-Class and People's Unity," *Political Affairs* XXIX (May 1950), 49.

74. Alexander Bittelman to [Eugene Dennis], March 3, 1950, Papers of Alexander Bittelman, BHL.

75. Dennis, "For Communist Clarity . . . ," 50.

76. Ibid., 53.

77. Gus Hall, "Through United-Front Struggle to the Victory of Peace," *Political Affairs* XXIX (May 1950), 18–19.

78. Henry Winston, "Building the Party—Key to Building the United Front of Struggle," *Political Affairs* XXIX (May 1950), 60.

79. Gilbert Green, "For Communist Vigilance," *Political Affairs* XXIX (May 1950), 129.

80. Ibid., 115.

81. *The Daily Worker*, March 30, 1950; Hall, "Through United Front . . . ," 27–28.

82. Edward E. Strong, "On the 40th Anniversary of the N.A.A.C.P.," *Political Affairs* XXIX (February 1950), 27.

83. Alexander Bittelman, "Lenin," January 19, 1950, Papers of Alexander Bittelman, BHL; Green, "Capitalism's Crisis . . . ," 77.

84. Peggy Dennis, *The Autobiography of an American Communist, A Personal View of a Political Life 1925–1975* (Westport, 1977), 237.

85. Eugene Dennis, "Let Us March Forward with Supreme Confidence," *Political Affairs* XXIX (July 1950), 10.

86. Gus Hall, "Raise the Struggle for Peace to New Heights," *Political Affairs* XXIX (July 1950), 22, 24.

87. Alexander Bittelman to William Z. Foster, May 29, 1950, Papers of Alexander Bittelman, BHL.

88. William Z. Foster, "People's Front and People's Democracy," *Political Affairs* XXIX (June 1950), 14–31.

89. *The Daily Worker*, June 8, 1950.

90. *United States v. Dennis, et al.*, "Brief for Appellants" in the United States Court of Appeals for the Second Circuit (October Term, 1949), 6.

91. *United States v. Dennis, et al.*, "Brief for the United States" in the United States Court of Appeals for the Second Circuit (October Term, 1949).

92. *The New York Times*, June 24, 1950; *The Daily Worker*, June 25, 1950.

93. Michal R. Belknap, *Cold War Political Justice, The Smith Act, the Communist Party, and American Civil Liberties* (Westport, 1977), 125.

94. Alonzo Hamby, *Beyond the New Deal: Harry S. Truman and American Liberalism* (New York, 1973), 409; McAuliffe, *Crisis on the Left*, 77; William R. Tanner, "The Passage of the Internal Security Act of 1950" (2 vols., Ph.D. Diss., University of Kansas, 1971), II, 381; Athan Theoharis, *Seeds of Repression: Harry S. Truman and the Origins of McCarthyism* (Chicago, 1971), 140.

95. Dick Neustadt, "Memorandum for Don Hansen," May 15, 1950, 31/National Defense-Internal Security and Individual Rights 2, Papers of Stephen J. Spingarn, HSTL.

96. Stephen J. Spingarn, "Memorandum for the President," July 14, 1950, 31/National Defense-Internal Security and Individual Rights 2, Papers of Stephen J. Spingarn, HSTL.

97. Stephen J. Spingarn, "Memorandum for Messrs. Murphy, Dawson and Elsey," July 20, 1950, 31/National Defense-S. 2311, Papers of Stephen J. Spingarn, HSTL.

98. Truman, *Public Papers . . . 1950*, 545.

99. Frank J. Donner, *The Age of Surveillance, The Aims and Methods of America's Political Intelligence System* (New York, 1980), 65–66; Athan Theoharis, *Spying on Americans: Political Surveillance from Hoover to the Huston Plan* (Philadelphia, 1978), 66–77.

100. "Statement of J. Edgar Hoover, Director, Federal Bureau of Investigation," July 26, 1950, 8/Internal Security File-FBI 1, Papers of Eleanor Bontecou, HSTL.

101. Stephen J. Spingarn, "Memorandum for the File on Internal Security and Individual Rights," July 22, 1950, 31/National Defense-S. 2311, Papers of Stephen J. Spingarn, HSTL.

102. *United States v. Dennis, et al.*, "Opinion of the Court of Appeals for the Second Circuit" (August 1, 1950), 1629.

103. Ibid., 1630.

104. Ibid., 1631–32.

105. Ibid., 1632–33.

106. "Notes on Cabinet Meetings," August 1, 1950, Post-Presidential File, Papers of Matthew J. Connelly, HSTL.

107. *The New York Times*, August 15, 1950.

108. Truman, *Public Papers . . . 1950*, 561.

109. Stephen J. Spingarn, "Memo," August 1, 1950, 32/National Defense-Internal Security and Individual Rights 3, Vol. 2, Papers of Stephen J. Spingarn, HSTL.

110. Truman, *Public Papers . . . 1950*, 571.

111. Ibid., 573.

112. Ibid., 574.

113. Ibid.

114. Ibid., 575.

115. Stephen J. Spingarn, "Memorandum for the File on Internal Security and

Individual Rights," 22/Internal Security, Files of Charles S. Murphy, Papers of Harry S. Truman, HSTL.

116. "Legislative Draft of Amendment to the Foreign Agents Registration Act of 1938," August 9, 1950, 32/National Defense-Internal Security and Individual Rights 3, Vol. 2, Papers of Stephen J. Spingarn, HSTL.

117. David D. Lloyd, "Memorandum to Mr. Spingarn," August 10, 1950, 32/National Defense-Internal Security and Individual Rights 2, Vol. 2, Papers of Stephen J. Spingarn, HSTL.

118. Spingarn, "Memorandum for the File . . . ," August 11, 1950, HSTL.

119. "Explanation of Substitute Bill," 31/National Defense-Internal Security and Individual Rights 1, Vol. 1, Papers of Stephen J. Spingarn, HSTL.

120. David D. Lloyd, "Memo to Mr. Spingarn," August 17, 1950, 32/National Defense-Internal Security and Individual Rights 1, Vol. 2, Papers of Stephen J. Spingarn, HSTL.

121. Spingarn, "Memorandum for the File . . . ," August 11, 1950, HSTL; Stephen J. Spingarn, "Memorandum for Honorable Millard E. Tydings," August 16, 1950, 31/National Defense-Internal Security 2, Papers of Stephen J. Spingarn, HSTL.

122. Stephen J. Spingarn, "Memorandum for J. Edgar Hoover," August 22, 1950, 33/National Defense-Internal Security and Individual Rights 3, Vol. 3, Papers of Stephen J. Spingarn, HSTL.

123. J. Howard McGrath to Scott W. Lucas, August 26, 1950, 33/National Defense-Internal Security and Individual Rights 3, Vol. 3, Papers of Stephen J. Spingarn, HSTL.

124. Stephen J. Spingarn, "Memorandum for the Internal Security File," September 6, 1950, 32/National Defense-Internal Security and Individual Rights, Vol. 3, Papers of Stephen J. Spingarn, HSTL.

125. *The Daily Worker*, September 7, 1950.

126. Truman, *Public Papers . . . 1950*, 620.

127. Stephen J. Spingarn, "Memorandum for the File on Proposed Commission on Internal Security and Individual Rights," July 12, 1950, 31/National Defense-Internal Security and Individual Rights 1, Vol. 1, Papers of Stephen J. Spingarn, HSTL.

128. Stephen J. Spingarn, "Memorandum for the Internal Security File," September 25, 1950, 32/National Defense-Internal Security and Individual Rights 1, Vol. 3, Papers of Stephen J. Spingarn, HSTL.

129. Stephen J. Spingarn, "Memorandum for the File on the Wood-McCarran Anti-Subversive Bill (H.R. 9490)," September 19, 1950, 32/National Defense-Internal Security and Individual Rights 1, Vol. 3, Papers of Stephen J. Spingarn, HSTL.

130. Stephen J. Spingarn, "Memorandum," September 20, 1950, 32/National Defense-Internal Security and Individual Rights 1, Vol. 3, Papers of Stephen J. Spingarn, HSTL.

131. Spingarn, "Memorandum for the Internal Security File," September 25, 1950, HSTL.

132. "Memorandum to Peyton Ford, Deputy Attorney General," September

11, 1950, 32/National Defense-Internal Security and Individual Rights 2, Vol. 3, Papers of Stephen J. Spingarn, HSTL.

133. Truman, *Public Papers . . . 1950*, 645.

134. Ibid., 649.

135. Spingarn, "Memorandum for the Internal Security File," September 25, 1950, HSTL.

136. *The Daily Worker*, June 28, 1950.

137. Ibid., July 31, 1950.

138. Gus Hall, "The Present Situation and the Tasks of Our Party," *Political Affairs* XXIX (October 1950), 6–7.

139. *The Daily Worker*, September 25, 1950.

140. Ibid., September 29, 1950.

141. Hall, "The Present Situation . . . ," 24.

142. *United States v. Flynn, et al.*, "Transcript of Trial," Testimony of Bereniece Baldwin (July 30, 1952), 7271; *United States v. Trachtenberg, et al.*, "Transcript of Trial," Testimony of Barbara Hartle (May 17, 1956), 3158.

143. Henry Winston, "Gear the Party for Its Great Tasks," *Political Affairs* XXX (February 1951), 51–52.

144. "Draft Resolution on the Present Political Situation and the Tasks of the Communist Party of the USA," October 11, 1950, Folder 3, Papers of Alexander Bittelman, BHL.

145. William Z. Foster to the National Committee, October 16, 1950, Folder 13, Papers of Alexander Bittelman, BHL.

146. "Draft Resolution on the Present Political Situation and the Tasks of the Communist Party of the USA," October 22, 1950, Folder 25, Papers of Alexander Bittelman, BHL.

147. "Notes on Cabinet Meetings," September 26, 1950, President's Personal File, Papers of Matthew J. Connelly, HSTL.

148. J. Howard McGrath to Lee Nichols, October 14, 1950, 136/Deputy Attorney General, Papers of J. Howard McGrath, HSTL.

149. Truman, *Public Papers . . . 1950*, 680.

150. *The New York Times*, October 20, 1950.

151. Ibid., October 24, 1950.

152. Don Whitehead, *The FBI Story, A Report to the People* (New York, 1956), 300.

153. *The New York Times*, October 24, 1950; *The Daily Worker*, October 31, 1950.

154. Irving R. Saypol, "Respondent's Memorandum in Support of the Attorney General's Authority Under the Internal Security Act of 1950 to Apprehend and Detain Aliens Without Bail Pending Deportation Proceedings," November 8, 1950, Folder 4, Papers of Alexander Bittelman, BHL.

155. *The New York Times*, November 18, 1950.

156. A. H. Belmont, "Memorandum to D. M. Ladd," October 15, 1952, in *Final Report*, III, 442.

157. Peyton Ford, "Memorandum to the FBI Director," December 7, 1950, in *Final Report*, III, 442.

158. *Dennis, et al. v. United States*, "Brief for Petitioners" in the Supreme Court

of the United States (November 20, 1950), 50; *Dennis, et al. v. United States*, "Motion of American Civil Liberties Union for Leave to File Brief as An 'Amicus Curiae' " in the Supreme Court of the United States (October Term, 1950), 2.

159. *Dennis, et al. v. United States*, "Brief for Petitioners" (November 20, 1950), 174.

160. Ibid., 36.

161. *Dennis, et al. v. United States*, "Brief for the United States" in the Supreme Court of the United States (October Term, 1950), 160.

162. Ibid., 172.

163. *The Daily Worker*, December 8, 1950.

164. "Working-Class and Peoples' Unity for Peace!" *Political Affairs* XXX (January 1951), 15.

165. Special agent Scheidt to FBI Director, Teletype, March 10, 1951, copy of document submitted to author by FBI.

166. Special agent Scheidt to FBI Director, Teletype, March 12, 1951, copy of document submitted to author by FBI.

167. Special agent Scheidt to FBI Director, Teletype, March 13, 1951, copy of document submitted to author by FBI.

168. SAC, New York to Director, FBI, March 12, 1951, copy of document submitted to author by FBI.

169. J. Howard McGrath to Emanuel Celler, January 31, 1951, 19/Internal Security Correspondence January-August 1951 Folder, Papers of Emanuel Celler, LC.

170. McGrath, *United States v. Communist Party*, "Proceedings," April 23, 1951, 1.

171. Ibid., Government's Opening Statement, 4.

172. *The New York Times*, April 28, 1951.

173. U.S. House of Representatives, 82d Cong., 1st sess., Committee on Appropriations, *Department of Justice Appropriations for 1952. Hearings . . .* (Washington, 1951), 335, 337. Hereafter cited as *Justice Apropriations*.

174. Ibid., 181.

175. Ibid., 191.

176. Ibid., 200.

177. Ibid., 194.

178. Ibid., 12–13.

179. Mr. Clegg, "Memorandum to Mr. Tolson," May 10, 1951, in *Final Report*, III, 443.

180. A. H. Belmont, "Memorandum to Mr. Ladd," May 31, 1951, in *Final Report*, III, 443.

181. Deputy Attorney General Peyton Ford, "Memorandum to the FBI Director," June 1, 1951, in *Final Report*, III, 443.

182. F. J. Baumgardner, "Memorandum to A. H. Belmont," June 8, 1951, in *Final Report*, III, 443–44.

183. FBI Director, "Memorandum to Deputy Attorney General Peyton Ford," June 28, 1951, in *Final Report*, III, 444.

222 The Great "Red Menace"

184. A. H. Belmont, "Memorandum to Mr. Ladd," March 19, 1952, in *Final Report*, III, 444; the Attorney General, "Memorandum to the FBI Director," November 25, 1952, in *Final Report*, III, 445.

185. *The New York Times*, March 23, 1951.

186. Executive Order 10241, in Eleanor Bontecou, *The Federal Loyalty-Security Program* (Ithaca, 1953), 282.

187. Murphy, Post-Presidential Conversations Memoirs 1, November 19, 1954, HSTL.

188. Harry S Truman, "Memorandum for Charles Murphy," May 24, 1951, OF 2750 A-(1945–July 1951), Papers of Harry S. Truman, HSTL; "Notes on Cabinet Meetings," August 10, 1951, President's Personal File, Papers of Matthew J. Connelly, HSTL.

189. *Justice Appropriations*, 336.

190. *The Daily Worker*, January 19, 1951.

191. Al Richmond, *A Long View from the Left, Memoirs of an American Revolutionary* (Boston, 1967), 300.

192. *The Daily Worker*, February 10, 1951.

193. Ibid., April 6, 1951.

194. Ibid., May 24, 1951.

195. William Z. Foster, "Truman's 'State of National Emergency,'" *Political Affairs* XXX (March 1951), 8.

196. Joseph R. Starobin, *American Communism in Crisis, 1943–1957* (Cambridge, 1972), 216–17.

197. *The Daily Worker*, February 18, 1951.

198. Starobin, *American Communism in Crisis*, 216–17.

199. George Watt to author, June 29, 1975.

200. J. Edgar Hoover to Rear Admiral Robert L. Dennison, February 28, 1951, 169/Personal, President's Secretary's Files, Papers of Harry S. Truman, HSTL.

201. George Watt to author, June 29, 1975.

202. Alexander Bittelman, "On the Decision," May 25, 1951, Folder 1, Papers of Alexander Bittelman, BHL.

203. John Gates to author, March 5, 1978; George Watt to author, June 29, 1975; Sidney Steinberg (National Committee alternate member in 1951) to author, December 25, 1974.

204. John Gates to author, March 5, 1978.

205. George Watt to author, June 29, 1975.

206. Ibid.

X

The Deep Freeze

Communist debates and plans were cut short on June 4, 1951. The Supreme Court, by a decisive six to two vote, upheld the Smith Act's constitutionality and denied the appeal of the CP leaders.[1] Chief Justice Fred Vinson, joined by three other justices, wrote the opinion of the Court. Separate concurring opinions were written by Robert Jackson and Felix Frankfurter. While Tom Clark did not participate in the decision, the three other judges appointed to the Court by Truman joined the majority opinion.

Vinson fully supported the lower court rulings of Harold Medina and Learned Hand. He agreed that conviction under the Smith Act required proof of "intent . . . to overthrow the Government by force and violence."[2] "Success or probability of success" was discarded as a criterion. Vinson said that the Communist Party presented a new and unique threat to the United States—"an apparatus designed and dedicated to the overthrow of the Government, in the context of world crisis after crisis."[3]

The Court's opinion commended Medina's charge to the jury that conviction required a finding that the communists would overthrow the government "as speedily as circumstances would permit," and Hand's new test for restriction of freedom of speech: "whether the gravity of the 'evil,' discounted by its improbability, justifies such invasion of free speech as is necessary to avoid the danger."[4] Vinson concluded that the "requisite danger" had been proven:

The formulation by petitioners of such a highly organized conspiracy, with rigidly disciplined members subject to call when the leaders, these petitioners, felt that the time had come for action, coupled with the inflammable nature of world conditions, similar uprisings in other countries, and the touch-and-go nature of our relations with countries with whom petitioners were in the very least ideologically attuned, convince us that their convictions were justified on this score.[5]

Apparently the Court had ruled that international conditions warranted the restriction of Americans' free speech.

Frankfurter and Jackson asserted that the Smith Act represented an exercise of congressional discretion with which the courts should not interfere. It was up to the legislature, they said, to balance the competing interests of security and freedom.[6] Jackson completely rejected the "clear and present danger" test when applied to "the subtlety and efficacy of modernized revolutionary techniques used by totalitarian parties." Communists were plotting, he said, at some time in the future to overthrow the government. The Justice maintained that government action was needed in the "period of incubation," lest it come too late to stop a revolution.[7]

The dissenters, Hugo Black and William O. Douglas, vigorously attacked the conclusions of the majority and the possible effects of their decision. Black pointed out that the communists were not charged with any overt acts, any revolutionary attempts, or even with "saying anything or writing anything designed to overthrow the Government." "No matter how it is worded," he said, "this is a virulent form of prior censorship of speech and press, which I believe the First Amendment forbids."[8] He reminded the Court and the American people that while "unfettered communication of ideas does entail dangers," the "free expression" gained was "worth the risk."[9] Black concluded with a call for a future reversal:

Public opinion being what it now is, few will protest the conviction of these Communist petitioners. There is hope, however, that in calmer times, when present pressures, passions and fears subside, this or some later Court will restore the First Amendment liberties to the high preferred place where they belong in a free society.[10]

Douglas noted that the convictions had been based on Marxist-Leninist texts which presumably were available in libraries and classrooms throughout the United States. "The crime then depends not on what is taught," he said, "but on who the teacher is. That is to make freedom of speech turn not on *what is said*, but on the *intent* with which it is said. Once we start down that road, we enter territory dangerous to the liberties of every citizen . . . . "[11] He particularly attacked the use of the conspiracy statute, declaring, "The doctrine of conspiracy has served divers and oppressive purposes and in its broad reach can be made to do great evil. But never until today has anyone seriously thought that the ancient law of conspiracy could constitutionally be used to turn speech into seditious conduct." [12]

The dissents were phrased powerfully, but they had little influence. An old New Deal official wrote to Black congratulating him for upholding "traditional" liberties, but few others supported him or his colleague. [13] The ADA engaged in a long internal struggle to determine its position. Some leaders who opposed the Court's ruling feared to take a position which would be politically damaging. The organization finally reached a consensus simply to oppose the Smith Act. [14] The American Civil Liberties Union continued to work against similar prosecutions, although apparently as quietly as possible. [15]

The unequivocal nature of the Court's decision destroyed the position of those Communist leaders seeking a moderate response. There seemed a certainty of mass prosecution and very little time to prepare for it. It would take twenty-five days for the Court's mandate to be handed down to the District Court for execution. In less than a month the Party's leadership would be sent to prison. The CP's heads reacted with a panic which was perhaps to scar their movement permanently.

The national leaders immediately ordered a new and complete registration of all Party members. Only those who sought to remain in the CP, and were approved by appropriate committees, would be allowed to stay. Those who were not approved for continued membership by August 8 were to be dropped. [16] The Party was paring its membership drastically to prepare it for the underground.

Discussion and bitter dispute within the top leadership intensified. The opposition to convicted leaders going underground apparently ended, but the struggle for leadership of the dwindling movement remained. Foster, Davis, and Thompson argued that all the Party's top leaders should submerge, while the majority held out for a compromise where some would go to prison, and others would become fugitives. Foster challenged the militancy of those who were to be incarcerated.

The communist chiefs finally agreed by a majority vote that roughly half of them should go underground, while the other half surrendered to federal authorities. "We thought this would be a signal to the Party of combining legal and illegal methods," said Gates. [17] It was believed that the rest of the Party would follow the same example with a portion going into hiding and the remainder working within the open structure.

Foster proposed that any leader who wished to go into the underground be permitted to do so, but this was rejected.[18] There was a fierce struggle over who would surrender. Thompson, apparently in the belief that those who "jumped bail" would control the movement, insisted on remaining free. He claimed that his experience during World War II uniquely qualified him to go into the underground. His colleagues reluctantly agreed, believing at first that his shorter sentence of three years and his position as a national war hero would be jeopardized if he became a fugitive.[19] Although initially opposed to the strategy, Green volunteered to go into hiding, perhaps in the hope of destroying the image of his earlier association with Earl Browder.[20]

Winston, Hall, and Dennis were selected to complete the subterranean leadership. The latter reluctantly agreed, but had to follow Thompson lest his leadership position be undermined.[21]

Separate underground teams were established to work with each of the designated leaders. Cars were "dry cleaned"—handled so that they could not be traced. Special housing for each fugitive was obtained. It was decided to use the Mexican escape route in preference to others.

Gates, who had been given the responsibility of completing escape arrangements with the Poles, had to inform them that they would not be used. He was supposed to attend a formal reception given by the Polish Ambassador to the United Nations, Dr. Julius Katz-Suchy, in order to give him a list of those leaders to be taken out of the country. Gates went to the Polish gathering, but deliberately avoided the Ambassador and his glances in the hope that Katz-Suchy would understand that the CPUSA had decided not to use his assistance. In each of its foreign contacts, the United States Party leadership gave no real thought to the dangers of a liaison with the Soviet Union or Poland—it was assumed that these efforts would succeed without becoming known generally.[22]

The CP membership was alerted to other dangers about to threaten the country and the Party. On June 14 the National Committee issued a statement warning: "Our country now stands on the edge of the precipice."[23] "Creeping fascism" had quickened its pace, said the Party declaration, and "all Americans—not just the Communists—face a wholly new situation."[24] Party members were advised of the CP's next steps: "We are . . . going to protect our members and our organization. We are going to guard the integrity and working class principles of our Party, and preserve its ability to function under any and all circumstances."[25] No clearer call to go underground could have been made.

Rumors of upwards of 25,000 communists' arrests, apparently emanating from the Justice Department, circulated in the press. They were deliberately given credence by Department spokesmen. Assistant Attorney General McInerney stated that the prosecution of CP members all over the United States would begin "within several weeks." He promised that forty of the United States' ninety-five judicial districts would be involved and said the number of indictments to be sought would be "nearer 2,500 than 25,000." [26] The Justice statement came on the same day as the Party's declaration, and seemed to provide convincing evidence to support the CP's conclusions.

A special task force to coordinate Smith Act prosecutions, headed by Tom Hall, was formed within the Department of Justice. Members of this group have insisted that there was "never a thought of mass prosecutions." They have claimed that only 150 leading Party members were being actively considered for prosecutive purposes. [27] In actuality, within a few months the FBI submitted prosecutive summaries involving 206 additional CP members. [28] It would seem that Department rumors and statements were intended to panic the CP and, perhaps, to drive it underground. "The Party believed obviously that thousands would be prosecuted," said an attorney active in the government's task force. "I can see where the Party would have been apprehensive." [29]

The Party's "apprehension" turned to dread on June 20, 1951, when the FBI sought to arrest twenty-one "second-string" CP leaders in New York. The rumors seemed ready to become fact. Seventeen of the newly indicted communists were quickly apprehended, but four escaped. Following instructions given long before, the four—Fred Fine, James Jackson, William Norman, and Sidney Stein—went to prearranged hiding places as soon as they received news of the indictments. Fine and Stein had been travelling by car to a midwest meeting. Jackson and Norman had made themselves "unavailable" as part of the rotation to avoid arrest of the entire leadership. Each contacted the National Committee's underground leadership and was told to go into hiding and remain there. [30]

Years later the government claimed that it had no knowledge of the whereabouts of these four fugitives until one was arrested two years later and the three others subsequently surrendered voluntarily. [31] All four had been under intense surveillance by the FBI for at least two years. Individual FBI men had been detailed to follow them, and these agents were supposed to make the arrests. [32] Two of the four were not underground when the indictments were filed. It is difficult to accept the government's claim that the FBI simply allowed them to slip through the fingers of the Bureau.

The unexpected problem of four fugitives presented difficulties for the Party's underground machinery. There was no prepared apparatus ready to handle them.[33] New plans had to be made in an increasing atmosphere of fear and confusion.

Elizabeth Gurley Flynn, formerly the only unindicted member of the National Committee, headed the new group of seventeen defendants. Among the overt acts charged against them was that as part of a conspiracy they "would agree upon and carry into effect detailed plans for the vital parts of the Communist Party of the United States of America to go underground in the event of emergency."[34] There was no suggestion that this procedure would be used for purposes other than carrying on CP activities.

The new arrests greatly increased Foster's prestige within the Communist Party. His estimate of the dangers of war and fascism, emphasized over a period of years, seemed supported by contemporary events. The Party chairman seemed to welcome the coming underground period.[35] Bittelman recalled Foster's view of the situation as: "Just one of those difficult periods in the life of a revolutionary party which it must have the stoicism to bear and sit out, until the inevitable next revolutionary upsurge will make its appearance."[36]

Foster did not remain idle as the Party's leadership was imprisoned, put on trial, or driven undercover. He pushed to gain control of the Party machinery. He told the National Committee that neither "sick people" nor "underground people" should run the Party, but that those left in open, legal positions should have the authority.[37] Personnel were brought into the national office who would take direction from the Party chairman—the only prominent figure still available.

The eleven convicted CPUSA leaders were ordered to surrender to federal authorities on July 2, 1951. For his last scheduled public appearance, Dennis prepared a speech in which he warned that a "qualitative change" had occurred in the United States. The Supreme Court's decision, he wrote, had "nullified" the First Amendment to the Constitution, and "signalizes the blotting out of constitutional guarantees and threatens the breakdown of all the institutions of bourgeois democracy." Dennis claimed to be too ill to deliver the address himself, but his bleak message was read to the assembled audience.[38]

Four days later, at midnight on June 30, Dennis left home to meet a "connection" who would take him to a safe hiding place. Although the contact was there, Dennis believed something was wrong and returned home. He sent his wife with messages to two trusted comrades to inform them that he would try again the next night. That evening the same sequence of events was repeated. Dennis returned home a second time. A few hours later he met Gates and told him that his escape plan had failed. The Party general secretary traveled to the federal courthouse to surrender, and on the way asked his wife to find out what had gone amiss. He wondered whether someone in the leadership had deliberately sabotaged his plans in order to move him out of the way. Other leaders asked if Dennis had chosen to stay out of the underground so that he could serve his prison time and come back to his Party position relatively quickly.[39]

Dennis may well have had reason to be suspicious on the nights of June 30 and July 1. He had been under intense FBI surveillance since his March 12 release from prison. On May 8 the Bureau's New York office reported that it would continue to follow the general secretary and to report on his activities.[40] It seems apparent that as the date for his surrender approached, as the Party's underground apparatus went into operation, and as the four leaders indicted on June 20 remained at liberty, the surveillance would have been intensified. It is doubtful that Dennis could have avoided the FBI's effort to follow him.

At 10:00 A.M. on July 2, 1951, Dennis and six of his colleagues surrendered to begin serving their prison sentences. The four leaders chosen by the National Committee, Hall, Thompson, Green, and Winston, did not appear, and their bail was forfeited. The success of these four in evading FBI surveillance was remarkable. It is fair to assume that each national committeeman was under the same kind of observation as Dennis. Gates was certain that he was being watched carefully at all times. He recalled that on a trip to Tucson, Arizona, shortly before the surrender, he was followed the entire way and that the FBI set up telescopic surveillance on a hilltop overlooking the house in which he stayed.[41] Hall reportedly left his Bronx apartment at 7:00 A.M. on June 30 carrying two suitcases. He walked to a nearby automobile, deposited the suitcases, returned home, emerged a few minutes later with some suits, and drove away.[42] He then disappeared.

Thompson had been subject to active surveillance throughout the year. As a "top functionary" in the CP, regular FBI reports were filed concerning his activities.[43] The Bureau was aware that he had disappeared for a time after his indictment in 1948.[44] Despite this, and the failure to apprehend the four newly indicted leaders in June, there is no indication in FBI files of any special precautions. It is striking that the last indication of Bureau activity concerning Thompson occurred in May. In the middle of that month Thompson was given the most dangerous listing in the FBI Security Index. He was put on the "Comsab" list as well as that of "Detcom" and "top functionary." His experience during the Spanish Civil War prompted the New York office to consider him a sabotage threat—marking him for immediate detention as a dangerous security risk in case of hostilities.[45] No other substantive materials concerning Thompson can be found in FBI files until after his disappearance. Following his failure to appear, the FBI notified Mexican authorities by secret air courier of the flight of the four fugitivies.[46] The fact that there is no similar evidence of notification of Canadian authorities may be an indication that the FBI was aware of the Mexican connection.

The disappearance of the four convicted leaders, in conjunction with earlier Party statements, was taken by many CP members as a signal that fascism was imminent. Party clubs stopped meeting. Without instruction, ordinary members went "underground." They dropped their Party activity, sometimes moved, changed occupations, and even assumed new names. There was "a massive development in 1951 far beyond what many of us thought it would be," recalled Gates.[47] Dennis questioned his wife closely on the developments as she visited him in the federal penitentiary at Atlanta. "I don't understand," he said. "It was not intended that way. We planned to safeguard a few, select cadre for the future, never to take the whole organization into illegality . . . ."[48]

Within months what remained of the open leadership was complaining bitterly of a breakdown in the Party's structure. CP clubs were coming close to self-liquidation, complained a writer in the communists' theoretical magazine. There was no distribution of leaflets or the Party press, and no recruiting. "The holding of the Party club meeting is a matter of profound, principled significance," he said.[49]

As the aboveground CP floundered, the underground structure attempted to organize itself. Long discussions were held on the correct strategy to be followed. A three-tier organization, centering around the eight fugitive leaders, was formed. Only the most trusted Party veterans were integrated into the apparatus. At the top of an inverted pyramid were the "UBO's"—those who were "unavailable" but open. These people would work as couriers between the legal Party and the underground leaders, and among the members of the secret organization. They left their homes and families, and assumed new identities. On the next rank were the "unavailables"—Party members who were to be saved from expected future indictment. Finally, there was the "deep freeze" which was composed of the eight fugitives who initially were not to be involved in Party work. They were to be safeguarded from immediate arrest and imprisonment, and their future role was to be determined. The predominant belief among Party leaders was that the fugitives would be able to emerge only when full civil liberties were restored either after a long period of repression or as a result of the defeat of the United States in a world war.[50]

A dual organization—one in exile and one within the United States—was to be established. The convicted fugitives were to be sent to the Soviet Union and possibly Mexico. Green insisted on remaining in the United States and established his own apparatus in the Midwest. The other three leaders were to be sent out of the country one at a time. Hall wanted to leave quickly and his escape plan was developed first. Winston was to follow, and Thompson was to be the third to depart.

Hall's escape route was planned through Mexico. A team was recruited to carry out the operation, including one man who lived along the border. "He was the only guy in the set up we did not know," said George Watt, who was in charge of the arrangements. Hall made the decision to use the border resident since he was needed as a guide in crossing the Rio Grande. A Hall look-alike was sent across the border to check the operation and it worked well. Two cars traveled toward the Mexican border with the riders acting as if they were typical tourists. Hall insisted that Watt travel with him. All the occupants, with the exception of Hall, went across the border legally. Led by a guide, the CP national secretary waded across the Rio Grande. He was picked up on the other side and driven to a motel on the outskirts of Mexico City. The plan was to take him to another connection who, in turn, would bring Hall to a rendezvous with a Soviet representative. The latter was to make the final arrangements to take the CP leader out of Mexico.

Hall's guide disappeared soon after they reached the motel. At 2:00 A.M. on October 8, men with guns entered the motel room and took Hall away. Watt attempted to generate publicity in order to stop Hall's extradition, but the FBI gave him no time.[51] Hall was taken back across the border to the United States immediately without any legal proceedings.[52]

The operatives in the Mexican apparatus which Watt had established a year earlier went into hiding for six months. The plan to take other communist fugitives out of the United States was abandoned. The effort to whisk Hall to a safe exile in the Soviet Union ended with his receiving an additional three-year sentence for "criminal contempt."[53]

The Justice Department used the "bail jumping" to attack further the crumbling defenses of the Communist Party. The bail of $80,000 for the communist fugitives was collected swiftly by the government.[54] Officials of the Civil Rights Congress, which had provided the bonds, were brought into court to furnish the names of those who had contributed to its bail fund. When they refused, four trustees—Frederick Vanderbilt Field, Alpheus T. Hunton, Dashiell Hammett, and Abner Green—were adjudged in contempt of court and sentenced to prison terms.[55]

Bail bonds provided by the CRC for fifteen of the newly indicted CP leaders were revoked, and the leaders were remanded to prison.[56] At the beginning of August, the government ordered thirty-nine defendants involved in deportation proceedings to surrender immediately. The bonds provided for them by the CRC were no longer considered valid. One defendant brought $5,000 in cash to replace the cancelled bonds, but this was not accepted either. The government insisted on receiving only United States Treasury bonds.[57]

The Justice Department moved in rapid-fire succession to arrest communists in four other parts of the United States. On July 26, fifteen heads of the California CP were taken into custody. On August 7 six in Maryland were arrested. Two days later six more were apprehended in Pittsburgh. Seven communists were seized in Hawaii on August 28.[58] In each of these cases the government requested bail of $75,000 to $100,000 for each defendant, citing the flight of the four convicted leaders as reason for the high bail demand.[59] The bail question ultimately was carried to the Supreme Court, which unanimously ruled that the district courts had to set reasonable bail requirements.[60]

Within a few months, the flight of the Party's leaders had led to an increased sentence for one, the incarceration of many for months, the imprisonment of sympathetic allies, and the movement of a significant portion of the Party membership into a secretive existence which destroyed any possibility of constructive work. Gates remarked: "This was a disastrous decision—to the extent that anything mattered—and precisely what the enemy wanted us to do."[61]

Statements by open Party leaders became more extreme as each new government step evolved. In early July Bittelman referred to the "process of fascization of bourgeois rule."[62] On August 30 Flynn wrote: "FBI agents swarm at mass meetings and funerals. The concentration camp and book-burnings are around the next corner. Fascism is let loose in America."[63] When on October 8 the Supreme Court refused a rehearing to the Party's eleven leaders, Foster, Flynn, and Pettis Perry declared: "This decision signalizes that Wall Street is ready to go full-speed ahead into a bloody war and a brutal fascism."[64]

There was a small element in the CP which did not accept the views of the national leadership. A center of opposition existed among the arrested California leaders. They were criticized angrily for their refusal to avoid apprehension through integration into the underground structure. In jail for several months awaiting the outcome of their appeal for a lessening of bail requirements, the Californians had an opportunity to reflect on the realities of the domestic and international situations. They found themselves in surprising agreement that the dangers of fascism and world war had been overestimated.[65] They concentrated their energies on establishing a "maximum defense" against their Smith Act prosecution in the belief that there was still a chance to win in the courts. Rejecting criticism from the California underground leadership that they were seeking "too many lawyers, too much money," and that this "reflected 'legalistic illusions,' " they determined to seek the best possible counsel, to wage a "full-dress public campaign," and to raise sufficient money to conduct a complete defense.[66]

Foster repeatedly criticized the attitudes and actions of his West Coast colleagues, mainly through communications with the National Committee. Terming their beliefs "legalistic nonsense," he demanded that they follow the example set by the CP's eleven heads. "In all these trials we have to take as our general pattern the trial of Comrade Dennis and our ten Board members," he wrote.[67]

The Californians sought to gain a hearing for their view that fascism was not imminent, but they were blocked by a chaotic leadership situation. The Party's national heads were either in prison, on trial, or on the run. Control of the CP's machinery was in process of being turned over to the underground leadership. Communications were haphazard and cumbersome. They were informed that the developing "underground centers" had the "authority to formulate, interpret, and execute policy." They were "to mind their own business."[68]

A few on the East Coast also joined the questioning of party policies, but they were isolated and ineffective. Bittelman—one of the indicted "second-string" leaders—publicly decried shrinking Party membership and called for an active campaign to involve the CP in "mass work" and to increase its size.[69]

In a series of private letters, Bittelman offered important criticisms of Foster's new book, *History of the Communist Party of the United States*, which he saw in galleys. He told Foster that his analysis necessarily led to the conclusion that war and fascism were inevitable. The book suggested that the "whole American capitalist class wants . . . world war," said Bittelman. He rejected this concept, saying that "certain sections of the bourgeoisie are not ready to risk a new world war," nor did he believe they were seeking a fascist state.[70]

Bittelman emphasized that the CPUSA should be seeking a "peaceful road of transition from capitalism to socialism, from capitalist democracy to socialist democracy." He criticized national leaders, particularly Betty Gannett, for negating the importance of "bourgeois democracy." Bittelman warned Foster that unless his book supported a "peaceful transition," and an "American road to socialism," "you will find that very soon it will not be adequate and behind times on the question of historic perspective and orientation."[71]

Bittelman's analysis was to be repeated by other American communists a few years later and by many foreign communists in the years to come, but it was largely rejected in 1951. Foster's book, which was published the next year, emphasized: "This is fascism in the making, the building of a police state in the United States."[72] "American imperialism," he wrote, was involved in a concerted drive toward "reaction and fascism," and was seeking "a fascist world."[73]

Bittelman attempted to use the second New York Smith Act trial to develop and express his ideas. In a letter to Elizabeth Gurley Flynn on October 25, 1951, he proposed that he be allowed to take the witness stand to explain the concept of an "American road to socialism" and the necessity for a peaceful transition from capitalism. "Peaceful coexistence and competition between the two systems," he said, "are both possible and desirable."[74] In an internal memorandum to his fellow defendants three days later, he argued that they had to be prepared to meet the "clumsy and false" charge that a Marxist-Leninist ideology "is tantamount to advocating the deed of violent overthrow."[75]

Despite Foster's wishes, none of the new Smith Act trials could be the same as the first. The bonds of party control had been loosened and they could not be retied easily. The further away the trial from the New York center, the more independently did the defendants proceed. Certain new common threads were applied to each of the cases. Outside attorneys were sought who often had no sympathy for the CP. They were necessarily given the freedom to fight the legal issues, only being bound to the Party's interpretation of its own doctrines.[76] Often this created serious strains within a Party leadership committed to the same type of political defense as in the Dennis trial. In his pretrial arguments for a dismissal of the second New York indictments, Professor Thomas Emerson of the Yale Law School argued that neither a "clear and present danger" nor a "probable danger" existed since the CP was so demonstrably small and weak. He noted its declining membership, lack of public officials, and loss of influence within the labor movement, as well as the government claim that it had the Party under effective control.[77] A substantial number of the defendants opposed this argument which seemed to undermine the CP's political position, but the professor was allowed to make his case.[78]

The position of Professor Emerson and other attorneys was made more difficult by the existence of the underground. In opposing Emerson's motion, Assistant U.S. Attorney Roy Cohn, later a key aide to Senator McCarthy, maintained that the existence of the underground provided "a sufficient showing of 'clear and present danger.' "[79]

The California defendants successfully reached beyond the left-wing in building a defense team. The chief counsel of the Southern California branch of the ACLU, A. L. Wirin, agreed to act, in a private capacity, as a trial attorney. He was joined by Alexander H. Schullman, who was a counsel for several AFL unions. A young black attorney, Leo A. Branton, Jr., accepted a position on the team, together with two lawyers, Norman Leonard and Ben Margolis, who had represented various left-wing causes. During the trial, Schullman took "personal umbrage" at a prosecution witness' characterization of Margolis as a "Marxist," only to have the latter indicate his acceptance of the designation.[80] The defense team was completed by William Schneiderman, California state chairman of the CP, who chose to defend himself and the Party, playing the same role as Dennis in the first trial.

Defendants and attorneys were agreed that the heaviest emphasis would be placed on defending "the right of advocacy." The legal system would be used, within that context, to present the Party's program.[81] The defense attacked the indictment and, for the first time, forced the court to dismiss it. Judge William C. Mathes, who had sought to maintain exorbitant bail on the California defendants, agreed in December 1951 that the original indictment failed to allege specific unlawful intent.[82] Within ten days a second indictment was filed. Each of the defendants was charged with eight violations of the Smith Act in conspiracy with the convicted national leaders and Foster. The indictments stated that the defendants were seeking the "overthrow and destruction of the Government of the United States by force and violence as speedily as circumstances would permit."[83] Twenty-three overt acts were alleged including seemingly innocent steps such as attendance at meetings, and the publishing of articles.[84] Despite its many delays, the California case was ready for trial more than two months before its New York counterpart.

The prosecution patterned itself on the Dennis case. Lawrence K. Bailey, a special assistant to the Attorney General, was included on the government team to insure uniformity. He had helped to prosecute the CP national board. Once again the prosecutors argued that "Communism cannot be established by peaceful evolution, but, on the contrary, can be established only by violent revolution."[85] A "gigantic conspiracy" was alleged as Ray Kennison discussed the Party's concentration policy, "Aesopian language," democratic centralism, schools, and the underground.[86] The government's heavy reliance on Marxist classics was shown as Kennison noted that "the evidences in this case goes back more than 100 . . . years."[87]

While the prosecution opening came purely out of past experience, the defense began on a slightly different tone. Wirin emphasized that the defendants "had the specific intent of functioning within our democratic system, of acting within the guarantees of the Constitution, of inducing Americans to make peaceful changes in matters that they thought were wrong."[88] Although Schneiderman defended all traditional Marxist concepts, including the dictatorship of the proletariat, he claimed that the CPUSA would interpret the principles of Marxism-Leninism and apply them to the United States. The concept of different roads to socialism was asserted, at the same time as the New York defendants were still debating internally whether this was an acceptable principle.[89] It was clear that subtle but important changes were taking place within the Party.

The government's presentation took more than three months as twenty-two witnesses were called. Six of them testified for less than a day and were subject to almost no cross-examination. They were used primarily to identify one or more of the defendants and to note a Party office or a defendant's presence at a particular meeting—matters generally not disputed by the defense.[90] Four of the remaining witnesses were used almost exclusively to testify to events prior to 1945, mainly in the 1930's. Eight had been minor club officials and had little extensive contact with the Party's state or national leadership. Almost all were used to introduce massive quantities of Marxist and CP literature. Most of the witnesses had been planted by the FBI and at least four of them had received substantial payments for their services.

John Lautner was the most impressive and effective government witness. He had joined the CP in 1929 at the age of twenty-seven and remained an apparently loyal worker in the movement until expelled early in 1950. Never a leader, he had held a series of middle-level Party positions throughout the nation, and had attended and taught in various Party schools. In 1946 he was assigned to New York State and placed in charge of security arrangements for both the state and national conventions of 1948. In 1949 he became head of the New York State Review Commission, a major position holding responsibility for security matters. He played an important role in the development of the underground structure and in securing necessary materials. Although he had no part in establishing policy, he was scheduled to play a key part in carrying it out in perhaps the most sensitive area. Then suspicion grew, apparently from foreign sources, that Lautner was a secret U.S. agent. Without substantial supporting evidence, it was determined to expel him from the Party. He was confronted in the cellar of a Cleveland house early in 1950 by three Party leaders and two others. He claimed a gun was held to his head and knives and rubber hoses were displayed prominently. He was forced to disrobe and accused of being a CIA agent.

Inexplicably, he returned the following morning for another meeting, but found no one there. Two days later he read in *The Daily Worker* of his expulsion. He wrote to the Justice Department in September offering valuable information and was placed on the Department payroll.[91] Lautner's first public appearance was before the SACB. He completed that testimony less than two weeks before being called to the stand in Los Angeles. He subsequently played a starring role in other Smith Act prosecutions.

Lautner was not only able to read and interpret Marxist and Party literature, but his was the most important testimony on the underground. He had been near the tactical center and the authority with which he spoke could not be shaken. He related that in mid–1948 Robert Thompson had briefed him on Foster's plan to establish an underground based on the European model of a "system of threes." As he would do again in the New York trial a short time later, he described the division of the state into regions, the assignment of individuals down to the seventh level, the gathering of mimeo machines and paper, and the acquisition of hiding and meeting places. He claimed that Dorothy Healey, one of the defendants, had been brought to him during a 1949 plenum for a demonstration of the new portable mimeo machines to be used in the underground. Thus the California defendants were tied to the national underground.[92]

The portrait emerging from the Lautner testimony was that of a dangerous, conspiratorial grouping, using the techniques of spies to further their secret ends. The defense, in cross-examination, tried to force Lautner to admit that the underground was only to be employed under conditions similar to Nazi control of World War II Europe, but the witness refused.[93] The fact that the underground had been put into effect already seemed to negate the defense point.

As presented by the prosecution, the underground was not an illegal operation, but it suggested an aura of illegality to the jury. Seven of the witnesses called by the prosecution testified about aspects of the underground. William Foard, who had joined the CP of his own volition in 1945 and had ceased activity in 1948, claimed his local club had begun a collection for a mimeo machine and paper as early as 1946. These were, he said, part of the security precautions being taken. He claimed that his Party club was informed in May 1947 "that the party was going to proceed on a program of going underground" and that Party cards were to be destroyed.[94] This was considerably before the CP had instituted its underground structure, making the testimony rather suspect. Another witness testified it was not until 1948 that her club formed "squads" composed of a few members each which were to operate if the Party submerged.[95] Howard Litt, who had been placed in the CP by the FBI, claimed that his club was first informed of the underground in late 1949 and that it was to be instituted if a guilty verdict was handed down in the Dennis case.[96] Two witnesses, Lloyd Hamlin and Daniel Scarlatto, both FBI informants, claimed they were asked to go "underground" in 1950. Each testified this meant giving up his normal Party functions and waiting for further instructions.[97]

The prosecutors sought to augment their portrait of the CP with a series of isolated statements relating to the use of violence. Hamlin claimed that defendant Loretta Stack had made a comment six years earlier which "in effect" said the CP would be "the instrument through which this capitalist government will be overthrown."[98] A Milwaukee policeman, Paul Estrada, said he had joined the CP, with the knowledge of the FBI, in 1947 and that shortly thereafter "a party member" had given him a government pamphlet entitled "The Land Mines and Booby Traps" and told him to study it "because it will be very useful to you in the event of a revolution in this country."[99] He claimed to have been invited for dinner to Frank Carlson's home following a club meeting in April 1947. Carlson, a defendant, allegedly had asked him to form a black veterans organization "because it will be necessary in the event of a revolution in this country to overthrow this country by the Communist Party, that the Negro boys in the North will have to be militant enough to guide the Negro people in the South." He said Carlson had informed him, in answer to a question, that the Party had "methods" of providing guns to southern blacks.[100] The defense then forced the production of Estrada's written report to the FBI, dated April 9, 1947, indicating that Carlson's remarks came as a result of "lead-on questions." The 1947 report quoted Carlson as saying: "Negroes in the South will have to be taught the Communist way of living. (Program which is now being carried on by CP, CIO, and AFL.) Before they can receive firearms in the event of revolutionary action by the Fascists in that part of the country."[101] The written report, if it was accurate, impeached Estrada's testimony and indicated a Communist desire to defend those who were victims of "fascist" violence—a position which they consistently claimed. Schneiderman was accused of saying, in 1947, that "socialism could only be established through violent revolution," but even here the witness noted that Schneiderman's point was that "finance capital would never give in without a fight."[102]

The government's final witness perhaps best summed up the nature of the prosecution case. Daisy Van Dorn was the sixty-seven-year-old superintendent of the Party's building in San Francisco. She had been induced by the FBI to join the CP in 1945 and had little understanding of its program or of Marxism. The main burden of her testimony was to identify a majority of the defendants, to describe the location of their desks, and to enumerate the times they had asked for night elevator service. Toward the end of her brief testimony, she dropped the one line that government attorneys apparently wished to remain with the jury. She claimed that "Mother" [Ella Reeve] Bloor, at an April 1945 reception had said they were "on the threshold of this revolution" and that "there will be blood flowing in the streets."[103] The fact that this comment was made during the pacific period of the Communist Political Association was not raised. The "blood flowing in the streets" phrase was quoted by various witnesses in widely different settings and proceedings. Such phraseology was put in the best perspective when Foard testified for the prosecution concerning a 1946 Party meeting where "humorous" comments were made such as, "comes the revolution, each person said he had his own special killing list made up and believe me he would show no mercy."[104] It was with such off-hand posturing and lengthy quotations from written works that the government's theory was to be supported.

The prosecution case was not impressive. The only figure of any importance in the Party was Lautner, and he had never been a policy maker. Most of the witnesses had a poor understanding of Marxist theory and had had few contacts with the defendants on trial. Their testimony, at times, was an embarrassment to the government. Louis Rosser, who had left the CP in 1945, implied that attorneys Wirin and Branton were communists because they had defended communists and had met with them on occasion. When Branton denied this and demanded that Rosser repeat a statement he had heard the attorney make at an NAACP meeting, the witness replied that Branton had given the "usual Communist answer, that it was your American right to defend anybody that you wanted to in the community."[105] Foard was forced to admit that defendant Ernest Fox in 1946 and Schneiderman in 1947 had both condemned left sectarians in the Party who were pushing for greater militance, and that each had emphasized that the time for revolutionary action had not come.[106] Stephen Wereb testified that two members in 1945 had arisen in the southern section of the State Convention and "urged that there would be a revolution of workers of the United States and the overthrow of the government." Under cross-examination by Margolis, he was forced to admit that at least one of those members had been expelled for "left sectarianism" in 1947.[107] Scarlatto, extremely anxious on the witness stand to please the prosecutors, volunteered that at a Marxist Institute he attended late in 1949 and early in 1950, they discussed the war in Korea at length. Defense attorney

Leonard pointed out that the Korean War began after the Institute ended.[108] FBI informant Margaret Ames, who had left the CP only months before, wrongly identified Leonard as defendant Al Richmond.[109] Scarlatto, one of the major prosecution witnesses, related a speech supposedly made by Rose Kusnitz in September 1951, while she was still in jail seeking a reduction in bail.[110]

The difficulties of the prosecution were compounded by a new defense strategy. Rather than risk contempt charges against their own witnesses, as in the Dennis trial, the prosecution's witnesses were used to introduce much of the defense case. Seven of the major prosecution witnesses—David Saunders, Hamlin, Scarlatto, Timothy Evans, Foard, Rosser, and Lautner—were required to read important segments of Marxist literature considered favorable to the defense position. They, and others, were led through a maze of more recent Party literature to prove that the CP had sought peaceful, beneficial reforms within the society. Foster bitterly condemned the new defense technique. Claiming that the failure to produce Party witnesses was "legalistic nonsense," he maintained that the California defendants had "made no effective, positive presentation of our Party's line and of our case in general. The trial was essentially on the defensive, instead of on the offensive as in the trial of the 'Eleven.' "[111] The Party's line may not have been presented as Foster would have wished, but the case was well presented.

The government rested its case on May 21, 1952.[112] As the defense prepared and presented its motions for acquittal, it was aware that while prosecution witnesses were testifying, a second Smith Act case had gone to trial and been completed with expected results. Six Baltimore defendants, Philip and Regina Frankfeld, George Meyers, Leroy Wood, Maurice Braverman, and Dorothy Blumberg were convicted after a three-week trial. Running what is still recalled admiringly by prosecutors as a "tight ship,"[113] Judge W. Calvin Chesnut tightly controlled both witnesses and evidence. Unlike the previous proceedings, jury selection was completed in one day. From the beginning the Judge made it clear that he would not allow repetitive evidence and demanded the limitation of readings. The trial began on March 10, 1952, and the first witness was on the stand the next day.

The theory, evidence, and many of the witnesses in Baltimore were familiar. Again the defendants were charged with conspiring to advocate violent overthrow of the government "as speedily as circumstances will permit." Once more the development of the underground was included in the indictment.[114] Three outside attorneys agreed to represent four of the defendants, while Braverman, who was a lawyer, and Meyers defended themselves. Judge Chesnut would permit none of them any latitude. When defense attorneys in their opening statements claimed this was a political trial, and an extraordinary case, the Judge would allow none of it. He interrupted defense attorney Harold Buchman to state: "No, it is not the ordinary case. I propose to keep before the jury the issues of the case, which are simple and clear as far as I have been able to get them."[115] At the conclusion of all the opening statements, the Judge again made his position clear. "The defendants contend or say that it is a political trial," he said to the jury. "If, when and as there is evidence bearing on that, I will undertake to rule on it as a matter of evidence . . . . Now let me say another thing. It is a criminal trial."[116] The government took its cue from the Judge and carefully limited its case.

Five of the ten prosecution witnesses had testified before. John Lautner appeared just ten days after his Los Angeles testimony was completed, and his relation of the underground structure as well as definition of Marxist terms and concepts was becoming familiar. He maintained that the purpose of the CP was violently to overthrow the government at some future date, in an emergency, when the Party had gained sufficient influence to be successful.[117]

Paul Crouch, the government's first witness, told far more lurid tales. He had been a member of the Party in the 1920's and 1930's and had left in 1942 to become a "consultant" with the Immigration and Naturalization Service. His role as a professional informer eventually was to be discredited as his stories became contradictory. Now he told the court of Moscow-directed plans to infiltrate the United States armed forces in the late 1920's. There was no question as to his view of the purposes of the CP. "Throughout the period of my membership," he related, "the attitude of the Communist Party toward the United States Government was that it was an enemy government which must be overthrown by armed insurrection within and with the aid of the Red Army of the Soviet Union with its defeat, its destruction, annihilation, and replacement by a Soviet America."[118]

William Nowell and Charles Nicodemus had testified in 1949 at Foley Square. They repeated, with small discrepancies, their earlier statements. Nicodemus' effort to repeat the story of a threatened 1945 Soviet invasion through Alaska was ruled out by Judge Chesnut.[119] Mary Stalcup Markward, an FBI informant placed in the Party in 1943 and who had testified extensively before the SACB, identified each of the defendants and their Party positions. She maintained that she was involved in discussions concerning an underground apparatus in 1946.[120] Three of the remaining witnesses had been FBI informants, another had been in the Party only two years and had left in 1948 at the age of twenty-two, and the last was a bank employee identifying those listed as local CP officials. Charles Craig, who testified most extensively, had been a Baltimore club official and knew each of the defendants. He had been expelled in 1950 as an informant, but might easily have been dropped for a lack of understanding of Marxism. He was forced to admit that the concept of violence had never openly been taught and that he had never heard the words "force and violence" used in the eight years he had been in the Party, but maintained that "when you read the Leninist-Marxist theory, you can take that conception of what it is supposed to be."[121]

The last of the major government witnesses, Harry Bartlett, proved to be an embarrassment. He testified concerning CP labor agitation and claimed that Philip Frankfeld had said he would always be a "professional revolutionist."[122] Under cross-examination he admitted reluctantly that he had been expelled from the Party in late 1949 for being "too revolutionary" and for advocating the use of force and violence.[123] No longer on the FBI payroll, and "broke," Bartlett had hoped that his testimony would bring him some needed money.

The entire defense case took less than four days. Meyers was the only defendant to testify—a striking departure from the Dennis case. He had joined the CP in 1942, after already achieving the position of a textile workers' union leader and a CIO state officer. His testimony was a curious combination of traditional Marxist jargon, the Party line, and a groping movement toward a more pragmatic approach. He defined Marxist terminology for the jury, but continued to defend such concepts as the "dictatorship of the proletariat." His major emphasis shifted to the possibility of achieving socialism through a peaceful "further extension of democratic processes."[124] Meyers reminded the court that "social change is brought about by the majority will of the people, and the majority of the people, under no circumstances, desire to resort to the use of force or violence to bring about such change." Violence, if it was to come, he said, would be initiated by the ruling class.[125] The effective impression Meyers might have made on the jury was largely destroyed during his second day on the stand. Under cross-examination he refused to identify the leaders of the Maryland CP when he joined in 1942 or to testify about his co-defendant Braverman. He was immediately adjudged in contempt, although the sentence was held in abeyance. The only other major witness called by the defense was Marxist historian Herbert Aptheker. With his challenge to government interpretations of Marxist theory, the defense rested.

The Baltimore case went to the jury on April 1 and in less than three hours each of the defendants was found guilty. On April 4, 1952, the defendants were sentenced to terms ranging from two to five years.[126]

The California defendants could not have been encouraged by the events in Baltimore. Judge Chesnut, while brusque and demanding, had been far more objective than Judge Mathes. The government case presented there had been far less extensive, yet the verdicts were decisive. The one major witness called by the defense in California was Oleta O'Connor Yates. As she prepared to begin her testimony on June 11, 1952, she knew the difficulties which lay ahead. Three of the defendants, Frank Spector, Kusnitz, and Richmond, already had rested their cases, claiming an insufficiency of evidence to convict them—a tactic again bitterly opposed by Foster.[127] A fourth defendant, Bernadette Doyle, had been severed by Judge Mathes as a result of poor health.[128] The defense had decided already that Yates would be the major witness they would present.

Attorney Leonard had reserved his opening statement and now used his time to propose a defense view that marked a serious departure from the previous trials. This was not a Party defense, but an individual defense that Leonard promised to the jury. Each of the defendants, he said, had his "own personal interpretation and understanding of this [Marxist] philosophy," and they totally rejected the use of violence and believed Marxism-Leninism to do so as well.[129] Time and again Leonard referred to the beliefs of the individual defendants, a position which must have distressed Foster deeply. There was no vacillation in Leonard's remarks. "They do not believe that fascism is inevitable in the United States," he said.[130] Here was a major section of the CP leadership pragmatically claiming the right to express their own interpretations of Party policy and basic philosophy, a position which portended much for the future.

With Leonard's words setting the stage, Yates took the stand. She had been a member of the CP for nineteen of her forty-two years, and had risen to the position of California state organizational secretary. Her parents had immigrated to the United States from Ireland in the mid-nineteenth century. She came from a long family history of trade unionists, with her grandfather a founder of the Union Labor Party. Born in a poor Irish neighborhood in San Francisco, she entered the University of California at Berkeley just prior to the onset of the Depression. The economic crisis drove her, as so many others, toward radicalism. While earning a B.A. and M.A., she read Marx and Engels, attended meetings of the unemployed, and by 1932 had joined the Socialist Party. A year later she became a CP member. Her experience, background, and education made her a forceful, articulate witness—and the defense relied on her. For two weeks she was allowed to testify on a wide range of CP activities from the 1930's through to the trial date. She explained Marxist classics in understandable terms of contemporary conditions and emphasized CP efforts to gain reforms within the existing system.

Yates' testimony, as a whole, marked a clear departure for the CP. She emphasized that contemporary leaders have a right to interpret Marxism and exercised that option. She rejected whole "programmatic sections of the Communist Manifesto" as "inapplicable" to the United States more than 100 years later.[131] Lenin's writings on revolution were discarded for the world of 1952, and Yates made clear that the principles of Marxism-Leninism were to be applied "as a result of study and experimentation" and "differently under different conditions."[132]

The Party's position on the imminence of fascism was modified severely. Yates asserted that "under this form of government there are still avenues through which the people can democratically express themselves." She could conceive of "no circumstances" which would cause her to advocate the violent overthrow of the existing form of government.[133] The failure to reach the masses, much less educate them or prepare them for revolutionary change was implicitly expressed. "I think the majority of the people at this stage of history do not understand what socialism is," she said, "much less are they convinced that it is necessary; and until the people do understand what it is, until the majority are convinced of the necessity, socialism cannot be an immediate issue."[134]

It was only when Yates was challenged with the statements of the national leadership that she lost some of her credibility. Even here, surprisingly, she did not fully embrace concepts at variance with her own views. Confronted with Foster's 1949 statement that the CPUSA would join the French and Italian parties in opposing U.S. aggression in any war with the Soviet Union, she reemphasized her own "understanding" that peace is possible and rejected a full concurrence.[135] Placed on the defensive by a 1950 Gus Hall article in which he termed the United States the "headquarters of the world camp of reaction, fascism and war," she defended the article, but put some distance between her own views, or at least emphasis, and those of Hall.[136] Despite these difficulties, her testimony was a complete, impresssive defense against months of government charges, readings, and interpretations.

The government's major weapon against Yates was not in the area of doctrine. Within a short time after the beginning of cross-examination, the prosecutors were demanding the names and identities of Party officials and her associates. Yates adamantly refused the role of "government informer," as they knew she would. Judge Mathes, following the precedent set by Judge Medina, struck hard at her refusal. He was willing, he said, to make a "martyr" of her "in the best sense of the word." He would make her suffer the "pain" as well as accept the glory for her refusal to name names.[137] Each refusal to answer a prosecution question was ruled to be a separate offense subject to a separate penalty. Adjudged guilty of four acts of contempt on the first day of cross-examination, she was immediately committed to prison for an indefinite period. All stays were denied. On the night of June 26, 1952, she was taken to the overcrowded county jail. Since the authorities were unable to find space in a cell, she was put on a cot in the corridor where she spent the night. She was brought to court the following morning after a sleepless night and suffering from a deep cold.[138] Despite the fact that Yates had already been committed to prison for the remainder of the trial, Judge Mathes continued to press the issue. He invited the prosecution to ask "leading questions as to the names of persons previously mentioned in the testimony," and the government attorneys accepted the suggestion. Yates was cited eleven additional times for contempt and the Judge announced he would now treat this refusal as "criminal contempt," contemplating more severe punishment.[139]

The Yates testimony had presented the views of the California defendants. They determined there was nothing to be gained by placing additional Party leaders in jeopardy or continuing the battle with the Judge. Schneiderman announced that the defense had intended calling ten or fifteen witnesses, but faced with the government determination to elicit names for the purpose of exposure, none would be called. After presenting a minor technical witness, the remaining defendants rested.[140]

Foster again was outraged by the trial strategy. He sharply commented that "it was a basic error in California to put only one witness on the stand. This wrong course originated in the legalistic illusion that 'the Government had made no case against us.' The error was doubly compounded," he maintained, "when, after Comrade Oleta O'Connor Yates was condemned for contempt we failed to back her up by putting other witnesses on the stand."[141] The California defendants had not followed the pattern set in the Dennis case, had charted a somewhat independent course, and had presented a differing Party estimate, but Foster's opposition to their actions was greatly strengthened when the outcome appeared to be essentially the same. The months of testimony had changed no positions. The government, in closing arguments, maintained that the Marxist classics provided a blueprint for revolutionary action. "Is that just a history book?" the prosecuting attorney asked. "A book that you are reviewing to find out what happened in

1902, 1905, 1917 or are you being told that is what to do?" The prosecutor claimed that "they are saying there you have got to take Marxism-Leninism as it is contained in the books, don't water it down or don't change it."[142] That is precisely what the attorneys and Yates had not said, but the subtle change was either not understood or simply made no difference to a prosecution intent on achieving its goals.

Judge Mathes patterned the major part of the jury charge on that developed by Medina in the first New York trial. It was only in two critical areas that he departed. One was unavoidable. It involved a definition of the term "organize" since these defendants were accused of having organized the CP with the intent of carrying out the illegal acts defined in the Smith Act. The statute of limitations had run out on the 1945 reorganization of the Party. Judge Mathes defined the term to include the recruitment of new members, the forming of new clubs and other ongoing activities.[143] The Judge cautioned the jurors that the mere "holding of a belief or opinion does not constitute advocacy or teaching" and that this was not barred by the law. It had to be proven that the defendants had a specific intent to bring about the violent overthrow of the government "as speedily as circumstances would permit."[144] Inexplicably, the Judge refused both defense and government suggestions to define more clearly the nature of the proscribed intent. He refused a defense proposal to include the concept that teaching or advocacy to "induce action," "rather than discussion or belief" had to be proven.[145] The critical question of abstract advocacy was thus left for future court decisions.

After more than five days of deliberation, surprising in its length to most observers, each of the defendants was found guilty.[146] Judge Mathes immediately remanded all defendants to prison without bail. Each was sentenced to a full five-year prison term with a $10,000 fine.[147] Despite pleas by the defense attorneys, Mathes refused to reconsider the denial of bail. As far as he was concerned, there was not even a "substantial question" to be considered by the appellate court. He rejected all defense motions to set aside the verdicts and when Wirin, Branton, and Margolis suggested an insufficiency of evidence, he asked, incredulously, "Are you suggesting that the Supreme Court is going to determine the facts, to determine whether there is any doubt?"[148] Four years later Judge Mathes must have been shocked when the Court did precisely this.

The Judge went beyond simple denials of defense motions. Nothing was more ominous to the CP than his answer to defense arguments concerning the insufficiency of the jury instructions. "There is nothing in the instructions," he said, "that tells the jury that they may not find that every member of the Communist Party is a member of this conspiracy."[149] The Judge's remarks, together with the verdicts, caused an important reaction within communist ranks. One of the California defendants noted that, "If the Supreme Court decision in the Dennis case signified it was five to midnight then our conviction, coming after one in Baltimore, plausibly moved the minute hand a notch or two closer to the upright position. Certainly, from our vantage point, the political situation in the country had not gotten better between June 1951 and August 1952."[150]

It seemed as if the government deliberately was spacing the scheduling of the trials so that the Party would never have a period to rest and gain some perspective. As the California trial ended, the second New York trial was continuing. The verdict on the West Coast gave Foster and his allies an opportunity to attack the fledgling independence movement within the Party. A week after the Los Angeles decision, Foster wrote to the National Committee to criticize the California defendants for not correctly expressing "the line" adopted by the national leadership. The verdict had been predetermined, he suggested. If that was so, his view of the imminence of fascism had been strengthened. "Very probably, no matter how well and militantly we had presented our case to the California court," he maintained, "the verdict would have been the same." The courts could provide no legal relief. What then was the purpose of an extended defense? Foster's answer was clear. "We have got to make such a defense as will clearly present our case, not only to the jury, but especially to the Party membership and the Party's general following. This was most emphatically not done in California."[151] Foster and his allies tried to dictate the defense strategy in the second New York case and had considerable success. Despite this effective control, the trial did not fully support Foster's analysis.

Nominal control of trial strategy rested in a policy committee composed, at first, of Elizabeth Gurley Flynn, Pettis Perry, Simon Gerson, and George Charney. Apparently this group had been chosen by Eugene Dennis, but it was not fully trusted by Foster and others who remained in the national office of the Party. Foster insisted that Betty Gannett and Claudia Jones be added to the committee and this was done.[152] The degree of national oversight over the trial was impressive. Unlike the California defendants who were able to gain a consensus concerning trial strategy, the New York defendants were subject to severe strains and conflicts—many of which were to mirror the later splits in the Party. Bittelman fought a lonely battle to meet the charge that the advocacy of Marxist-Leninist theory "is tantamount to advocating the deed of violent overthrow." He emphasized that the defendants had to find an effective means of meeting this charge.[153] His solution was to develop more fully the concept of a peaceful transition to socialism through the creation of a "People's Democracy." This was not simply to be an abstract theoretical possibility, but Bittelman argued that the conditions for such a transformation were "being created in the major struggles of the present period—the struggles for peace and democracy."[154] Despite the fact that the national leadership did not approve his formulation, Bittelman sought to gain its acceptance as trial strategy. On January 7, 1952, he presented an elaboration of his developing theoretical position at a defendants' meeting. A bitter struggle ensued and the proposals were rejected.[155] Bittelman pressed for an opportunity to take the witness stand. His effort initially was rebuffed by the policy committee. Flynn was to be the major witness, to be followed by Gerson, testifying on political activities, and Charney on theory and the Party program. The national office intervened to demand that Bittelman, Jones, and Gannett be added to the defense witness list. There was to be a full exposition of the Party line. By the time the trial opened in April 1952, there was no agreement by the defendants as to how to proceed. Some wanted to follow the California strategy of seeking to increase "ties with the liberal community." Others, supported by Foster, were concerned with presentation of the Party line, with no deviations.[156]

It has been suggested that all the Smith Act trials after the Dennis case "were but variations of a single trial, with the CPUSA as the defendant."[157] The analysis has validity when applied to the government position, but begins to break down when subtle changes in the defense are examined. The Justice Department's task force coordinated government strategy for all the trials and the testimony of prosecution witnesses was remarkably similar. A small group of key witnesses travelled from trial to trial, and they were supplemented by a few local witnesses. The government's basic theory was unchanging. The defendants believed in and taught Marxism-Leninism. Socialism can be established only by violent revolution. The communist leaders studied and taught from the classics of Marxist-Leninist literature. These writings were "studies in minute detail as a model for the revolution in this country."[158] In one way or another the defense in the various trials attempted to meet the issue, but the differences in approach were important. Yates in California had emphasized her belief that a peaceful transition to socialism would take place, and Bittelman had sought to expand this concept. In opening remarks at the second New York trial, Flynn, acting as her own attorney, moved back to the earlier Dennis position. She emphasized the communist desire for a peaceful transition, but accepted the concept that violence, initiated by "the enemies of the people," would develop since they would never peacefully accept the loss of their power.[159] The prediction of violence negated the peaceful image being projected.

The government's case in the second New York trial was presented through ten witnesses, many of them familiar. As in the first trial, the star witness was Louis Budenz, and he was followed by John Lautner, Mary Markward, William Cummings, and Thomas Younglove, all of whom had testified before. The presentation of the prosecution case, with a dreary repetition of readings as well as testimony, went on for more than four months, and through a hot summer. The Judge, Edward Dimock, provided a far more open and objective atmosphere than had the three previous Smith Act jurists. He allowed both sides to put into the record enormous quantities of readings. As the prosecution case wound down, toward the end of the summer, internal defense conflict grew. The trial policy committee decided that Bittelman should not be allowed to testify. His participation in the Communist International in the 1920's and 1930's would leave the defendants open to serious attack. For Foster this was an unacceptable position. "The best possible defense of our Party, before our Party, before the public, and also before the jury," he wrote to the National Committee, "is a militant exposition of our Party line, as laid down in our Party history [which he had written] just newly off the press."[160] Foster thought that the matter of Bittelman testifying had been settled, but found that there was growing opposition again. Now he demanded that both Bittelman and Gannett take the stand to defend the Party. He was aware of Bittelman's evolving differences. Bittelman had written to him privately to criticize his formulations in the Party history. He had written numerous articles for *Political Affairs*, only to have his references to an American road to socialism omitted.[161] Foster was confident that Bittelman would do what he had always done, defend the Party line on theory as well as program no matter what his personal views. "The main thing to consider . . . is the political line, and there can be no doubt but that he can defend and explain that line as well as any of us," Foster argued. "He is one of the very best developed comrades theoretically in our entire Party."[162] Despite Foster's demands, the question was not settled until well into the defense case, perhaps because his analysis was shown to be partially faulty.

At the conclusion of the prosecution case, the defense made a series of routine motions for directed verdicts of acquittal. John T. McTernan, an outside attorney who had agreed to join the defense team, argued that these defendants were not an "identifiable inside group" as in the Dennis case and could not automatically be considered as part of a conspiracy simply due to the holding of Party positions.[163] The argument must have distressed Foster. Judge Dimock indicated considerable interest in it. He noted that mere officership in the CP was not a crime and asked the prosecution for evidence of "personal knowledge of each one of the defendants of the content of the alleged conspiracy."[164] When the special assistant U.S. attorney general assigned to the case argued that the existence of an underground structure proved the illegality of the Party, the Judge disagreed, and forced David Marks to qualify his assertion with the statement that the underground "verges on the illegal."[165] Dimock stunned the courtroom on September 22, 1952, when he directed verdicts of acquittal for Gerson and Isidore Begun on the grounds of an insufficiency of evidence.[166] Only two of the sixteen defendants had been released, but the ruling gave greater impetus to those beginning to challenge Foster's views.

Several of the defense attorneys had reserved their opening remarks and presented them as the defense opened its case. Allowed to argue legal issues, they were still tied by the defendants to Party definitions of theory and program. Again it was argued that the CP would not initiate violence unless majority will is "suppressed by a tyrannical dictatorship." At the same time it was admitted, and Marxist-Leninist literature was said to state, that "history has demonstrated that no privileged group has relinquished its power or control without desperate resistance."[167] The CP again seemed to be arguing the government case.

Abraham Magil, a *Daily Worker* journalist and experienced Party member, was called as the first defense witness to dispute some of Budenz' assertions concerning the operation of the communist press. His most extensive testimony came under cross-examination as the prosecutors questioned him closely about Marxist theory. Flynn followed him to the stand and she was to serve much the same role as Yates. In testimony ranging over a period of two months, she reviewed a life of struggle for labor rights and put forward the positive program of the CP. While emphasizing the theoretical possibility of a peaceful transition to socialism through the creation of an antimonopoly third party growing out of a united front movement to extend democratic rights, Flynn felt it necessary to defend the full range of Party policies and Marxist theory. The "dictatorship of the proletariat" was again supported as was the belief that violence would be initiated by the minority against a majority decision to move to socialism. She refused to move away from a full acceptance of Marxist-Leninist theory although

Dimock gave her the opportunity. When the Judge asked if changed conditions in the United States permitted the "abandonment of any theory of Marxism-Leninism," she replied there would be no abandonment, although there might be "different application under different times, conditions, and circumstances."[168] The impression she gave after two months of testimony was of a warm, concerned human being who was unyielding, in the final analysis, on the beliefs she had held for many years.

Under cross-examination, Flynn faced the same difficulties as previous defendants, although this was somewhat ameliorated by Dimock. Once again the prosecution immediately demanded the naming of names, and Flynn refused. The Judge was conciliatory and sought some form of accommodation, forcing the prosecutors to hold these questions in abeyance for a short time. Eventually the issue had to be faced and Flynn was cited for contempt, with a thirty-day sentence to commence upon leaving the witness stand.[169]

The conclusion of the Flynn testimony, in early December 1952, left the defense in the midst of its continuing conflict. Foster, with the support of some defendants, demanded the trial strategy he had outlined. The defendants joined in a meeting lasting much of the night and adopted, by a one-vote margin, a course of action where no other witnesses would be called. Thus neither the witnesses desired by Foster, nor those wanted by the policy committee, would appear. Members of the defendants' majority were called before Foster and others from the national office and severely berated for the decision, but it stood.[170]

The conclusion of the case was anticlimactic. Summations given both by prosecution and defense were a restatement of previous positions and Dimock delivered a Medina charge to the jury. After six days of deliberation, each of the remaining defendants was found guilty. Dimock sentenced them to terms from a year and a day to three years.[171] As the trial ended, President Truman was leaving the White House and a new Republican administration was moving in. The prosecutive actions begun by the Democratic administration were continuing. The trial of the Hawaiian communists had begun in November 1952 and was still going on as Truman left office. In September 1952, the Justice Department had indicted an additional eighteen communist functionaries in Seattle, Detroit, and St. Louis. All these cases, together with that of Pittsburgh, were tried in 1953 and 1954 and the Eisenhower administration continued the process with indictments in Philadelphia, Cleveland, Denver, Connecticut, Puerto Rico, and Boston. Additionally, eight CP leaders were indicted and tried under the "membership clause" of the Smith Act during the Eisenhower years. President Truman had left behind a considerable legacy and one which he had done little to lessen as his term ended.

The President had feared the onset of an "alien and sedition" type of hysteria for years, but found just such a political atmosphere developing. An historian described the new climate: "Everywhere in the United States, the fury against Communism was taking on—even more than it had before the Korean War—elements of a vendetta against the Half-Century of Revolution in domestic affairs, against all departures from tradition in foreign policy, against the new, the adventurous, the questing in any field."[172] Despite all this, Truman never changed his tactics. He still defended himself by attacking the "Red Menace." At a December 1951 press conference, he recalled that his administration had taken "drastic action" in the past to protect the United States' internal security. "The Communists who have been tried and convicted," he said, "were tried and convicted by the Attorney General, not by any outside agency."[173]

Those persons in the internal security establishment who had worked hardest to attack the "Red Menace" were promoted and honored. A. Devitt Vanech, for example, who had been an obscure special assistant to the Attorney General early in 1947, was confirmed in the position of deputy attorney general on September 24, 1951.[174] He had served as an effective conduit for information to and from the FBI. His new position did not change that role. On December 27, 1951, he received a request from the Attorney General to "informally talk" with Hoover on the question of future prosecution of members of the Communist Party. "I know he is deeply concerned about these matters," wrote McGrath, "and we should be very careful that he receives adequate cooperation."[175]

As the nation entered the presidential election year of 1952, Truman was on the defensive again with regard to the communist issue. McCarthy, quickly followed by a host of Republican candidates, reopened the "soft on communism" issue. McCarthy attacked the White House staff, specifically naming David D. Lloyd and Philleo Nash. The President shot back at a January press conference that McCarthy was "pathological" and a "character assassin," but he would allow neither characterization to be quoted directly. He had more difficulty in answering the reporter who quoted McCarthy as claiming to have secret FBI reports. The President may have been speaking wishfully when he said, "I doubt very much whether he received any information."[176]

A strategy had to be found to answer the Republicans, and the Democrats resorted to the means they had used before. The nation was to be reassured by stressing confidence in the security agencies at the same time as the administration would reassert both its record in fighting communism at home and abroad and its determination to continue the struggle.

Speaking on March 29, 1952, before a Jefferson-Jackson Day Dinner in Washington, President Truman announced that he would not seek re-election. The President reminded the nation that "We have fought communism abroad. We have fought communism at home. We have an FBI and a Central Intelligence Agency defending us against spies and saboteurs. The Federal loyalty program keeps communists out of Government."[177] The Republicans would have to run against his anti-communist record, although he would no longer be the candidate.

As the presidential campaign heated up in the fall, Truman began a series of speeches on behalf of the Democratic ticket. The issue of communism was a favorite topic. Repeatedly taking material from his 1948 Oklahoma City speech on communism, Truman defended his record by pointing to the prosecution of communist leaders and the low ebb of the CP. "Communism inside this country has been badly beaten," he asserted in Washington on September 17. Some leaders had been tried already, he said, and others were undergoing trials. Communists had been driven from the nation's labor unions and the government loyalty program "stands as a firm barrier to Communist infiltration." Truman defined communists as "a definite and disciplined group of people who are fanatically dedicated to carrying out the purposes of the Soviet Union," and promised that they would be "identified, isolated, and prosecuted in many cases, and rendered harmless."[178] Less than a week later communist functionaries in Seattle, Detroit, and St. Louis were arrested and accused of violation of the Smith Act.

The next month the President repeated almost the same statements in a Boston speech, now terming the CP "a small, insidious underground conspiracy." He gave credit to the FBI for "skillfully and systematically" rooting out the communist danger, and noted that this process had started with President Roosevelt's 1939 directive for the FBI "to take charge of all investigative work in matters relating to espionage, sabotage, and subversive activities." The fact that the 1939 directive had not authorized investigation of "subversive activities" apparently continued to be unknown to the President. Truman lauded the FBI and Department of Justice for sending the leaders of the CP to jail.[179] The next day the President quoted Herbert Philbrick to suggest that "McCarthyism" was a great danger because it "does not hurt the Communists—it helps them."[180] The same themes were struck time and again as Truman whistle-stopped along the eastern coast. As he had four years before, the President suggested that the communists were trying to defeat the Democratic Party.[181] None of these efforts could stop the election of Eisenhower. The anticommunist Democratic campaign had helped to create an issue which ultimately aided in the Democratic administration's undoing.

On the evening of January 15, 1953, President Truman delivered his farewell address to a nationwide audience. Earlier that day a jury in New York City had begun to deliberate in the trial of fourteen communist defendants. The President had no need to refer to this now. Instead, he spoke in general terms of the continuing "menace of communism." He spoke of communism as "a godless system; a system of slavery." He spoke of the "Iron Curtain," the Soviet "secret police," and the "free world."[182] There was no recognition that the fears he had helped to create and for which his administration had served as a vehicle, had made his own part of the "free world" significantly less free.

On Christmas day 1951, a little more than a year before the President's farewell address, Elizabeth Gurley Flynn had recalled that she was "lonesome for old-fashioned mass meetings with real fighting speeches."[183] The American people, too, would soon become "lonesome" for the kind of give and take which is the lifeblood of political democracy.

NOTES

1. *Dennis, et al. v. United States*, 341 U.S. 494 (1951).
2. Ibid., 499.
3. Ibid., 510.
4. Ibid., 510, 516–17.
5. Ibid., 510–11.
6. Ibid., 539–40, 578.
7. Ibid., 567–70.
8. Ibid., 579.
9. Ibid., 580.
10. Ibid., 581.
11. Ibid., 583.
12. Ibid., 584.
13. Ben V. Cohen to Hugo Black, July 2, 1951, Container 308, Folder No. 336 October term, 1950 *Dennis v. U.S.* Hereafter container number and folder designations will be cited as 308/No. 336 . . . . Papers of Hugo Black, Library of Congress, Washington, D.C. Hereafter cited as LC.
14. Alonzo Hamby, *Beyond the New Deal: Harry S. Truman and American Liberalism* (New York, 1973), 469–70; Mary S. McAuliffe, *Crisis on the Left, Cold War Politics and American Liberals, 1947–1954* (Amherst, 1978), 86–87.
15. McAuliffe, *Crisis on the Left*, 96.
16. *The Daily Worker*, June 21, 1951.

17. John Gates to author, March 5, 1978.

18. John Gates to Joseph Starobin, October 12, 1970, in Joseph R. Starobin, *American Communism in Crisis, 1943–1957* (Cambridge, 1972), 306 n.10.

19. George Watt to author, June 29, 1975.

20. John Gates to author, March 5, 1978.

21. Sidney Steinberg to author, December 25, 1974.

22. John Gates to author, March 5, 1978.

23. National Committee, CPUSA, "America's Hour of Peril—United! Save Democracy and Peace!" *Political Affairs* XXX (July 1951), 1–2.

24. Ibid., 5.

25. Ibid., 6.

26. *The New York Times*, June 15, 1951.

27. Lawrence Bailey and Kevin Maroney to author, July 24, 1974.

28. A. H. Belmont, "Memorandum to D. M. Ladd," October 5, 1951, copy of document submitted to author by FBI.

29. Kevin Maroney to author, July 24, 1974.

30. Sidney Steinberg to author, December 25, 1974.

31. *United States v. Trachtenberg, et al.*, "Transcript of Trial," Government's Opening Statement (April 30, 1956), 1284.

32. Ibid., Testimony of Special Agent Joseph P. McCane (June 6, 1956), 4743–45.

33. George Watt to author, June 29, 1975.

34. *United States v. Flynn, et al.*, "Transcript of Trial." Hereafter cited as *Flynn Transcript*. Reading of the Indictment (April 15, 1952), 757.

35. *The Daily Worker*, June 26, 1951.

36. Alexander Bittelman, "Autobiography" (Unpublished Typescript, 1963, Tamiment Library, New York University), 745.

37. John Gates to author, March 5, 1978.

38. Eugene Dennis, "Our Cause is Invincible," *Political Affairs* XXX (August 1951), 2.

39. Peggy Dennis, *The Autobiography of an American Communist, A Personal View of a Political Life 1925–1975* (Westport, 1977), 208–9; John Gates to author, March 5, 1978; George Watt to author, June 29, 1975.

40. FBI New York office, "Eugene Dennis," May 8, 1951, copy of document submitted to author by FBI.

41. John Gates to author, March 5, 1978.

42. *United States v. Hall*, 100 F. Supp. 671 (1951).

43. FBI New York office, "Robert George Thompson," January 13, 1951, May 7, 1951, copy of documents submitted to author by FBI.

44. FBI Pittsburgh to Director, SACs, New York and Cleveland, Teletype, September 18, 1951, copy of document submitted to author by FBI.

45. SAC, New York to Director FBI, "Memorandum," May 15, 1951; To Inspector Naughten, "Inspection Report," New York Office FBI, May 14, 1951, copies of documents submitted to author by FBI.

46. John Edgar Hoover to Legal Attaché Mexico, D.F., July 6, 1951, copy of document submitted to author by FBI.

47. John Gates to author, March 5, 1978.

48. Peggy Dennis, *Autobiography*, 204.

49. Martin Fisher, "Urgent Tasks for Strengthening the Party," *Political Affairs* XXX (November 1951), 35.

50. George Watt to author, June 29, 1975.

51. Ibid.

52. *The Daily Worker*, October 10, 1951.

53. Ibid., December 20, 1951; *United States v. Hall*, 101 F. Supp. 666 (1951).

54. *The New York Times*, July 3, 1951.

55. "The Democratic Record Against Communism, Appendix A, List of Prosecutions Involving Communist Activity—1941–1953," December 9, 1953, 27/Anti-Communism, Papers of Charles Murphy, Harry S. Truman Library, Independence, Missouri. Hereafter cited as HSTL. *The Daily Worker*, December 4, 1951.

56. *The Daily Worker*, July 12, 1951.

57. *The New York Times*, August 3, 1951.

58. "The Democratic Record Against Communism . . . ," December 9, 1953, HSTL.

59. Philip B. Perlman (Solicitor General) to Charles E. Cropley (Supreme Court Clerk), October 26, 1951, 310/October Term 1951 Conference Memoranda, Papers of Hugo Black, LC.

60. *Stack v. Boyle*, 342 U.S. 1 (1951); *The New York Times*, November 6, 1951.

61. John Gates to author, March 5, 1978.

62. Alexander Bittelman, "Who Are the Conspirators?" *Political Affairs* XXX (July 1951), 13.

63. *The Daily Worker*, August 30, 1951.

64. Ibid., October 10, 1951.

65. Al Richmond, *A Long View from the Left, Memoirs of an American Revolutionary* (Boston, 1967), 312–13.

66. Ibid., 314.

67. William Z. Foster to the National Committee, August 15, 1952, Folder 7, Papers of Alexander Bittelman, Alexander Bittelman Home Library, Croton, New York. Hereafter cited as BHL.

68. Richmond, *A Long View from the Left*, 312–14; George Watt to author, June 29, 1975; Sidney Steinberg to author, December 25, 1974.

69. Alexander Bittelman, "Mass Tasks Facing the Party Today," *Political Affairs* XXX (September 1951), 16.

70. Alexander Bittelman to William Z. Foster, October 4, 1951, Folder 3, Papers of Alexander Bittelman, BHL.

71. Alexander Bittelman to William Z. Foster, November 14, 1951, Folder 3, Papers of Alexander Bittelman, BHL.

72. William Z. Foster, *History of the Communist Party of the United States* (New York, 1968), 467.

73. Ibid., 463.

74. Bittelman, "Autobiography," 748–49.

75. Alexander Bittelman, "On the Overt Acts," October 28, 1951, Folder 5, Papers of Alexander Bittelman, BHL.

76. George Charney, *A Long Journey* (Chicago, 1968), 216.

77. *Flynn Transcript*, Pretrial hearing before Hon. Edward A. Conger, District Judge, November 8, 1951, 46–59.

78. Charney, *A Long Journey*, 213.

79. *Flynn Transcript*, Pretrial hearing before Hon. Edward A. Conger, District Judge, November 8, 1951, 72.

80. *United States v. Schneiderman, et al.*, "Transcript of Proceedings," United States District Court, Southern District of California, Central Division. Hereafter cited as *Yates Transcript* [the case was later known as *Yates v. United States*]. Colloquy, April 8, 1952, 4779.

81. Richmond, *A Long View from the Left*, 329–30.

82. *Yates Transcript*, December 11, 1951, 10.

83. Ibid., Indictment, December 21, 1951, 2.

84. Ibid., 3.

85. Ibid., Government Opening, February 5, 1952, 240.

86. Ibid., 246, 252–55.

87. Ibid., 242.

88. Ibid., Defendants' Opening, February 6, 1952, 289.

89. Ibid., 313–20, 325; Bittelman, "Autobiography," 748–49.

90. *Yates Transcript*, testimony of Bessie Honig, Alfred W. Addy, Teresa M. Scagnelli, Vernon Sutherland, Otis E. Phillips, Jr., Edgar Brandt, April 16–May 9, 1952, 5430–7763.

91. Ibid., Testimony of John Lautner, February 26–March 3, 1952, 1987–2707; *Flynn Transcript*, Testimony of John Lautner, June 11, 1952, 4576–93; Starobin, *American Communism in Crisis*, 218–19.

92. *Yates Transcript*, Testimony of John Lautner, February 28, 1952, 2258, 2272–74, 2282–84, 2287, 2292.

93. Ibid., March 3, 1952, 2560.

94. Ibid., Testimony of William Foard, April 1, 1952, 4369–70.

95. Ibid., Testimony of Margaret Louise Ames, May 5, May 7–8, 1952, 7093–7101, 7509–7609.

96. Ibid., Testimony of Howard Litt, April 9, 1952, 5029–30.

97. Ibid., Testimony of Lloyd Norman Hamlin, February 15–21, 1952, 1272–1961; Testimony of Daniel Scarlatto, March 7–13, 1952, 2712–3355.

98. Ibid., Testimony of Lloyd Norman Hamlin, February 15, 1952, 1341.

99. Ibid., Testimony of Paul Estrada, May 6, 1952, 7270.

100. Ibid., April 29, 1952, 6480.

101. Ibid., May 7, 1952, 7444–48.

102. Ibid., Testimony of William Foard, April 1, 1952, 4380.

103. Ibid., Testimony of Daisy Van Dorn, May 9–13, 1952, 7763–8048.

104. Ibid., Testimony of William Foard, April 1, 1952, 4447.

105. Ibid., Testimony of Louis Rosser, April 24, 1952, 5935, 6014–15.

106. Ibid., Testimony of William Foard, April 1, 1952, 4379, 4386.

107. Ibid., Testimony of Stephen A. Wereb, March 24, 1952, 3858–59.

108. Ibid., Testimony of Daniel Scarlatto, March 11, 1952, 3000–3003.

109. Ibid., Testimony of Margaret Louise Ames, May 5, May 7–8, 1952, 7093–7101, 7509–7609.

110. Ibid., Testimony of Daniel Scarlatto, March 7–13, 1952, 2712–3355.

111. Foster to the National Committee, August 15, 1952, BHL.

112. *Yates Transcript*, May 21, 1952, 8659.

113. Kevin Maroney to author, July 24, 1974.

114. *United States v. Frankfeld, et al.*, "Transcript of Proceedings Before the Court," United States District Court for the District of Maryland, at Baltimore, Government Opening, March 10, 1952, 221.

115. Ibid., Defendants' Opening, March 11, 1951, 313.

116. Ibid., 320.

117. Ibid., Testimony of John Lautner, March 13–17, 1952, 661–1007.

118. Ibid., Testimony of Paul Crouch, March 12, 1952, 493.

119. Ibid., Testimony of William Odell Nowell, March 17, 1952, 1007–83, Testimony of Charles W. Nicodemus, March 17–18, 1952, 1083–1107, 1287–90.

120. Ibid., Testimony of Mary Stalcup Markward, March 19, 1952, 1370–71.

121. Ibid., Testimony of Charles Craig, March 18, 1952, 1179.

122. Ibid., Testimony of Harry Owen Bartlett, March 18, 1952, 1247.

123. Ibid., 1273.

124. Ibid., Testimony of George Meyers, March 24, 1952, 1780.

125. Ibid., 1751.

126. United States Department of Justice, "List of Smith Act Cases Involving Communist Party Leaders," 2, document submitted to author by Department of Justice.

127. *Yates Transcript*, June 10, 1952, 10075.

128. Ibid., April 24, 1952, 5887.

129. Ibid., Defendants' Opening, June 10, 1952, 10109.

130. Ibid., June 11, 1952, 10138.

131. Ibid., Testimony of Oleta O'Connor Yates, June 11, 1952, 10193.

132. Ibid., June 16, 1952, 10293; June 23, 1952, 10947.

133. Ibid., June 19, 1952, 10703.

134. Ibid., June 18, 1952, 10576.

135. Ibid., July 1, 1952, 11664–67.

136. Ibid., June 26, 1952, 11359.

137. Ibid., June 27, 1952, 11383.

138. Ibid., June 26–27, 1952, 11283–84, 11312–19, 11372–73, 11380.

139. Ibid., June 30, 1952, 11619, 11634.

140. Ibid., Defense Statement, July 2, 1952, 11887; July 8, 1952, 12162.

141. Foster to the National Committee, August 15, 1952, BHL.

142. *Yates Transcript*, Government Closing, July 18, 1952, 12617, 12665.

143. Ibid., Judge's Charge, July 31, 1952, 13756.

144. Ibid., 13738.

145. Ibid., Defendants' Proposed Instructions, July 31, 1952, 13822.

146. *The New York Times*, August 6, 1952.

147. *Yates Transcript*, Sentencing, August 7, 1952, 14155.

148. Ibid., Defense Motions, August 6–7, 1952, 13958, 13964, 14161, 14171.

149. Ibid., August 6, 1952, 13991.

150. Richmond, *A Long View from the Left*, 351.

151. Foster to the National Committee, August 15, 1952, BHL.

152. Charney, *A Long Journey*, 215.

153. Alexander Bittelman, "On the Overt Acts," October 28, 1951, Folder 5, Papers of Alexander Bittelman, BHL.

154. Alexander Bittelman to Elizabeth Gurley Flynn, October 25, 1951, in Bittelman, "Autobiography," 748–49.

155. Bittelman, "Autobiography," 752–53.

156. Charney, *A Long Journey*, 224–25.

157. Michal R. Belknap, *Cold War Political Justice, The Smith Act, the Communist Party, and American Civil Liberties* (Westport, 1977), 162.

158. *Flynn Transcript*, Government Opening, April 24, 1952, 1618.

159. Ibid., Defendants' Opening, April 24, 1952, 1707.

160. Foster to the National Committee, August 15, 1952, BHL.

161. Bittelman, "Autobiography," 753–54.

162. Foster to the National Committee, August 15, 1952, BHL.

163. *Flynn Transcript*, Defense Motion, September 22, 1952, 9760.

164. Ibid., 9939–40.

165. Ibid., September 23, 1952, 9972.

166. Ibid., Judgment of Acquittal, September 22, 1952, 10008.

167. Ibid., Defendants' Opening, September 25, 1952, 10160.

168. Ibid., Testimony of Elizabeth Gurley Flynn, November 7, 1952, 11841, 11848–52; December 2, 1952, 13182.

169. Ibid., November 19, 1952, 12555–12609.

170. Ibid., Defense Rests, December 3, 1952, 13264; Charney, *A Long Journey*, 225.

171. Department of Justice, "List of Smith Act Cases," 2.

172. Eric F. Goldman, *The Crucial Decade—And After, America, 1945–1960* (New York, 1966), 214.

173. Truman, *Public Papers . . . 1951*, 643.

174. *The New York Times*, September 25, 1951.

175. J. Howard McGrath, "Memorandum for Mr. Vanech," December 27, 1951, 136/Deputy Attorney General, Papers of J. Howard McGrath, HSTL. Vanech suddenly resigned his position as deputy attorney general on August 4, 1952, while under a cloud of suspicion. It had been revealed that he had failed several bar examinations in Virginia and the District of Columbia before gaining a license in Tennessee in 1940 under what some deemed fraudulent procedures.

176. Harry S. Truman, *Public Papers of the Presidents of the United States 1952–3* (Washington, 1965), 134.

177. Ibid., 223.

178. Ibid., 578.

179. Ibid., 857.
180. Ibid., 889.
181. Ibid., 896.
182. Ibid., 1201.
183. *The Daily Worker*, December 25, 1951.

XI

An Epilogue: The Fruits of Repression

On June 17, 1957, the Supreme Court, by a 6–1 vote, reversed the conviction of the California Smith Act defendants. Five were set free immediately, and a retrial was ordered for the remaining nine under restrictive conditions that ultimately led to a government decision to seek dismissal of the indictment.[1] As a practical matter, the *Yates* decision marked the beginning of the end of government prosecution of American communists. One of the California defendants freed by the Court suggested that the impetus for the decision resulted less from changing legal interpretation than from changing world and domestic conditions.[2] The ebbing of the Cold War together with a domestic reaction against McCarthy and "McCarthyism" had its legal equivalent in a series of liberal court decisions. The open legal repression of communists came to a practical end at a time when the CP virtually had destroyed itself. Tom Clark, the only dissenting justice in the *Yates* case, put the matter best when he noted that there was "no point in picking an overripe orange."[3] Although the FBI continued its secret war against the CP, the government had seen the achievement of a major goal already, the destruction of the largest organized left-wing resistance to government policy. Despite this success, only partial "credit" belonged to the government.

The prosecutions alone had not destroyed the CP. They had accentuated "left sectarian" policies within the organization which had helped to isolate it from mass work and organizations. They had driven all but the most committed members out of the Party. They had caused the dropping of thousands by the Party itself. The McCarthyite atmosphere had ended almost all liberal cooperation with the CP or its members. The Party had been encouraged to initiate what has been termed a "suicidal" descent into an underground structure from which it could never fully emerge.[4] Early in 1953, J. Edgar Hoover estimated, probably correctly, that there were more than 24,000 members left in the CP.[5] Three years later there were still more than 17,000.[6] These numbers, as relatively small as they had become, could have been significant. A political party's influence and value may not always be measured by its membership rolls, but the Communist Party's influence had ended already. It had become a small political sect waiting for the final blows to fall. Many of these blows, accentuated by government repression, had been self-inflicted. Within five years following Truman's exit from the presidency, most CP members and leaders came to believe there was no longer anything worth saving. During the 1956–57 period a desperate final struggle over what had become a lost cause was waged within the Party's entire remaining membership. Although greatly enlivened by Soviet actions, divergent participants agree that its origins lay a decade before and may, in fact, have been postponed by government repression.[7]

There has been considerable debate over the practical, as distinguished from actual dissolution of the CP. David Shannon has written that "it was still a going concern after the frequency of new indictments declined in 1955."[8] A second historian agreed and suggested that it was the CPUSA's response to the 1956 Soviet invasion of Hungary that marked the end, while a third observer wrote that the effort to save the CP was not over until the end of 1959.[9] The lively struggle to which these observers referred was fought over a largely lifeless organization. It was conducted within a predominantly unconcerned nation. The communists already had separated themselves from the main concerns of the American people.

Just as the CP isolated itself from the people, the decision to go underground had separated the communist leadership from the membership. The underlying thesis of the imminence of war and fascism was never fully accepted by many within the movement. From the East Coast to the West, loyal Party functionaries felt themselves forced to act and think independently. The California Party leaders were not the only ones to reject the mandate to go underground or to react to it with less than total acceptance. Otis Hood, a Massachusetts CP leader later to be indicted under the Smith Act, was "ordered" to go underground. He insisted that the removal of the Party's most effective leaders was "not logical in [the] way it was applied" and did not carry out the order. He ignored further directives carried personally by messenger from the national office. Later he recalled that it was the "first time I did not obey a Party order."[10] Most did, with severe repercussions.

The existence of the underground was a message to all Party members that "public" activity no longer was truly possible. Some meetings were held and there were efforts to sell *The Daily Worker*, but little else.[11] There was little effective national leadership as local districts often were left to devise their own policies.[12] CP leaders called upon the membership to respond with greater "mass work." The small Party clubs which had been established for security purposes were asked to issue leaflets and take part in activities in their own name.[13] There was almost no response. Bittelman wrote to Foster in early 1952 to complain that while the political situation in general seemed to be improving, "the only sector in which little is being done politically is on the Left. And that is awful."[14]

The real leadership of the Party went underground. Despite the isolation of many of those who submerged and the difficulties of communication, this is where the major decisions were made. "Daily operative financial and political decision-making [was placed] into the hands of the subterranean structure." The relative few who remained within the open Party came to call themselves the "expendables."[15] What remained of the CP's image suffered irreparable harm. It had become an inconsequential sect on the run, a political grouping viewed as essentially operating in an illegal fashion.

With the entire National Committee either in prison, in hiding, or on trial, a National Administrative Committee, composed of lesser officials who were still available, became the leading open Party body. The Committee met weekly to discuss the major issues of the day, but had no real authority.[16] Within that body, and more significantly within the underground leadership, dissent began to arise. The Republican victory in the 1952 elections caused a reappraisal of party policy. The insignificant vote received by the Progressive Party ticket of Vincent Hallinan and Charlotte Bass, supported by the CP, had proven to some the sectarian nature of Party policies. Bittelman arose within the Administrative Committee to break with Foster decisively. He emphasized his belief in "the non-inevitability of war and fascism," and proposed an American road to socialism through the creation of a "United Front Marxist Party." Although not proposing the end of the CP, and still tied to the concept that the Soviet Union was to hold a leading position in the socialist world, Bittelman's position was a forerunner of the more independent thought which would begin to flourish just a few years later. His 1953 proposal was greeted as "liquidationist" by the remaining Party leaders and rejected.[17]

From the underground, a second voice arose to challenge the direction of Party policy. Gilbert Green, the subject of a massive FBI hunt, was able to bring his views before the Party membership. Using the pseudonym "Jonathan Swift," his first article from the underground appeared in *Political Affairs* in February 1953. While not directly criticizing the underground, Green noted the difficulties in speaking out created by the "semi-legal conditions" which existed.[18] He attacked the growing isolation of Party members within narrow left-wing organizations, presumably such as the Progressive Party, to the exclusion of mass organizations. Green noted that a good many comrades "do not think of mass work as starting with the masses themselves and the issues that are uppermost before them."[19] The "main danger" faced by the Party, he emphasized, was "left sectarianism."[20] The article coincided with the production of a National Committee "draft resolution" criticizing the CP role in the 1952 elections in a limited sense. Green's comments provided the impetus to strengthen the document and to include, against Foster's opposition, an analysis that "The mistakes made by the Party in the election campaign must be ascribed to strong sectarian tendencies within its ranks."[21] Despite this conclusion, the program maintained that the decision to support the Progressive Party had been correct and attacked Adlai Stevenson as a supporter of the "bipartisan war program."[22]

The outlook of many leaders was beginning to change, but the change was painfully slow and was little understood by those outside the inner circles of the CP.[23] Despite the inertia within much of the leadership, events not under their control were pushing the Party toward change. On August 27, 1953, two of the remaining fugitive leaders of the Party, Robert Thompson and Sidney Stein, were captured by the FBI in a mountain cabin in Twain Hart, California. Three of the eight major fugitives were once again in prison. The remaining five were operating under severely restrictive circumstances. It was clear that the underground operation had achieved little purpose and would soon come to an end. It symbolized the Party's isolation and lack of understanding of existing conditions. Some of this was recognized in the Party's significant 1954 draft program. Even the name of the statement, "An American Way to Jobs, Peace, Democracy," indicated a shifting emphasis. The position of a peaceful transition to socialism was fully, and belatedly, accepted. The CP dissociated itself from the third party movement and called for New Deal-style Democratic victories in 1954 and 1956. The program, as much as it marked an advance in thinking, was also the product of compromise. The Foster forces were accommodated as the program re-emphasized that "the danger of McCarthyism, of American fascism, is real, grave and growing."[24]

The "draft program," although it was adopted, did not change Party policies. It did begin a debate within the CP. Foster was angered by the signs that his analysis was being rejected. As the "draft program" was issued, he emphasized those aspects of the program which supported his position and ignored the implied criticisms. He publicly attacked those who suggested that a serious war danger had passed, claimed the government was already "in the hands" of "semi-McCarthyite pro-fascists," and warned that "the atomaniacs controlling the monster military machine might well throw our country into war."[25] In a message to the CP's "national election conference," which approved the program, Foster predicted that "broad and vital class struggle" would occur soon within the United States.[26] Within months he went on to cite a growing fascist danger in the nation when most observers saw the lessening of both internal repression and international tension.[27]

No Party leader effectively could stop the growing expression of independent viewpoints. Claude Lightfoot, the Illinois Party leader and a member of the National Committee, strongly supported the "draft program" and implied serious criticism of Foster and others. He attacked the national leadership for "a certain panic" in the face of repression. Lightfoot said there had been a failure to organize a collective leadership, the haphazard promotion and shifting of cadre, and isolation from the struggles of the people. "We are unwanted citizens in most of the broad people's mass organizations," he noted, and demanded active involvement in the struggles against "McCarthyism" and the spreading war in Indo-China, and for Negro rights.[28]

The Senate censure of McCarthy at the end of 1954 set the stage for even more dramatic changes the following year. The heads of the United States, the Soviet Union, Britain, and France met in July, leading to the "spirit of Geneva" as the concept of peaceful coexistence began to gain strength. Domestically, prominent attorneys agreed to represent defendants in the continuing Smith Act trials and in their appeals. The Supreme Court signalled a possible change by agreeing to hear the appeal of the California Smith Act defendants.[29] Party leader Green, still underground, reacted in a book, published early in 1956. "The year 1955," he said, "marked a turning point away from the postwar hysteria and witchhunt."[30] The book mirrored both the changes taking place and the contrasting currents within the communist movement.

Green supported an American road to socialism without dissociating himself from the Soviet Union. "The special history, culture, tradition and experience of the American people" would cause "Socialist democracy" to differ from that in other nations. Green contended that neither Marx, Engels, Lenin, nor Stalin had intended Marxism to be applied mechanically.[31] Continuing the analysis he had begun in 1953, Green criticized the CP for "incorrect practices" which had led many to believe that communists were seeking to control mass organizations. Green maintained that this had never been the Party's purpose, only a corrupted view of the CP's energy and discipline created by the "Big Business enemy of the people." The analysis stopped far short of exploring the basis of the sectarian policies Green had criticized. To do so would have meant a critical examination of the communists' attitude toward the Soviet Union, and Green was not prepared to go that far. The book carefully defended the Soviet Union and its contributions and excused its defects. "The change in political climate which began in 1954, and continued through 1955," he wrote, "was made possible only because the unreal fear of Soviet aggression has subsided."[32]

The developing split in Party ranks was becoming sharper as conditions in the world changed more rapidly. Foster had been left behind, but his views remained unchanged. He railed against the "pressing Right danger" within the Party—those seeking changes. Calling on his guns from the past, he resurrected the specter of "collaborationist ideas cultivated by Browder" to attack the "illusions" he saw emanating from the meetings at Geneva. There could be no "liquidation of the basic antagonisms between the forces of democratic progress and those of reactionary monopoly."[33] Foster was by no means alone. There were many left in the Party who could not understand the changes taking place. The Yugoslav-Soviet rapprochement, initiated by Khrushchev after seven years of verbal warfare, was bewildering. A Party spokesman could do no more than accept the Soviet "explanation" that Lavrenti Beria had been responsible for the "errors" that led to the break. Previous Soviet assessments of the split were accepted, and the Soviet Union was given full credit for the resumption of relations. There was almost a conscious effort among sections of the Party to gain shelter from the winds of change.[34]

The CPUSA could not remain unaffected. Party leaders began to emerge from prison, and the changes which had taken place were painfully clear to them. The underground, which had only heightened the Party's isolation, was abandoned. The remaining fugitives surrendered to the authorities at the end of 1955 and the beginning of 1956. Foster publicly claimed this represented "an expression of confidence in the rising democratic strength of the American people."[35] In fact, it represented a conscious effort to break with a disastrous analysis which had led to this reckless, self-defeating adventure. The return of the Party to full legal operation meant that the divisions which had become increasingly apparent would now be the basis for an internal struggle.

It seemed for a time that the CP was ready for a radical, independent departure from previous policies and attitudes. On January 20, 1956,

Dennis and Gates were "welcomed back" as their restrictive paroles ended. The Carnegie Hall gathering provided an emotional setting for the promise of change from some of the architects of past destructive policies. Dennis candidly admitted to the thousands who had kept the faith through the bitter period of repression that "We have, like others, made not a few mistakes." He promised "a new look" at the problems of the nation as well as Party policy.[36] Deliberately, nothing was said of the Soviet Union. This was to be a new examination of the reality of the United States and their Party.[37] The promise of a new Party came out of internal needs created by the disasters which had befallen them. The "new look" was initiated before the following month's far-ranging re-examination by the Soviet Party of its history, and particularly of the role of Joseph Stalin. By the time the XXth Soviet Party conference met on February 14, 1956, the CPUSA was already engaged in a serious, critical examination of past policies. Reports from the Soviet Union encouraged the effort to go forward.

Gates used his editorship of *The Daily Worker* to encourage the growth of internal criticism and debate. With an enthusiastic newspaper staff, the Party's paper began in March its own highly critical examination of policies and leaders. Published reports from the Soviet's XXth Congress had made clear that a basic re-evaluation was taking place. The "cult of the personality" had been exposed, although Khrushchev's secret speech denouncing Stalin's crimes had not yet been printed.[38]

The Daily Worker's open approach, while highly unusual, did not come in a vacuum. It occurred as the leading body of the CP prepared an unprecedented exposure of its own failures. Dennis readied a major report for the first meeting of the National Committee since he had gone to prison. As all such reports, it was the product of joint consideration and approval of the Party leadership.[39] In the midst of these preparations, the publication of fragmentary reports from the Soviet Union already was making the membership restive. Dennis and the National Committee chose to make the revelations coming from the Soviet Union a part of their own re-evaluation, without giving them too much emphasis. Through the means of answering a series of questions posed in *Politial Affairs*, the general secretary agreed that the Soviet revelations "without any doubt come to us all with something of a shock and raise many questions."[40] He emphasized again the errors committed by the CPUSA and reiterated the promised "new look." He sought to turn attention to the key doctrinal and policy questions which had harmed his own party. Dennis contended that the main focus should be on important Soviet conclusions concerning the lack of inevitability of war and peaceful transition to socialism. It was only in one key area that Dennis held back, and it was to mark a major division between him and others who sought serious changes. He continued to defend Soviet policies. He supported the decision not to publish Khrushchev's secret speech, one which he might not have read as yet, and continued to emphasize the positive role of the Soviet Union. This continuing and largely uncritical tie to the Soviets made a full understanding of the basic causes of Party errors impossible.

Some 120 leading members of the Party gathered on April 28, 1956, in New York City for a National Committee plenum. The report delivered by the Party's general secretary was a devastating critique of CP errors during the prior decade. Dennis spoke for the overwhelming majority of the leadership in seeking basic answers to explain the Party's isolation. His conclusions were clear. "Left sectarian" tactics and analyses had been a major cause of CP isolation since 1945. "Doctrinaire" policies in the labor movement, characterized by the use of "foreign policy as an acid test," had helped to drive the left out of organized labor. The Party repeatedly had overestimated "the imminence of a new cyclical economic crisis." While often claiming that war and fascism were not inevitable, Dennis admitted that Party actions and even statements had led to the inescapable conclusion that these dangers were imminent. This overestimate of the process of fascization or imminence of war was coupled with an underestimation of "the nationwide, mass strength of American democratic traditions, sentiments, and processes." One result was that the Smith Act trials had been seen as a defense of Party doctrine rather than "constitutional liberties."[41]

While Dennis did not condemn the underground structure completely, he did attack its extreme nature. Recognizing that security measures were necessary so that the Party could continue "to function under all conditions," he said the "drastic measures" which had been taken and their maintenance, without change, over an extended period of time, had not been justified. This action, coupled with "arbitrary and undemocratic measures" to pare Party membership, had cost the CP dearly. Dennis noted the steps taken to re-evaluate Party policy, particularly those embodied in the 1952 statement and 1954 resolution, but even these had been inadequate. The 1952 effort, which had attempted to modify sectarian political policies, was sabotaged by "sectarian attitudes in the leadership," surely an attack on Foster and his allies. The 1954 resolution, in examining the eased international situation, inexplicably had concluded that the dangers of "McCarthyism" had increased. Dennis and the National Committee admitted that the Party had "suffered heavy organizational losses and . . . [loss of] political influence."[42]

There was a seemingly genuine outpouring of support for the Dennis analysis. The desperate position of the Party was clear. Only Foster, with minimal backing from a few, opposed the severity of the self-criticism. The more difficult part of the report was in determining those policies which might again bring the CP the influence it had helped to destroy. It was here that Dennis was weakest and for good cause. It was understood that a "doctrinaire" application of Marxism and a devotion to the Soviet experience had handicapped the CPUSA, but the solution was difficult for some to accept. The first step to end a "doctrinaire" approach was to establish inner-party democracy. Dennis asked for the creation of a democratic atmosphere which would allow the submission of alternative and "unorthodox" policies or proposals. The goal was a Marxist analysis of developments within the United States and the creation of an American peaceful road to socialism through the eventual development of "a broader mass party of socialism." It was significant that Dennis gave credit to Foster for his advancement of the American road concept in 1949, although he backed away from it subsequently, while no credit was given to Bittelman who had gone much further both on this and the creation of a mass socialist party.[43] Dennis was seeking to lead the movement toward reform, but could not really free himself from the past.

Although the Party, according to the general secretary, was to avoid sectarian approaches, it was still to occupy a "vanguard" role. It was still to lead, not simply to join—as unrealistic as this idea was. Recognizing the errors of the past, Dennis still could not entirely cast the CP in a new role. The same was true of his evaluation of the Soviet Union, and perhaps more critically. The CP's use of the "acid test" of foreign policy had allowed it to be driven from organized labor in the late 1940's. While it no longer wished a division on this basis, others outside of the Party were not ready to comply. Now the reverse was taking place. The "acid test" was the degree to which the CPUSA could and would differentiate itself from the Soviet Union. Nothing less than full independence could bring the CP within the orbit of the American political scene. Dennis found this impossible. He had nothing but praise for the XXth Soviet congress. "The re-evaluation of past ideas and practices, which was infinitely greater than just the re-evaluation of the Stalin leadership," he wrote, "had the purpose and effect of putting an end to those violations of socialist democracy which did serious damage and were an intolerable hindrance upon the further advance of socialism."[44] Khrushchev's words alone were enough to satisfy Dennis, but it would not be enough to satisfy the American people or even many of his comrades. Within two days, the leaders of the Party were shaken and Dennis' position weakened. The top Party leaders had received a detailed summary of Khrushchev's secret speech. While the National Committee had heard a sharply critical analysis of the Soviet congress from theoretician Max Weiss, this had not included the secret speech. The Party leaders from throughout the nation gathered on the last day of the plenum to have read to them the extensive summary, presented as a letter from a British friend, presumably John Williamson who had been deported at the conclusion of his prison sentence a year earlier. Although they had heard rumors of the speech, they were unprepared for the details which they heard. Tears streamed from their eyes as Stalin's bloody crimes were sketched in detail.[45] Leaders who had faced their own nation's repression with a rare stoicism were forced to question the value of their actions. They were brought face to face with their own complicity of silence and their own justifications for the crimes committed.

It seemed for a time that Foster had been isolated and defeated. His was the only vote against the Dennis report, while three other members of the National Committee abstained.[46] In order to effect the changes promised in Dennis' report, the National Committee decided to call the first national convention in six years and to open the Party press to a wide-ranging discussion of the issues. Despite his initial defeat, Foster neither retired nor reversed his position. More important, the tactics and policies which he had supported did not end automatically. Although the Party's leaders had heard the secret Khrushchev report, they did not immediately publicize it. For more than a month they held its contents without sharing them with the CP's members. The promise of inner party democracy had been compromised already by the desire for direction from the top. It took the U.S. State Department to release the text of Khrushchev's speech on June 4, 1956. The next day, *The Daily Worker*, acting without National Committee approval, printed a condensed version of the speech and within days printed the full text. Gates was attacked by both Foster and Dennis for his action. The full membership would now be drawn into the debate over the Soviet Union, not simply internal Party policy. Gates offered to resign his editorship and Foster fought for an acceptance, but the National Committee refused, fearing a public split.[47] An official reaction to the Khrushchev revelations was necessary. Dennis already had come out with an article mildly critical of Soviet actions while defending the historic role of the Soviet Union. A majority of the National Committee wanted more. With Foster the sole dissenting vote, the Committee demanded a "further and deeper examination" by Soviet authorities and called for an explanation of reports of Soviet anti-Semitism. The CPUSA leaders rejected

any analysis which placed blame for the crimes committed on "the ca-
pricious aberrations of a single individual, no matter how much arbitrary power he was wrongly permitted to usurp."[48] It was a bold statement, reaching out for a sense of independence and expressing an
unwillingness any longer to be the far away tail on the Soviet kite. It
was to be perhaps the last National Committee statement to reflect near
unanimity of the desire for significant change.

Three days after the National Committee statement, *Pravda* published Dennis' earlier article, although leaving out some of his significant criticisms. The article was the first printed notice to the Soviet people of Khrushchev's special speech to the Soviet congress. In choosing
to print Dennis' remarks, the Soviets deliberately ignored both the
American Party's National Committee as well as far more critical published views of Italian Communist leader Palmiro Togliatti and others.[49] It was clear that the Soviets were seeking to limit foreign criticism
and had used Dennis for their own purposes. The following day riots
broke out in Poznan, Poland, partially attributed to the widespread reports of Khrushchev's remarks. The Soviet Communist Party reacted
quickly with a resolution adopted on June 30, 1956. The Soviet leaders
lauded their own actions and all aspects of their socialist society. The
development of the "cult of the personality" was attributed to the difficulty of building the first socialist state, threatening conditions from
surrounding capitalist states, Lavrenti Beria, and "individual traits" of
Stalin. No long-lasting effects on Soviet society were admitted and no
complicity on the part of the existing leadership which claimed that
"many facts and wrong actions of Stalin, especially as regards the violation of Soviet law, became known only in recent times, after his death."
Sharp criticism was offered for foreign communists who "have not got
to the bottom of the question of the personality cult and its consequences and are tolerating at times a wrong interpretation of certain of
its aspects." Togliatti was attacked by name, while Dennis was the only
foreign leader specifically praised. His "well-known article" was quoted
once more where it had praised the Soviet Congress for strengthening
"universal peace and social progress."[50]

For some the Khrushchev revelations broke their ties to the Soviet
Union. Others, led by Dennis, had been shaken briefly, but were more
than ready to return to the habits of a lifetime. Now honored by the
Soviet Central Committee, and understanding the significance of its
statement, Dennis sought to limit the critical line of the CPUSA.

The response of the CP's National Committee to the Soviet statement
was indicative of the changing attitudes within a portion of the leadership. The sharp, challenging tone of their June statement was gone.

It was replaced with a mild, rather tentative statement which rejected extreme criticism of Soviet policies. While asking "further study and discussion" in areas such as "bureaucratic distortions" and anti-Semitism, although carefully avoiding the latter term, the NC clearly supported the actions taken by the Soviet leaders.[51] The Committee members most committed to basic change were engaged in the writing of a draft resolution for the coming Party convention. Soviet actions were considered secondary to, although associated with, the task of internal reform. Foster's lone vote of opposition to the resolution seemed to justify its passage.

The major portions of the draft resolution were ready for consideration by a National Committee plenum at the end of August. For many of the Committee members it represented a last hope—an opportunity for basic change which could not come again. The opportunity was seized with enthusiasm and an acute awareness that time was extremely short. The resolution was the product of years of dissatisfaction and searching. The main impetus for it came before the Khrushchev revelations and thus represented an American response to the desperate conditions of the CPUSA as well as changing world conditions. The denunciation of Stalin had disabled the opposition temporarily, allowing more freedom to the draftsmen. The result was what has been described as a "remarkable document." The major sections were approved by majority vote of the National Committee, with the final document to be presented to the Committee in September. Considering the character of the resolution, there had to be sufficient time for Party debate. The convention, scheduled for later in the year, was postponed until February 1957. Foster bitterly attacked the draft at the September meeting, but the demand for real change was too strong. Only Ben Davis joined the Party chairman in voting a "qualified yes" for the resolution. All others, in a remarkable display of apparent unity, supported the resolution.[52]

The resolution, brought before the entire Party in September and opened for the most wide-ranging debate in CP history, went beyond Dennis' April report. There was no question where the blame was placed for the errors of a decade. *"The most important mistakes made in the period under review were left-sectarian in character,"* declared the report.[53] The great loss of Party membership and influence was attributed, in largest part, to CP errors, the most important of which was the overestimation of the dangers of war and fascism. These fears had led to the deliberate paring of Party membership and to the underground, both termed "wrong organizational decisions."[54] Sectarian policies had made easier the CP's isolation within the labor movement. The Party had exaggerated its influence and support within even left-led unions and its *"in-flexible insistence on the adoption of a third party perspective and a condem-nation of the Marshall Plan* facilitated the objectives of the cold war splitters."[55] It was a devastating self-criticism, but made necessary, the resolution added, by the desperate condition in which the Party found itself.[56] The criticism was extended to its relations with the Soviet Union. "Our Party had also suffered from an oversimplified approach to and an uncritical acceptance of many views of Marxists and Marxist parties in other countries." The result had been that the CPUSA was "entirely unprepared for and deeply shocked" by Khrushchev's revelations. De-claring that some Marxist-Leninist theory had "become outdated and rendered obsolete by new historical developments," the document most significantly promised that in the future the American Party would "in-terpret" and "apply" Marxism-Leninism itself. There would no longer be an acceptance of direction from abroad.[57]

The Party was to be committed fully both to internal and external de-mocracy. Its support for a peaceful, constitutional road to socialism was stated forcefully.[58] The objective of the CP was an American socialism in which "full civil liberties to all, including the right to dissent" would be guaranteed.[59] Internal democratic practices were to replace the con-cepts of "monolithic unity" and "democratic centralism" as practiced previously. Both the majority and minority were to have access to the membership and there was to be a conscious effort to encourage op-position viewpoints.[60] The "vanguard role" of the CP was re-empha-sized, but there was to be no mechanical, unrealistic, or arrogant ap-plication, and the Party was to join existing organizations in the struggle for a better society already being waged.[61]

For the authors of the resolution, it was a beginning. For some of those who supported it in September, it was an end. It was further than many had ever imagined they would go. It reflected many of their in-nermost feelings, yet wrenched deeply ingrained ties which could not be destroyed easily. It envisioned radical changes within the theory, practice, and structure of their organization. Perhaps as much as any-one else, Foster understood this and used it to his advantage. As an observer has written, "Foster had inertia and tradition on his side,"[62] but he also had something else—the Soviet Union. A week following National Committee approval of the draft resolution, *Pravda* reviewed a Foster book printed a year earlier and took the opportunity to praise him as a "noted theoretician and Marxist historian." With this message from Moscow, Foster changed his vote to a "no" and prepared a mas-sive attack on the resolution.[63]

In a 14,000-word article printed in the October *Political Affairs*, Foster led off the discussion. It was a masterful attack by an experienced leader of factional warfare. He would retreat where it could not be avoided, but attacked with the greatest force where his opponents were weakest. Admitting "left sectarian" errors during the Cold War period, Foster blamed them on government repression rather than a self-sacrificing membership which had shown "a high degree of political unity and fighting morale." The "worst mistakes" which had been made—1948 support of the Progressive Party, failure adequately to put forward the concept of a peaceful road to socialism in the first Smith Act trial, and the extreme security measures taken—were all blamed on the members of the National Board before 1951, four of whom had voted to support the draft resolution. Foster accepted no blame himself and, indeed, congratulated himself for his 1949 espousal of a parliamentary road to socialism.[64] The chairman sharply attacked Dennis' April report for its criticism of the Party's role during the previous decade and for a "serious underestimation" of the war dangers and the degree of repression with which the CP had been faced. He noted, significantly, that the "exaggeration of mistakes" would never have been tolerated by the Soviet or other parties.[65]

Foster insisted there was no danger from the left, but only from the right, from those who were seeking to "liquidate" the Party. These were the new "Browderites" and they were concentrated in *The Daily Worker*. Their agitation, he said, had begun as early as 1954 with criticism from Joe Starobin and Joe Clark, both former foreign editors of the Party newspaper. Now the "right tendency" was led by Gates who had led a factional attack against Dennis until Dennis, presumably, joined them at the August National Committee meeting which had approved the essentials of the draft resolution.[66] The fact that neither Gates nor Dennis had been responsible for the resolution mattered not at all. Everyone who opposed Foster's position was now labeled a "rightist." Foster attacked the heart of the resolution in rejecting the right of the CPUSA to "interpret" Marxism-Leninism, claiming this would have reduced it to "the status of a Russian Socialist philosophy" and destroyed "proletarian internationalism."[67] The article put the debate on his grounds, and international events kept it there.

The use of Soviet troops in Hungary to quell growing demonstrations and riots divided the world communist movement and dealt a severe blow to the efforts to reform the American Communist Party. During the first few days following the October 24, 1956, Soviet move, *The Daily Worker* generally attributed the violence to "reactionaries" taking advantage of the "widespread popular demonstrations and pressure for democratization." By October 29, the Party newspaper was deploring the Soviet use of troops.[68] The battle over the invasion began to rage within the leadership of the Party, as it did all over the world. The Soviet agreement to withdraw its troops at the end of October gave the National Committee an opportunity for comment and a majority of its New York members demanded a public declaration. The November 1, 1956, statement supported *The Daily Worker* position and asserted that the Hungarian government decision to request Soviet troops "to put down the popular demonstrations was a tragic error." The Soviet response was criticized harshly, although it was acknowledged that reactionary elements had sought to take advantage of the situation. Major responsibility for the uprising was placed on Stalin's "wrong policies" and those who had "mechanically followed the experiences of the Soviet Union." Foster was not present, but Dennis joined Davis in abstaining, while James Jackson voted "yes with qualifications."[69] The massive reintroduction of Soviet troops three days later and the crushing of the Hungarian uprising split the National Committee even more deeply. "Stormy meetings" of the Committee members followed, but the rift was too deep to allow a quick statement. Gates, with the obligation of putting out a daily newspaper, would not wait for a National Committee decision. In a front page editorial on November 5, *The Daily Worker* condemned the Soviet action in strong terms and declared that "socialism cannot be imposed by force."[70]

The Soviet invasion did not create the basic division within the Party, but it served to sharpen it greatly. The essential question of the relationship between the CPUSA and the Soviet Union and, indeed, among socialist parties or states in general, had been raised already. Important positions had been expressed and taken. The occurrence of the Hungarian revolution forced that issue to the forefront. It was an issue which had to be raised. Its timing was fortuitous for Foster and his supporters. They could now charge that those seeking reform were anti-Soviet and antisocialist. This was a critical issue for many who had remained within the CP. Dennis represented at least some when a week later he wrote to *The Daily Worker* to dissociate himself from its editorial. He claimed it had not presented the facts concerning Hungary, had not analyzed the developing situation, and had not recognized the threat of "an imperialist salient" directed against "the vital security of all the peoples' democracies and the USSR." While recognizing "past mistakes" of the Soviet and Hungarian communist parties, Dennis supported fully "the anti-fascist and pro-peace intervention of the Soviet Army units after November 1."[71] He simply would not oppose the Soviet Union, and there were others who stood with him. The National Committee was divided hopelessly. The major authors of the draft resolution demanded a condemnation of the Soviet Union, Foster and Davis called for support, and Dennis and his followers were unwilling to accept any major criticism of recent Soviet actions. The result was an unprecedented National Committee open letter to the membership which admitted deep differences. It reiterated its earlier conclusion that the initial use of Soviet troops had been an act of "repression" and a "tragic error for which the Soviet Union must also take responsibility." The National Committee neither "condoned nor condemned" the second use of Soviet troops intended "to head off the White Terror" in Hungary. *The Daily Worker* editorial which had taken such a forthright stand was criticized.[72] The compromise resolution was introduced by William Schneiderman, head of the California organization. He insisted that a refusal to support the Soviet action marked a dramatic break with the past and would be sufficient, while maintaining Party unity.[73] On this basis, the compromise received the support of all National Committee members with the exception of Foster. While those seeking basic change believed the resolution to represent a major victory, it may have achieved the opposite result. The coalition in support of the draft resolution had been split. Gates had been isolated. The movement toward a full independent analysis of Soviet policy had been halted, and a new platform for Foster's struggle had been erected.

Many of those who took part in the CP struggle and historians viewing it have concluded that the Hungarian crisis provided the impetus for the Party's final disintegration. Many who had stayed in the CP through the most repressive of times and who had been given hope by the Khrushchev revelations and the draft resolution found that hope destroyed. The Soviets seemed to have demonstrated a very short-term commitment to "socialist democracy" and fraternal relations. The CPUSA had reacted with indecision and timidity rather than resoluteness. The result was a mass exodus mainly of those most supportive of reform.[74] Despite this, there was no immediate collapse. The leadership remained intact and continued to struggle toward the Party convention, but now the debate took on far sharper and more bitter tones.

The events in Hungary pushed Dennis toward ever greater expressions of faith in the Soviet Union. Within a year of the revolt, he was ready to weigh in with a paean to the socialist nations. Dennis hailed the corrective measures taken following the XXth Congress and, in a remarkable paragraph, praised "socialist democracy—as well as the bold and flexible moves and notable achievements registered in unfolding the resolute peace policy of the USSR." The American people, he said, had been "compelled" to take a "second look" to see the reality of socialist advance.[75] The article was vintage Dennis and represented the logical progression of his views. Although he was often accused of vacillation, he rarely equivocated on the issue of loyalty to the Soviet Union. With the exception of the first several months of 1956, Dennis' position on this issue was consistent.

As Soviet troops crushed the Hungarian revolt, *Political Affairs* appeared with Gates' major pre-convention article. He argued, as had others throughout the year, for a full democratization of the Party. To achieve this, he called for an end to "democratic centralism" and proposed that the Party's name and form be changed. The CP had been so discredited through the previous decade, Gates maintained, that to continue with its existing form would make no sense. Instead, he demanded a movement toward the "mass party of socialism" envisioned in Dennis' April report. For Gates there could be no equivocation over the path of socialism in the United States. It would have to be a "peaceful and constitutional struggle."[76] Dennis answered the following month with a blistering attack on Gates and a rejection of his proposals. The Dennis article came close to accusing Gates of having abandoned a Marxist approach. The joint commitment to the development of a new party, so bravely announced a year before at Carnegie Hall, had died a swift death.[77] As the convention approached, the National Committee sought to compromise the differences within the leadership to avoid an open split. The proposal to change the Party's name and form was not to be considered at the convention, although it was agreed this would be studied after the convention.[78]

The effort to bring a temporary peace was almost blown apart from the outside as the convention opened. Once again Jacques Duclos intervened as he had twelve years earlier, but this time in the form of a "greeting" to the convention. The words were almost the same. He still warned of "liquidationist revisionism" and demanded that the "universal truth" of Marxism-Leninism be recognized. Only some of the issues differed, as he specifically attacked the draft resolution and the Party positions on events in Poland and Hungary.[79] Foster demanded support for Duclos, while many of the delegates deeply resented this direct intrusion into their affairs. Dennis, in his opening address, rejected the Duclos criticism and, to great applause, promised that "our decisions will be our own, made by the collective judgment of this convention, and will be based on *our* Marxist understanding of American reality and the needs of our people and nation."[80] The effects of his promise were muted somewhat when he proceeded to hail the thwarting of "imperialist designs in Hungary."[81] While supporting the draft resolution, Dennis showed his reappraisal during the past months. He mildly criticized his April report and agreed that he had not warned sufficiently against "right opportunist tendencies" nor had he emphasized the "positive" CP contributions during the Cold War period.[82] Although he tried to strike a hopeful note, the Party's general secretary had to recognize the divisions and desperate conditions within the Party. The shrinking of membership as well as the "bitter and divisive internal struggle" could not be avoided.[83] The very meeting room in which he spoke symbolized the Party's circumstances. The convention gathered in a dimly lit converted catering hall on the lower East Side of Manhattan. All major halls and hotels had closed their doors to them.

While most speakers on the convention floor, with the exception of Foster, struck a note of limited unity, the committee meetings, dealing with different aspects of the draft resolution and a proposed new constitution, were forums for bitter dispute. The subcommittee on "theory" divided 14–12 in favor of the Party's right to "interpret" Marxism-Leninism.[84] A convention resolution forced a compromise "consensus" which, while continuing to recognize left sectarianism as the Party's main error, placed somewhat greater emphasis on possible dangers from the right and identified objective conditions as a partial cause of the CP's mistakes.[85] There was no question that a majority of the convention backed the reform proposals, although much of that support was concentrated in the large California and New York delegations. A new Party constitution providing far more democratic practice was adopted. A resolution was accepted calling for equality among socialist parties and, by implication, real independence for the CPUSA.[86] On the surface the convention seemed to be a triumph for the forces of change. In fact, it marked a real end to the effort.

Just a few months before Foster had been isolated within the national leadership. Now his supporters had demonstrated that they remained a potent, although still minority force. In an attempt to maintain unity, issues such as Hungary were buried, despite the protests of a few.[87] It was revealed that the circulation of *The Daily Worker*, the most visible center of protest, had fallen to 6,700.[88] Instead of wiping away the vestiges of anachronistic policies and leaders, the convention ended with the election of a twenty-member "unity" slate to the new National Committee, with another forty to be elected later from the districts— districts often controlled by more leftist elements. Dennis, Foster, Davis, and Gates were all chosen, as were some of the principal authors of the draft resolution and constitution.[89] As the convention ended, Dennis, Davis, Gates, and Foster stood together and each issued words of unity. A sole figure arose to warn that many members who had wanted real change would now "take a walk" from the Party.[90]

The prediction quickly came to pass. Within months large numbers of

Party members who had stayed for the convention left the CP. The New York organization was soon controlled by the Foster forces.[91] More than half the Party members remaining at the end of 1956 were gone by the end of 1957.[92] As each new member left, the demand for a return to traditional ideological and policy positions grew stronger. In a letter written in May, Betty Gannett, long-time Party functionary and supporter of Foster, said that she was troubled that "Ideological unity" had not been achieved in the American Party as it had in other parties.[93] In that same month, Herbert Aptheker's book, *The Truth About Hungary*, was published with a laudatory accompanying review in *Political Affairs*. The work largely represented an acceptance and justification of Soviet actions. Its political position had never been approved by the National Committee, but the author of the accompanying article, Hyman Lumer, was elected the same month to serve as one of seven members of the National Administrative Committee (NAC). He joined Dennis, Fine, Gates, Jackson, Davis, and Stein in a leading body with no officers. Those supportive of basic change, Fine, Gates, and Stein, no longer had a majority on the body although, at times, Dennis and Jackson might join them.[94] Dennis apparently had played a key role in the encouragement of Aptheker's book. Stein had confronted Dennis while the latter was going over galleys of the book with the author. Dennis made it clear that he would not allow the other members of the NAC to examine it prior to publication.[95] By the end of the year Foster was claiming that the 16th Party Convention, with the exception of a few vestiges of revisionism within the resolutions, had been a clear victory for his leftist forces.[96]

In the midst of the growing disarray of the CPUSA, and perhaps as the most positive consequence of it, the Supreme Court struck a "devastating blow" against the prosecution of American communists.[97] In June 1957, the Court reversed the convictions of the California Smith Act defendants. Speaking for a 6–1 majority, Justice John Marshall Harlan applied a narrow interpretation to the law, making the possibility of successful prosecution far more difficult. Harlan, who had been a member of the majority in the *Dennis* decision, did not wish to reverse that ruling. Instead, he allowed the effect of his new opinion to accomplish that end. The Justice ruled that the three-year statute of limitations had run out on the charge of organizing the Communist Party since it had come into being in 1945 and the indictment was not returned until 1951. This part of the indictment should have been withdrawn before submission to the jury.[98] Harlan emphasized that abstract advocacy of forcible overthrow, even with the hope of achieving such a future result, is not punishable. "Those to whom the advocacy is addressed must be urged to *do* something, now or in the future, rather than merely to *believe* in something."[99] The Court found Judge Mathes' instructions to the jury fatally defective and noted that he had not given the same directives as had Medina in the Dennis trial. Harlan considered this a vital question due to the "equivocal character of the evidence" presented. There were extremely few instances of "advocacy of action" as contrasted to doctrinal discussion,[100] he wrote, yet the nature of the evidence was essentially that provided in the first and all subsequent Smith Act trials. By refusing to reverse the *Dennis* decision, Harlan had avoided a "knock down, drag out fight,"[101] yet accomplished much the same result.

Five of the defendants were freed by the Supreme Court, while the other nine had their indictments dismissed by the trial court before the end of the year.[102] As the formal proceedings against them were coming to an end, five of the California defendants, including Yates, were preparing to resign from the CP. Others soon followed.[103] The continuing Party crisis had been heightened, characteristically, by international events.

In October and November the world's twelve leading communist parties met and issued a declaration clearly intended to end the debates raging since the denunciation of Stalin. The greatest danger, they declared, came from the right, from those seeking to revise the universal truths of Marxism-Leninism. They called upon all communists to join in the struggle to maintain the world unity of the communist movement. The challenge to American communists went to the heart of their convention resolutions. All they had opposed was represented by the new declaration. Dennis, Jackson, Davis, and Lumer combined in the National Administrative Committee, without discussion with the other members, to issue a public statement welcoming the declaration and, by inference, supporting its major conclusions.[104] The final struggle was now joined. The National Executive Committee, composed of twenty members of the National Committee and directly responsible to it, was called into session toward the end of December. The clearest outlines of the basic differences in the Party were presented in separate reports given to the NEC by Dennis and Stein. Dennis' wife later recalled that "he sought from within himself plausible explanations for the Soviet viewpoint. He found it difficult to put into practice that new independence of action he had proclaimed."[105] There were certain universal truths, he told the NEC members, which had to be accepted by the Party. The situation had changed from that existing a year earlier. There had to be waged a two-front struggle, against the extremists on the left and against the revisionists on the right. The Party had achieved some notable successes during the period since the convention and great new possibilities were open to it, but the dangers of a continuing split within the movement had to be overcome. The speech was delivered in a low-key, quiet manner.[106] Stein's response was angry. The convention resolution had been betrayed by Dennis and others, he said, and the Party was in a "worse position" than it had been in at the time of the convention. As of the morning of the meeting, 3,474 members nationwide had paid their dues. While some members were not dues-paying, and others would still be heard from, it was clear that the Party had collapsed around them. Stein argued that the CP had developed good positions on all the major issues. "Our problem is that we can't find our way into the mass movements; that we can't get a hearing." Endorsement of the Twelve Party Statement, he said, had closed "millions of ears to anything we have to say."

Stein identified three "root causes" of the Party's continuing decline and isolation—the same causes stated in the convention resolution. He cited these as the "dogmatic application of Marxist theory to the American scene," the uncritical acceptance of the views of foreign Marxists, and a lack of inner party democracy. He claimed that "our party is being turned upside down." The convention resolution had represented a binding majority position, but the minority had not only refused to accept it, but had maintained that it had the only truth. This minority, led by Foster and Davis, had thus made a determined effort to rid the Party of the majority. "The source of bureaucracy . . . is the idea that somebody can do your thinking for you, that there is a Pope, that there are cardinals . . . . " he said. "Once you accept that idea, there can be no democracy. There can be no free discussion. There can be no majority rule." He demanded that the Party remain true to its stated goal, the creation of a broad socialist movement, including the thousands who had left the CP and been reviled by some Party leaders. "Where is the Dennis of the April report?" he asked. "Where is the brave talk about the need for changing, of making changes within the Party, for making it possible to build a broader socialist movement within the United States?" Instead, Stein claimed, Dennis was seeking to reestablish a "political secretariat" which would rule the Party as it had been ruled a decade before. Stein charged Dennis had joined the struggle against the convention resolution.[107]

By an 11–7–2 vote the NEC rejected Dennis' position and adopted a resolution strongly asserting the right of the CPUSA to make its own evaluation and interpretation of Marxism and world events. The view that a "rightist" danger had become paramount was rejected for the American scene.[108] The vote was the last significant triumph of the reform forces. Davis and Robert Thompson, representing the Foster wing had joined Dennis and Elizabeth Gurley Flynn in opposition. With the decline in Party membership, they represented the majority of those who remained, not the leadership majority elected at the national convention. The same NEC meeting was forced to recommend suspension of *The Daily Worker*. "The unsatisfactory situation within the party" had made the financial situation of the newspaper intolerable. [109] Those in opposition to the paper's reformist viewpoint had strangled it. The action symbolized the collapse of a free internal debate. When the NEC action concerning the newspaper was approved by the National Committee in a mail ballot, Gates resigned from the Party. His letter of resignation declared that "The party is a futile and impotent sect of no importance in this country." [110]

Dennis carried his fight to the full National Committee in mid-February. This time a resolution endorsing his views was passed by a 32–20–3 vote and the action of the NEC was reversed. The Party again was the "vanguard." There were equal dangers on both left and right. The Twelve Party Statement was supported fully and hailed as "a major Marxist-Leninist contribution to the fight for world peace, democracy, national freedom and socialism." The Party was turned on its head. Those who sought independent analysis were now termed "sectarian." [111] The circle had become complete. Stein, Fine, George Charney, and others resigned their positions and soon left the CP, and a new executive committee was chosen. [112] A few remained to continue the struggle for change, but recognized the impossible nature of the effort. One of those, Dorothy Healey, complained a month after the climactic NC meeting that "the theft of the Convention Resolution is taking place" and that the leftist forces continued to gain strength "as more and more Comrades leave the Party." Plaintively she called for divergent views. [113] Three months later, at the next NC meeting, an effort, opposed by Dennis, was made to remove her from the leadership. The Party leaders at that meeting voted 28–10 to support the execution of Imre Nagy, the Hungarian leader deposed and later seized by Soviet troops. [114]

Only two groups remained to allege that the CPUSA had any significance. One was composed of the few who remained in the Party. In their own minds they would always remain the "indispensable vanguard," the true defenders of the faith. The other was the FBI which had recently developed its COINTELPRO program designed to "disrupt and discredit Communist Party activities" through "covert action." [115] Both J. Edgar Hoover and Foster could never accept the fact that the CP had done more to discredit itself than had been achieved by the immense pressure of the FBI.

It has been suggested that the disparate group which sought basic changes in the CPUSA failed because its tactics were not as politically astute as those of its opponents.[116] This analysis fails to recognize that the reformers could not have won. There was nothing of consequence over which to win control. The prosecution of American communists had both heightened and delayed the essential contradictions which destroyed the movement, but it had not created them. Those who wanted the CPUSA to be a truly independent American socialist movement in 1957 were seeking a new political existence, not control of the party which had operated throughout most of its history. Their views prevailed for a short time, but the view of the American people, including the thousands cut adrift by the Party in 1951, and the thousands who left in 1956, would not change. By 1957 it was widely accepted that an internal "Red Menace" no longer existed. The only image left was of an aging group of cold warriors who would never change.

NOTES

1. *Yates v. United States*, 345 U.S. 298.

2. Al Richmond, *A Long View from the Left, Memoirs of an American Revolutionary* (Boston, 1967), 362.

3. Tom Clark to author, March 28, 1975.

4. Michal Belknap, *Cold War Political Justice, The Smith Act, the Communist Party, and American Civil Liberties* (Westport, 1977), 193.

5. U.S. House of Representatives, 83d Cong., 1st sess., Appropriations Committee, *Departments of State, Justice, and Commerce Appropriations for 1954. Hearings . . .* (Washington, 1953), 135.

6. John Gates, *The Story of an American Communist* (New York, 1958), 173; Maurice Isserman, "The Half-Swept House: American Communism in 1956," *Socialist Review* XII (January-February 1982), 72.

7. Gates, *The Story of an American Communist*, 157; Peggy Dennis, *The Autobiography of an American Communist, A Personal View of a Political Life 1925–1975* (Westport, 1977), 226–27.

8. David A. Shannon, *The Decline of American Communism, A History of the Communist Party of the United States since 1945* (New York, 1959), 202.

9. Isserman, "The Half-Swept House," 95; Peggy Dennis, "A Half-View of History is not Good Enough," Unpublished article submitted to *Socialist Review*, April 5, 1982.

10. Otis Hood, Oral History, Tamiment Library, New York University.

11. George Charney, *A Long Journey* (Chicago, 1968), 209.

12. Steve Nelson, James R. Barrett, Rob Ruck, *Steve Nelson, American Radical* (Pittsburgh, 1981), 317–18.

13. Martin Fisher, "Urgent Tasks for Strengthening the Party," *Political Affairs* XXX (November 1951), 34–35.

14. Alexander Bittelman to William Z. Foster, January 12, 1952, Papers of Alexander Bittelman, Folder 17, Alexander Bittelman Home Library, Croton, New York. Hereafter cited as BHL.

15. Dennis, *Autobiography*, 203.

16. Charney, *A Long Journey*, 230, 232.

17. Ibid., 235; Alexander Bittelman, "Autobiography" (Unpublished Typescript, 1963, Tamiment Library, New York University), 768.

18. John Swift, "The Struggle for a Mass Policy," *Political Affairs* XXXII (February 1953), 27.

19. Ibid., 28–29.

20. Ibid., 33.

21. National Committee, C.P.U.S.A., "Resolution on the Situation Growing out of the Presidential Elections (Final Text)," *Political Affairs* XXXII (July 1953), 12; Charney, *A Long Journey*, 236.

22. National Committee, "Resolution," 7.

23. Alexander Bittelman to the members of the National Committee, October 11, 1953, Papers of Alexander Bittelman, Folder 3, BHL.

24. National Committee, CPUSA, "The American Way to Jobs, Peace, Democracy (Draft Program of the Communist Party)," *Political Affairs* XXXIII (April 1954), 9; Bittelman, "Autobiography," 736.

25. William Z. Fostser, "The War Danger in the Present World Situation," *Political Affairs* XXXIII (May 1954), 13.

26. William Z. Foster, "Message to the Conference of the C.P.U.S.A.," *Political Affairs* XXXIII (September 1954), 10.

27. William Z. Foster, "Is the United States in the Early Stages of Fascism?" *Political Affairs* XXXIII (November 1954), 9–10.

28. Claude Lightfoot, "Leadership Quality and the Draft Program Perspectives," *Political Affairs* XXXIII (June 1954), 36, 38, 40, 42.

29. Richmond, *A Long View from the Left*, 358–59; Belknap, *Cold War Political Justice*, 224–26.

30. Gilbert Green, *The Enemy Forgotten* (New York, 1956), 21.

31. Ibid., 293, 314.

32. Ibid., 28, 54, 307.

33. William Z. Foster, "Geneva: Background and Perspectives," *Political Affairs* XXXIV (September 1955), 27.

34. Nemmy Sparks, "The Yugoslav-Soviet Rapprochement," *Political Affairs* XXXIV (December 1955), 27–34.

35. *The New York Times*, December 5, 1955.

36. Eugene Dennis, "After Five Years," *Political Affairs* XXXV (February 1956), 7.

37. Gates, *The Story of an American Communist*, 160–61.

38. Isserman, "The Half-Swept House," 77, 81; Shannon, *The Decline of American Communism*, 272.

39. Gates, *The Story of an American Communist*, 164.

40. Eugene Dennis, "Questions and Answers on the XXth Congress, CPSU," *Political Affairs* XXXV (April 1956), 21–26.

41. Eugene Dennis, *The Communists Take a New Look* (New York, 1956), 22–25, 27, 29, 35.

42. Ibid., 20, 24, 25, 32.

43. Ibid., 21, 36–37, 41–42, 43, 45–47.

44. Ibid., 6–7, 39.

45. Joseph R. Starobin, *American Communism in Crisis, 1943–1957* (Cambridge, 1972), 242 n.10; Charney, *A Long Journey*, 243–44; Nelson, Barrett, Ruck, *Steve Nelson*, 386–87; Gates, *The Story of an American Communist*, 165.

46. Gates, *The Story of an American Communist*, 164; Shannon, *The Decline of American Communism*, 289.

47. Gates, *The Story of an American Communist*, 167–68; Isserman, "The Half-Swept House," 88.

48. "Statement of the National Committee, C.P.U.S.A.," *Political Affairs* XXXV (July 1956), 34–35.

49. *The New York Times*, June 19, June 28, 1956.

50. Ibid., July 2, 1956.

51. National Committee, CPUSA, "On the Resolution of the Central Committee, CPSU," *Political Affairs* XXXV (August 1956), 48–49.

52. Gates, *The Story of an American Communist*, 172, 182; Charney, *A Long Journey*, 285; *The New York Times*, August 28, 1956.

53. *Proceedings (abridged) of the 16th National Convention of the Communist Party, U.S.A., February 9–12, 1957* (New York, 1957), 315.

54. Ibid., 313–15.

55. Ibid., 281–82.

56. Ibid., 312.

57. Ibid., 317–19, 321.

58. Ibid., 304.

59. Ibid., 306.

60. Ibid., 325.

61. Ibid., 296, 323.

62. Isserman, "The Half-Swept House," 91.

63. Charney, *A Long Journey*, 290; Starobin, *American Communism in Crisis*, 309 n.9; *The New York Times*, September 28, 1956.

64. William Z. Foster, "On the Party Situation," *Political Affairs* XXXV (October 1956), 15, 30–32, 42.

65. Ibid., 16–17, 34.

66. Ibid., 16, 19, 27–28.

67. Ibid., 20, 22.

68. *The Daily Worker*, October 25, October 29, October 30, 1956.

69. Ibid., November 5, 1956.

70. Ibid.; Gates, *The Story of an American Communist*, 178.

71. *The Daily Worker*, November 12, 1956.

72. National Committee, CPUSA, "On the Events in Hungary," *Political Affairs* XXXV (December 1956), 3.

73. Sidney Steinberg to author, September 1, 1982.

74. Peggy Dennis, *Autobiography*, 232; Maurice Isserman, "The 1956 Gen-

eration, An Alternative Approach to the History of American Communism,"
Radical America XIV (March, April 1980), 49; Isserman, "The Half-Swept House,"
94; Gates, *The Story of an American Communist*, 177–78, 180; Charney, *A Long Journey*, 251, 258, 292, 296.

75. Eugene Dennis, "Sputnik, the USA and the USSR," *Political Affairs* XXXVI (November 1957), 6.

76. John Gates, "Time for a Change," *Political Affairs* XXXV (November 1956), 49, 53–54.

77. Eugene Dennis, "What Kind of a Change?" *Political Affairs* XXXVI (January 1957), 27–42.

78. Shannon, *The Decline of American Communism*, 322.

79. *Proceedings, February 9–12, 1957*, 43.

80. Ibid., 50–51.

81. Ibid., 48.

82. Ibid., 55.

83. Ibid., 46, 56.

84. Ibid., 173.

85. Ibid., 145.

86. Ibid., 205–21.

87. Ibid., 101.

88. Ibid., 240.

89. Ibid., 195.

90. Ibid., 232–37.

91. Charney, *A Long Journey*, 301.

92. "Speech of Sid Stein, in debate with Eugene Dennis, December 1957, National Executive Committee, CPUSA," copy of tape submitted to author by Sidney Steinberg.

93. Betty Gannett to Bob [Thompson], July 25, 1957, Papers of Betty Gannett, State Historical Society of Wisconsin.

94. *The New York Times*, June 4, 1957.

95. Sidney Steinberg to author, September 1, 1982.

96. William Z. Foster, "The Party Crisis and the Way Out, Part I," *Political Affairs* XXXVI (December 1957), 47–51.

97. Belknap, *Cold War Political Justice*, 501.

98. *Yates v. United States*, 354 U.S. 312.

99. Ibid., 324–25, 318.

100. Ibid., 319–20, 327.

101. Tom Clark to author, March 28, 1975.

102. United States Department of Justice, "List of Smith Act Cases Involving Communist Party Leaders," 4, document submitted to author by Department of Justice.

103. Richmond, *A Long View from the Left*, 381.

104. "Speech of Sid Stein . . . December 1957."

105. Peggy Dennis, *Autobiography*, 234.

106. "Speech of Sid Stein . . . December 1957."

107. Ibid.

108. *The Daily Worker*, January 31, 1958; National Executive Committee, CPUSA, "Statement on the Declaration of 12 Communist Parties," *Political Affairs* XXXVII (January 1958), 2.

109. *The Daily Worker*, January 31, 1958; Isserman, "The Half-Swept House," 95.

110. *The Daily Worker*, January 13, 1958; Gates, *The Story of an American Communist*, 189.

111. National Committee, CPUSA, "On Uniting and Strengthening the Party and Its Mass Base," *Political Affairs* XXXVII (March 1958), 1–6.

112. *The New York Times*, February 22, 1958.

113. Dorothy R. Healey, "On the Status of the Party," *Political Affairs* XXXVII (March 1958), 47–48.

114. Peggy Dennis, "A Half View of History is not Good Enough," 4; *The New York Times*, July 12, 1958.

115. U.S. Senate, 94th Cong., 2d sess., *Final Report of the Select Committee to Study Governmental Operations with Respect to Intelligence Activities* (6 vols., Washington, 1976), II, 40.

116. Isserman, "The Half-Swept House," 90–91, 97.

Conclusion

The tragedy of the years 1947 to 1952 was that both the Truman administration and the American Communist Party sought to stop the development of "McCarthyism," but could not do so. The policies of each
actually encouraged its growth.

Truman's failure to protect adequately the essential freedoms included in the Bill of Rights was a larger failure of the American political
process. The representative nature of democratic practice was hampered by the growth of an internal government bureaucracy, led by the
FBI, which set its own standards and policies—often untouched by
elected public officials. J. Edgar Hoover had determined his course of
action long before the Cold War's development. He was intent on shifting political thought in the United States to the right by eliminating a
persistent "leftist" opposition. The Communist Party was only an initial target—made easier by the growing United States-Soviet conflict.
Hoover intended to silence all "Marxists"—all those who challenged the
dominant capitalist ideology.

Revisionist historians often do not sufficiently credit Truman with a
sincere effort to limit the growth of political hysteria. The problem was
not his intentions but his understanding of the needs of a political democracy. Truman had nothing but contempt for American communists. He perceived them as foolish purveyors of a foreign ideology, and
as an inconsequential sect. He was willing, as were some other liberals,
to destroy the CPUSA in order to maintain basic liberties of all other
citizens. It was a form of internal appeasement which could work no
better than its international counterpart a few years earlier.

The administration believed that defending the constitutional rights of noncommunists would be sufficient to safeguard the essence of democracy, while what was needed at the time was a militant defense of the freedoms of all Americans. Historian Alonzo Hamby has argued that "an administration and a liberal movement clinging tenaciously to Popular Frontism would have suffered lethal right-wing assaults long before 1949."[1] He posed the alternatives incorrectly. The government did not need to embrace the CP in order to defend its right to exist. Liberals did not have to support the policies of the Soviet Union in order to protect the right of others to do so.

The communists were a vital element in the post-World War II internal political community, not because they exercised any great influence—they did not—but because they presented a coherent, internationally important critique of American society. Their unhindered presence within the United States could have legitimized an international policy of "peaceful coexistence." The removal of their viewpoint meant the practical destruction of such a policy, leading inevitably to a critical deepening of the Cold War. The possibilities for criticism of American programs and assumptions concerning the nature of communism and the reality of Soviet intentions, as a result, were severely limited. The internal Cold War immeasurably strengthened the external one.

The basic freedoms—speech and press—cannot exist in a vacuum. Although the CPUSA's national leaders were sent to prison during the early 1950's, the Communist Party remained in quasi-legal existence. Its newspapers published, and its members continued to work for their socialist ideal. All this did not mean that full political democracy existed. While communists spoke and wrote, there were few who were willing or believed themselves able to listen. The "marketplace of ideas" was restricted. Americans certainly had a right to reject communist concepts, but to do so without a full hearing and an opportunity for consideration was to destroy the intellectual atmosphere in which freedom has meaning.

In a political democracy all ideas must be permissible, all advocacy should be encouraged. To allow some to set limits for others is to restrict the freedom of everyone. In the postwar years, American communists sought to do no more than spread their ideas and advocate their solutions to the United States' problems. They openly believed in a revolutionary political and economic theory, but never gathered guns, nor trained for military action, nor urged violence of any kind. They dreamed of a coming socialist revolution, but often labored to make American democracy work better. Their actions may sometimes have been foolish, but they presented no threat to the United States. It was in their suppression that the real peril existed.

The CPUSA's failure was not in its effort to express and further its philosophy, but in its inability to grasp opportunities for developing its own thoughtful, independent policies. Its psychological ties to the Soviet Union and the international communist movement blocked 1945 efforts to develop programs suitable to the needs of the United States and based on a realistic appraisal of the world situation. It could have proposed an "American road to socialism" and broken away from a monolithic dependence on the Soviet model, but it did not do so.

The CP's blind defense of Soviet actions alienated many potential supporters and, more important, many who otherwise might have supported its right to exist and operate freely. Its rigid adherence to Marxist-Leninist concepts such as the "dictatorship of the proletariat" made it an easy target for its enemies and helped to discredit ideological politics. The communists' underestimation of the innate strength of democratic traditions led the CP to fall into the trap of an underground structure from which there could be no real emergence. The existence of the Party's secret apparatus added significantly to the growing domestic hysteria.

Hamby has written:

The historical situation in which Truman and the liberals found themselves by the middle of 1950 was complex in its nature and origins. Given the frailties of American democracy, which seems able to handle complicated issues of diplomacy in only the most simplistic, moralistic manner and is susceptible to demagoguery, the rise of McCarthyism was at least to some extent an inevitable tragedy.[2]

This analysis comes close to the historical determinism which precipitated the CP's disastrous actions. Essential elements in the development of "McCarthyism" were the internal security establishment's deliberate creation of a sense of panic among the American people and the use of that hysteria over the "Red Menace" by self-seeking politicians. There was nothing "inevitable" in these events. They were allowed to occur.

General Douglas MacArthur was removed from his Korean command for exceeding his authority, but J. Edgar Hoover maintained his position until he died. Truman had similar suspicions concerning both, but while seeing the peril of world war, he did not understand fully the dangers of an expanded internal conflict.

William C. Sullivan, former head of the FBI's Domestic Intelligence Division, wrote to Hoover in 1971:

More than one of us at the Bureau were disturbed when you identified yourself with Senator McCarthy and his irresponsible anti-Communist campaign. His method was not the method which should be used to combat Communism and he did grave damage to national security in the sense that reflective men said if this is anti-Communism I want none of it. Yet, you had us preparing material for him regularly, kept furnishing it to him while you denied publicly that we were helping him. And you have done the same thing with others. This is wrong and one day the "chickens may come home to roost."[3]

Sullivan was right. The events surrounding Watergate finally led to a public unearthing of at least some of the secrets of the government's internal security apparatus. By that time, enormous damage had been done.

As a result of the events of 1947 to 1952, the whole focus of American politics shifted right. An ideological approach—never very popular in the United States—was totally discredited. A "silent generation" grew in the shadow of the Cold War. The furious rebellion in the 1960's among some youth may well be traced to the destruction of ideology during the Truman administration. With no coherent social philosophy to which to relate, with little historical framework in which to operate, there was a resort to an almost anarchistic violence. Shutting off effective means of communication and debate for a generation had frustrated the peaceful growth of political thought, organization, and change.

The American Communist party was the first victim of political repression, but society as a whole eventually suffered the consequences of the minority's suppression.

NOTES

1. Alonzo Hamby, *Beyond the New Deal: Harry S. Truman and American Liberalism* (New York, 1973), 401.
2. Ibid.
3. William C. Sullivan to J. Edgar Hoover, October 6, 1971, in Sanford J. Ungar, *FBI* (Boston, 1976), 649.

Bibliographical Essay

A complete examination of the development and execution of federal government policy is highly dependent upon the government itself. This self-evident proposition illustrates both the opportunities for, and limitations placed on, scholars, particularly those seeking to study sensitive areas of national policy. More than thirty years after the initial conviction of the leaders of the American Communist Party, officials in the Department of Justice are still reluctant to allow consideration of the full record. All government documents with relation to the CP remain classified and only a difficult freedom of information procedure, made more restrictive by the Reagan administration, has allowed some information into the historical process. For this study I obtained FBI files relating to CP leaders Claudia Jones and John Williamson for the year 1947. These memoranda and reports shed some important light on the government's deportation drive. Bureau records dealing with Eugene Dennis and Robert Thompson were processed and obtained for 1951. These documents contain limited information of value concerning FBI procedures, but may be more important for what they do not hold. There are many, sometimes massive, excisions in the material and curious lapses indicating what may be a continuing cover-up of investigative techniques and policies. Similar problems exist with regard to the 1951 files dealing with the CP and the "Prosecution of Additional Functionaries under the Smith Act." A ten-volume FBI "Brief to Establish the Illegal Status of the Communist Party of the United States of America," submitted February 3, 1948, to the Attorney General, is particularly valuable for the rather complete history of the CPUSA which is provided. It also documents conclusively the extent to which J. Edgar Hoover guided the government's Smith Act prosecutions.

The difficulties in gaining access to classified material have increased the historical profession's debt to the U.S. Senate's Select Committee to Study Government Operations with Respect to Intelligence Activities. Its seven volumes of *Hearings . . .* , 94th Cong., 1st sess., 1976, and particularly volume 6 on the "Federal Bureau of Investigation," and its six-volume *Final Report . . .* , 94th Cong., 2d sess., 1976, especially volumes II and III, are replete with hitherto classified material proving the development of a dangerous political police.

A major part of our understanding of government purposes and practices is dependent on manuscript collections. The papers held in the Harry S. Truman Library are most important. Stephen J. Spingarn's collection of internal memoranda during the years 1948 to 1951 is particularly vital. In examining the Dennis Smith Act prosecution, the papers of John F.X. McGohey provide significant insights. Other papers of value are those of Eban A. Ayers, Eleanor Bontecou, Tom Clark, Clark M. Clifford, Matthew J. Connelly, George M. Elsey, John W. Gibson, Kenneth Hechler, Paul M. Herzog, David D. Lloyd, James H. McGrath, Charles S. Murphy, Philleo Nash, the President's Commission on Internal Security and Individual Rights, Samuel I. Rosenman, Charles G. Ross, Sidney W. Souers, David H. Stowe, Harry S Truman, and A. Devitt Vanech. Also consulted were the Library of Congress collections of Hugo L. Black, Emanuel Celler, Lewis B. Schwellenbach, and Robert A. Taft. Although of more limited value, the Truman Library's collection of oral history interviews was of some use. Material was found in the recollections of Clark, Judge Richmond B. Keech, Edwin A. Locke, Jr., James I. Loeb, Max Lowenthal, H. Graham Morison, Murphy, Rosenman, and Spingarn. This was supplemented by a valuable personal interview with Justice Clark (Washington, D.C., March 28, 1975) and a considerably more restricted talk with government attorneys Lawrence Bailey and Kevin Maroney (Washington, D.C., July 24, 1974).

The outlines of and justifications for policy were often delivered at congressional hearings. The many investigations conducted by the House Un-American Activities Committee give necessary insights into the public positions of not only government personnel but also many private individuals and organizations. The annual hearings held by both House and Senate Appropriations committees were often used as propaganda forums by the FBI. The Senate Judiciary Committee served much the same function as HUAC during the period 1948–53. The record of its investigations is instructive. Its *Hearings on Communist Underground Printing Facilities and Illegal Propaganda*, 83d Cong., 1st sess., 1953, present a detailed description of CP activities by FBI informants.

Congressional hearings into specific areas helped to establish much of the atmosphere which allowed the growth of "McCarthyism." This is shown in such hearings as those conducted by the House Education and Labor Committee during the 80th Congress. The Committee's *Conference Report*, Report No. 245, 80th Cong., 1st sess., 1947, also provides a good summary of the Taft-Hartley Act.

An examination of the prosecution of communists necessarily involves a detailed understanding of the trials which took place. As repetitive and lengthy as are the trial transcripts, they are invaluable for both the information and strategy which are revealed. Their importance is tempered only by a need to understand the internal dynamics at work on both government and defense sides. The complete transcript for the Dennis case is printed in the "Joint Appendix on Appeal from Judgments of Conviction of the United States District Court for the Southern District of New York" in the United States Court of Appeals for the Second Circuit (July 14, 1950). The second New York trial, *United States v. Flynn, et al.*, has its "Transcript of Trial Proceedings" in the United States District Court for the Southern District of New York (1951–52). The same court has the transcript of the third Foley Square trial, *United States v. Trachtenberg, et al.* (1956). The "Transcript of Proceedings" for the California Smith Act trial can be found as *United States v. Schneiderman, et al.* in the United States District Court, Southern District of California (1952). For the Baltimore case, *United States v. Frankfeld, et al.*, the "Transcript of Proceedings" is in the United States District Court for the District of Maryland, at Baltimore (1952). The Hawaii trial is printed as *United States v. Fujimoto, et al.*, "Transcript of Proceedings," held in United States District Court, Honolulu (1952–53). The "Official Report of Proceedings Before the Subversive Activities Control Board" (1950–51) in the case of *J. Howard McGrath, Attorney General of the United States v. The Communist Party of the United States of America* provides a complete record of those lengthy hearings which came close to constituting a trial proceeding.

Particularly in the Dennis and Yates cases, the many motions filed in the courts of appeal and the Supreme Court by defense, government, and outside groups offer significant legal points as well as much additional information. The decisions of the courts remain important historical documents. These include *American Communications Assn., et al. v. Douds, Regional Director of the National Labor Relations Board*, 339 U.S. 382 (1950); *Dennis, et al., v. United States*, 341 U.S. 494 (1951); *Gitlow v. New York*, 268 U.S. 652 (1925); *Jencks v. United States*, 353 U.S. 657 (1957); *Schenck v. United States*, 249 U.S. 47 (1919); *United States v. Dennis, et al.*, "Opinion" of the United States Court of Appeals for the Second Circuit (August 1, 1950); and *Yates, et al. v. United States*, 354 U.S. 298 (1957). Helpful in providing statistical data are the annual reports of the Attorneys General.

Valuable documents are contained in Tyrus G. Fain, ed., *The Intelligence Community* (New York, 1977). The annual volumes of *Public Papers of the Presidents of the United States* similarly save much time and effort.

Secondary literature on the period of "McCarthyism" continues to grow. Frank Donner's comprehensive work, *The Age of Surveillance, The Aims and Methods of America's Political Intelligence System* (New York, 1980), is an intelligent, highly critical consideration of government policies and actions. Stanley I. Kutler, *The American Inquisition: Justice and Injustice in the Cold War* (New York, 1982) provides an effective contribution as well. Somewhat more specialized but well researched and provocative in its views is Athan Theoharis' *Spying on Americans: Political Surveillance from Hoover to the Huston Plan* (Philadelphia, 1978). Theoharis' article on "The FBI's Stretching of Presidential Directives, 1936–1953," *Political Science Quarterly* LXLI (Winter 1976–77), 649–72, provides the basis for a portion of his later work. Barton Bernstein's "The Road to Watergate and Beyond: The Growth and Abuse of Executive Authority Since 1940," *Law and Contemporary Problems* XL (Spring 1976), 58–86, is particularly good in its consideration of Truman's reaction to Hoover's letters on political matters.

Former head of the FBI's Domestic Intelligence Division William C. Sullivan allows insights into the psychology of the Bureau in *My Thirty Years in Hoover's FBI* (written with Bill Brown, New York, 1979). Other works on the Bureau include Max Lowenthal's *The Federal Bureau of Investigation* (New York, 1950); Sanford Ungar's massive *FBI* (Boston, 1976); and the *American Police State, The Government Against the People* (New York, 1976) by David Wise. All are critical of political intelligence gathering. The other side is told in the semi-official *The FBI Story, A Report to the People* by Don Whitehead (New York, 1956). Examinations of the Department of Justice can be found in Victor Navasky, *Kennedy Justice* (New York, 1971), and Luther Huston, *The Department of Justice* (New York, 1967). The latter is written by a former Justice official.

The genre of anti-communist informer operations is exemplified by Angela Calomiris' *Red Masquerade, Undercover for the F.B.I.* (Philadelphia 1950), and *I Led 3 Lives* (New York, 1952) by Herbert Philbrick. Both were witnesses at the Dennis trial. Hoover's works, including *Masters of Deceit, The Story of Communism in America and How to Fight It* (New York, 1958), and *On Communism* (New York, 1969), as well as numerous articles, although written by FBI subordinates, illustrate his state of mind.

A good, popularized work on the McCarthyite period is David Caute, *The Great Fear, The Anti-Communist Purge Under Truman and Eisenhower* (New York, 1978). Thoughtful contributions are included in Robert Griffith and Athan Theoharis, eds., *Original Essays on the Cold War and the Origins of McCarthyism* (New York, 1974). Theoharis' *Seeds of Repression: Harry S. Truman and the Origins of McCarthyism* (Chicago, 1971) and Griffith's *The Politics of Fear, Joseph R. McCarthy and the Senate* (Rochelle Park, New Jersey, 1978) suggest challenging interpretations. A Ph.D. dissertation, Leslie Adler, "The Red Image: American Attitudes Toward Communism in the Cold War Era," University of California, Berkeley, 1970, gives an effective analysis of postwar psychology. Other works of value include the contributions of Richard Hofstadter, David Riesman, Nathan Glazer, Seymour Lipset and others in Daniel Bell, ed., *The Radical Right* (Freeport, New York, 1971); James E. Bristol, et al., *Anatomy of Anti-Communism, A Report Prepared for the Peace Division of the American Friends Service Committee* (New York, 1969); Fred Cook, *The Nightmare Decade, The Life and Times of Senator Joe McCarthy* (New York, 1971); Richard Freeland, *The Truman Doctrine and the Origins of McCarthyism, Foreign Policy, Domestic Politics, and Internal Security 1946–1948* (New York, 1972); John Lewis Gaddis, *The United States and the Origins of the Cold War, 1941–1947* (New York, 1972); Earl Latham, *The Communist Controversy in Washington From the New Deal to McCarthy* (Cambridge, 1966); and Richard Rovere, *Senator Joe McCarthy* (New York, 1959). A positive portrait of McCarthy appears in Roy Cohn, *McCarthy* (New York, 1968).

Robert Carr, *The House Committee on Un-American Activities 1945–1950* (New York, 1952), and Walter Goodman, *The Committee, The Extraordinary Career of the House Committee on Un-American Activities* (New York, 1968) have become standard works. The federal loyalty program is explored in Eleanor Bontecou, *The Federal Loyalty-Security Program* (Ithaca, New York, 1953); Alan Harper, *The Politics of Loyalty: The White House and the Communist Issue, 1946–1952* (Westport, 1969); and Francis Thompson, "Truman and Congress: The Issue of Loyalty,

1946–1952," Ph.D. dissertation, Texas Tech University, 1970. The latter is of minor quality, but the former two are good studies although somewhat dated in their documentation.

The most impressive study of the CP and prosecutions is Michal Belknap, *Cold War Political Justice, The Smith Act, the Communist Party and American Civil Liberties* (Westport, 1977) and his Ph.D. dissertation, "The Smith Act and the Communist Party: A Study in Political Justice," the University of Wisconsin, 1973. Although perhaps too centered on his thesis that the CP was destroyed by the prosecutions, it is solidly researched and presented. Harold Chase, *Security and Liberty: The Problem of Native Communists, 1947–1955* (Garden City, New York, 1955), and his earlier dissertation, "Controlling Subversive Activities: An Analysis of the Efforts of the National Government to Control the Indigenous Communists, 1933–1952," Princeton University, 1954, were written too early to permit full documentation. Some merit can be found in Thomas Holmes, "The Specter of Communism in Hawaii 1947–53," Ph.D. dissertation, University of Hawaii, 1975; Herbert Packer, *Ex-Communist Witnesses, Four Studies in Fact Finding* (Stanford, California, 1962); and John Somerville, *The Communist Trials and the American Tradition, Expert Testimony on Force and Violence* (New York, 1956). The latter testified as a defense witness in three Smith Act trials, while Packer provides interesting analyses of Louis Budenz and John Lautner, as does Joseph Alsop in "The Strange Case of Louis Budenz," *Atlantic Monthly* CLXXXIX (April 1952), 29–33. Judge Harold R. Medina's views are expressed in *The Anatomy of Freedom* (New York, 1959).

Among the best, and most friendly, works on the Truman presidency are Alonso Hamby, *Beyond the New Deal: Harry S. Truman and American Liberalism* (New York, 1973), and Robert Donovan's *Conflict and Crisis, The Presidency of Harry S Truman, 1945–1948* (New York, 1977), and *Tumultuous Years, The Presidency of Harry S Truman, 1949–1953* (New York, 1982). Other works of particular value include: Francis Biddle, *In Brief Authority* (Garden City, New York, 1962); Clifton Brock, *Americans for Democratic Action: Its Role in National Politics* (Washington, D.C., 1962); William Berman, *The Politics of Civil Rights in the Truman Administration* (Columbus, Ohio, 1970); Barton Bernstein, ed., *Politics and Policies of the Truman Administration* (Chicago, 1970); Eric Goldman, *The Crucial Decade—and After, America, 1945–1960* (New York, 1966); Susan Hartmann, *Truman and the 80th Congress* (Columbia, Missouri, 1971); R. Alton Lee, *Truman and Taft-Hartley: A Question of Mandate* (Lexington, Kentucky, 1966); Mary McAuliffe, *Crisis on the Left, Cold War Politics and American Liberals, 1947–1954* (Amherst, Massachusetts, 1978); Arthur F. McClure, *The Truman Administration and the Problems of Postwar Labor, 1945–1948* (Rutherford, New Jersey, 1969); Cabell Phillips, *The Truman Presidency: The History of a Triumphant Succession* (New York, 1966); I. F. Stone, *The Truman Era* (New York, 1972); William Tanner, "The Passage of the Internal Security Act of 1950," 2 vols., Ph.D. dissertation, University of Kansas, 1971; Harry Truman, *Memoirs . . . .*, 2 vols. (Garden City, New York, 1955–56); and Allen Weinstein, *Perjury, the Hiss-Chambers Case* (New York, 1978).

The election of 1948 is dealt with effectively in Curtis D. MacDougall, *Gide-*

on's Army, 3 vols. (New York, 1965); Norman Markowitz, *The Rise and Fall of the People's Century: Henry A. Wallace and American Liberalism, 1941–1948* (New York, 1973); Irwin Ross, *The Loneliest Campaign: The Truman Victory of 1948* (New York, 1968); Karl Schmidt, *Henry A. Wallace: Quixotic Crusade 1948* (n.p., 1960); Richard Walton, *Henry Wallace, Harry Truman, and the Cold War* (New York, 1976); and Allen Yarnell, *Democrats and Progressives, The 1948 Presidential Election As a Test of Postwar Liberalism* (Berkeley, 1974). Arthur M. Schlesinger, Jr., *The Vital Center, The Politics of Freedom* (Boston, 1962) contains a clear statement of the anticommunist liberal creed. The conflict among liberals in the early Cold War period is well illustrated and defined by a series of short articles in *The New Republic*, all under the title "Progressives and Communists." Stanley Isaacs, *The New Republic* CXIV (May 20, 1946), 733; James Loeb, Jr., *The New Republic* CXIV (May 13, 1946), 699; and Roger Baldwin, *The New Republic* CXIV (June 17, 1946), 871, sharply etch the liberal dilemma and response. Geoffrey Smith has provided a helpful bibliography in " 'Harry We Hardly Know You': Revisionism, Politics and Diplomacy, 1945–1954," *American Political Science Review* LXX (June 1976), 560–82.

An accurate history of the American Communist Party is made more difficult by the paucity of primary sources. Due to the existence of persecution and danger of prosecution, as well as a lack of inner democratic practice, relatively little was committed to paper and that which was, often was soon destroyed. It is for this reason that the papers of Alexander Bittelman, a Commmunist leader for close to forty years, are so important. Somewhat haphazardly maintained in his home in Croton, New York, they remain a valuable, if relatively untapped, resource. Following his expulsion from the CP, Bittelman authored a 1963 "Autobiography" which was not published. It is held in the Tamiment Library at New York University. Long and sometimes tedious, it nonetheless contains a wealth of information. The papers of Party functionary Betty Gannett, at the State Historical Society of Wisconsin, hold little of value. The oral history of Massachusetts leader Otis Hood, at Tamiment Library, contains some interesting illustrations of life in the CP, but is not substantial.

A tape of a portion of a December 22, 1957, meeting of the CP's National Executive Committee, provided to the author by Sidney Steinberg, is an unusual and rare source. Interviews with Steinberg (Spring Valley, New York, December 25, 1974, September 1, 1982); John Gates (Oyster Bay, New York, March 5, 1978); and George Watt (Spring Valley, New York, June 29, 1975) were invaluable in offering information available from no other sources.

Books by six former communists provide a necessary understanding of those who joined and led the Party, life in it, and the political crises through which the CP moved. George Charney, *A Long Journey* (Chicago, 1968); Peggy Dennis, *The Autobiography of an American Communist, A Personal View of a Political Life 1925–1975* (Westport, 1977); John Gates, *The Story of an American Communist* (New York, 1958); Steve Nelson, James R. Barrett, Rob Ruck, *Steve Nelson, American Radical* (Pittsburgh, 1981); Joseph Starobin, *American Communism in Crisis, 1943–1957* (Cambridge, 1972); and Al Richmond, *A Long View from the Left, Memoirs of an American Revolutionary* (Boston, 1967) give personal insights and examples which are of great importance. The publishing of their recollections may have been possible only after they left CP discipline. Quite different are the works of Harry Haywood, *Black Bolshevik, Autobiography of an Afro-American Communist* (Chicago, 1978); Nell Painter, *The Narrative of Hosea Hudson, His Life as a Negro Communist in the South* (Cambridge, 1979); and John Williamson, *Dangerous Scot: The Life and Work of an American "Undesirable"* (New York, 1969). Haywood was expelled from the Party in 1959 as an ultra-leftist, while Hudson remained a Party member. Unfortunately, his story is concluded in 1948, apparently due to space limitations, and it is strongest in social rather than political aspects. Williamson remained a loyal Party member following his deportation in 1955; his book, written in Britain, adds little. More significant material comes from Len DeCaux, *Labor Radical From the Wobblies to CIO* (Boston, 1970).

Highly significant are the mass of articles which appeared in the Party's theoretical organ, *Political Affairs*, during the entire period covered by this study. Within its pages most of the programs, beliefs, and conflicts of the movement were displayed, but the articles must be read with care. It is often their nuances which are of great importance and it should be understood that they were generally screened carefully for political orientation before publication. *The Daily Worker* and *The Worker* provide information and analyses concerning continuing activities. To these sources should be added theoretical books and numerous pamphlets such as Earl Browder, *In Defense of Communism* (Yonkers, New York, 1949); Gilbert Green, *The Enemy Forgotten* (New York, 1956); Alex Parker [pseudonym], *Organizing the Party for Victory Over Reaction, Report delivered at the National Conference of the Communist Party* (New York, 1953); and Eugene Dennis, *The Communists Take a New Look* (New York, 1956).

William Z. Foster, *History of the Communist Party of the United States* (New York, 1968) deals best with early CP history. His treatment of the post-World War II period has little value and the entire work is limited by an overt effort to serve the author's political purposes. Better histories and analyses come from outside sources. These include Theodore Draper's books, *The Roots of American Communism* (New York, 1957) and *American Communism and Soviet Russia, The Formative Period* (New York, 1960); Nathan Glazer, *The Social Basis of American Communism* (New York, 1961); Irving Howe and Lewis Coser, *The American Communist Party, A Critical History (1919–1957)* (Boston, 1957); and David Shannon, *The Decline of American Communism, A History of the Communist Party of the United States Since 1945* (New York, 1959). The latter gives the most objective effort, although not wholly successful, of the general histories. Philip Jaffe, *The Rise and Fall of American Communism* (New York, 1975) rarely rises above the level of an apologia for his close friend Earl Browder. A far more objective consideration is found in Maurice Isserman, *Which Side Were You On? The American Communist Party During the Second World War* (Middletown, Connecticut, 1982). Isserman's work is an effective piece of scholarship with a fair, though sympathetic approach both to the height of the Browder period and his fall from grace. It is particularly strong in discussing the effects of rejection of the Teheran thesis.

Communist Party relations with organized labor are examined by Frank Emspak, "The Break-up of the Congress of Industrial Organizations (CIO), 1945–

1950," Ph.D. dissertation, University of Wisconsin, 1972; Max Kampelman, *The Communist Party vs. The C.I.O., A Study in Power Politics* (New York, 1957); and Harvey A. Levenstein, *Communism, Anticommunism, and the CIO* (Westport, 1981). The latter is solidly researched and written and has an independent, critical outlook. His conclusion that the destruction of left CIO unions and CP influence led to disastrous consequences by shifting domestic and foreign policy as well as unionism far to the right is well argued. Other aspects of the communist experience are considered in Ronald Johnson, "The Communist Issue in Missouri: 1946–1956," Ph.D. dissertation, University of Missouri, 1973; Wilson Record, *Race and Radicalism, The NAACP and the Communist Party in Conflict* (Ithaca, New York, 1964); and David Saposs, *Communism in American Politics* (Washington, D.C., 1960). The Record effort is marred by a conscious attempt to absolve the NAACP of all charges of communist infiltration.

The critical 1957 CP Convention can be examined through the *Proceedings (abridged) of the 16th National Convention of the Communist Party, U.S.A.* (New York, 1957), but one would have hoped for a far more complete record. The events of that period are dealt with by Isserman in "The 1956 Generation, An Alternative Approach to the History of American Communism," *Radical America* XIV (March, April 1980), 43–51, and "The Half-Swept House: American Communism in 1956," *Socialist Review* XII (January–February 1982), 71–101. A reply to the latter is contained in Peggy Dennis, "A Half-View of History Is Not Good Enough," unpublished article prepared for and submitted to the *Socialist Review*, April 6, 1982. Much of what has been written about the disintegration of the CP is marked with a desire, among the combatants, for personal and political vindication.

Throughout any study of this period, *The New York Times* provides a necessary chronological setting and record. Although not nearly as objective as claimed, it remains an invaluable resource.

Index

Acheson, Dean, 5
Aesopian language, 163, 170, 172, 235
Alien Registration Act, xiii, 47
American Civil Liberties Union (ACLU), 121-22, 225
Americans for Democratic Action (ADA), 49, 188, 225
Ames, Margaret, 240
Aptheker, Herbert, 242, 279
Association of Catholic Trade Unionists, 20
Attorney General's list, 27, 29-30, 81. *See also* Loyalty program

Bailey, Lawrence, 97, 235
Balint, Alex, 93
Bartlett, Harry, 242
Bass, Charlotte, 263
Begun, Isidore, 250
Bentley, Elizabeth, 22, 128, 129
Beria, Lavrenti, 266, 271
Bittelman, Alexander, 66, 67, 70-71, 191, 192, 194, 195, 206, 232; argues for concept of peaceful transition to socialism in defendant discussions, 247-48; breaks with Foster, 263; criticizes Foster's *History of the Communist Party of the United States*, 233, 249;

deportation efforts, 89-91, 131; prediction that communist convictions will be upheld, 212-13; seeks to testify at second New York Smith Act trial, 234, 248, 249; on significance of Wallace vote, 134
Black, Hugo, 189-90, 224
"Blood flowing in the streets," 239
Bloor, Ella Reeve ("Mother"), 239
Blumberg, Dorothy, 240
Bondy, William, 93, 94
Branton, Leo A., Jr., 235, 239, 246
Braverman, Maurice, 240, 242
Bridges, Harry, 134-35
Browder, Earl, 62-63, 65, 66, 82
Brown, Peter Campbell, 208
Buchman, Harold, 241
Budenz, Louis, 103, 109, 143, 249; testimony in *Dennis* case, 161-63
Bureau of the Budget, U.S., 41
Byrd, Harry F., 186

Canadian Royal Commission, 22
Carlson, Frank, 238
Catholic Church, 20
Chafee, Zechariah, Jr., 187
Chaka, Edward, 171
Chambers, Whittaker, 128, 129